IN HONOR OF

JOHN BAIRD

Charity and Children in Renaissance Florence

STUDIES IN MEDIEVAL AND EARLY MODERN CIVILIZATION
Marvin B. Becker, General Editor

Charity and Children in Renaissance Florence:
The *Ospedale degli Innocenti,* 1410–1536
  Philip Gavitt

Humanism in Crisis: The Decline of the French Renaissance
  Philippe Desan, editor

Upon My Husband's Death: Widows in the Literature
and Histories of Medieval Europe
  Louise Mirrer, editor

The Crannied Wall: Women, Religion, and the Arts
in Early Modern Europe
  Craig A. Monson, editor

The Rhetorics of Life-Writing in Early Modern Europe:
Forms of Biography from Cassandra Fedele to Louis XIV
  Thomas F. Mayer and D. R. Woolf, editors

Defining Dominion: The Discourses of Magic and Witchcraft
in Early Modern France and Germany
  Gerhild Scholz Williams

Charity and Children in Renaissance Florence

The Ospedale degli Innocenti,
1410–1536

Philip Gavitt

Ann Arbor
THE UNIVERSITY OF MICHIGAN PRESS

Copyright © by The University of Michigan 1990
All rights reserved
Published in the United States of America by
The University of Michigan Press
Manufactured in the United States of America

1999   1998   1997   1996   4   3   2

Library of Congress Cataloging-in-Publication Data
Gavitt, Philip, 1950–
    Charity and children in Renaissance Florence : the Ospedale degli
Innocenti, 1410–1536 / Philip Gavitt.
        p.   cm. — (Studies in medieval and early modern civilization)
    Includes bibliographical references and index.
    ISBN 0-472-10183-8 (alk. paper)
    1. Ospedale degli Innocenti (Florence, Italy)—History.
2. Orphans—Italy—Florence—History.   3. Abandoned children—Italy—
Florence—History.   4. Charities—Italy—Florence—History.
I. Title.   II. Series.
HV1195.F5620874   1990
362.7'31'094551—dc20   90-39785
                                                                                                              CIP

To my parents

Acknowledgments

This book would be inconceivable without Marvin Becker's patient support and encouragement, not to mention his depth and breadth of historical vision. I have also benefited greatly from his colleagues and my patrons in the Department of History at the University of Michigan: Charles Trinkaus, Thomas Tentler, and the late James Vann; and in the Department of Anthropology, Vern Carroll and William Lockwood. I would be remiss if I did not mention the importance of the work of Diane Hughes in using notarial sources and other official documents to illuminate the history of private life. The Department of History has been generous with fellowship money, which sustained a second year of research in Florence. A grant from the Horace H. Rackham School of Graduate Studies at the University of Michigan made possible a third trip to Italy in the spring of 1980.

Other institutions also played a vital role in the completion of this book, foremost among them Boston University. Without slighting the contributions of any of my colleagues there, I especially wish to thank Anthony T. G. Pallett, Frederic A. H. Siegel, George Schiller, and Carol Doherty, all of whom have lent support and encouragement to this enterprise. Jean Conlin never faltered in her generosity, technical expertise, and sense of humor, and I am forever in her debt for granting me virtually unlimited access to the resources and materials of the Word Processing Center. I am also indebted to Jean Ireland, who made many valuable suggestions.

Who wants a book, wants money, to paraphrase Alessandra Strozzi. In addition to the generous support provided by the University of Michigan, a grant from the Renaissance Society of America in the summer of 1976 made it possible to learn paleography and archival research under the expert guidance of Anthony Molho, Gino Corti, and Riccardo Fubini. The Fulbright Commission funded the first year of my research in Italy and, more importantly, made the experience of culture shock almost imperceptible.

The material richness of the Archivio di Stato is matched only by the friendliness and helpfulness of its staff, in both Florence and Siena. In particular, Francesca Morandini placed her enthusiasm in the service of unrestricted access to the archives of the Ospedale degli Innocenti. The employees of the Ospedale degli Innocenti, which until quite recently functioned as a day-care center and preschool, were unfailingly cheerful and cooperative not only with my research, but in hosting an endless number of impromptu tours of the hospital for friends and family. Attilio Piccini often gave me the benefit of his familiarity with the archive of the hospital, which he served with great protectiveness as well as diligence and love.

The Istituto Europeo Universitario in Florence provided many lively opportunities for scholarly exchange, and I wish especially to thank Professor Thomas Riis for his many suggestions. The Kunsthistorische Institut of Florence's incomparable collection of published primary sources has no doubt saved many months of waiting for interlibrary loans in the United States. The cooperation and helpfulness of the staff at the Baker library of the Harvard Business School was exemplary.

A number of researchers in or of Florence took time and energy away from their own research to ponder issues of common interest and to offer valuable help. They include, but by no means are limited to: Richard Goldthwaite, Judith Brown, Sam Cohn, John Henderson, Sharon Strocchia, Gene Brucker, James Banker, Anthony Molho, and Edward English. Katharine Park, in particular, provided valuable information on individual physicians as well as more general insights into the history of hospitals. Judith Brown offered many valuable suggestions for strengthening the book's argument and presentation, and David Herlihy saved me from a particularly egregious error regarding the attribution of the pseudo-Pandolfini *Trattato del governo della famiglia*. Such quantitative sophistication as is here is due largely to his expertise, as well as that of Maris Vinovskis. Limitations both of data and of time prevented my following many of their extremely valuable suggestions, and any inadequacies are mine, not theirs. My editor at University of Michigan Press, Mary Erwin, exhibited reserves of patience and loyalty above and beyond the call of duty.

Finally, another book would be required to express the debt of gratitude to my wife Terry, who endured years of separation during the research phase yet still found the resources within herself to support, in very concrete terms, the completion of the project. My son, Brendan, moreover, made the delight and love Florentines had for their children a shared experience.

Contents

Introduction

When the silk guild and the commune of Florence collaborated in 1419 to begin the construction of the Ospedale degli Innocenti, their activities signified much more than the laudable intention to provide for the care of orphans and foundlings. The establishment of charity on this magnificent scale came out of a society, economy, and culture very different from the conditions that had prevailed three-quarters of a century earlier. The differences can be most strikingly observed through changes in the character of religious devotion: the fifteenth century saw far fewer displays of mass religious enthusiasm and much more deliberate zeal in the extension of charity beyond the confines of confraternal membership. Wealthy Florentines were leaving less money to religious orders and giving more to institutions that specialized in social problems.[1]

These relatively short-term changes assume even more interest when set against the background of long-term changes in the ideology of wealth and poverty from the thirteenth through the fifteenth centuries. Two features of the earlier period stand out: the popularity of voluntary poverty, and a developing notion of the "poor in spirit." The former represented a confidence that values heretofore nurtured only in the cloister could survive in the world of urban lay men and women. The twelfth-century collection of sermons in Honorius of Autun's *Speculum Ecclesiae* suggests the extreme tenuousness of the layman's position in the race for salvation. If the regular and secular clergy could achieve eternal blessedness through devotion to the rules of the order or the fulfillment of parochial duties, laymen were beset by the temptations of avarice and the profit inherent in laic occupations. Only frequent almsgiving could efface the disadvantage of lay status.[2]

Among the cultural features that converged to make the appeal of voluntary poverty stronger was an emphasis on the imitation of Christ. As Southern and Becker have suggested, the shift in the idea of penitence from literal, concrete, and public forms to a more individual, interior, and experiential form is critical here. The Crusades were only one expression of a desire to make the life of Christ and the Holy Sites more tangible and more accessible.[3] The extremes of a stern and unforgiving Christ and Christ as triumphant victor gave way to the middle ground emphasizing Christ's compassion and suffering on the Cross, and to a yearning to emulate the poverty of Christ and the Apostles. Although lay penitential groups met before the period of Saint Francis, the Franciscans did much to popularize the notion that a strictly penitential life could be pursued within the confines of lay occupations and conjugal relationships.[4]

By the fourteenth century, the radical Franciscans had forced a reconsideration of the entire notion of apostolic poverty. The papal bull of 1322, *Ad conditorem,* sought to establish that Christ and the Apostles had owned property both individually and in common. If the Spirituals' solution was a refusal to compromise with wealth or with a Church that wealth had corrupted, more orthodox preaching moved away from the glorification of literal poverty and toward the notion that true poverty depended on one's interior attitude.[5] A hagiographer of San Lucchese in 1320 distinguished three kinds of poverty, in ascending order of desirability:

> The first kind is that of the poor, deprived of temporal goods. We call this indigence, because they have indigence of good will, the greatest wealth of this world. A second sort of poverty the philosophers call frugality, or moderation, which is voluntary poverty. The last kind is that of those who possess the most goods, but remain poor in spirit. This poverty can well be called golden poverty, because if riches abound, they refuse to set their hearts on them.[6]

For the preacher Giovanni di San Gimignano, even voluntary poverty courted the dangers of pride and envy; for him, "poverty is nothing in itself. It is solely the love of poverty, of humility, that is of account."[7]

As Hans Baron has noted, early humanism saw in moderate voluntary poverty the reconciliation of the precepts of Christianity and those of classical antiquity. The fusion of Stoicism and asceticism persisted into the fifteenth century in the writings of Antonio da Romagno, which placed the Romans and Saint Francis in each other's distinguished company. Salutati, writing in *De Saeculo et Religione,* suggested that both the Church and the Roman Empire were "established by the poor and spoilt by the rich."[8] Baron argues that as the social position of the humanists improved, and they found positions in the service of the Florentine state, their attitudes to voluntary poverty became less favorable. Fifteenth-century humanists focused on the centrality of wealth to sustaining the active life of the individual and to the glorification of community. Leonardo Bruni's gloss on the *Economics* of Aristotle, for example, proposed that "in order to accomplish deeds we need many external goods, and the greater and more excellent the acts of virtue are, all the more do we depend on these means."[9]

Matteo Palmieri's *Della vita civile,* book 4, also connects wealth and deeds. Although in book 3, Agnolo argues that "money is itself neither good nor bad, except by virtue of the uses to which its possessor puts it,"[10] the fourth book stresses that:

> riches and abundant resources are the instruments with which valiant men occupy themselves virtuously. The virtues that require the help and subsidy of the goods of fortune are numerous and without them are found to be ineffective.[11]

The virtuous man should observe two rules concerning the acquisition of possessions: first, to acquire them honestly, and second, to put them to good use in providing a modicum of creature comforts:

> Vain and valueless are the riches that at death are hidden without being used for the comfort and welfare of our lives, and worse still to use them in vile occupations and trades according to the use of many who, with such stinginess in attending to their needs, appear born more to acquire riches than to afford themselves the proper comforts.[12]

Book 3 makes clear that the proper uses of wealth extend beyond the comforts of the rich themselves:

> Those who have some natural defect of illness or of age, and thus are not able to provide for themselves, deserve public subsidy. In the former case their misery should provoke compassion; in the latter

case, if they are small children, their preservation is [at stake] ... for the [future] comfort and betterment of the common weal; if they are old, those who have passed the prosperous age of human life should be aided charitably.[13]

But the approbation of wealth in the service of a community's charitable obligations was not limited to lay humanists. In his preaching on usury, San Bernardino of Siena described the wealth of a city as its lifeblood, whose maldistribution left the body politic vulnerable to a variety of social ills.

The fourth harm is the diversion of these monies and riches to a single place. It is the general rule that as more and more riches are finding their way to fewer people and fewer purses, the worse is the evidence of the condition of the land.[14]

Sant'Antonino's position was similar. Avarice, he wrote:

consists in this: that whoever does not help his neighbor in the necessities of this life when he is able: such proceeds commonly from avarice, from him who loves temporal substance more than his neighbor.... For when temporal goods are not able to be possessed in the same degree by everyone, one man is not able to have an overabundance of temporal goods unless another is lacking, and thus avarice is directly contrary to one's neighbor.[15]

The concern of these two clerics that available wealth was becoming concentrated in the hands of a few was more than hypothetical. If attitudes toward wealth were changing, they were a partial reflection of the changing structure of the medieval economy, a change that was sharper in fourteenth-century Italy than in countries to the north, especially after the Black Death. These economic shifts demand our attention on two grounds. First, they provide a more precise sense of the extent of need to which charitable initiatives attempted to respond. Second, they provide an account of the resources at the disposal of philanthropic individuals and institutions.

The problems of identifying the extent of need are various and complex even in the twentieth century.[16] But they revolve around two problems: one is how to arrive at a definition of poverty; the other is to settle on a comprehensive description of the economic climate. Richard Trexler's article on Charity and Elites, for example, argues that both canon law and charitable practice distinguished between three types of poor: the religious, the lay miserable, and the lay poor.[17] The first category corresponds to practitioners of voluntary poverty, as well as secular clergy of modest means. The lay miserable, however, were to be sharply distinguished from the lay poor. The poverty of the first category was the poverty of helplessness: beggars, widows, orphans, and the disabled. The lay poor, on the contrary, could experience economic conditions ranging from ease to distress. Trexler's sources for this distinction, however, are Anglo-Saxon; when he refers to fourteenth- and fifteenth-century Italian sources, he indicates only that charitable aid was plentiful for fallen nobility. When the lawyer Baldus was asked whether a noble who could support himself but could not marry off his daughters was poor, Baldus replied that such a noble was indeed poor, because he could not continue to live in the style appropriate to his social station. But however careful these legal distinctions may have been, in practice the definition of *paupertas* was more fluid than Trexler suggests. Sant'Antonino, for example, frequently uses the word *pauper* to describe the "salaried indigent" in the trades and occupations he evaluates in the *Summa Moralis*. In the same opus, Antonino wrote that the poor are to be kept in their social station; hence, they are not to be given lavish banquets. Moreover, the research of Amleto Spicciani on the Buonomini di San Martino, that noble confraternity assembled to help the *poveri vergognosi*, or fallen nobility, shows that sums were dispersed to other categories of poor; the frescoes on the walls of the confraternity's headquarters near the Casa di Dante reveal the same. Thus a juridical definition does not necessarily bring us closer to the realities of fifteenth-century poverty.[18]

Attempts to arrive at a strictly economic definition, however, have so far been no more productive. Charles M. de la Roncière's articles on poverty in fourteenth-century Florence have attempted to combine wages and grain prices into a caloric formula to define the poverty line. He argues that both the Church and lay philanthropists addressed themselves to traditional categories of poor, such as widows, orphans, and foundlings, but neglected a large underclass of workers whose wages were insufficient to hold them back from the brink of starvation. This perceptual misalignment between those who distributed charity and those who received it, he argues, had its tragic outcome in the Ciompi revolt of 1378.[19] A closer look at the economic situation of wage-earners, however, shows that their fortunes were not increasingly or unremittingly bleak over the years 1350 to 1378.[20] De la Roncière's own calculations demonstrate a doubling, even tripling of wages immediately after the Black Death, with a much less dramatic increase in prices, so that workers were substantially more prosperous after the Black Death than before.[21] In short, the economic prospects of even the lowest-paid workers in Florence followed the model for which Braudel argues in *Capitalism and Material Life:* the most direct result of a catastrophe such as the Black Death was the economic benefit to survivors. The drastic decline in population stabilized the balance between resources and consumers, while resulting labor shortages pushed up wages.[22]

Another way to arrive at an economic definition of poverty might be to use the Catasto of 1427. Gene Brucker, for example, has estimated the percentage of poor in Florence at about 50 percent, including those who were too poor to have to pay any tax either on the basis of straight income or by using deductions.[23] The problem with this approach is that deductions were substantial—up to two hundred florins per dependent—so that families that paid no taxes may have possessed considerable patrimony.

Other research confirms a cautiously optimistic portrait of the economic situation for wage-earners. E. H. Phelps-Brown and Sheila V. Hopkins also found an increase of wages in England for construction workers, though the increase was much more gradual,[24] and Richard Goldthwaite's research documents the stability of grain prices throughout the fifteenth century. Giuliano Pinto's careful research on the Opsedale di San Gallo's workers also demonstrates that wages remained consistently elevated after the Black Death.[25] Between 1395 and 1406, for example, even a wet nurse's wages of 55 soldi per month could support two or three people. Finally, Goldthwaite's data, taken from various projects in the construction industry, have shown an average daily wage in 1346 of 3 soldi, 8 denarii for unskilled workers. In 1348, the average jumped to 6s. 11d., increased to 8s. 5d. the following year, and dropped below that level only four times before 1400. After the turn of the century, wages dipped below this level only nine times: in 1425, 1426, 1431, 1454, 1455, 1474, 1475, 1495, and 1496. Not once between 1349 and 1577 did the average daily wage for unskilled workers go below eight soldi.[26]

Many of the economic gains of workers might be effaced, however, if the general contraction of the economy through shrinking markets substantially eliminated a number of jobs. In certain industries, such as the wool industry, this may well have been the case. But other enterprises managed to prosper. Corti and da Silva's work on the silk industry shows much more prosperity than other historians have suggested, while the tremendous building programs of the early fifteenth century provided yet further opportunities for employment. The devaluation of silver was also not a major factor in this period: the value of a florin rose only from 74 soldi in 1389 to 83 soldi in 1431, and to 90 soldi in 1466.[27]

Although the level of wages and the behavior of prices constitute an issue separate from the performance of the economy as a whole, there is now considerable evidence to counter the very pessimistic view of the Renaissance economy put forward by Armando Sapori and Robert S. Lopez, who argued from the premise that investment in luxury goods and artifacts indicated a failure of nerve in taking those larger risks that built the financial empires of the Bardi and the Peruzzi a half-century earlier.[28] Quite apart from the inaccuracy of traditional stereotypes of such merchants as Francesco Datini and Cosimo de' Medici, there is a serious methodological problem in the assumption that cautious investment equals economic decline. Such an assumption is more appropriate to a fully industrial economy than to the economy of the preindustrial age. As more individual studies come to fruition, the portrait that emerges is one in which Florentine merchants developed increasingly subtle and sophisticated mechanisms of credit and banking to compete successfully in international commerce. Moreover, those symptoms one might expect from investors lacking confidence in the economy did not appear in fifteenth-century Florence. There was no move to return to land as the primary source of investment opportunity, nor, until the sixteenth century, did the great landowners jealously protect their patrimony through systems of impartible inheritance.[29]

Nor did wealth accrue exclusively in the hands of the few. Although it is true that in the Catasto of 1427, one quarter of the total wealth of the city lay in the hands of a hundred men, and one half of the city's liquid wealth in the hands of two hundred to three hundred men, distribution of high levels of wealth was fairly widespread. Thus, 1,649 Florentines were worth at least a thousand florins each, a distribution that, as Goldthwaite indicates, compares very favorably with the distribution of wealth in Nuremberg in the same period.[30]

In short, there is considerable evidence to suggest that the problem of poverty was less pressing in fifteenth-century Florence at a time that substantial resources could be developed to address social problems. This peculiarly favorable economic climate shaped the unique responses of Florentine philanthropists, whose generosity sprang less from a perception of acute economic distress than was true for their successors in sixteenth-century Lyons or Venice. If charitable giving in Renaissance Florence became in some sense more laicized or more rationalized during the fifteenth century, the absence of outright starvation may have left a greater margin of safety for imagination and innovation. However that may be, certainly the building of charitable institutions in the fifteenth century became suffused with the desire for personal and collective glory and immortality.

An older tradition of writing the history of charity has placed rationalization and laicization at the heart of charitable giving. W. K. Jordan, in his *Philanthropy in England, 1480–1660,* inherited not only the terms but also the theoretical framework that viewed the passing of control over bequests from ecclesiastical to lay institutions as an improvement in the efficiency and discrimination of almsgiving:

> The Middle Ages were acutely sensitive to the spiritual needs of mankind while displaying only scant, or ineffectual concern with the alleviation or cure of the ills that beset the bodies of so large a mass of humanity. The medieval system of alms, administered principally by the monastic foundations, was at once casual and ineffective in its incidence, never seeking to do more than relieve conspicuous and abject suffering.[31]

Jordan was, of course, responding to the views of R. H. Tawney and others that the Protestant devaluation of the efficacy of good works represented a hardening of attitudes after the Reformation toward the poor.

Jordan's response was to paint in rosy hues the motives and generosity of seventeenth-century Puritan merchants, whose investment and zeal he set against a medieval background of monastic charity that was not only meager, but also failed to make important distinctions between the able and the disabled poor. This distinction is also traceable to Troeltsch, who described Catholic charity as undertaken principally for the salvation of the giver, and Protestant charity as conscious social policy based on the principle of lay and governmental intervention in the disbursement of alms.

As Brian Tierney has pointed out, however, the assertion of a specifically Catholic form of charity falls apart in the face of wide variations in medieval theory and practice. Following Gratian, the twelfth-century canonists insisted that discrimination ought to be exercised in the distribution of charity, and warned of the corrupting influence of alms given to the undeserving poor. This distinction between deserving and undeserving poor was central to humanist thinking in fifteenth-century Florence as well, as Palmieri's remarks demonstrate:

> All others, who, on account of the forces of nature, are perfectly able to take care of themselves, should not receive sustenance from the *patria,* if first they have not placed themselves at its service.... Whoever of these is shiftless and without virtue [and] seeks welfare, deserves to be driven from the city; [such a man] is useless.[32]

Moreover, it would be a grave mistake to assume that monasteries were the only institutions to distribute charity in the earlier period. John H. Mundy's work on charity in Toulouse notes that "the basic resource for public charity and social work was pious giving by layfolk" in the twelfth and thirteenth centuries. A shift seems to have taken place between 1100 and 1250 from charity inter vivos to an increasing frequency of testamentary charity. Although charitable institutions in Toulouse remained under the administrative control of clergy throughout the period, the older system of eleemosynary services by monasteries and cathedral chapters became "much more specialized and articulated," with the result that charitable services were increasingly offered through hospitals, leper-houses, and rest homes. As early as the end of the twelfth century isolated charitable institutions in Toulouse were regulated and controlled by boards of laymen, and sometimes governed by married couples. It was also in this period at Toulouse that confraternities began to be associated with charitable activities, although municipal and guild government had yet to take an active role.[33]

Two studies of sixteenth-century charity address the issues that Jordan raised. The Aumône-Générale of Lyons, argues Natalie Davis, was a coalition formed in the early sixteenth century to synthesize earlier and more haphazard patterns of giving. Two hospitals undertook the care of orphans and foundlings and provided dowries for their female charges, and the Aumône-Générale invested its capital in the silk industry to provide employment opportunities for poor girls. A humanistic model of education inspired a charitable administration that cut across denominational lines and attempted to engage the energies of the lay community as a whole. Davis traced the connection between humanism, laic sanctity, and community to Florentine models and Florentine figures.[34]

Pullan's study of Venice also notes the importance of Tuscany and Northern Italy in the fifteenth century as centers of innovation in charitable practice, but his main concern is testing Jordan's hypothesis against the reality of charitable giving in the context of a Catholic state. The main Venetian arteries for charitable giving in the late fourteenth and early fifteenth centuries were the *Scuole Grandi*, which were in many ways analogous to Florentine confraternities. The Scuole, however, were to develop along very different lines: specifically, the Venetian sodalities appeared to have been more corporative and less subject to municipal regulation than were their Florentine counterparts. In the earlier period, the Scuole founded small hospitals, and at the same time began to divide into cadres of rich and poor, with the express intention that the Scuole were to be the channels by which the rich were to transmit their surplus wealth to the poor.[35]

As Pullan's own figures show, the charity dispensed by the Scuole cannot have reached the majority of the poor, though his monograph fails to provide the sort of economic analysis that would suggest the extent of poverty in sixteenth-century Venice. Given that in 1575, the membership of all the Scuole combined was equal to 3 percent of the Venetian population and to 10 percent of the Venetian adult male population, a suspicion emerges that the primary focus of the Scuole Grandi's efforts was the respectable poor, the *poveri vergognosi*. This is further borne out by the edict of the Council of Ten in 1527 ordering the Scuole to distribute bread to *miserabili*, implying that the Scuole did not routinely practice charity to this class of the indigent, even as late as the early sixteenth century.[36]

The Scuole were not the only form of succour to the poor: the sixteenth century in Venice saw the development of large general hospitals, which in Pullan's view were more advanced than the scattered, smaller institutions of the fourteenth and fifteenth centuries. Venice received its inspiration, however, from cities in Tuscany and Lombardy, where the trend toward large general hospitals dates from the end of the fourteenth century and even earlier. In Tuscany especially, Pullan sees the major stimuli as agricultural depression after the Black Death and the influence of Observant Franciscans. In the Lombard foundations, such as that of the *Officium Pietatis Pauperum* in Milan, Pullan notes the close cooperation between lay and ecclesiastical bodies, a pattern to be repeated in Venice after the Council of Trent. Large general hospitals were founded in Brescia in 1447 and in Milan in 1448, while a decree founding the hospital of San Marco in Bergamo expressed dissatisfaction with the inefficiency and corruption inherent in several small, unconnected hospitals. The decree charged that because of these abuses, large numbers of poor were inadequately served. Lombard officials turned to Florence and Siena for models of centralization: a Sienese, Alberto of Sarteano, urged Brescians to copy the hospitals of both cities. An edict of Gian Galeozzo Visconti ordered that Milanese hospitals "shall be governed and regulated in the same way as the hospital of the city of Siena."[37] Pullan argues, finally, that Venice did not adopt the model of the general hospital sooner because the impulses for such institutions were clerical, and Venetian piety and society gave greater prominence to lay people.[38]

This latter view is somewhat curious in light of the close cooperation among laymen cited in Brescia and Milan and the high frequency in both Tuscany and Lombardy of lay foundations of large general hospitals. A number of fifteenth-century Florentine institutions that could be said to represent part of the "new philanthropy," such as the hospitals of San Matteo and Bonifazio Lupi, and, of course, the Innocenti, were noted for their specialized services. The large general hospitals, such as those of Santa Maria Nuova in Florence and Santa Maria della Scala in Siena, were not new foundations at all. Santa Maria Nuova was founded in 1288, and the foundation of Santa Maria della Scala of Siena can be dated back well into the eleventh century. Although both hospitals underwent considerable administrative reorganization in the early fifteenth century, they were both large general hospitals well before that date. Nor did centralization and the aggrandizement of real estate holdings necessarily imply efficiency and honesty. In the early fifteenth century, the Bigallo-Misericordia company of Florence supervised at least ten hospitals, but its real estate ventures brought the company to the verge of bankruptcy and required the hasty intervention of the communal authorities.[39] Pullan's ascription of the foundation of these Tuscan charities to the pressure of agricultural depression and the influx of rural workers into cities and towns is hardly borne out by the experience of Florence, whose guilds were constrained to offer tax exemptions to encourage workers to settle and work in Florence.[40]

A close comparison of Venetian and Florentine charity might well reveal shared humanist influences and concerns, but little else in common. Venetian charity in the Scuole does not seem to have extended beyond the membership of those bodies, where Florentine confraternities and guilds, even in the fourteenth century, stepped outside their corporate boundaries.[41] The Scuole primarily aided the *poveri vergognosi*, while in Florence the Buonomini di San Martino, though perhaps formed for that purpose, assisted other categories of poor.[42] Municipal intervention in Venetian poor relief was scarce in normal times and ad hoc in times of crisis, although Venice had a magistracy of public health long before Florence. The Florentine government intervened frequently in the activities of charitable organizations, alternately assuming political and fiscal control as circumstances dictated. This did not, however, stifle the creative philanthropy of lay men and lay women. Despite these problems in *Rich and Poor,* Pullan's achievement was to open the question of money-lending and other unofficial enterprises as forms of providing easy access to credit. Also illuminating is the suggested connection between anti-Semitism and charitable initiative, prominent and direct in the way that the Monti di Pieta were to supplant Jewish moneylenders, but no less so than San Bernardino's sermons on usury declaring that Jews were "the chief enemy" of all Christians. Not only Siena, but Florence, too, experienced the linking of anti-Semitism to charitable impulse. Pullan's suggestion that the urgent and demanding pressures of charity may have had their psychic cost in hatred does not seem at all far-fetched in the Florentine context.[43]

Reinhold Mueller's review article in the 1972 issue of *Studi Veneziani* suggests that Florence and Tuscany may not necessarily have served as models for Venetian charity, and, by extension, that Pullan may have underestimated the role of Venice's own earlier tradition of charity in shaping the philanthropy of the sixteenth century. Moreover, a greater variety of charitable organizations than the Scuole Grandi may have extended charity beyond their very limited membership. Mueller mentions in this context the guilds, the *scuole piccole,* the Procuratie di San Marco, and the ecclesiastical *decima dei morti.* By the year 1500, Venice could boast more than 150 *scuole piccole,* some of which were not devotional institutions but whose sole purpose was to attract alms. The

Procurators of San Marco as early as the fourteenth century invested in trusts set up for "pious causes" and distributed some of the return of these investments as charity. Finally, the *decima dei morti*, or tithes, controlled by the Venetian commune included distributions to the Bishop of Castello, the clergy of Venice, and the maintenance of churches and the poor.

Municipal intervention in the fourteenth century was also much more striking than Pullan's study would suggest. In 1300, the Great Council of Venice forbade the poor from "wandering about the city" and decreed that they should be placed in hospitals and that any additional facilities were to be constructed on the islands. The commune of Venice seems to have made a conscious effort to control the direction of charitable monies to already existing institutions. The Procurators of San Marco would also exercise indirect municipal control when testators entrusted to them the execution of their philanthropic bequests.[44]

In Florence, the principle of municipal intervention was well-established before the Black Death. In 1294, for example, the Arte della Seta was placed in charge of both the Ospedale di San Gallo and the city's foundlings. As early as 1318 the Society of Or San Michele had to petition for permission to receive charitable bequests and to acquire tax-exempt status as a *locus ecclesiasticus*.[45] It is, rather, the scope of municipal intervention that changed after the Black Death, and one can detect a subtle but discernible shift from a crisis mentality to both an increased interest in building and a pattern of more direct central control over the patrimony of charitable groups.

The specific application of the trend of municipal intervention to Florence would by necessity include the transformation in the 1350s of Or San Michele, at the geographic center of the Renaissance city, from a market center for the sale and distribution of grain into a religious and communal center for the guilds. In both a symbolic and a literal sense, the monumental replaced the quotidian, the communitarian and public the restricted and corporate. Each guild, it is true, spent fortunes on self-glorification for the part of the facade to which it was assigned, but the initiative for the project came from the commune's decree of 1406 ordering the guilds to adorn their niches.[46]

Municipal intervention also took the form of asserting communal control over the burgeoning patrimonies of confraternities and charitable institutions. The history of two of the city's most important confraternities, the Bigallo and Or San Michele, provides a vivid illustration of the scope of the problem and of the determination of the commune to intervene. The Bigallo had begun supervising the city's hospitals as early as 1245, and by 1350 the confraternity's captains administered at least five hospitals of ten to twenty beds each. Between 1350 and 1400 another four were added. The Bigallo was entrusted with these enterprises through a combination of purchase and donation by both monastic communities and lay testators. The leadership of the confraternity was based on a system of drawings by chance from a pool consisting of the membership, a managerial flaw that may itself have contributed to the confraternity's increasingly dire straits in the early fifteenth century.[47]

In 1417, eight of the confraternity's officials petitioned the Signoria to enforce various measures concerning the organization's distribution of resources. The enabling legislation's preamble noted that both the devotion and the reputation of the company had fallen on hard times, "for which reason almost nothing is bequeathed to them."[48] The *Provvisione* elaborated thus: the reason for this was the confraternity's maldistribution of alms and the lack of enthusiastic and devoted officials. "They [the eight captains], desirous that the Company should be maintained and increased, had recourse to your Magnificence to prevent it from being completely ruined."[49] Henceforth, the captains could not give any alms without the express permission of a governing board to be chosen from the Guelf party, the Mercanzia, the seven major guilds, and the fourteen minor guilds. Out of a pool of twenty-six nominated from these groups, sixteen were actually to be chosen for office. In addition to seeking approval from this board of overseers, the bursar also had to swear an oath that the company was not in debt. Only then could the captains disburse alms at their pleasure, on the condition that they swore them to be for worthy causes. The captains were also forbidden to choose a bursar, notary, or treasurer without the board's consent. Together the captains and the board would "elect and delegate in each of the said offices whomever shall appear to be good, useful, and suitable."[50] The same provision applied to choosing the *spedalinghi* of the Company's various hospitals. The governing board's consent was also required for the sale or alienation of any of the company's mobile or immobile goods. Finally, all testaments and contracts were to be sealed and brought to the Company within two months from the day they were notarized.

Tight as these measures were, they did not suffice to resuscitate the confidence of testators, and in 1425, the Bigallo was unified with the hospital of Santa Maria della Misericordia, and its responsibilities became limited to the care of orphans and abandoned children, whereas previously its functions had been considerably more diverse.[51]

Three *Provvisioni* before 1350 suggest the confidence Florentines had in the second great charitable confraternity, the Captains of Or San Michele. In 1318 the commune authorized the Society to receive bequests. In 1329, the commune decreed that the estate of a condemned murderer could not go to his descendants, but had to be divided up between the commune, which received two-thirds, and the poor, who received the other third. In 1339 legislation provided that anyone who initiated litigation against the Society had to pay a deposit, which was forfeited if Or San Michele won the suit.[52]

Such was the confidence of testators in Or San Michele, wrote the chronicler Matteo Villani, that legacies drawn up during the Black Death yielded the Society the huge sum of 350,000 florins, earmarked for distribution to the poor. Villani ascribed the size of the sum to the reputation of Or San Michele as an especially efficient and humane administrator of alms. As the Society was accumulating this vast treasure, Villani wrote, the begging poor:

were almost all dead, and every poor woman was so laden with things that she did not seek alms.... And there being no needy poor in that time, they [the captains] distributed alms liberally, each captain where it pleased him the most, and with little concern for the favor of God and His Holy Mother. Much treasure was thus consumed in little time, and when it came time to create new captains, they were from among the friends of the old captains.... The possessions of the Company they farmed out for friendship and a quick sale, and sales were made quite dishonestly. Those citizens [whose affairs] were entangled in the hands of the captains for inheritances, dowries, debts, and shares of property ... were not for a long time able to free themselves from them, and everything suffered in protracted default, without resolution.... The citizenry, perceiving the shameful operation of the captains, ... ordered them called before the council, and in the passage of time the commune took part of the personal property of the Company, seeing that it was badly distributed by the captains. For the above reasons the faith towards the Company among citizens and *contadini* began to decline precipitously, poisoned by the Company's disordered fiscal affairs, and by its avaricious overseers.[53]

Villani also noted that the Company paid Orcagna eighty-six thousand florins to build the marble tabernacle inside the church of Or San Michele, a sum that Ghiberti a half-century later would record as greater than that paid to any artist in living memory.[54]

At least five *Provvisioni* in the year 1348 concerned the hasty intervention of the commune in the Society's fiscal affairs, and the following half-century is replete with other provisions concerning them. Legislation multiplied in inverse ratio to its effectiveness and, in 1384, the Signory, because of the continued disorder of this confraternity's transactions, ordered that before accepting property left to it, the Society had first to ascertain whether it could sustain the burdens imposed on it by the testator. The nineteenth-century historian Passerini noted that the books of the captains were in such disorder that it was impossible to gauge the amount spent annually by the Society for almsgiving.[55] In 1415 communal intervention extended, as in the case of the Bigallo, to determining the manner of electing officers. The procedures established in 1415 were not changed until the end of the sixteenth century, and were incorporated into the statutes of 1415.[56]

This pattern was repeated in a large number of cases, embroiling the Florentine government more and more in the business of taking control of charity. In 1419 it dissolved all the confraternities in the city. The intention was not to eliminate the role of confraternities in providing charity, since most of them survived the dissolution. Rather, the legislation stipulated that they could only operate by special license of the Signory, which effectively meant that confraternal political activities would no longer be tolerated. Their subordination to a larger sense of community and charity, like that of the guilds, was conscious policy on the part of the commune. In the measure providing for the dissolution, motives of charitable reform and political uniformity were clear:

The Lord Priors ... desire to eliminate the cause and occasion of scandals and to remove all suspicion from the minds of authorities so that everyone can live peaceably. ...

Item, the Lord Priors are authorized, between now and the end of

November, to dispose of all property, both real and personal, and for the remissions of sins, of those who had given that property to those confraternities.[57]

Florence was not unique in these respects. In 1404, the commune of Siena undertook a reform of the hospital of Santa Maria della Scala that greatly extended communal authority over the institution.[58] In Pistoia, the Bishop of Pistoia and the commune struggled tenaciously over the Ospedale del Dolce and the Ospedale della Misericordia. To view the conflicts as traditional ones between Church and State, however, provides too narrow a focus.[59] Municipal intervention is only one facet of the larger impulse on the part of the laity to push outward the boundaries of its areas of legitimate concern. Parallel to the extension of lay spiritual power was an equally important shift taking place in the pattern of charitable giving.

The task of fully substantiating such an assertion would be truly staggering: surely a study of wills over the period 1300–1500 would be a minimum requirement. Nevertheless, a comparison of the foundation of the hospital of Santa Maria Nuova in 1288 with the foundation of the hospital of Bonifazio Lupi in 1377 is highly suggestive of an important shift in the attitude of testators and founders of charitable institutions.

The document by which Folco Portinari founded the hospital of Santa Maria Nuova was not a will, but a simple, notarized "public instrument." On 23 June 1288, it states, Folco Portinari, son of Recupero de' Portinari of the parish of Saint Margaret in Florence "placed before the Venerable Father, Lord Andrea, by the grace of God Bishop of Florence, a certain petition."[60] The document then discusses the *domus* that Portinari had built for "the lodging and support of the poor and indigent," with a description of its boundaries. The Bishop conceded to Portinari and his descendants the full rights of patronage, including the right to appoint the rector of both the Church of Sant'Egidio and the rector of the hospital. In addition, no *converso* could be placed in the service of the hospital without the consent of Portinari or his descendants. Although certainly this provided considerable lay independence, Portinari also petitioned the Bishop to grant Santa Maria Nuova the immunity "that other hospitals and religious places subject to you have, that it may enjoy ecclesiastical liberty, and be free and exempt from every secular tie and servitude." Although such provisions were employed even in the fifteenth century to avoid municipal levies, Portinari specifically compared Santa Maria Nuova to other religious places subject to the Bishop of Florence.

Less than a hundred years later it is extremely difficult to find a testator so anxious to entrust his charitable enterprise to a cleric. In 1377, Bonifazio Lupi, a *condottiere* for the Florentines, but who hailed from Parma, petitioned the Signory of Florence for permission to build a hospital dedicated to Saint John the Baptist. In the *Provvisione* that resulted, the Signory agreed to defend the hospital "against the presumption of those clerics, who, heedless of God's judgments, seek for themselves what has already been allocated for pious works, converting it not only to other uses, but also for illicit purposes."[61] One hears echoes of Mazzei's warnings to Francesco Datini not to leave his estate to the Bishop of Pistoia or Florence, who were likely to spend it on "banquets and horses." Bonifazio's will stipulated that the administration of his hospital should be undertaken by the Calimala guild. In general, testators anxious to leave a charitable enterprise as their memorial turned not to the Church but to the secular authority of guild and commune. Yet the designated successors of these philanthropists did not always find secular authorities sympathetic to their demands for tax exemptions, and the frequency with which they sought recourse through petitions suggests that lay stewardship could often be financially precarious. On more than one occasion the Innocenti would require the intervention of the Archbishop of Florence to save its potential patrimony from taxation.[62] One must therefore be careful not to emphasize that pious impulse on the part of laymen was necessarily anticlerical. Lay piety is a phenomenon considerably more complex, and the central issue for the fifteenth-century giver was not so much to whom he should leave his patrimony but whom should he entrust with its administration.

As Kristeller and Trinkaus have shown, lay piety sought a redefinition, a redistribution of sacred and secular space. Philanthropy and the proper uses of wealth were central to this process of redefinition. Brucker's *The Civic World of Early Renaissance Florence* shows the practical application of the humanist vision at work in the Florentine councils. Christian Bec's *Les marchands écrivains* has illuminated the shared moral and practical concerns among humanists and the merchant elite of Florence. Humanist treatises and merchant diaries both stressed the centrality of family and pedagogy to the creation of an ideal civil polity.[63] A discussion of attitudes toward poverty, wealth, and charity may illuminate motives for philanthropy, but does not explain why charity toward children should be an issue of such moment. Two recent approaches, one primarily using demographic evidence, the other literary and legal evidence, suggest different hypotheses.

The first hypothesis stresses the necessity for a foundling hospital; this derives from Ariès's argument that high infant mortality deadened parental feelings toward infants, especially female infants, and left them more vulnerable to abandonment. The second hypothesis relies on the evidence of literature, law, and high infant mortality rates in the early modern period to suggest that the premodern foundling hospital depersonalized and undermined medieval systems of abandonment and adoption that had previously worked to the benefit of abandoned children and their unfortunate parents.

Certainly the most thorough and comprehensive contribution to the demographic argument is David Herlihy and Christiane Klapisch-Zuber's *Les Toscans et leurs familles,* which sharpens the distinction, somewhat blunted in Klapisch-Zuber's earlier work, between attitudes toward infants and attitudes toward older children. This distinction results in the more sophisticated argument that very high infant mortality caused parental indifference to children in the most vulnerable age group: one month to two years old. A love too strong and too liberally dispensed to these fragile creatures risked intolerable parental suffering. A participant in Alberti's dialogue on the family describes the intense depressive state that fathers experienced at the deaths of their infants, and suggests that for this reason marriage is to be avoided altogether. Sending infants out to wet-nurse, Herlihy and Klapisch-Zuber argue, reflected not so much a lack of love for them as a deep fear of loving them. The authors insist with equal vehemence on the lavishness of parental affection for children who had crossed the threshold of vulnerability and whose chances for survival were relatively promising.[64] It is, perhaps, for emotional as well as practical reasons that Alberti advised that children were better off placed under a mother's care until the age of two.

In this respect the records of the Ospedale degli Innocenti provide the materials for a crucial test of the "demographic" hypothesis, which has been the central working hypothesis of the secondary literature on the history of childhood since the publication of Ariès's *Centuries of Childhood.* The series of *Balie e Bambini,* or "wet nurses and babies," in the hospital of the Innocenti's archive, is the record of depositions taken by hospital officials from porters who abandoned children there. These depositions, if not exactly verbose, do, in about 55 percent of the cases, enable us to identify the parents of the children brought to the Innocenti and the circumstances of each child's birth.[65] The crucial test for the argument that children were abandoned at the Innocenti because of widespread and accepted parental neglect would be to determine what proportion of abandoned children were illegitimate, forcing at least a crude distinction between motives of economic hardship, social shame, and parental neglect.

Richard Trexler's two brief studies of child abandonment in Florence found that "with the exception of slave and clerical parentage, illegitimacy does not seem to have furnished moral or material justification for abandonment."[66] Yet, of the cases in which the child's parentage is known, 60 percent were children of slaves and servants.[67] Contemporaries also ascribed to "the larger than usual number of slaves and servants in the city" the Innocenti's success in attracting infants.[68] As Trexler himself notes, these proportions were far from immune to change by external pressures. In the first of his two studies, Trexler advances the thesis that the expanded facilities of the Innocenti encouraged parents to abandon more boys there than they had at the foundling hospitals of San Gallo and Santa Maria della Scala. He notes in this respect a drop from 61 percent to 58.9 percent in the number of female foundlings at San Gallo compared to those of the Innocenti.

Trexler's second study is more closely tied to the Ospedale degli Innocenti than the first. He charges that the Innocenti "institutionalized" female infanticide by sending a greater proportion of female than male infants to wet nurses. The hospital's putative motivations lay in the greater willingness of fathers to write notes for boys imploring the hospital not to send them out.[69] In general, Trexler's work fails to distinguish intention and effect. I hope in the following pages to give a more detailed account of who the hospital's clients were and what effect the dynamics of the institution's administrative organization had on the disposition of children placed under its care. This requires not only a discussion of admissions decisions, but also of the entire network of adoption and apprenticeship and its relationship to the society and economy of Renaissance Florence. The documentary and literary evidence left by fifteenth-century Florentines suggests that among the middle and upper strata, the importance of heirs to maintaining family standing and importance in

Florentine politics would make parental neglect of legitimate children a most unlikely motive for abandonment.

A final consideration is necessary to make an effective distinction between foundling hospitals of the fifteenth century and those of the eighteenth. As will be shown, mortality rates within foundling hospitals in the seventeenth, eighteenth, and nineteenth centuries were considerably higher than those at the Innocenti in the fifteenth century. In Paris between 1710 and 1780, the proportion of children abandoned to those baptized rose from 10 to 30 percent.[70] In the decade 1841 to 1850, the proportion of admissions at the Ospedale degli Innocenti to baptisms in Florence was as high as 38 percent.[71] Contrast these proportions with those of 1451, in which 4.8 percent of baptisms were abandoned to the Innocenti, and those of 1465, when 8.9 percent were abandoned. If foundling hospitals in the eighteenth century were caring for a third of a city's infants, in fifteenth-century Florence the Innocenti was burdened with a mere tenth, even a mere twentieth of the number of children baptized at San Giovanni.[72]

Other historians have preferred a broader cultural and legal perspective to a more strictly demographic approach. John Boswell's recent volume, *The Kindness of Strangers,* is a magisterial survey of the theme of abandonment from antiquity through the middle ages. Boswell's study, using bold and sophisticated analysis of literature and law to illuminate the frequency and effects of the actual practice of abandonment, discerns what amounts to a social system of abandonment. Families who could not afford to support surplus children recycled them through abandonment into families and institutions better equipped to provide for the necessities of childhood. In late antiquity, abandoned children might be sold into slavery or adopted into families of higher social standing.

In the early middle ages, some wealthy families who practiced partible inheritance abandoned their surplus males to monasteries in order to preserve the integrity of the family patrimony. During the high middle ages, the evidence of literature shows less concern and interest in the problem during this era of incipient urbanization. Not until the mid-thirteenth century, when population growth peaked and resources became increasingly strained, did abandonment resurface as a literary or legal *topos.* Both population pressure and endemic plague combined in the fourteenth and fifteenth centuries to motivate urban laymen and municipal authorities to establish orphanages and foundling hospitals.

These large and well-endowed charitable institutions, Boswell argues, allowed parents to abandon children anonymously and coldbloodedly, given the horrifying mortality of which parents must have been aware. These new institutions, then, undermined what had been a less deadly and more compassionate form of abandonment that had prevailed in the middle ages.[73] Yet to compare the mortality of two systems of abandonment, as Boswell implicitly does, can hardly be illuminating when, for the later period, we have the detailed demographic evidence of institutional archives but have none for the earlier. What the institutional evidence from the Ospedale degli Innocenti does show, however, is that the abandonment of children elicited responses from parents that ranged from the callous to the compassionate. Chapter 5, in particular, will show that parents remained involved with their abandoned sons and daughters for years, even decades, after abandonment had taken place.[74]

The Kindness of Strangers, as a general work of cultural and social history, could not take into account the particular milieu in which Florentine concern for children thrived. The concerns of Florentine historians concerning family structure, however, suggest that a number of factors converged to place children at the center of family life. Even though the view that the isolated nuclear family defined the limits of the affections of Florentines is no longer tenable,[75] one needs only to read the letters of Alessandra Strozzi to her sons to draw the connection between high infant mortality and the centrality of children to the preservation of lineage solidarity and, ultimately, the Florentine state.[76]

Preserving lineage solidarity, however, was not merely a matter of having children, but also a matter of educating them to further the family's social, economic, and political fortunes. One of the most important cultural and social phenomena of modern European history is surely the careful attention devoted to pedagogy, and the revival of the classical ideal of *paideia.* It is this revival of classical pedagogy that reconciles the approaches of demography and family structure. The spiritual and educational interest in the salvation of children reflected the demographic realities of high infant mortality and the precariousness of family solidarity. The "preservation of our city and its state," a recurring phrase in nearly every piece of communal legislation concerning the Ospedale degli Innocenti, was no mere spiritual sloganeering, but a recognition of the demographic reality that the future of the city depended on the preservation and education of its youth. For this reason the issue of nuclear versus extended family was less important to contemporaries than it has been for some modern historians. Alberti's *Della Famiglia* argued the interdependence of the father's domestic role and its contribution to lineage and family solidarity:

> I also have no doubt at all that by good management, careful and diligent rule by the father, good habits, and the utmost integrity of conduct, culture, courtesy and responsibility, the family can become great and fortunate. . . . Seek the well-being, increase the honor, magnify the fame of our house. Listen, also, to what our Alberti ancestors thought that learned, educated, cultivated persons owed to the family. . . . The old cannot more appropriately acquire, increase, and conserve great authority and dignity than by caring for the young. Thus must they draw them toward the greatest and the highest ambitions, [and] keep them to the study of the best things and those of highest esteem.[77]

Although this passage is a clear statement of the importance of the household to the position of lineage in public life, Alberti is describing a hope rather than a reality. His deep interest in relationships between fathers and sons is a reflection not of the strength of those bonds, but of their fragility.[78] As a consequence of late male marriage and an average superiority of thirteen years over female marriage age, many Florentine fathers never lived to see their sons fully grown.[79] About 20 percent of Florentine households contained only a single person.[80] Thus Alberti himself, for example, never knew his own father; his branch of the family, moreover, suffered considerable injustices at the hands of malicious kinsmen. The depressing demographic profile of the Alberti family is movingly described by Adovardo Alberti in *Della Famiglia:*

> It grieves me to see so many of you younger Alberti without an heir, not having done what you could to increase the family and make it numerous. . . . According to a count I took a few days ago not less than twenty-two young Alberti no younger than sixteen or older than thirty-six are living alone and without a female companion, since they have no wife. I think we should gladly bear all the discomforts and unpleasant burdens in the world rather than allow our family to stand desolate, with none to succeed in the place and name of the fathers. I

particularly hope that you . . . will adorn and increase the Alberti family, not only as now with your fame and honor but also with sons like yourself.[81]

In evaluating this treatise as evidence, moreover, one must be aware not only of its idealistic rather than descriptive character, but also of the motives and intentions of its composition. Alberti's concern is less with either household or lineage as modes of familial organization, and more with using the idea of the family to organize important humanist themes of education in *civiltà*. The family is only secondarily a form of social organization; first and foremost it is the stage on which the drama of skillful political management versus the power of fortune is acted out. The family is also the training ground for education in full *humanitas:* as Man expresses the image and likeness of the Heavenly Father, so does an earthly father "take delight in seeing them [his own children] express his very image and likeness."[82]

The qualities of fatherhood and the successful management of lineage are political, civic, and public. The good father "knows how to steer according to the winds' favor, the waves of popular opinion, and the grace given him by his fellow citizens, toward the harbor of honor, prestige, and authority."[83] The new appreciation of marriage and domesticity of such thinkers as Leonardo Bruni, Matteo Palmieri, and Alberti marked less a new sentimentality than it did a keen perception of the importance of the family to public life. The demarcation between these intellectual sensibilities and awareness of demographic crisis was far from sharp; Palmieri also valued children for this reason: "A useful thing it is to have fostered children, [thereby] having increased the population and given citizens to the *patria*."[84] As Christian Bec has noted in *Les marchands écrivains*, merchant pedagogy was not only moral education, but also political insofar as its ultimate end was to develop in the young merchant the skills of civility and sociability. Culture and education were not ends in themselves, but the means of maintaining, extending, and perpetuating the discourse among men that constituted an enduring civil polity.

The centrality of humanist sensibilities and of the pedagogical thinking of Florentine merchants to the conception and execution of the charitable enterprise of the Innocenti is clear above all in the bequests upon which it was founded, discussed in detail in the next two chapters. The earliest founders of the institution envisioned extensive lay stewardship and set up several mechanisms for recourse to various municipal authorities. The histories of subsequent bequests demonstrate how frequently governmental intervention was summoned to the aid of the institution in guaranteeing that its share of patrimony should remain intact.[85] In addition to supervising bequests, the commune was also perforce involved, as we shall see in chapter 2, with the administration of Monte credits bequeathed to the orphanage, and with sharing with the Arte della Seta the burden of maintaining a sufficient flow of revenue.[86] The Arte della Seta, in turn, governed the Ospedale degli Innocenti with a board of *operai,* or trustees, whose tasks were distributed among the upper echelons of guild membership on a rotating basis. Offices within the hospital's administrative structure were filled using the same criteria as those in force for higher guild offices.[87]

The organization of care at the Ospedale degli Innocenti, discussed in chapter 4, attempted to replicate insofar as was institutionally possible the experience of family life. Although the sexes were rigidly separated as far as living quarters were concerned, the hospital referred to itself as "tutta la famiglia," or as "tutta la brigata." An outsider who married one of the hospital's girls was even referred to as "our son-in-law." If the separate cloisters and the strict vows of obedience taken by the staff were reminiscent more of monasteries than of homes, the orphanage nevertheless encouraged a lay monasticism that allowed married couples to take their vows of service together and to retain quarters permitting the sustenance of the conjugal relationship.[88] It was not until the early 1450s, as we will see in chapter 5, that the Innocenti began to acquire anything like a permanent resident population. When children were abandoned there, almost without exception as newborns, they were sent out to wet-nurse, and did not return to the hospital, (except for brief interludes between foster parents), until the age of five. By the age of six or seven not only boys but girls had either been apprenticed to local tradesmen or adopted as domestic servants to local families.[89]

The symbolic importance of children to the city and its foremost charitable enterprise transcended the demographic and the pedagogical, uniting them within the larger context of civic and collective salvation.[90] Numerous depictions of the massacre of the Innocents in late fourteenth-century and early fifteenth-century painting must have lent compelling emotional force to the plight of contemporary children. Just as on the individual level humanists perceived in children the potential satisfaction of yearnings for personal immortality,[91] their contemporaries discovered in their dead and dying children the occasion for both inexpressible grief, legitimized by Giannozzo Manetti's *Consolateria*,[92] and spiritual consolation.[93] Spirituality and civics combined in this 1456 piece of legislation, which expressed the hope that:

> because of the prayers of these infants who shine in purity, our most high and omnipotent Lord God will see fit in His tender compassion and mercy not only to preserve, but also to increase, this city and its state.[94]

NOTES

1. Gene Brucker, *Renaissance Florence* (New York, 1971), 209–10.

2. Robert Manz, "Almsgiving as Part of Lay Spirituality in the *Speculum Ecclesiae*," unpublished.

3. R. W. Southern, *The Making of the Middle Ages* (London, 1953), 50–52; Marvin B. Becker, *Medieval Italy* (Bloomington, 1981), 99–125; Colin Morris, *The Discovery of the Individual, 1050–1200* (New York, 1972), passim.

4. Becker, *Medieval Italy*, 46.

5. Charles M. de la Roncière, "L'église et la pauvreté à Florence au XIVe siècle," *Recherches et débats: Cahier du Centre Catholique Intellectuels Francais. La pauvreté: des sociétés de penurie à la société d'abondance* 49 (1964): 47–66.

6. Ibid., 53. All translations, unless otherwise attributed, are by the author.

7. Ibid., 55.

8. Coluccio Salutati, *De Saeculo et Religione*, ed. T. F. Rich and B. H. Ullman (Leipzig, 1934), cited in Hans Baron, "Franciscan Poverty and Civic Wealth as Factors in the Rise of Humanistic Thought," *Speculum* 13 (1938): 16.

9. Cited in Hans Baron, "Franciscan Poverty and Civic Wealth as Factors in the Rise of Humanistic Thought," *Speculum* 13 (1938): 20. Baron points out that the attribution of the *Economics* to Aristotle is no longer tenable. For a discussion of Alberti's rejection of the use of wealth for charity, see G. Ponte, "Etica ed economica nel terzo libro 'Della famiglia' di Leon Battista Alberti," in *Renaissance Studies in Honor of Hans Baron*, ed. Anthony Molho and John Tedeschi (De Kalb, 1971), 306–7.

10. Matteo Palmieri, *Della vita civile* (Milan, 1825), 94.

11. Ibid., 211.

12. Ibid., 240.

13. Ibid., 191–92.

14. San Bernardino da Siena, *Opera omnia* (Florence, 1956), 4:252. Philip Gavitt, "Economy, Charity, and Community in Florence, 1350–1450," in *As-*

pects of Poverty in Early Modern Europe, ed. Thomas Riis (Florence, 1981), 79–118.

15. Sant'Antonino, *Summa Theologica* (Verona, 1749), vol. 2, col. 13a; Gavitt, "Economy, Charity, and Community," 109.

16. Wilfrid Beckerman, "The Measurement of Poverty," in *Aspects of Poverty in Early Modern Europe*, ed. Thomas Riis (Florence, 1981), 47–64.

17. Richard Trexler, "Charity and the Defense of Urban Elites in the Italian Communes," in *The Rich, the Well-born, and the Powerful*, ed. F. Jaher (Urbana, 1973), 64–109.

18. Amleto Spicciani, "The Poveri Vergognosi," in *Aspects of Poverty in Early Modern Europe*, ed. Thomas Riis (Florence, 1981), 126–27. See especially the plates between pp. 126–27.

19. Charles M. de la Roncière, "Pauvres et pauvreté à Florence au XIVᵉ siècle," in *Etudes sur l'histoire de la pauvreté*, ed. Michel Mollat (Paris, 1974), 2:661–745.

20. On the social and economic composition of the Ciompi, see Gene Brucker, "The Ciompi revolution," in *Florentine Studies*, ed. Nicolai Rubinstein (Evanston, 1968), 314–56.

21. Gavitt, "Economy, Charity, and Community," 83–96.

22. Fernand Braudel, *Capitalism and Material Life, 1400–1800*, trans. Miriam Kochan (New York, 1973), passim.

23. Gene Brucker, *The Society of Renaissance Florence* (New York, 1971), xv.

24. M. M. Postan, "Some Economic Evidence of Declining Population in the Later Middle Ages," *Economic History Review*, 2d ser., 2 (1950): 221–46; E. H. Phelps-Brown and Sheila V. Hopkins, "Seven Centuries of Building Wages," *Economica* 22 (1953): 195–206, and "Seven Centuries of the Price of Consumables, Compared with Builders' Wage Rates," *Economica* 23 (1956): 296–314; Carlo Cipolla, *Before the Industrial Revolution, 1000–1700* (New York, 1976): 202–3; Richard Goldthwaite, "I prezzi del grano a Firenze dal XIV al XVI secolo," *Quaderni Storici* 28 (1975): 5–36.

25. Giuliano Pinto, "Il personale, le balie, e i salariati dell'Ospedale di San Gallo di Firenze negli anni 1395–1406. Note per la storia del salariato nelle città medievali," *Ricerche Storiche* 4, no. 2 (1974): 113–68.

26. Richard Goldthwaite, *The Building of Renaissance Florence* (Baltimore, 1980): 295ff., 436–39.

27. Gino Corti and J. G. da Silva, "Note sur la production de la soie à Florence au XVᵉ siècle," *Annales: Economie, Société, Civilisations* 20 (1965): 309–11. See Goldthwaite, *Building*, 41–66.

28. See Armando Sapori's contribution to *Atti del III Convegno Internazionale del Rinascimento* (Florence, 1953), 126–32. See also Robert S. Lopez, "Hard Times and Investment in Culture," in *The Renaissance: A Symposium* (New

York, 1953), 19–32, and Robert S. Lopez and Harry A. Miskimin, "The Economic Depression of the Renaissance," *Economic History Review*, 2d ser., 14 (1962): 408–26. Finally, note the debate between Lopez and Carlo Cipolla in *Economic History Review*, 2d ser., 16 (1964): 519–35.

29. J. P. Cooper, "Patterns of Inheritance and Settlement by Great Landowners from the Fifteenth to the Eighteenth Centuries," in *Family and Inheritance: Rural Society in Western Europe, 1200–1800*, ed. J. Goody, J. Thirsk, and E. P. Thompson (Cambridge, 1976), 193–305.

30. Goldthwaite, *Building*, 60–61. Cf. Lauro Martines, *The Social World of the Florentine Humanists* (Princeton, 1963), passim; H. H. von Hallerstein, "Grösse und Quellen des Vermögens von hundert Nürnburgen Bürgern um 1500." *Beiträge zur Wirtschaftsgeschichte Nürnbergs* (Nuremberg, 1967), 1:117–76. Goldthwaite points out that one quarter of the total wealth of the city of Florence was in the hands of 100 men, or about 1 percent of the men who filled out tax returns. At the next level of wealth, Florence far outperformed Nuremberg. Alice Hanson Jones has published similar data for colonial and twentieth-century America. In 1774 among the free wealthholders of the Thirteen Colonies, distribution of total wealth was more even: the wealthiest 1 percent held 12.9 percent of the wealth. In 1962, the percentage of wealth possessed by the upper 1 percent of the population was about one quarter, a figure virtually equal to that of Florence in 1427. The widest differences, of course, come at the next level of wealth. In the United States, in 1962, the richest 10 percent of the population held 62 percent of the wealth, whereas in Renaissance Florence, the upper 3 percent of taxpayers held about 50 percent of the liquid wealth reported in the 1427 Catasto. See Alice Hanson Jones, *Wealth of a Nation to Be: The American Colonies on the Eve of the Revolution* (New York, 1980), 162–65, 289.

31. W. K. Jordan, *Philanthropy in England, 1480–1660* (London, 1959), 17.

32. Brian Tierney, *Medieval Poor Law* (Berkeley, 1959), passim. See also his "The Decretists and the 'Deserving Poor,'" *Comparative Studies in Society and History* 1 (1958–59): 360–73. Palmieri, *Della vita civile*, 192.

33. John H. Mundy, "Charity and Social Work in Toulouse, 1100–1250," *Traditio* 22 (1966): 203–87.

34. Natalie Davis, "Poor Relief, Humanism and Heresy: The Case of Lyons," *Studies in Medieval and Renaissance History* 5 (1968): 217–69.

35. Brian Pullan, *Rich and Poor in Renaissance Venice: The Social Institutions of a Catholic State* (Oxford, 1971), passim.

36. See Marvin B. Becker's review of Pullan's *Rich and Poor* in the *Journal of Economic History* 32 (1972): 1005–8.

37. Pullan, *Rich and Poor*, 206.

38. Ibid., 65–156.

39. Howard Saalman, *The Bigallo* (New York, 1969), 5.

40. Raymond de Roover, "Labour Conditions in Florence ca. 1400," in *Florentine Studies*, ed. Rubinstein 277–313. The model proposed by Bronislaw Geremek in "La popolazione marginale fra il Medievo e l'era moderna," *Studi Storici* 9 (1968): 623–40, does not appear to fit the Florentine case in the early fifteenth century.

41. Pullan, *Rich and Poor,* 65–156.

42. Spicciani, "Buonomini di San Martino," 119–82.

43. Pullan, *Rich and Poor,* 626ff.

44. Reinhold Mueller, "Charitable Institutions, the Jewish Community, and Venetian Society: A Discussion of the Recent Volume by Brian Pullan," *Studi Veneziani* 14 (1972): 37–81. See idem, "The Procurators of San Marco in the Thirteenth and Fourteenth Centuries: A Study of the Office as a Financial and Trust Institution," *Studi Veneziani* 13 (1971): 105–220.

45. Archivio dell'Ospedale degli Innocenti di Firenze (AOIF), Liber Artis Portae Sanctae Mariae (V,2), fol. 1r. The Book of the Silk Guild, series V of the hospital's archive, has three volumes containing the *Provvisioni* that affected the hospital, as well as *Provvisioni* of similar institutions, legislation the guild used as legal precedent.

46. Archivio di Stato di Firenze (ASF), Provvisioni Registri, 95, fols. 1r–1v, 23 April 1406; Goldthwaite, "I prezzi del grano," 24–25.

47. Luigi Passerini, *Storia degli stabilmenti di beneficenza e d'istruzione gratuita della città di Firenze* (Florence, 1853), 793ff.

48. Ibid.

49. Ibid.

50. Ibid.

51. Ibid.

52. AOIF, Liber Artis Portae Sanctae Mariae (V,2), fols. 1r–2v, 5v–6v, 8v–17r.

53. Matteo Villani, *Cronica,* bk. I, chap. 6, cited in Passerini, *Storia degli stabilmenti di beneficenza,* 413–15.

54. Millard Meiss, *Painting in Florence and Siena After the Black Death* (New York, 1964), 78.

55. Passerini, *Storia degli stabilmenti di beneficenza,* 418–19.

56. Ibid.

57. ASF, Provvisioni Registri, 109, fols. 160v–161v. Cf. Marvin B. Becker, "Aspects of Lay Piety in Renaissance Florence," in *The Pursuit of Holiness,* ed. Charles Trinkaus and Heiko Oberman (Leiden, 1974), 177–80. Brucker, *Society,* 83–84.

58. *Statuti dell'Ospedale di Santa Maria della Scala di Siena* (Rome, 1964).

59. Iris Origo, *The Merchant of Prato,* rev. ed. (New York, 1979), 321.

60. This notarial act is fully transcribed in Passerini, *Storia degli stabilmenti di beneficenza,* 834–39.

61. ASF, Provvisioni Registri, 28, fol. 241v; Passerini, *Storia degli stabilmenti di beneficenza,* 825: "Et propter ambitiosas importunitates multorum potissime clericorum, qui divina judicia non verentes, ea que ad pietatis opera disponantur impetrare sollicitant, ipsa etiam ad illicita convertentes, appetit ipse Dominus Bonifatius providere pro posse suae intentionis propositum adminiculis possibilibus Deo propitios roborare."

62. Infra, 96.

63. Paul Oskar Kristeller, "Lay Religious Traditions and Florentine Platonism," in *Studies in Renaissance Thought and Letters* (Rome, 1956), 99–122. Charles Trinkaus, *In Our Image and Likeness: Humanity and Divinity in Italian Humanist Thought* (Chicago, 1969), passim. Gene Brucker, *The Civic World of Early Renaissance Florence* (Princeton, 1977), especially chap. 1. Christian Bec, *Les marchands écrivains: affaires et humanisme à Florence, 1375–1434* (Paris, 1967), 279–349.

64. Christiane Klapisch-Zuber, "L'enfance en Toscane au debut XVe siècle," *Annales de demographie historique* (1973): 99–122. This study of childhood in fifteenth-century Tuscany was the first attempt to apply the results of demographic research from the Catasto of 1427 to the experience of childhood itself. Its central argument stems from the curious imbalance in the sex ratios shown in the Catasto. Klapisch-Zuber argues that once one rules out mortality and abandonment as factors, underregistration represents a tendency on the part of parents to forget those fragile creatures whose lives were so precarious and uncertain, especially if they were female. One might be tempted to conclude from the evidence of underregistration itself that a general and pervasive cultural indifference to newborns might signal the practice of widespread abandonment. But the argument that the cause of underregistration was parental indifference due to the fragility of infants would be considerably more compelling if the imbalance in the sex ratios were not present in nearly all stages of the life cycle. In her collaboration with David Herlihy, *Les Toscans et leurs familles* (Paris, 1978), Klapisch-Zuber also suggests the greater likelihood of female monachation as an explanation of imbalance in the sex ratios for older persons.

65. AOIF, Balie e Bambini A (XVI,1), passim.

66. Richard Trexler, "The Foundlings of Florence," *History of Childhood Quarterly* 1 (1974): 259–84.

67. AOIF, Balie e Bambini A (XVI,1), passim.

68. ASF, Provvisioni Registri 139, fols. 46v–47v, 29 April 1448; fol. 46v: "propter maiorem numerum solito ancillarum sed sclavarum et aliarum servitialium."

69. Richard Trexler, "Infanticide in Florence: New Sources and First Results," *History of Childhood Quarterly* 1 (1974): 98–116.

70. Claude Delasselle, "Les enfants abandonées à Paris au XVIIIe siècle," *Annales: Economie, Société, Civilisations* 30 (1975): 187–218.

71. Carlo Corsini, "Materiali per lo studio della famiglia in Toscana nei secoli XVII–XIX," *Quaderni Storici* 33 (1976): 998–1052.

72. David Herlihy and Christiane Klapisch-Zuber, in *Les Toscans,* 184–85, provide a chart of baptisms at San Giovanni based on Marco Lastri, *Ricerche sull'antica e moderna popolazione della città di Firenze per mezzo dei registri del battistero di San Giovanni dal 1451 al 1774* (Florence, 1775). Data concerning admissions to the Innocenti may be found in AOIF, Balie e Bambini A–F (XVI,1–6).

73. John Boswell, *The Kindness of Strangers: The Abandonment of Children in Western Europe from Late Antiquity to the Renaissance* (New York, 1988), passim.

74. Infra, chap. 5, 187–272.

75. On the emergence of the nuclear family and of individualism, see Richard Goldthwaite, *Private Wealth in Renaissance Florence: A Study of Four Families* (Princeton, 1968); M. B. Becker, *Florence in Transition,* 2 vols. (Baltimore, 1967). See also Goldthwaite, "The Florentine Palace as Domestic Architecture," *American Historical Review* 77 (1972): 977–1012. On the importance of lineage solidarity, see F. W. Kent, "The Rucellai Family and its Loggia," *Journal of the Warburg and Courtauld Institutes* 35 (1972): 397–401; F. W. Kent, *Household and Lineage in Renaissance Florence* (Princeton, 1977); and Dale Kent, *The Rise of the Medici* (Oxford, 1978). Although F. W. Kent's view is now generally accepted, the economics of families, at the center of Goldthwaite's view, was not, in my view, adequately treated in *Household and Lineage.*

76. Alessandra Strozzi, *Lettere di una gentildonna fiorentina,* ed. C. Guasti (Florence, 1877).

77. Leon Battista Alberti, *Della famiglia.* Translated by Rene Watkins as *The Family in Renaissance Florence* (Columbia, S.C., 1969), 30, 32, 38.

78. David Herlihy, "Mapping Households in Medieval Italy," *Catholic Historical Review* 58 (1972): 1–24.

79. Christiane Klapisch-Zuber, "Fiscalité et demographie," 1327–29.

80. David Herlihy, "Viellir à Florence au Quattrocento," *Annales: Economie, Société, Civilisations* 24 (1969): 1338–52.

81. Alberti, *Della Famiglia,* 50–51.

82. Ibid., 47.

83. Ibid., 37.

84. Palmieri, *Della vita civile,* 222.

85. Infra, 107–40.

86. Ibid.

87. Infra, 61–105.

88. Ibid.

89. Infra, 187–271.

90. See Richard Trexler, "Ritual in Florence: Adolescence and Salvation in

the Renaissance," in *The Pursuit of Holiness,* ed. Trinkaus and Oberman (Leiden, 1974), 200–264.

91. Infra, 273–306.

92. James Banker, "Mourning a Son: Childhood and Paternal Love in the *Consolateria* of Giannozzo Manetti," *History of Childhood Quarterly* 3, no. 3 (1976): 351–62.

93. Infra, 273–306.

94. ASF, Provvisioni Registri, 147, fols. 169v–171r, 29 December 1456: "de eximiis operibus pietatis et caritatis que in hac civitate fiant . . . quod ipsis mediantibus et propter preces dictorum infantium qui puritate nitent altissimus et omnipotens dominus noster dignetur sua molita pietate ac misericordia non solum conservare civitatem ipsam et statum suum sed augere . . ."

Chapter 1
Francesco Datini and the Foundation
of the Hospital of the Innocenti

If, in the years following the Black Death, charitable giving was becoming more laicized, in the sense that lay institutions such as communes,
guilds, and confraternities were drawing the control of charitable patrimony away from ecclesiastical bodies, nevertheless, the beneficiaries of
this generosity also had to rely on private sources of support. Historians
have largely neglected the problem of the relationship between individual
and civic charity, perhaps because, as Brian Pullan has suggested, our
knowledge of the institutional machinery available to testators is so
incomplete. Yet a careful charting of the territories of these two forms
of charity is indispensable to a clear definition of "laicization." Even
during periods in which the Ospedale degli Innocenti relied heavily on
the generosity of individuals, the commune of Florence was involved in
the administration of their patrimonies, not only as trustee, but also as
administrator of the public debt and of testators' shares in it. In a more
general sense, the quality and quantity of private support that an institution could generate shaped the strategy of public bodies and determined
their effectiveness in satisfying the claims of both testators and recipients.

No less important, however, was the role of testamentary charity in
defining the layman's stake in the divine economy of salvation. The
concern with mortality and immortality so characteristic of the humanist
outlook sought, in civic life and children, the perpetuation of an individual's glory beyond the grave. In the mid-fifteenth century Matteo
Palmieri wrote:

Numerous and varied are the things in our present life, Alessandro,
that are by nature delightful and valuable to mankind, but no other
love binds us so tightly as love for our country and love for our own

33

children. This is easily enough discovered, because all our other possessions and desires end with death, [but] our country and children
we hope and desire to endure, and be graced with fortune and true
glory.... Certainly in our minds is a firm desire for future centuries,
which constrains us to desire our eternal glory, the happiest circumstances for our country, and the continued health of our offspring.[1]

To Rabelais in the sixteenth century, children were the partial compensation that God provided Man after the Fall for the loss of bodily immortality.[2]

The will of Francesco Datini, which left a thousand florins to the
superintendent of the hospital of Santa Maria Nuova in Florence to begin
a new foundling hospital, was the culmination of Datini's lifetime concern with personal issues of children, earthly immortality, and the relationship between charity and salvation, a concern expressed repeatedly
in the two volumes of correspondence published by Guasti in 1880 between Datini and his notary and close advisor, Ser Lapo Mazzei.[3]
Francescso Datini's role in the foundation of the Ospedale degli Innocenti is not widely known: not until Cornelius von Fabriczy's biography
of Brunelleschi[4] did this information appear in even a footnote, and
Datini's biographers make only scant mention of it. No one to date has
drawn on the rich source material of the Mazzei letters to draw the
connections between Datini's lay piety and the foundation of the hospital
of the Innocenti.[5]

If those letters yield valuable insights into Datini's motives and anxieties, the will itself, dictated to Mazzei from Datini's deathbed, presents
a clear portrait of Datini's position in the spectrum of lay concerns and
humanist values. Even as Datini was nearing the end of life, he and
Mazzei weighed issues concerning the proper balance between individual
and corporate initiative, and between clerical and lay administration of
the bequest. Moreover, Datini's selection of his beneficiaries makes
clear that his charitable concerns were ultimately less familial and more
comprehensive than recent scholarship has attributed to fifteenth-century charity.[6]

Finally, any discussion of Francesco Datini's will must take into account the actual disposition of the bequest, since Datini did not envision
the silk guild's eventual stewardship of the institution. From the cluster
of details emerges the critical role of civic and public institutions over

the administration of bequests; equally important, however, was private initiative. Most striking is the coincidence of interest between testator and commune to turn private initiative to public advantage by erecting a monument reflecting the glory of the city of Florence. More than one commentator linked the salvation of the city and its earthly fortunes to the magnificence of its hospitals, and to the diligence and care lavished by foundling hospitals on their children.[7]

The correspondence between Ser Lapo Mazzei and Francesco Datini published in the Guasti edition forms a small fraction of the 125,000 letters discovered in the middle of the nineteenth century in a cupboard underneath the stairs of Datini's residence in Prato. The collection published by Guasti contains, with a few exceptions, only the letters Ser Lapo Mazzei wrote to Datini. Mazzei and Datini first became acquainted in 1373, when Datini was living as a merchant in Avignon and Mazzei was pursuing the study of law at the University of Bologna. One of Datini's relatives requested that Datini assist Lapo Mazzei in obtaining a scholarship to the Papal College in Bologna.[8] Mazzei began to practice law in Florence at the age of twenty-three, and the Signory apppointed him ambassador to Faenza and Genoa, as well as making him its own notary. Mazzei also assisted the Florentine Chancellor of the republic, Coluccio Salutati, from whom he undoubtedly acquired his characteristic mix of Christian piety and humanist values. Certainly Mazzei's views of charity and lay piety, if absorbed from his mentor Salutati, were strongly reinforced by Mazzei's occupation as notary to the hospital of Santa Maria Nuova. In this position Mazzei would have acquired both the practical knowledge involved with the process of testation as well as a clear impression of the snares and dangers that could befall the imprecisely worded or misdirected bequest.[9]

The formal relationship between Mazzei and Datini began in 1390, when Datini was fifty-five and Mazzei forty. Datini had no legitimate and two illegitimate children; Mazzei had eight legitimate children. Mazzei's financial position and origins were modest; Datini had assets of 40,000 florins and a net worth, once the claims of creditors were deducted, of perhaps 25,000 florins.[10] Both Mazzei's experience as assistant to the Chancellor of the Republic and as notary to the Signory gave him the personal connections and intimate working knowledge of Florentine government and politics to which Datini, as a citizen of a subject town, could not hope to aspire, even if he possessed the interest. In exchange, Datini's wealth assisted Mazzei from time to time, so that Datini and Mazzei were by turns client and patron.

Central to this relationship, as Trexler has quite rightly noted, was each man's utility to the other, to which the conventions and protestations of love, though genuine, were ancillary.[11] Both the classical ideals of friendship, as expressed in Alberti's *Della Famiglia*, and the ritual conventions of friendship reflected Florentine beliefs and practices that friendship widened one's circle of influence and reputation, which were both critical factors in avoiding crippling tax assessments and political prejudice. Yet if such ritual and formal conventions dictated emotion, they also intensified it.

As Datini's notary, Ser Lapo Mazzei not only handled his legal affairs, but was also Datini's intimate friend, spiritual counselor, and in the turbulent and treacherous world of Florentine politics and finances, his advocate. To the hospital of Santa Maria Nuova, Datini occasionally lent his financial support, entrusted his illegitimate daughter, Ginevra, and, finally, bequeathed the thousand florins that began the Ospedale degli Innocenti.

These letters are remarkable not only for the detail with which they convey the intensity of emotion involved in the relationships between Datini and his circle of partners and friends. They also reveal Datini's constant preoccupation with establishing, in the presence of riches and in the absence of legitimate heirs, some sort of memory on earth as well as the divine favor sought for the testator's life hereafter. The second half of the correspondence, coinciding roughly with the turn of the century, became more and more concerned with arranging Datini's financial and testamentary affairs to assure that his best intentions would be honored.

As early as the 1370s Niccolozzo di ser Naldo had written to Francesco, then living in Avignon, and as of that date unmarried: "Pray hasten [home] to find a wife, for the time is ripe, that some memory may remain of you, and some fruit of your labors be bequeathed to your lawful heirs."[12] In April 1392 Guido di Tommaso Deti, who would himself leave a considerable fortune to the Ospedale degli Innocenti, suggested to Ser Lapo Mazzei the considerable extent to which Datini sought to realize in his monumental and frenzied building programs the earthly immortality denied him by his lack of legitimate children:

And this is [the reason I am writing to you], that in these past few days, when I was alone at table with Guido di Messer Tommaso, he spoke these words to me, if I can recall them exactly: 'Ser Lapo, you said to me that since he has no children, he has [by building] given himself a child and a posthumous memorial. I wish you would tell him on my behalf, that I have thought a lot about the subject, and that I wish he would acquire a spiritual child, which at his death he could see begin to bear fruit... to establish some pious place for regular clergy or other devout persons or some restored chapel, or sanctuary for the soul, where in his life he could undertake to the honor of God, the salvation of his own soul, either through the saying of divine offices, or through the dispensing of alms. And this would be a child that would not die [but] would come to fruit in its time. I answered Guido that I would write it to you, not in the elegant Latin that he can boast, but as God might allow me. And I am as impressed with these thoughts of his as I am with all his others.[13]

Three years later, in 1395, Ser Lapo again pressed Datini on the subject of creating a religious foundation:

Here is my proposal. If you buy land for a hundred florins, or a little more or less, and it is of the said church, inasmuch as a priest resides there; this priest will be obligated forever to say mass in the said chapel or oratory that you will make.... And you may call it as you wish, either the chapel of Francesco, or Santa Maria delle Grazie, or Santa Maria degli Umili, or Santa Maria Beata, or della Romita; however you wish. Here [in Florence] is a large hospital that will always be known as the hospital of Messer Bonifazio.[14]

As Ser Lapo's shrewd observations suggest, the proper focus of Datini's concern was not earthly immortality through monuments bearing his name, but a much deeper concern for the state of his soul. The rich man was, as San Bernardino expressed it, God's almoner, and in his letters, Ser Lapo repeatedly stressed the heavy burden of responsibilities borne by the rich. Writing to Francesco in 1406, he quoted a letter of advice written by Saint Bernard to Pope Eugenius III on the subject of how to treat the riches that had been entrusted to him:

[One should say] I do not love them [i.e., riches] and it would not bother me to lose them. And he [also] said: "Act so that transitory things, that cannot last, pass away from you and not through you. As the river, wherever it passes erodes the earth, so do the flux and loss and gain of temporal things erode the conscience." And if you, Eugenius, can act so that the river runs through your own field without ruining it, then rest assured that you can hold [possessions] without harm![15]

Ser Lapo interpreted this to mean that although the clergy should possess nothing:

to us laymen he would write: Do not willingly possess anything beyond your needs. And you [Francesco] would do well to say, as you are wont to do, that whoever wants to become richer should come to you for advice, because you would discourage him in every way.[16]

Once again, as one finds in the tradition of writing and advice on poverty and wealth, laymen occupy a place in the divine economy different from that of the clergy, and are encouraged not to accumulate wealth beyond what is necessary. Moreover, these considerations were a central topic of Mazzei's and Datini's correspondence, and caused anguish to both. As early as 1391, Mazzei was moved to write:

Francesco, I have considered your state a hundred times since leaving your house: on my walks, in bed, and in my study when I was most alone. And charity compels me to speak the truth, which seems to me the most precious thing among friends....

I have already heard from you, through letters, of the anxieties and obstacles placed before you by the things of this world: but having seen them with my own eyes, they are far more than I had realized; with regard to the cares of the house that you are building, of the establishments you have in foreign lands, of your banquets, of your accounts, and other things, that seem to me so far beyond what is necessary that it is not possible for you to take an hour from the world and its snares. Yet God has given you an abundance of earthly goods, and a thousand warnings to awaken you; you are nearing sixty, free from thoughts of children, and would you wish to wait until you are at death's door, when the latch of death will be open, to undergo a change of heart? You saw your own wife, a few days ago, nearly at the point of coming to us. . . . I would that you see fit to bring to a conclusion many of your affairs, which you yourself say are in order, and even sooner I wish that you would put an end to more building, and from your riches and revenues disburse alms with your own hands; and that you value these riches at their worth, that is, own them as if they were not yours. . . . The wheel turns for you as it does for the others you see die every day. I am not telling you to become a monk or a priest, but I say to you, that what is Caesar's you give to Caesar and what is God's you give to God, that is, you give part of your honestly acquired riches per week or per day to God, part to relatives and friends.[17]

Much in the same vein Mazzei wrote to Datini, "God did not give you your wealth to increase your own prosperity, but to trouble you and scourge you with it."[18] Datini clearly took these warnings to heart, for in the same letter Mazzei was able to credit him with the survival of over twenty-five families, and with giving help to another hundred a year. Indeed, this letter of 1405 was addressed to "Francesco di Marco, padre di molti."

Behind Mazzei's exhortations lay an indubitable moral economy, in which the notary conceived of the will as the testator's last opportunity to settle up accounts. No single document presents a clearer view of this ledger approach to moral theology than Mazzei's letter of 26 December 1406:

We have one chance to settle this account with Him. . . . God's *de dare* is completely just and full of love, when He made and created us who were nothing; and He made us like the angels, and more than angels. . . . Item, His *de dare* says that He sent His son Christ to cancel out our sins; suffering He made the sacrifice, for the sin of the first man, father of all, for which we were deprived of His vision after death. And living amongst us here, He gave us the structure of justice, truth, and equity. And an account of what was given on our side would find there considerable ingratitude, crime, and madness. . . . We see that all our brothers, friends, and partners have done is as a dream where there has been no love of God or remembrance of him. . . . [Francesco], the time of day you stay in bed grieves me, when you are perfectly healthy. If for God's sake you could spare a half hour for mass [so that] when God sees your alms, followed by your sacrifice, He will thank you heartily for not valuing false riches, deceptions, and frauds. . . . God's love cancels out our multitude of sins. For the sake of His love, forgive me. Your friend, on the 26th of December [1406].[19]

The outline of a complete moral theology for fifteenth-century lay people is here: the humanist strain stressing the equality, even the superiority, of men to angels; and the view of almsgiving as a settling of accounts, as a completion of the neglected side of the ledger.

Ser Lapo suggested to Datini in the correspondence various worthwhile enterprises for charitable giving inter vivos, and so yields considerable insight into assessments of both the nature and extent of poverty, and its most worthwhile remedies. In addition to the initiation of building programs for charitable purposes, Ser Lapo frequently exhorted Datini to provide dowries for poor girls. In 1392, for example, Mazzei wrote that as notary of Santa Maria Nuova:

I [have under my care] more than fifty legacies and their beneficiaries, and in these, according to the will of the testator, they have to be given for God, through us, money and clothes and dowries. . . . And thus I have seen several merchants come to me who at the time of year they review their accounts, want to set aside a certain share of their profits, and with it to support a good cause. . . . I have told them that there are so many girls to be dowered that it would move a stone.[20]

Five days later, on 11 December 1392, Lapo wrote, "Had I a hundred tongues and an iron voice, as that fellow said, I could not render sufficient thanks for your love and your offerings."[21] But in 1396, Ser Lapo wrote to Margerita, Datini's wife, that,

in the last few days that poor widow from the Serraglio . . . arrived at my doorstep, and she has four daughters to dower. . . . I beseech and pray on God's behalf, and on behalf of the love among us all, that if that woman is needy, as I believe, you encourage Francesco to extend his generosity to one of those girls, and I promise you that I think he himself will be happier than with all the building he has ever done.

Churches and paintings are all very good, but for every time Christ mentioned them, he mentioned the poor a hundred times.[22]

Datini's notebooks reveal a charity inter vivos that was both personalized and direct. Most often, alms would go to his own laborers and immediate neighbors, or, in the case of dowries, to those needy cases that were brought to his attention by Ser Lapo. Although there is some indication that Datini was concerned that his alms reach the truly needy (as when he told one of his *fattori* before giving alms to a hermit that the *fattore* should "mark well what sort of life he leads: and only if he is a good charity to give some bread and wine"),[23] he seems to have made little effort to address the problems of poverty in a systematic, formal, or institutionalized fashion. Mazzei's letters did insist that Datini's gifts to churches be matched by a commitment to direct succour of the truly miserable. Moreover, Datini spread his charity among several classes of poor rather than restricting it to any one particular class such as the *poveri vergognosi*.

The process of drawing up Francesco Datini's will presents a stark contrast to the informality of his daily giving. The early stages of this process, which took place in the mid-1390s, suggest that the question of whether to commit one's patrimony into the hands of clerical or lay institutions was an occasion of considerable moment and conflict for testators. The abbot of the monastery of San Fabiano, for example, encouraged Datini to deposit his fortune with the clergy of Prato, and to allow them to distribute it to "a hospital, or perhaps to give it to some religious order" such as that of the Angeli in Florence:

There is another way, if it should please you: buy the place called la Sacca, which is a beautiful monastery and devout place, and endow it as you see fit... or once again, if it should happen that God does not grant you children, leave to be done that which makes you the most content. And above all, do not ever make a congregation of females, which does not seem to me to be a good devotion.[24]

The abbot also suggested that the clergy be allowed to distribute his patrimony "to marry girls, succour the sick, or in other works of mercy."

One of the early versions of Datini's will must have contained such a provision, for in a letter of 7 November 1395, Ser Lapo wrote to him thus:

Here is a man [Datini] who has enjoyed all the delights of the body; riches and estates he knows are nothing because they have to be left behind; a man who from God has had an abundance of these transitory things, and with his lips always disdains them and esteems them as nothing; a man who possesses so much treasure, that one could make of it a flame and a wellspring that would leap up to eternal life; a man whom God for thirty years or more has lent the time to arrange the manner of his dying and the distribution of his patrimony, and he finds himself with a testament in which his heir is the holy Bishop of Pistoia.[25]

Mazzei had other misgivings about Francesco's testamentary wisdom, which he expressed vehemently in a letter six days later:

For God and for the love that will reign between the two of us unto death, and perhaps even beyond, I beg you and entreat you to wait and be careful about such a thing as the Sacca; that throwing these good thoughts behind you, you believe that in such an undertaking there is harm and shame unto life and death. The very best advice is required, so as not to spend huge sums of money on these great affairs, only not to have them bear fruit. You see what happened to Lemmo [Balducci], who spent more than twenty-five thousand florins on his great hospital; and I believe, because of its location, that it will never bear fruit there.[26]

Nevertheless, Datini allowed his will to remain unchanged for another three years, until Mazzei wrote to him again on 25 November 1398:

I have seen you several times these days, and I have been meaning to talk to you about something, and then every time I see you are so busy with your work that I have remained silent. Francesco, I often feel my mind fighting to remind you of the good of your soul, and the honor of your reputation, and I would be afraid not to say it, having already had once from God a warning blow.[27]

Having seen Ser Paolo, the superintendent of the hospital of Santa Maria Nuova, die in such distress from his disease that he could not speak his last wishes, Mazzei continued to write with evident anxiety:

I have had in mind to tell you that, if you do not make some provision to place some brief words in that testament you have drawn up, I see that it would be all too easy for the bishop of Pistoia or Florence to take all you have, and to spend it paying his debts on horses and banquets. . . . And should you be inclined to say "I have time, I trust in God!" I would answer, you claim to have enough time, as if God did not know how you have spent the time He has given you. I am not saying you've spent it in usury and gluttony, but you yourself know, and say every day, that you've pursued vain things that pass away and dry up like straw or flowers.[28]

Lapo then described his plan in which Christ's poor and not "the devil's rich" would benefit from his testament and his patrimony. In the postscript to the letter above, he wrote:

And what I have in mind is this, that you write a brief note to this effect, that we will call a codicil, that is, insofar as you need, in sickness or in health, not to change or have changed the testament that you have already drawn up. Where the poor of Christ were your heir, that in this case . . . you desire the said poor be nominated by either the commune of Prato, or such Consuls, or such men from Prato or from Florence, or whomever you wish to name. Or even better, that you desire that they must nominate certain persons written by your own hand, sealed and closed by your seal, of which you will keep one copy in your cash box, and one sealed to the prior of the Agnoli, so that twenty to thirty years from now it won't happen that there be not at least one [copy] to be found. And all [I've said] doesn't apply if you change your will.[29]

Some time during Lent Datini apparently sought the advice of Giovanni Dominici and received much the same answer he had from Ser Lapo. On 18 June 1400 Ser Lapo wrote again to Datini and mentioned approvingly a codicil of Francesco da Mantova that Ser Lapo had notarized himself, and which may well have served as a model for Datini's will. Ser Lapo had notarized the codicil only eight days before, on 10 June, and it provided 600 florins to the hospital of Santa Maria della Scala in Florence for dowries and to feed children. To the hospitals of Bonifazio Lupi and San Gallo the testator gave 200 florins each, and to the company of the Bigallo 400 florins to be spent over a period of twenty years in providing baked bread for the prisoners of the Stinche. A further 800 florins went for cloth to clothe 500 of the city's poor, while the proceeds of his farm at Montughi were to be enjoyed by the previous owner until his death, and then by the monastery of the Angeli. Should they wish to sell the land, half of the proceeds would go to Or San Michele, and the other half to the poor. Two hundred florins were set aside for Santa Croce to be used for a *rinovale*. The Frati dei Servi were to use their 200 florins solely for the purpose of buying books necessary to their order. The Bigallo was entrusted with 500 florins to dower poor girls to be named by the executors of the will, as well as another 200 florins to be spent on alms for the poor. This codicil names four lay executors, and the prior of the Frati degli Angeli.[30]

The letter Ser Lapo wrote to Francesco Datini the day before Datini signed his will expressed the anxieties that gnawed at them both:

> *Deus in adiutorum vestrum intendat.* As you know better than I do, if God does not place his guiding hand on our needs, in vain do we initiate and arrange our good intentions, which cannot be had, according to Scripture, without Him. Pray go tomorrow morn to hear Mass with devotion and to commend yourself to Him, who has no other intent but His boundless goodness, that He may strengthen you to devote your heart and fortune to His glory after your death, and in such a manner that God's poor, whom you have had so much in mind, may have the greatest benefit and comfort, and that all your care and toil may not have been in vain. Francesco, remember that God of necessity hears just prayers, because He is all-just. I have already offered up this prayer, and tomorrow, by God's grace, I will do my part, since you have chosen me to help you. And you, trust in God without fear. Tears keep me from writing more.[31]

The very next day, 27 June 1400, Francesco signed his will and began a journey with his household to escape the plague. This first will left half his fortune to the foundling hospital in Florence, Santa Maria della Scala, rather than his whole fortune to his own foundation as he would do in his last will, in 1410. Although in most other respects the two wills are similar, the earlier will provided for a dowry to a girl who had been secretly placed with the hospital of Santa Maria Nuova. She is not mentioned by name, but the girl in question was Francesco's own illegitimate daughter, Ginevra. The will of 1400 states that Datini:

> leaves one thousand gold florins to the Hospital of Santa Maria Nuova, for marrying a certain girl who was placed in secret with the *spedalingo* of the said Hospital. . . . And if she should die before the consummation of her marriage, the said money reverts to beneficiaries of the said testator as named below. And in the meantime [the testator] wills that she be honorably fed and brought up, either with his wife, or with Ser Niccolò di Piero of Prato, to be decided by the executors to be mentioned, as they shall deem fit.[32]

In 1407, three years before the final version of the will was drawn up, Datini used the thousand florins to marry Ginevra to Lionardo di ser Tommaso Giunta.[33]

Datini's bequest to establish a new foundling hospital, however, did not appear in the earlier will, but only in the will of 1410 he dictated from his deathbed. Far from being the central provision of the will, the bequest that began the Ospedale degli Innocenti was one of nearly fifty separate bequests brought under the umbrella of a charitable trust called the Casa del Ceppo. Although the executors of the estate and the Ceppo later transferred control of the Ospedale degli Innocenti to the Arte della Seta in Florence, Datini's instructions regarding the administration of the Ceppo articulate the connection between charity and lay piety so conspicuously that his entire will warrants a full discussion.

In the provisions he made in his last will and testament, Datini clearly saw the commune of Prato's role as fiduciary rather than pecuniary. His intention was to finance the Casa del Ceppo entirely through his vast fortune by donating his mobile and immobile goods,[34] and by dissolving his companies.[35] The Consiglio Generale, or General Council of Prato, however, exercised considerable control over the patrimony in a number of ways. The council was to administer the annual election of four *terrazzani*, "the best and most honest in the land." Datini gave the commune full authority to administer the bequest, as well as conferring on the commune the obligation of defending the Casa del Ceppo, at the Ceppo's expense, and recovering its possessions, accounts, or anything else that might belong to it.[36]

The four honorable citizens so chosen took the title of *presidenti*. By the authority the commune vested in them, their charge was to review, calculate, and settle all Datini's accounts, and to "take, receive, and recover all the interest in his credits in the *Monte Comune* of Florence and its treasurers."[37] In turn, the *presidenti* were to apply this interest to his remaining debts in the *prestanze*, in order to remove Datini's name from the list of lenders and to protect his estate from further claims. Datini's impoverished friends were to benefit from the remainder, but he empowered the *presidenti* to recover his debts even to the point of repossessing the goods of his debtors. Finally, Datini placed the *presidenti* in charge of appointing a guardian, either married or unmarried, but of good standing and reputation. This guardian had the responsibility of keeping the buildings in good repair without incurring ruinous expenses. Free lodging in the Casa del Ceppo and a stipend to be decided by the commune of Prato were among the benefits to be enjoyed by the incumbent.

The "maintenance, defense, and administration" of the Casa del Ceppo fell to the commune of Prato, Datini said, because of his confidence in the commune and its important citizens, a confidence that moved him to extend the powers of the commune and the Casa del Ceppo to the administration of the entire estate.[38] Not only confidence, but also "the love he bears toward the said commune of Prato and toward the men of that city"[39] inspired Datini to entrust them with the task of protecting the Casa del Ceppo from the encroachment of any magnate, whether he acted under the cloak of ecclesiastical or secular authority, who coveted the Ceppo's possessions.[40] Datini appointed the commune of Prato his agent *in perpetuo* and entrusted it with the power to decide whether to invest in full or partial shares in the public debt of Florence. The commune was also empowered to recover debts owed by the commune of Florence to the estate, "or by any other person, commune, guild, company, or place."[41]

Datini built in another layer of safeguards by providing for nine trustees from the commune of Prato who would oversee the election of the four *presidenti*. These nine trustees were to be notified of the date of all elections,[42] and they also enforced the decisions of the *presidenti*. As "guardians, defenders, and friends of the Casa del Ceppo" the trustees could demand from the *presidenti* a full account of their actions during their terms of office.[43]

Datini's will did not envision that any civil authority would have to call for an outlay of funds to support the Casa del Ceppo. The fiscal initiative was strictly private: even the cost of services provided by the commune was paid by the trust fund. The role of the commune of Prato and of the trust's administrators was to oversee the execution of the will's every detail. Datini's confidence in the ability and inclination of the commune to carry out his intentions was boundless. If the ultimate recourse of authority was to the will's executors, Datini's wife, son-in-law, and two of his business partners, the commune of Prato still had extensive powers to organize and administer the estate, and to decide how best to defend the interests of the "Casa o granaio dei poveri del Ceppo."

Datini's confidence in the ability of municipal appointees to manage his huge patrimony was, as one might expect from the tone of his correspondence with Mazzei, in stark contrast to his perceptions of the abilities of ecclesiastical institutions:

Item, this testator, Francesco, willed and commanded, for the love of God and so that he might give to the poor all that was his by the grace of God, that his major habitation and residence in Prato, with its garden and *loggie*, . . . is to be a Ceppo, granary, or private house. It is no way to be considered holy, nor to be placed in any way under the Church, ecclesiastical offices, prelates, or any other ecclesiastical personage. In no way should it be reduced to that state, but rather should belong to Christ's poor, and be for their perpetual use and benefit.[44]

The importance Datini attached to the lay character of the institution can be inferred not only from the unequivocal language of the above provision, but also from its position in the first paragraph establishing the Ceppo. He clearly felt the prohibition merited repetition, for in the provision leaving his possessions to the Ceppo, he wrote:

The Casa del Ceppo and its aforementioned goods [are] to be private and not sacred, and in no way to be said to be ecclesiastical, but thought of secularly, for the love of God, to the aforementioned perpetual use of the poor, and to be subject neither to the church nor to clerics in any way.[45]

In case future generations should doubt his intentions, the testament was to be bound into a book, and chained securely in the Casa del Ceppo, so that Datini's wishes would be unmistakable. In addition to Datini's last will and testament, this book was also to contain an annual list of the names of the *presidenti,* and any record of events or transactions the commune of Prato might wish to include.[46]

Yet if Datini was scrupulous in his attempts to prevent ecclesiastical interference in the administration of the Ceppo, his anti-clericalism was not of sufficient intensity to preclude bequests to ecclesiastical foundations. He left 500 florins, for example, to the "brothers, chapter and monastery of Santa Maria degli Agnoli" in Florence. But Datini earmarked the bequest for the purchase of a suitable vineyard, and if the land was subsequently sold or otherwise alienated, the substance of the bequest would revert to the Ceppo.[47]

The monastery of San Francesco da Prato received a bequest of twenty-five florins per year to buy food and clothing for the friars, and to cover the expense of an annual memorial to Datini's soul "as the officials of the Ceppo shall arrange."[48] The Ceppo also undertook the expenses of maintaining two altars that Francesco had left to the monastery, and the Ceppo's rectors were left to carry out work on the choir and cloister vaults, according to arrangements Datini had already made. Another ten florins subsidized a Saint Gregory mass to be said by a certain Friar Ventura of the Order of the Umiliati of Ognissanti.[49] Fifty florins went to the monastery of Santa Anna to rebuild the larger chapel, and to build a vault or a loggia. In this case also the Ceppo was to arrange and supervise the project.[50]

Four other monasteries, San Domenico, Sant'Agostino, the Carmine, and the Servi received twenty lire each, to be spent as the rectors of the Ceppo and the four executors of the will would decide. Three other monastic establishments, Santa Chiara, San Niccolò, and San Matteo, each received fifty lire.[51] The last two bequests to ecclesiastical institutions mentioned in the will were for works of art. San Matteo would have an altarpiece painted for it, and San Niccolò was to have certain benches painted. In both cases, the four executors of the will were placed in charge of the arrangements.[52]

Unless the testament itself specified the uses to which a bequest was to be applied, every gift to an ecclesiastical institution in Datini's will came under the purview of the laity: the officials of the Ceppo or the four executors of the will. Only one institution, Santa Maria degli Angeli, received a bequest the size of 500 florins. To all the others he left amounts of less than 100 florins each. Even the last paragraph of the will "prayed and cautioned" the Calimala guild, the commune of Prato, the four overseers of the Ceppo, and the executors not to erect there "an altar, oratory, or even the appearance of any ecclesiastical structure." They were to do nothing else "on which account the said Casa del Ceppo could be considered an ecclesiastical place."[53] Datini feared that "persons of ill will, acting under the rubric of good intentions might take possession of it. This [would be] completely contrary to the testator's intention." He exhorted his trustees in the event that this danger materialized "to avoid this trap, and to exert every effort and incur any expense so that it might please God to remove it."[54]

The Ceppo's act of foundation forbade the sale, alienation, or dispersal of its immobile goods "so that for eternity Christ's poor may be fed and nourished from them."[55] Datini's definition of *poveri* specified no particular class or type of poor person to whom the Ceppo's funds should be distributed. If any of the Ceppo's possessions were sold or in any other way alienated, they were to be conceded to the company of Or San Michele in Florence, to be distributed "among the poor of Jesus Christ" as much to the public (*poveri piuvichi*) as to the secret and shame-faced poor (*poveri vergognosi*).[56] The distinction in canon law and statutory legislation may have been what Datini meant here, but his stipulation was that the Ceppo was to provide for each.

The remainder of the will uses the term *povero* in a much more fluid manner than the strict juridical categories cited by Professor Trexler, categories that included "the miserable, divided between those who were economically destitute...*miserabiles personae,* and the poor, those propertied individuals who could not live according to their social position."[57] For example, Datini describes his widowed servant, Mona Domenica, as a *povera persona.* Indeed, in making provision for her in his will, Datini articulated the definition of poverty closest to the canonists' hearts when he stipulated the rectors of the Ceppo were to take care that Mona Domenica "lack nothing without which one may live comfortably, according to the condition of her status."[58] Andrea di Simone of the Porta Santa Trinita in Prato, was described as a *povero giovane* whom Datini had fed "almost from boyhood." Datini left to him and his sons "a bushel of grain and a large barrel of wine."[59] Chiarito di Matteo, "a poor and not intelligent man," however, seems at one time to have been sufficiently propertied to be taxed, as Datini's will tells us, "he has come into a bad state because of the *estimo* and other reasons."[60] His daughters each received a hundred gold florins for their dowries. Betto, a trumpeter from Prato whom Datini freed from all his debts to him is called a *poverissima persona.*[61] Certainly nothing in Datini's will necessarily supports the conclusion that *poveri* were or had previously been *uomini da bene.* It seems true enough that poverty in the fifteenth century meant insufficient resources to live according to one's social station and, therefore, that extremely well-placed men and women could be said to be "poor" by virtue of recent economic or political catastrophe. But charity's purpose went far beyond "the defense of elites"—on the civic level it was as much an affirmation of community and municipal cohesion as it was an affirmation of the preservation of status.

Immediately after "providing for the health of his soul" by recommending it to the "entire celestial court, and his body to the tomb in the church of San Francesco da Prato," Datini made arrangements that all his debts and debtors should be satisfied and made whole. Conversely, anyone owing money to Francesco was called upon to pay in full his debt.[62]

Equally important were the arrangements to be made for relatives. As he had done in his first will of 1400, Datini made provisions for his illegitimate daughter Ginevra, who had at one time been placed in secret with the *spedalingo* of Santa Maria Nuova. She inherited possessions and real estate worth a thousand gold florins, whether her status was married or widowed. After her death these goods would revert to the Ceppo, which was to manage her estate during her lifetime. The Ceppo, in addition to defending diligently her inheritance, was further charged with seeing that any daughters she had *"leggitimi e naturali"* should have a dowry of five hundred florins for the first daughter and an amount to be determined by the Ceppo's officials for daughters after that.[63]

To Margherita, "his beloved wife," Francesco left a hundred florins a year to feed herself and her household as long she remained "a widow and upright person." Moreover, she was to have anything she wished from her husband's estate, of which Datini furnished a brief inventory: two beds and all the tools and utensils she required to continue managing the household. All the clothes that had belonged to her and to Francesco she was to keep and use for purposes of almsgiving. Datini also bequeathed to her one of their two houses, which she could inhabit providing she remained a widow. The will also entitled Margherita to the usufruct of a purchase of land Datini had made, divided into scattered parcels, near the Porta Santa Trinita of Prato. Datini also required the Ceppo to pay all her taxes and, at the estate's expense, to defend his wife from any claims made against her portion. Finally, Datini provided another house for her in the countryside should she choose to dwell in Florence and maintain simultaneously a country residence.[64]

Apart from the bequest to Chiarito di Matteo, "his kinsman," Datini's charity to relatives outside his household was nonexistent. He provided generously for members of his household unrelated to him; similarly, he provided liberally for future generations in the families of his friends, as well as for the children of his illegitimate daughter, Ginevra. Yet he provided only for her daughters, not for her sons. To his son-in-law, apart from the responsibilities and benefits as one of the four executors of the will, he left only 500 florins, which were to be used in increasing the fortunes of his partnership with Luca del Sera and Francesco di Ser Benozzo. Even the *sustanza* of this five-year company, called "La esecuzione e fedecomissaria di Francesco di Marco e Compagni" was to revert to the Ceppo.[65]

Nearly all the other bequests in the will were to people who were vital links in the network of trade that had made Datini's fortune, and a good many of these amounts were intended to make up for salaries not paid or for other money owed. What is striking, if one considers the testament as a vehicle for the posthumous memory of the testator, is that lacking children, Datini dissolved the companies that made his fortune, and entrusted his earthly immortality to the four executors of the will and to the commune of Prato. Moreover, the beneficiaries of Francesco Datini's charity beyond the poor were not confined to the testator's relatives. His network of charity, the means for establishing equilibrium and balance in the economy of his personal relationships, encompassed friends and business partners as comfortably as family. Datini did not, either within or without his immediate family, establish a patrimony to last more than two generations after his death.[66] Once the imbalances were righted, once his friends and partners and their sons and daughters were provided for, the entire patrimony came under the umbrella of the Ceppo, to such an extent that the Ceppo was to be the penultimate administrator and arbiter of these private claims, and the commune of Prato the ultimate recourse.

It is in this context that one must place the comparatively brief provision in the will that founded the Ospedale degli Innocenti. The clues in the will to Datini's interest in charity to illegitimate children are scarce.

Such as they are, they consist in Datini's testamentary solicitude toward his daughter Ginevra. The Mazzei letters certainly evoke a world in which children were valued.[67] When Ginevra gave birth to a female child in 1410, Francesco Datini noted in his *ricordanze* that "Ginevra, daughter of Francesco di Marco and wife of Lionardo di Ser Tommaso gave birth to a female child." Eleven days later she was "baptized by Ser Viviano, Proposto di Prato, in the name and stead of the Cardinal of Puy ... and she had the name Lapa."[68] Although the Cardinal was unable to be present at the occasion, he wrote to Datini, "Having recently received your letter ... my heart is filled with an abundance of rejoicing ... that your beloved daughter, by the grace of God healthy in body, gave birth to a beautiful girl."[69]

Datini was clear, if not elaborately profound, concerning his motives for founding the Ospedale degli Innocenti. He left the bequest, he wrote in his will, "in order to increase the alms and devotions of citizens, rural dwellers, and others who have compassion for the boys and girls called 'throwaways' and so that these little children shall be well fed, educated, and disciplined."[70] He linked his concern for these small children with the larger question of the trustworthiness and value of municipal charity, expressing his wish that through the bequest, "the effects of giving alms shall be unencumbered, and that the givers should not fear that their alms will be sent outside the city."[71] A thousand florins were to be left to the *spedalingo* of the hospital of Santa Maria Nuova, who was to be "prior, rector, governor, and sustainer ... of the said new place." This superintendent had the responsibility of seeing that the children who were to be left at the new hospital "shall be nourished there with diligence and care." The thousand florins Datini specifically earmarked to be spent on planning and building the new hospital, and nothing else. Finally, the Ceppo and its rectors were named "patrons, caretakers, and founders."[72]

Datini clearly hoped, both with the Casa del Ceppo and the Ospedale degli Innocenti, to give his institutions tax-exempt status without the usual obligation of declaring them ecclesiastical sites and thus subject to clerical control. After Francesco's death, Ser Lapo Mazzei wrote in a reassuring letter dated 5 May 1411 to the officials of the Ceppo:

If I have not written to you in the past, honorable friends, it is not because I have forgotten you, but because I was waiting to be able to give you more firm news: first of all, about being freed from Francesco's *prestanza*. Just last evening, the matter was in the hands of the person who is helping this project of justice and compassion. He said: stay alert, because I will send for you shortly, for your own good; if you come before I send for you, you will undo us. We were not thinking of accomplishing this exemption by vote, but of going beyond that. At this I thought the matter settled, and the enterprise in a good position.[73]

The tension between the charitable impulses and the fiscal needs of the commune of Florence was evident not only in the discussion over Datini's estate but also would become a major issue in the relationship between the Ospedale degli Innocenti and the commune throughout the fifteenth century.

In the years immediately following Datini's death, both the commune of Prato and the officials of the Ceppo kept a watchful eye on the administration of the testament. Ser Lapo himself felt a very deep obligation to preserve the testator's best intentions, especially in periods of potential crisis, as when he wrote in August 1411 to the Otto di Guardia of Prato. Addressing them as "my eight noble defenders and standard-bearers of justice,"[74] he expressed his concern about the upcoming election of the four new executors of the Casa del Ceppo, pointing out that in the codicil to Datini's will:

I am bound to act with all possible diligence in every matter concerning this estate. I heard yesterday at Grignano that you were preparing for the election of new officers, on which election all the hopes of the city are pinned.[75]

Ser Lapo especially hoped the new officials would be solicitous of Francesco Datini's intentions that his estate was "for the eternal care of the poor,"[76] and wrote that never before had there been such a need for cautious deliberation, in view of:

the scourge God has sent us in the harvest. Whomever you elect should show considerable foresight in carrying out his duties this year ... because, as you know, that patrimony is the poor's and I fear enough in this year for their good will.[77]

Although there is very little evidence to trace the history between 1411 and 1419 of the provision in Datini's will that founded the Ospedale degli Innocenti, the enactments providing for the supervision of the orderly transfer of that portion of the patrimony suggest that the commune of Prato's role in the administration of the estate remained of paramount importance in the intervening years. In June 1419, after the silk guild of Florence had bought a tract of land on the Piazza de' Servi for 1,700 florins from Rinaldo degli Albizzi, the guild petitioned the commune of Prato to become the legal recipients of Datini's bequest.[78] The commune of Prato, on 13 June 1419, transferred to the Ceppo "full, free, and unrestricted mandate, sanction, and authority" to distribute the thousand florins to the Arte della Seta, stipulating that "neither the Guild, the superintendent of the hospital of Santa Maria Nuova, nor any other person may seek more than the said legacy."[79]

Since Datini's will had specified that the superintendent of the hospital of Santa Maria Nuova was to use the bequest to build a new foundling hospital, the transfer of the bequest also required the assent of Santa Maria Nuova's officials. On 26 July 1419, Michele di Fruosino, who was the superintendent, and three witnesses drew up the terms of Santa Maria Nuova's "cessation of rights concerning the legacy of a thousand gold florins left to the *spedalingo* of Santa Maria Nuova of Florence."[80] At least one of the notaries, Ser Lodovico Bertini, was notary for the silk guild of Por Santa Maria. The document also noted that the project of building a new foundling hospital was already well under way in the Piazza de' Servi and that the silk guild had already spent twenty thousand florins in its construction. This document also spelled out the reasons that the hospital of Santa Maria Nuova had repudiated the burdens of the legacy.

In entrusting the bequest to the silk guild, Michele di Fruosino argued that Datini's legacy was "more inconvenient than commodious and useful to the hospital of Santa Maria Nuova." In the first place, even if the superintendent had wished to establish a foundling hospital, the thousand florins would not even underwrite the foundations.[81] Even if the construction could be financed, Michele di Fruosino:

could not possibly attend to the administration and support of the new place without great injury, prejudice and inconvenience to the said hospital of Santa Maria Nuova and its poor and infirm.

If he were so to abandon this responsibility to which he was not only entrusted but also bound by oath, he would be acting not just to the detriment of Santa Maria Nuova's patients, but:

> to the shame of the said superintendent and of the people of the city of Florence, since the said hospital of Santa Maria Nuova is, among other things, a reflection of that city and its people.[82]

In ceding the legacy of a thousand florins to the consuls of the silk guild, the hospital of Santa Maria Nuova also transferred away its claims to the "governance, support, maintenance, and administration of the hospital of the Innocenti."[83] Finally, the hospital of Santa Maria Nuova agreed to observe all the conditions of the agreement and not to bring litigation against the silk guild and its consuls.[84]

On 3 August 1419, just a week after the above document was drawn up and signed, the rectors and officials of the Ceppo, the executors of Datini's will, and the consuls of the Arte della Seta met in the guildhall to complete the transfer of the legacy from the officials of the Casa del Ceppo to the consuls of the Arte della Seta. The four officials from Prato, the overseers of the Ceppo, were Ser Paolo di Stefano Torrigiani, "Doctor of Laws," Ser Jacopo Landi dei Landi, Stefano di Geri, a wool-worker, and Lapo di Nofrio, a craftsman. The representatives from the guild were the first *operai,* or board of trustees, of the new Ospedale degli Innocenti: Goro di Stagio Dati, Francesco della Luna, Agnolo di Ghezzi della Casa and Filippo di Giovanni Carducci. Goro di Stagio Dati, as the guild's agent, was stipulated as the recipient of the legacy, and the consuls of the silk guild were hereafter "to be thought of as the true patrons, Lord Protectors, and defenders of the said new place they have begun from the legacy of one thousand gold florins."[85]

To trivialize the act of medieval charitable giving by reducing it to a question of guilt does a grave injustice to the complexity of motive involved in fifteenth-century giving. In its deepest sense, charity extended beyond the grave the cultural reciprocities of everyday life. This system of cultural reciprocities included both the testator's relationship with future generations and his relationship with the Almighty. In the former, Datini sought to recover the immortality he lost through childlessness; first through his grandiose plans for his residences and, finally, at Ser Lapo Mazzei's insistence, through charity. In the latter relationship operated a detailed divine economy of salvation in which wealth emphasized the distance between the layman and God, a distance that one could only attempt to close through the distribution of riches in good works.

If medieval theologians such as Honorius of Autun addressed the problem of charity in terms of an individual's salvation, fifteenth-century thinkers increasingly saw charity as an issue of municipal and collective salvation. We have already seen that Michele di Fruosino, the superintendent of Santa Maria Nuova, saw reflected in the success or failure of the hospital the reputation and honor of the city of Florence. According to the Innocenti's *operaio,* Goro di Stagio Dati, the splendor of Florence's charitable institutions brought down the continued favor and benevolence of the Divine, on whose mercy depended the earthly fortunes of Florence. Communal legislation concerning charity was replete with similar language.

This spiritualization of the secular was central to the shifting territories of human and divine that so characterized the cultural history of early Renaissance Florence. Unavoidably, these shifts thrust into prominence the connection between charity and lay institutions. Datini's anxiety that the Ceppo should not in any way be considered an ecclesiastical institution reflects not only his confidence in the ability of the commune to distribute his patrimony according to his best intentions; it also reflects the legitimation of lay authority in mediating between life and death, and suggests that lay authority could be trusted in matters vital to the testator's salvation.

NOTES

1. Matteo Palmieri, *Della vita civile* (Milan, 1825), 133.

2. M. A. Screech, *The Rabelaisian Marriage* (London, 1958), 16–22.

3. Lapo Mazzei, *Lettere di un notaio a uno mercante,* ed. C. Guasti, 2 vols. (Florence, 1888).

4. Cornelius von Fabriczy, *Filippo Brunellesco: Seine Leben und Seine Werke* (Florence, 1892).

5. See, however, Attilio Piccini, "In nome di Dio e del guadagno," *Progress* (1978) 68–72. *Progress* is an internal publication of the Cassa di Risparmio di Prato.

6. Richard Trexler, "Charity and the Defense of Urban Elites in the Italian

Communes," in *The Rich, the Well-born and the Powerful,* ed. F. Jaher (Urbana, 1973), 64–109.

7. Goro di Stagio Dati, *Istoria di Firenze dal 1380 al 1450,* ed. Luigi Pratesi (Norcia, 1902).

8. Iris Origo, *The Merchant of Prato,* rev. ed. (New York, 1979), 205.

9. Ibid., 206–8.

10. Richard Trexler, *Public Life in Renaissance Florence* (New York, 1980), 134.

11. Ibid., 136.

12. Archivio Datini, File 1117, Nicolozzo di ser Naldo to Datini, 6 August 1375, cited in Origo, *Merchant of Prato,* 47.

13. Lapo Mazzei, *Lettere,* 1:25: Mazzei to Datini, 25 April 1392.

14. Ibid., 1:109: Mazzei to Datini, 1 September 1395.

15. Ibid., 2:70: Mazzei to Datini, 26 December 1406.

16. Ibid.

17. Ibid., 1:13: Mazzei to Datini, 24 June 1391. Cited and translated by Origo, *Merchant of Prato,* 221. All other translations are by the author unless otherwise noted.

18. Mazzei, *Lettere,* 2:47: Mazzei to Datini, 21 August 1405.

19. Ibid., 2:68: Mazzei to Datini, 26 December 1406.

20. Ibid., 1:38: Mazzei to Datini, 6 December 1392.

21. Ibid., 1:39: Mazzei to Datini, 11 December 1392.

22. Ibid., 2:182: Mazzei to Margherita Datini, 8 April 1396.

23. Origo, *The Merchant of Prato,* 281.

24. Mazzei, *Lettere,* 1:xcvi–xcvii: Abbot of San Fabiano to Datini, undated.

25. Ibid., 1:116: Mazzei to Datini, 7 November 1395.

26. Ibid., 2:119: Mazzei to Datini, 13 November 1395.

27. Ibid., 1:210–12: Mazzei to Datini, 25 November 1398.

28. Ibid.

29. Ibid.

30. Ibid., 1:253: Mazzei to Datini, 18 August 1400.

31. Ibid., 1:242: Mazzei to Datini, 26 June 1400.

32. Ibid., 2:283, n. 2.

33. Origo, *The Merchant of Prato,* 191–95.

34. Mazzei, *Lettere,* 2:297.

35. Ibid., 2:288.

36. Ibid., 2:290.

37. Ibid., 2:294.

38. Ibid., 2:291.

39. Ibid.

40. Ibid., 2:292.

41. Ibid.

42. Ibid., 2:293.
43. Ibid.
44. Ibid., 2:289.
45. Ibid., 2:297.
46. Ibid., 2:297–98.
47. Ibid., 2:275.
48. Ibid., 2:277.
49. Ibid., 2:279–80.
50. Ibid., 2:280.
51. Ibid., 2:280–81.
52. Ibid., 2:281.
53. Ibid., 2:300.
54. Ibid.
55. Ibid., 2:290.
56. Ibid.
57. Trexler, "Charity," 74.
58. Mazzei, *Lettere*, 2:276–77.
59. Ibid., 2:277.
60. Ibid.
61. Ibid., 2:282.
62. Ibid., 2:274.
63. Ibid., 2:283–85.
64. Ibid., 2:285–86.
65. Ibid., 2:289.
66. Ibid., 1:lxvii. C. Guasti, in the preface to this volume, writes that, "Ginevra and her husband, Lionardo di Ser Tommaso di Giunta, bequeathed his estate and recommended as his heirs Christ's Poor. This recommendation was far from useless, perhaps, for the descendants of a child that Ginevra and Lionardo had orphaned . . . named Brigida, who was six years old in 1427. The entry made in her name in the Catasto describes her as 'orphan and daughter of the late Lionardo di Ser Tommaso di Rosso and heiress of Madonna Ginevra her mother for her dowry.'"
67. For example, see Mazzei, *Lettere*, 1:195: Mazzei to Datini, 15 March 1397 [modern = 1398]: "El vostro figlioccio, il quale io non vidi mai se non una volta n'è tornato da balia dall'Alpe, il più bello tassello ricciuto ch'io avesse ancora [visto]. Pregate Iddio per lui."
68. Ibid., 2:335, n. 2 (Datini's *Ricordanze*): "Richordanza che a dì 9 di febraio in mercholedì la sera alle 3 ore di notte, detta Ginevra figliuola di Francescho di Marco e moglie di Lionardo di Ser Tommaso partorì una fanciulla femina. A dì 20, il giovedì mattina, la facemo batezzare alla Pieve di Prato: e tenela a battesimo Messer Andrea di ser Viviano Proposto di Prato in nome e vecie del Cardinale dal Puy . . . ed ebe nome Lapa."

69. Ibid. Guasti quotes the Cardinal's letter as well: "Honorabilis vir et conpater specialissime. Nuper receptis vestris gratiosis litteris atque visis, repletum extitit cor meum magna plenitudine gaudiorum, accepto quod predilecta conmater mea filia vestra, cum sanitate corporis et salute, per Dei gratiam, peperit puellam decoram et etiam speciosam."

70. Ibid., 2:275–76.

71. Ibid.

72. Ibid.

73. Ibid., 2:266: Mazzei to the officials of the Casa del Ceppo, 5 May 1411.

74. Ibid., 2:268: Mazzei to the Otto di Guardia of Prato, 13 August 1411.

75. Ibid.

76. Ibid.

77. Ibid.

78. Archivio dell'Ospedale degli Innocenti di Firenze (AOIF), Debitori e Creditori (CXX, 1), fol. 2 left, 1 January 1421.

79. AOIF, Testamenta et Donationes (IX,1), fol. 22r, 13 June 1419.

80. AOIF, Testamenta et Donationes (IX,1), fol. 23r, 26 July 1419.

81. AOIF, Testamenta et Donationes (IX,1), fol. 23r-23v, 26 July 1419.

82. Ibid.

83. AOIF, Testamenta et Donationes (IX,1), fol. 24r-24v, 26 July 1419.

84. AOIF, Testamenta et Donationes (IX,1), fol. 24r-26v, 3 August 1419.

85. AOIF, Libri delle Muraglie (VII,1), fol. 9 left ff., 13 August 1419.

Chapter 2

Hospital, Church, and Commune

The issue of administrative intervention by municipalities in charitable activity is greatly complicated by a configuration of political dividing lines between corporation and government that is very different from our present manner of thinking about them. When one tries to emphasize too forcefully the anticlerical strain in lay administration of charitable enterprises, the usual indicators that clearly define the proper spheres of church and state become indistinct and misleading. If the blending of corporate and municipal administrative methods worked to the distinct advantage of the institution, the inconsistencies and confusions of the church-state relationship in fifteenth-century Florence, especially during all too frequent periods of fiscal instability, capriciously determined the effectiveness of care the institution was able to provide.

Relationships between church and state were also complex, making Francesco Datini's and Lapo Mazzei's hope that the Innocenti might be free from ecclesiastical interference rather more difficult to sustain than Datini had envisioned. In 1398, the hospital of Bonifazio Lupi petitioned the Signory for the right to be considered a "locus pius," or what in today's terms might be thought of as a nonprofit, tax-exempt institution.[1] The hospital of Santa Maria Nuova followed suit in 1425,[2] and in 1430 the Innocenti petitioned for the same status.[3] Although all three petitions were granted, the tax exemptions for hospitals were by no means assured, not because the hospital's nonprofit status was in doubt, but because in fifteenth-century Florence the principle that ecclesiastical property was not to be taxed was far from established. The issue of taxation was to take on a certain urgency in the late 1420s and early 1430s with the Lucchese war and the imposition of the Catasto. Since the Catasto was an integral part of the system of public finance, and ecclesiastical and other nonprofit corporations could receive interest payments from the public debt that were willed or donated to them, the

61

issue was by no means straightforward. "I fail to see," Andrea de' Pazzi argued, "why ecclesiastical properties should bear no taxes. These are defended from enemies just as are others," a view in which others concurred.[4]

The compelling moral force of these councillors' views was hardly weakened by the relatively common practice of falsely declaring that property had been made over to a nonprofit organization when in fact it had not been. The supposed beneficiary was only too happy to attest to the veracity of the donation. In 1431, the Catasto officials pronounced that by a two-thirds vote they could declare any transfer of property to a nonsupporting institution to be fictitious and fraudulent.[5] If this provision was perhaps too broad, a narrower one in 1434 declared any fictitious donation to be a true donation and thus the actual property of the false beneficiary. Two amendments gave the tax evader a one-month grace period to pay the tax.[6]

The ineffectiveness of this legislation is well-documented by a subsequent proposal in 1437 to levy a graduated tax on property transferred to nonsupporting institutions since 1427, and by a provision of 1451 that attempted to place a 25 percent gabelle on all contracts transferring property from a taxpaying to a non-supporting entity. This provision was withdrawn in 1454 due to the objections of the Archbishop of Florence, Sant'Antonino.[7]

Not all clerical intervention was uninvited. In the 1440s the consuls of the silk guild petitioned the pope to determine the best method of electing the most important officials of the Innocenti;[8] in 1454 a bull of Nicholas V treated the issue of taxation of property left to the Innocenti during a donor's lifetime while the donor retained its usufruct.[9] There is no little irony in the notion that Datini sought the protection of the commune in defending his patrimony from the greed of clerics; in 1451 the Archbishop of Florence would be trying to protect the patrimony of the Innocenti from the insatiable fiscal demands of the commune. Yet the government of Florence would also intervene on at least one occasion to defend the city's hospitals from papal taxation. It is no wonder, in this world of tangled, overlapping, and competing jurisdictions that the provision of 1421 that founded the Innocenti prescribed capital punishment for anyone who acted to challenge the guild's administrative and protective power over the hospital.

In October of 1421, during Giovanni di Bicci de' Medici's tenure as Gonfalonier of Justice, the guild consuls of the Arte della Seta petitioned the Signory to be considered the protectors and patrons of the new hospital. In language that was common to many succeeding Provvisioni, the guild consuls argued that, "as is well-known and obvious to the entire populace of Florence, it is through the exercise of pious works that Divine Providence shall deign not only to conserve but also to increase your republic and this guild."[10] Mindful of this, the guild had begun constructing a hospital for those children whose parents, "against the laws of nature have deserted them," but acknowledged that these charitable intentions had scarce hope of being transformed into reality "without the help and favor of your benign Lordships."[11]

Specifically, the guild, as "founders, originators, and principals" of the hospital of the Innocenti, petitioned to be recognized as the "true and sole patrons, defenders, protectors, and supporters of the hospital, its executive administrators, children, and staff."[12] Already in this founding document, it is clear that the fundamental details of the hospital's organization had been clearly thought out, envisioning a system of *commessi*, or resident lay employees, at its core.

The guild also sought in this legislation to be accorded the power to choose the hospital's superintendent. This power was to be exercised entirely at its own discretion, without any confirmation of the institution by either ecclesiastical or secular authority. Similarly, the consuls also petitioned for sole power to review the administration of the hospital, and that the administrators of the hospital be considered accountable to no other superior, secular or ecclesiastical.

The major thrust of the provision, indeed, was to prevent outside interference of any kind. "No man, of whatever authority, power, rank, or status, even ecclesiastical,"[13] could presume to seek either the title to, or the control over, the property or administration of the hospital. Such was reserved to the consuls, and any other person undertaking such a presumption was to be decapitated. Despite the strong impulse for autonomy, the consuls enlisted the authority of any communal official to force and compel restitution of rights by anyone who might succeed in usurping them; any communal official who was derelict in this duty was also to forfeit his head. The guild also asked the Florentine government to confer upon it every privilege that had been extended to the hospital of Santa Maria Nuova.[14]

The harsh penalties meted out by this legislation surely reflect a precariousness of authority and what must have been a widespread perception that charitable institutions were particularly vulnerable to abuse, specifically from clerical sources. Datini's anticlericalism finds a strong echo here, but even stronger is the fear that secular and ecclesiastical authority might come into the sort of conflict that would ultimately vitiate the charitable work of the hospital, as had happened in Pistoia a half-century earlier.[15] Indeed, charitable institutions were vulnerable to far more than clerical interference. Without clearly defined regulations and without strongly worded legislation concerning the appointed protectors of a hospital, any overmighty layperson might turn a charitable enterprise to his own advantage.

The 1374 statutes of Santa Maria Nuova, for example, forbade the burial of anybody in the church or cemetery of the hospital who was not a patient, staff member, or patron. Moreover, no one could construct or even decorate a chapel within the complex of Santa Maria Nuova without express permission of the patrons, and any painting could not include family coats of arms. The writers of the statutes felt it necessary to mention by name those types of organizations that were forbidden even to hint at control over the institutions: "persons, communes, colleges, or collectivities."[16]

As the guild attempted to establish the construction of the hospital on a more solid fiscal foundation, the officers of Por Santa Maria found themselves increasingly accountable to the tax authorities between 1427 and 1430. The Catasto required not only individuals, but also corporations and tax-exempt institutions to make declarations of their assets. Once these declarations were submitted, the commune organized them by *quartiere* and *gonfalone,* just as it organized the *Monte* records. Tax officials maintained separate volumes for *non-sopportanti,* i.e., institutions traditionally exempt from taxes. More importantly, officials used these records to keep track of patrimony passing from taxpaying to nontaxpaying institutions. In the 1427 Catasto, the Innocenti declared three houses, two of which produced rental income, and the third which the hospital owned but reserved for the use of its previous owner. In the Innocenti's case, the assessed value of rental property was calculated on the basis that rent was 7 percent of the house's assessed value, although the documents do not make clear whether the commune required the Innocenti to pay taxes on it.[17]

In 1429, the guild also declared those estates that owed taxes before they were transferred to the Innocenti. These included the estate of the goldsmith, Piero di Goro, who specifically provided in his will that the hospital pay his illegitimate son Antonio eighteen florins per year, as well as his widow's taxes. The hospital had an additional thirty-florin debt due to taxes, but the remainder of the estate, that portion "left to charity" would actually be spent on the hospital. The implication is that inheritances were subject to the back taxes owed by the deceased at his death. A specific bequest to charity, however, was treated as immune from taxation.

The Catasto assessed Francesco di Lencio di San Miniato's *Monte* credits at 5,517 florins. Included in this bequest were both of the guild's hospitals: Sant' Antonio a Lastra a Signa and the Innocenti. In addition, the sales of produce from the Innocenti's garden were valued, according to the standard calculation, at 7 percent of the total value of the property, 15,500 florins. The calculation of the Innocenti's assets also included a house donated by the silk-thrower, Domenico Grazianello, which was valued at 378 florins. The total worth of Francesco's estate, plus the value of produce sold and real estate owned, amounted to 7,700 florins.

The Catasto also listed the hospital's obligations: various masses and offices left by testators as obligations, which amounted annually to 145 florins; a debt with Sandro di Giovanni degli Strozzi for 1,864 florins; and other debts amounting to a hundred florins. The remainder of the proceeds from these estates was being used, according the guild's declaration, in the building program of the hospital.[18]

Another Catasto volume spanning the years 1427–1430 lists property transferred to "pious places," as well as a comprehensive and detailed list of the credits on which the *Monte* had to pay dividends to nontaxpaying institutions. The Innocenti, for example, held shares amounting to 816 florins and worth a face value of about 2,000 florins. By comparison to Santa Maria Nuova, whose holdings amounted to 24,000 florins, the Innocenti's participation at this point was on a comparatively small scale.

This volume also lists in great detail the holdings of Bartolomeo di Matteo, who had donated to the Innocenti in 1422 a farm in Scandicci with both a vineyard and arable land, and from which the hospital realized an annual income of fifty-five florins in sales of produce. The list of income-producing property also included another parcel of land with a vineyard and small house "at the foot of the Scandicci bridge," a farm located in San Donato di Cerreto Guidi, numerous other parcels of cultivated land, as well as the rights to licensing fees paid by certain shops and stalls in the Mercato Vecchio. In addition to this massive amount of real estate, Bartolomeo also held fourteen hundred florins of *Monte* credits as a part of this donation.[19] This very case prompted the guild officials, on 29 October 1430, to petition the Florentine councils for official tax-exempt status. Although Bartolomeo had made the donation inter vivos in 1422, it was made with the explicit understanding that the donor retained the usufruct of all his possessions until his death. In return, Bartolomeo entered the service of the hospital as a *commesso*, and agreed that his estate would revert to the Innocenti at his death. No legal problems would therefore have surfaced until his death on 1 August 1430.

In petitioning the Colleges, the consuls of the guild and the administrators of the Innocenti pointed out that the legislation of 1421 naming the Arte della Seta as patrons and founders of the Innocenti also provided that every legislative decree and favor extended to the hospital of Santa Maria Nuova also applied to the Innocenti. In 1425, the consuls argued, Santa Maria Nuova and its officials were decreed exempt "from every impost, forced loan, and subsidy that the hospital of Bonifazio Lupi had been made exempt from in 1398."[20] That these two pieces of legislation were a compelling model for the guild consuls is attested to by their presence in the *Liber Artis Portae Sanctae Mariae,* the guild's book containing all provisions that affected the Innocenti. Both the 1398 and the 1425 legislation excluded from taxes any donation made inter vivos, unless the estate itself owed taxes. This was especially at issue with regard to the gabelle on contracts.

The consuls of the guild did not waste an opportunity to remind the Colleges that:

from such a praiseworthy enterprise, divine mercy might not unreasonably be hoped for, to the end of preserving the liberty of the people of Florence and also preserving [the patrimony of] the benefactors of that hospital.[21]

In the legislation cited as a precedent by the hospitals of the Innocenti and Santa Maria Nuova, the petitioners had complained that the hospital of Messer Bonifazio "beyond its usual burdens and expenses" had to endure demands for forced loans from the officials of the commune of Florence. "It seems neither just nor fair," wrote the authors of the 1398 petition, "that what is the poor's should be spent for other things."[22]

The governors of the hospital of Messer Bonifazio received exemption not only from all communal and civic impositions, burdens, demands, loans, subsidies, or gifts, but also any sort of revenue-producing devices invented "by the clergy or other persons of any ecclesiastical dignity individually, or severally, under any color of any authority whatsoever."[23]

The legislation of 1430 therefore had ample precedent in the Florentine councils. It is a measure of the fragility of the principle that "pious establishments" should be tax-exempt, that each institution had to apply separately for tax-exempt status, even when prior legislation had implicitly guaranteed it. The situation in which the hospital of Messer Bonifazio Lupi had found itself in 1398 represented a more clear-cut and blatant form of civic pressure than either Santa Maria Nuova or the Innocenti would face in 1425 and 1430, respectively. Both the petitions of Santa Maria Nuova and of the Innocenti turned on the murkier question of how, if at all, donations made *inter vivos* should be taxed.[24]

In any event, when the Innocenti took the case of Bartolomeo di Matteo's donation before the *regulatores* of the commune's income and expenditures, the hospital's administrators came fortified with the legislation passed a few months earlier. The hospital's advocate, representing "the superintendent of the said hospital and the consuls of the guild, who are the patrons, defenders, and protectors of the said hospital and its patrimony," complained that the tax collectors had been overly zealous in their pursuit of the tax obligations of the deceased. The hospital argued that in 1427, when the Catasto was levied, the property already belonged to the hospital, and Bartolomeo di Matteo no longer enjoyed ownership, but only the right of usufruct:

Bartolomeo retained only the use and enjoyment of the property . . . which ceased at his death. The full estate, with its usufruct . . . since his death, belonged and now belongs to the said hospital by the right of true domain and possession. Such goods are not taxable for the Catasto, nor are his obligations payable, because he alienated the property before the Catasto was enacted. Had Bartolomeo even wanted to obligate these goods to the commune, he could not have done so legally, nor could he in any way have transferred said goods to the officials of the Catasto to the hospital's disadvantage. [Moreover], the said hospital was and is, by the authority of the commune of Florence, and of the appropriate councils...exempt from any Catasto, levy, loan, solicitation of funds, or any other taxes whatsoever.[25]

On the basis of these arguments, the *regulatores* agreed that the property of the hospital, especially that donated by Bartolomeo di Matteo, could not legally be "pledged, harassed, or in any way disturbed by any Catasto, loan, or impost."[26] The regulatory officials did make the exception that if the hospital derived a profit from the estate by virtue of Bartolomeo's donation that otherwise would have rightfully been Bartolomeo's, such profit would be taxable.

In 1431, the hospital's declaration of the estate of Ceppo di Guido, a pharmacist, noted that it came with so many obligations that it should be considered "more damaging than useful" to the hospital's financial condition.[27] This suggests not only a new variation of the old theme of avoidance of taxation, but also a deeper economic and fiscal crisis that turned the commune from enthusiastic supporter to reluctant adversary.

The origins of this fiscal crisis are already well known to students of Florentine political and military history. Following a nine-year period of relative tranquillity and prosperity, Florence experienced a series of devastating military reverses at the hands of the Milanese from 1423 to 1428, which were capped in 1429 by a disastrous attempt to annex Lucca to the Florentine dominion. Even in the least trying wartime years, military expenditures were double the income produced by the standard sources of communal income. Giovanni Morelli estimated military expenditures at 2.5 million florins for the three-year period, 1423 through 1425, and in 1431 war expenditures sometimes reached 100,000 florins per month.[28]

Nor did military defeats alone account for chronic fiscal shortages. In the 1420s, the relationship between communes and their hired soldiers drastically altered, to the disadvantage of the communes' treasuries. *Condottieri* such as Sir John Hawkwood and Niccolò da Tolentino, celebrated by Paolo Uccello's frescoes in Santa Maria del Fiore, could command enormous sums of money. So could the soldiers under their command, whose pay increased proportionately. Thus, in the 1390s, knights, squires, and shield-bearers drew twelve to fourteen florins monthly, compared to the sixty florins per month for the *lancia* that Florence promised to the Lord of Faenza in 1430. In 1433, the commune paid Niccolò da Tolentino 50,000 florins, and another *condottiere* 60,000.[29]

In addition to these enormous new military expenditures, the commune also faced a mountain of public debt, a necessary outcome of heavy military spending. In 1347, the commune's total indebtedness stood at 450,000 florins. By 1380, this amount had doubled to a million florins, and by 1425 stood at 2.5 million. The interest alone amounted to an annual expenditure of 200,000 florins. The Catasto of 1427 attempted a more equitable distribution of the ever-increasing burden of forced loans.[30]

Forced loans were only one source of communal income, but as other sources yielded a smaller proportion of the commune's total expenditures, the commune relied more heavily on the generosity of its wealthier citizens. Direct taxes imposed on Florence's subject territories and gabelles, which were indirect taxes levied on contracts, as well as on the consumption or importation of certain products, provided two dwindling sources of revenue in the fifteenth century.

Direct taxes depended on a stable population and its stable or expanding patrimony. Yet postplague Florence could not sustain either. From 1404 to 1414, the number of households in the *contado* decreased from 40,711 to 36,333, with a total patrimony that decreased from 3,330,358 florins to 2,362,822.[31] Even the most successful and militant expansionism could not keep pace with these declines. At the same time, property held by Florentine citizens in the *contado* was added in increasing proportions to the city's tax rolls, which reduced the tax base on which the *estimo* could be imposed in the *contado*.[32] By the 1420s and 1430s, subject territories were anywhere from years to decades behind in paying their assessments.[33] The inhabitants of the Florentine *contado* itself resorted to pawnbrokers and moneylenders as well as the city's larger banking firms for loans.[34] As early as 1419, the newly formed *Ufficiali del contado* passed legislation authorizing only the Florentine Signory and Councils to impose taxes on subject territories. This legislation also forbade private individuals to lend any sums to territories without prior authorization from the officials of the *Monte*. The harshness of communal policy in the 1420s toward subject territories found its reply in the revolt of Volterra in 1429, and the near revolt of Arezzo in 1431.[35]

The Florentines could ill afford to squeeze the *contado* when another source of communal income was becoming even less reliable. In the period 1420–1433, annual income from gabelles reached a high in 1420 of 215,687 florins. In 1424, the annual income from this source had dropped to 159,000 florins, and from 1424 to 1433 it never rose above 150,000 florins. Legislative decrees modifying the structure of gabelles resulted in only very short-term gains.[36]

The effects of the fiscal crisis on individual taxpayers suggests the desperation of the communal fisc as much as it does the desperation of the taxpayers themselves. In the early 1420s, Palla di Nofri Strozzi had been one of Florence's most prosperous citizens. In 1431, he petitioned the Signory to be allowed to sell his Monte credits to foreign investors. His taxes were so high, he complained, that he had to borrow to pay them. His investments were only in land but he was unable to sell his real estate. Nor was he able to unburden himself by selling his *Monte* credits in Florence, and saw his only avenue of escape to be the sale of *Monte* credits to foreigners. The petition was granted, but Strozzi was still forced to request a reduction of his tax assessment, since his credits only sold for 27 percent of their face value and not 30 percent as he had anticipated. From 1424 to 1432, Palla di Nofri Strozzi had paid 158,000 florins in tax assessments. His inability to find buyers for his credits is corroborated by the precipitous decline in their value. In 1431 they fell from 27 to 24 percent, and by 1433, to 15 percent.[37] In those same years, Giovanni di Bicci de' Medici found himself in similar straits. From 1425 until 1433, he and his son, Cosimo, paid 91,441 florins in *prestanze* and *catasti*. The interest and partial amortization of their *Monte* investments yielded only 15,981 florins. Thus the commune's fiscal policy cost the Medici nearly 10,000 florins a year, exceeding their profits from a very successful company. Still another measure of this hardship is that in the 1427 Catasto, Palla Strozzi declared his net capital to be 101,422 florins, and Giovanni di Bicci de' Medici 79,472 florins. Thus over eight years Palla Strozzi paid in taxes one and a half times his net worth.[38]

The government resorted to several extraordinary expedients to maximize its return on taxes. Not only did it offer higher interest rates to its investors than it could pay, it also enforced more strictly and severely the penalties for tax delinquency. The commune, just as the silk guild, could disenfranchise debtors. Several new officials and commissions created from 1423 to 1433 could confiscate goods. In 1432 the officials of the *Monte* succeeded in empowering themselves to seize the property of tax delinquents.[39] As Palla di Nofri Strozzi wrote to Neri Acciaiuoli in 1424, "these are times one's own efforts should be engaged in providing for one's affairs in every way possible. [Yet] already it could be said we have been assessed [the equivalent of] forty forced loans."[40]

Thus the harassment of nonprofit institutions was neither unexpected nor without precedent. Andrea Pazzi was not the only citizen to complain that tax-exempt institutions still benefited from the military expenditures from which they were exempt. In August 1431, a member of the Signory stated that "ecclesiastical goods are one fourth or one fifth of all goods, and they are defended just as ours are. It is thus suitable that no one should be exempt. Let there be a tax on clergy. There are [even] some clerics who wish to be required to pay taxes and who fully agree [with me]."[41]

In the same year, 1431, that tax officials approved the exemption from taxes of Bartolomeo di Matteo's estate, they also pursued with some enthusiasm those estates and properties they felt had been transferred illegitimately to charitable institutions. By a two-thirds vote, the Catasto officials could deem fraudulent any transfer of property from taxpaying to nontaxpaying entities. In April 1434 this ruling was strengthened to provide that any such transfer legally belonged to the stated recipient, notwithstanding any prior written agreements. The Signory was to judge all appeals to this rule. The ruling also declared an amnesty for all those who reported their fraudulent alienations within a month of the measure's enactment.[42]

When the *balìa* of 1434 exiled Rinaldo degli Albizzi, it was statutorily understood that the state was to dispose of, as well as benefit from, his confiscated property.[43] Less clear was how the creditors of those estates were to have their claims satisfied. Rinaldo's brother Luca, fearful that once the government disposed of Rinaldo's possessions, Rinaldo's debtors would place claims against him as heir to the estate, sought the help of the Signory. The Signory appointed six men to handle the problem, who satisfied themselves that no known obligations remained. To cover any unknown claims, they published a notice to the effect that all men having claims on Rinaldo's possessions must submit such claims by a certain date or forever hold their peace.

A month before this notice was published, the Innocenti had already taken its own case before the *Signoria*, which had begun selling the confiscated property back to Rinaldo's brothers. Although Rinaldo had sold the parcel of land on which the Innocenti was situated to the silk guild in 1419, the original sale must have rested on sufficiently insecure foundations to compel the silk guild to seek protection from the sale of

Rinaldo's confiscated land. On 28 September the guild's consuls went through the channels provided by the legislation to avoid either eviction or the financial burden of repurchase.

The consuls argued that the sale had been documented by a public instrument detailing the boundaries of the property and outlining provisions that the property was guaranteed to be immune from eviction proceedings. Moreover, argued the guild, legislation passed on 3 September 1432 specifically approved the guild's purchase of the parcel, so that the commune was obligated not to proceed further in the attempt to sell it.

On 3 October the *Signoria* accepted the consuls' pleas and granted the petition in its entirety. In addition, the *Ufficiali dei Rebelli* were to purchase two thousand florins of *Monte* shares to be used as security to be applied against any sales or legal costs incurred by the guild or the hospital in recovering property or defending claims.[44]

The guild not only turned to communal government as a model, but also specifically sought the advice of the Pope concerning matters of hospital administration. The presence of Pope Eugenius IV at the Council of Florence occasioned several papal bulls and apostolic letters that addressed local issues. The consuls of the Arte Por Santa Maria entreated Eugenius to provide a set of guidelines for electing a superintendent, because, as the Pope wrote in his reply:

> it is fitting that his Holiness should advance the cause of particular pious places, especially the hospital and its poor and abandoned infants of both sexes . . . so that the practice of charity might be more effective, as we hope to alleviate the unhappy condition of these poor and miserable creatures.[45]

The papal bull also noted that the guild had spent twenty thousand florins in the hospital's construction and that it planned to spend a similar amount of money "to bring this work to completion," after which the institution would "become notable and outstanding among the hospitals found in the region of Italy."[46] For this reason, the guild sought not merely competent administration, but also some guidelines concerning the procedures for electing a superintendent.

The Pope recommended that the guild should place the names of nominees into a bag and begin drawing until it reached thirty-six names, twelve from each constituency of the guild. Each elector had to be at least thirty-five years of age and had to have previously held a major guild office. At least three-quarters of the electors had to be present before a vote could be taken, and no two electors could be a member of the same *consorteria*. The electors, in considering nominations for the post of superintendent, had to vote on each candidate three times. Whichever nominee finally received the most votes became appointed as superintendent. Unlike other major guild offices, the office of superintendent could be filled by someone outside the guild, which did not seem to be the case in the 1420s. The hospital's "ecclesiastical" status, granted in principle by the commune in 1430 and officially by the Pope in 1439, meant that a cleric could be chosen, and Eugenius's brief urged that the guild should choose a cleric. Laymen were just as likely as clergy to become superintendents, however, until the end of the fifteenth century. To fill the position required no confirmation, ecclesiastical or otherwise.

The brief further recommended that the consuls and the *operai* be given the power to remove immediately a superintendent suspect of maladministration and to declare the post vacant. In addition, the superintendent had to swear that he would renounce any other office or benefice within four months of his appointment. His failure to renounce the other post by the deadline was considered sufficient grounds for dismissal.

The Pope suggested this latter stipulation because the prior would then "exert himself more energetically and for the greater benefit of the administration of that hospital."[47] A guild petition presented to the Pope in 1446 complained, however, that "no candidate can be found who is not obstructed by this rule." If the superintendent were allowed to retain other benefices, "many more suitable and able men could be found to govern and direct the said hospital in a praiseworthy and effective manner." The Pope approved the petition in full, writing that future superintendents could "possess, have, receive, hold, and obtain any other ecclesiastical benefices." This apostolic brief also changed the official title of "Rector" to "Prior."[48]

In late January 1445 the hospital finally opened its doors (one presumes that the slow progress of construction is accounted for by Florence's heavy expenditures on the Milanese war after 1426); on 27 January a guildsman from Castelfiorentino, Lapo di Piero Pacini, and his wife, Dianora became *commessi* of the hospital. In accepting obedience to the superintendent, and pledging their entire lives and property to the Innocenti, this devout couple contributed both administrative energy and supplies and funds to the new hospital.

In order to leave their estate to the Innocenti, however, Lapo and Dianora had to seek the explicit approval of the *Signoria*. The *Signoria* "reached a decision among themselves according to the procedures and ordinances of the commune of Florence."[49] They considered especially a Provvisione of 1438, one of many passed to control the flow of estates from taxpaying families to charitable institutions. In 1437 the commune had asked two lawyers to submit recommendations concerning how to prevent the fraudulent transfer of property to charity. The lawyers proposed to levy a graduated tax on all property transferred since 1427 to religious persons, corporations, or places. This proposal never passed, but the legislation of 1438, which is no longer extant, was undoubtedly an attempt to monitor the flow of such property, and to verify the legitimacy and good faith of such transactions. At the same time, the *provvisione* would presumably have avoided the major confrontation between Church and State, hospital and commune, that would have resulted from the imposition of a graduated tax.[50] The *Signoria* allowed Lapo and Dianora to donate their worldly goods providing they had paid any back taxes and their "current contribution to the *decima*," which in their case amounted to twenty-five florins.[51]

Just as sensitive as the issue of the transfer of property from taxpayers to charity must have been the issue of whether charitable institutions should reap the advantages of interest payments from the *Monte*, especially in those cases in which estates leaving *Monte* credits to the Innocenti were heavily burdened with tax debts. Established in 1343, the *Monte* began as a list of all the creditors of the commune, broken down by quarter. Early in the development of this institution, the commune hoped to make good on at least the interest payments, and more ambitiously, to amortize the entire debt using revenue from direct and indirect taxes, customs tolls and gabelles in particular. Such measures hardly sufficed, especially during wartime, and the government was forced, in addition to reducing the annual rate of interest, to levy forced loans in order to balance the confidence of its creditors with its ever-growing military expenditures.[52] The *prestanza* of 1403 was only one of many such assessments. The Catasto of 1427, often heralded as the first graduated income tax, was in fact another assessment levied for the purpose of reducing the public debt. The Catasto differed from earlier assessments insofar as the criteria for assessment were more uniform and were verified by declarations and demands for proof of a taxpayer's total assets. In both forms of direct taxation, however, the taxpayer was inscribed as a creditor of the commune and thus rendered eligible for annual dividends.[53] The fiscal managers of early Renaissance Florence employed considerable creative imagination in attracting new investors by offering high interest rates. The *Monte delle Doti*, or dowry fund, was only one of several such schemes designed to attract the capital of wealthy citizens.[54]

Credits in the funded debt could be sold or exchanged for a market value that fluctuated in the range of 25 to 35 percent of face value. The *Monte* employed a special officer, the *camarlingo alle promute*, to oversee such transactions, for which the government collected a nominal fee. Wealthy creditors routinely bequeathed their shares in these government securities to charitable institutions, which benefited tremendously from reliable sources of income generated by regular interest payments. From this standpoint, the Catasto of 5 percent levied on taxpayers' assets represented, for those taxpayers who bequeathed credits to the Innocenti, a sort of investment upon which the hospital could eventually hope to draw.

Much of the discord between the commune's fiscal managers and the administrators of the Innocenti is traceable to the uncertain status of nonprofit institutions. Legislation passed in 1446 implies that the *Monte* paid interest to these institutions with less urgency than to its taxpaying creditors. The consuls of the guild noted in their petition that:

In the year that has passed since the hospital first opened, or rather, began to admit children, up until today, ninety have been left under our care, all of whom are at wet nurse and who are being raised with the greatest of care. Each one of these children costs at least one florin per month, between payments for the salaries of the wet nurse and the diapers and swaddling clothes. It seems likely that almost all the little children of this sort will be abandoned there in the future, if the first year is any indication, for in the same year no similar influx was reported at the hospitals of San Gallo and Santa Maria della Scala. This fact depends, we believe, on the reputation [the Innocenti] has throughout the entire region for being the best governed.[55]

The guild asserted that the hospital depended on the interest from *Monte* shares for three-quarters of its revenue, and that currently interest payments for tax-exempt institutions were kept in a bag separate from those of the taxpayers. Consequently, the hospital received payments well beyond the due date. Everyone knows, argued the gu .d, what a notable work of charity the hospital is and how much honor it brings to the city and the commune. The hospital's revenues must keep pace with its expenses, argued the consuls, so that it is not forced to cut back services or close altogether.

The legislation enacted as a result of the guild's petition stipulated that interest owed the Innocenti could be withdrawn from the tax-exempt bag and placed among the amounts owed to regular taxpayers and other creditors of the *Monte Comune*.[56] Striking in this legislation, first, is that in the first year of operation the administrators had already calculated the cost per child, and that the hospital's swelling population was attributed to its rational and efficient administration. Even more surprising is the willingness of the *Monte* officials to pay out the interest on *Monte* shares as though the Innocenti paid taxes. This commitment could not and did not last beyond the end of the decade, when once again the fiscal pressure of war moved the commune to neglect its pursuit of honor and collective salvation.

In 1448, the guild complained that:

> great is the number of tiny infant foundlings now abandoned there. At wet nurse are 260 or more, and this increases daily, due, we believe, to the presence of a larger-than-usual number of slaves and servants in the city.[57]

Perhaps, as the consuls had previously argued, the reputation of the hospital itself attracted admissions. This reputation was insufficient, however, to ensure that its "very heavy expenses" could be met by its "exceedingly scarce resources. Without some form of public assistance, the hospital would have to close and desert" those who had themselves already been deserted. Yes, the guild had levied its own taxes, but these did not suffice. In a rare preamble, the legislative councils, approving the petition, wrote:

> Knowing the aforesaid narration to be founded in truth, and considering that to foster piety and compassion concerning the abovesaid little children is most pleasing to Almighty God and his Most Blessed

Mother, and is known to redound to the honor and exaltation of this republic, and in no small way to the aforesaid guild and its membership, [the petition is approved].[58]

The legislation directed the guild to spend "the alms, subsidy, and subvention of the aforesaid hospital" on "the education and upbringing of the aforesaid children." The legislators placed not the commune, but the guild and hospital in charge of collecting a gabelle on every piece of commercial clothing material that passed thorough the city gates. The gatekeepers placed these sums in special cash-boxes designed for this purpose. "From time to time," the law specified, "the consuls of the guild will open the cash-boxes and hand over their contents to be converted to the education and sustenance of these children."[59] This gabelle was in force for only five years, and was renewable only by a similar petition.

This far from all-encompassing solution to the Innocenti's short-term financial crisis was at least superficially innovative insofar as it enabled communal government to support this worthy charitable enterprise without diminishing the communal treasury. The preamble implied not direct subsidy, but the fostering of "sufficient compassion and devotion" among citizens by involuntary voluntarism. Yet if the consuls' estimates that it cost more than a florin per month to maintain a child at the Innocenti were accurate, the amount voted by the commune was sufficient to sustain fewer than 50 of the 260 children the hospital had to support. A census of 260, moreover, implies that the hospital was already operating on a much more vast scale than that for which its patrons, benefactors, and administrators had planned. Finally, the guild had planned the hospital during the relatively prosperous decades between 1410 and 1430, when both business conditions and the stability of the communal fisc could provide a generous flow of cash for the building program.

Even if the late 1440s had not witnessed the significant economic contraction that squeezed the very guildsmen who supported the institution with their taxes, donations, and ultimately their estates, war and plague still diverted not only cash but energy and attention from the problems of institutions that paid no taxes. By March 1449, the *Consulte e Pratiche* record a concern that "considering the prolongation of war and the suspicion of plague ... our citizens should experience as little harm as possible." A week later this same advisory body noted "the lively temper in which the city is found, due to war and the small amount of gain that people are able to make, and the suspicion and fear there is of the plague."[60] A year later, the debaters of the *Consulte e Pratiche* considered proposals to lighten the tax burden on its most pressed lenders for six months, because of "the very evident dangers in which the city is placed because of the disorders of the people."[61]

Nevertheless, despite continuing economic problems in the early 1450s, the guild continued to reorganize the administration of the hospital. Lapo di Piero Pacini was reinstated and made treasurer for life, accountable, as in previous reforms, not to the prior but directly to the guild.[62] In April 1451, "at the insistence of the guild," Sant'Antonino, the Archbishop of Florence, consecrated the church's chapel,[63] a scene recorded in the *predella* of Ghirlandaio's *Adoration of the Magi*. Perhaps the guild insisted on consecration to legitimize the hospital's status as a "locus ecclesiasticus," under ever-increasing siege from communal legislation that threatened to place a 25 percent gabelle on transfers of property to charitable and religious organizations.

If the guild could provide controls autonomously, it still required the help of the commune in its charitable mission, especially when the guild became involved in the *Monte delle Doti,* the communal dowry fund. The consuls petitioned the guild in late 1451, complaining that "at present the dowries cannot be provided for the hospital's children as they can be for the children of the city and *contado.*"[64] The chief obstacle to the participation of the foundlings in the dowry scheme was the wording of the early *Monte* legislation, which forbade investments in the dowry fund if someone could not provide the name of one of the parents of the intended recipient.

This was not the only obstacle, however. The wording of general *Monte* legislation passed in 1380 and 1415 allowed suspension of interest payments to *non-sopportanti* whenever the *Monte* found itself unable to satisfy its taxpaying creditors.[65] The hospital wished to avoid such suspensions because "great are the expenditures of the hospital and great is the number of children to be provided for." The guild officials clearly viewed the right to continue receiving interest payments during a suspension of payments as a kind of subsidy. The consuls had already sought and obtained the permission of the *Monte* officials, who, according to the consuls, were concerned "to assist good government and proper maintenance" of the hospital. The legislation set up a procedure to handle petitions on a case-by-case basis. Every time the consuls wished to abridge an order of suspension, they had to present a petition to the legislative councils. Moreover, the hospital could invest in the *Monte delle Doti* provided the quantity of each girl's dowry did not exceed fifty florins. Apart from this limitation, girls for whom the Innocenti made a deposit in the dowry fund could receive a dowry just as girls outside the hospital could. Where the *Monte delle Doti* provided that in the event of a girl's death the father could retrieve the capital, this legislation appointed the superintendent of the Ospedale degli Innocenti the legal father of the hospital's foundlings, "just as if the aforesaid hospital were the true and natural father of the aforesaid girl."[66]

In order to qualify for paternal status, however, the hospital was subject to the same reporting requirements as other fathers. The legislation required the hospital to assign a number to every child, boy or girl, abandoned there. The number was to be recorded in the *Balie e Bambini,* along with a notation of the day the child was abandoned, the day he or she was baptized, and both forenames. The *Monte*'s register also had to contain the names of all the girls for whom the hospital had created a dowry account, noting what pages and volumes of the *Balie e Bambini* the child was in, as well her number. The hospital's duty was to notify, in writing, the *Monte*'s scribe of all the information kept in the *Balie e Bambini.* To collect a dowry, or to retrieve the capital, the hospital had to bring written proof that an account had been created for the girl in question.[67]

The clause limiting the amount of the dowry to fifty florins, despite the rest of the legislation, provided a clear and drastic separation of the girls of the Innocenti from those of the city and *contado.* In 1452, when the burgeoning debt of the *Monte delle Doti* had brought its officials to the extremes of placing a ceiling of 1200 florins for legitimate girls and 500 for illegitimate girls, the girls of the Innocenti could command only a fraction of their illegitimate counterparts in Florence.[68] Whatever concessions one makes to the charitable impulses of the Florentine state with respect to the Innocenti's children, one must keep in mind this enormous distance of fortunes.

The dowry was the cornerstone of family honor in fifteenth-century Florence. The anxiety of Florentines to dower the foundlings of the Innocenti illustrates both the pervasiveness of honor as a cultural value and the centrality of the hospital's charitable mission to the preservation of the family and the survival of the Florentine city-state. For Giovanni Morelli, a woman was suitable for his descendants to marry only if she was "well-born, of well-to-do parents, and of an honorable family."[69] Certainly few of the female children of the Innocenti could satisfy all three criteria. The legislative limits placed on their dowries reflected their low value in the fifteenth-century marriage market. As was the case with more general charitable practice, the poor woman's dowry was not designed to enhance her social mobility but to keep her from being vulnerable to the dishonor of being unmarried or unmonachated.[70] As the following example makes clear, such dishonor was to be feared more than death itself.

At the end of October 1435 the Signory heard an appeal on behalf of the twin daughters of Giovanni di Matteo dello Scielta, Oretta and Lorenza. These two girls, the advocate argued:

> can deservedly and worthily said to be orphans...deprived of a father...for crimes it is alleged that Giovanni committed...as well as deprived of brothers and of all their property. They are for all intents and purposes abandoned and bereft of every person related to them....
>
> Your Magnificent Lordship and the Honorable Colleges...would not wish for suffering and punishment where there has been no sin. They have heard that the Officials of Rebels and Condemned Persons sold the major portion of their father's goods...required by these girls for their nourishment, and more importantly[!] for their dowries ...so that they will neither die of hunger nor live the rest of their lives in wretchedness.[71]

The story of St. Nicholas of Bari established the model for charity toward poor girls. He anonymously gave an impoverished citizen enough money to dower his three daughters to avoid their imminent descent into prostitution. The implicit moral equation was inescapable. Women who remained unmarried or who did not enter convents were morally unaccountable and therefore likely to be promiscuous. To enter a convent or a marriage, a young woman required a dowry to guarantee that her life so far had been honorably led. This explains much of the pressure, less intense in Northern cultures, to decide a girl's adult fate by the time she was fifteen or sixteen years old. Without a dowry, honor, and therefore marriage, was impossible.

More practical considerations embellished the deeper cultural and moral imperatives. Dowries enabled new husbands to establish economic independence with their capital. When the husband died, the dowry reverted to the widow and her family, guaranteeing her patrimony, safeguarding her honor, and reflecting the stark demographic reality that 50 percent of Florentine women were widows by the time they reached the age of fifty.[72]

The interests of fiscal solvency and family honor coincided in the late 1420s with the establishment of the dowry fund. The fund became enormously successful after 1433, when the stipulation was introduced that a father could retrieve his capital in the event his daughter died before the dowry matured. The idea of a dowry fund financed by government bonds was not peculiar to Florence: in 1422 the Council of Ten in Venice granted permission to the Scuola of San Giovanni to administer a dowry fund called the *sacho*.[73] The scale on which the Florentine dowry fund operated, however, involved the entire fiscal structure of the commune, and nowhere else but in Florence did the state of a city's finances affect so deeply the marriage plans and family strategies of its citizens.

As had been the case with the *Monte Comune* in the fourteenth century, war and fiscal crisis were crucial variables in the initiation of the plan. In 1425, when the Florentine treasury needed more funds to wage war on Milan, the dowry fund was one of several expedients, including the 1427 Catasto, that Florentines hoped would shore up a deteriorating fiscal structure. Not until 1433, however, did the government come up with a workable scheme that was capable of attracting more than a handful of investors. Florentine fathers were encouraged to deposit sixty florins for terms of 5, 7.5, 11, or 15 years for their daughters. If the daughter died, the father received the sixty florins back. If she married, the sixty florins, plus interest compounded at annual rates ranging from 15 to 20 percent, were paid to the husband after the marriage was consummated. Thus a deposit of sixty florins for a term of fifteen years would result in a dowry of five hundred florins.[74]

The scheme had two major objectives: first, its promoters hoped to attract cash deposits to be used in the diminution of the *Monte Comune* and its carrying charges, which amounted to 175,000 florins per year. Secondly, the originators hoped to stimulate the marriage market and thereby to attempt a recovery from the drastic population losses incurred by the plagues that ravaged Florence between 1348 and 1424. The economics of supply and demand worked their havoc on the price of marriage: dowries of under a thousand florins, considered the norm during the fourteenth century, were meager by the standards of the fifteenth.

Moreover, the insolvency of fathers-in-law under the new legislation no longer presented an insurmountable obstacle to payment, as the government itself put all its power and authority, however rashly, behind guarantees of prompt and full repayment. In achieving its first objective, the government was spectacularly successful, if only for the short term: subscriptions during the first two months of 1433 equalled one-third of the *Monte Comune*'s annual carrying charges.[75]

In 1438, the fund faced its first major test: it had to pay the dowries of those investors who had chosen the five-year option, and had to return capital to a large number of fathers whose daughters had died of plague. The fund met both its obligations. Additional legislation passed in 1438 and 1441 further increased the confidence of investors, and by 1451 the commune had committed itself to paying interest on 2,542,000 florins of *Monte delle Doti* shares. So successful was this fund in attracting investors that legislation enacted in 1449 noted its benefit to public and private persons, as well as noting that the many marriages made possible through its operation had increased the number of children and future citizens. In short, honor and distinction to the city of Florence resulted from the preservation of the honor of its families and from the increase in population necessary to its survival. The charity on behalf of poor children that redounded to the honor of the city also assured both its spiritual and temporal salvation.[76]

The Ospedale degli Innocenti had the misfortune to begin participation in this dowry scheme scarcely a year before the government began to foresee the enormous drain that satisfying the fund's creditors would place on the communal fisc. In addition to the 1452 legislation limiting the amounts of dowries paid, emergency legislation had to be enacted in 1456 transferring more money from other sources into the dowry fund. Barely a year after the Innocenti had begun its participation in the fund, the consuls of the silk guild invoked the procedure to provide for the payment of dowries during the suspension to *non-sopportanti*. The guild again petitioned the commune to set aside the constraints of the early *Monte* legislation so that the dowries of the hospital's poor girls would continue to be paid.[77]

The *Monte delle Doti*, however, sank ever more deeply into debt. By late 1456, a sense that the fund was out of control dominated the debates of the government's advisory bodies. The protocol for 17 November 1456 records "an agitated session in the communal hall . . . concerning the Monte shares." Citizens made suggestions to expropriate 35,000 florins from the *Monte delle Doti,* which "this year" was already running a deficit of 75,000 florins. For the year to come, 1457, "40,000 florins shall be spent for the diminution of the first *Monte delle fanciulle.*" Altogether, "the carrying charges for the coming year would amount to 87,000 florins, of which 5,791 would go to tax-exempt individuals, and 28,986 florins to tax-exempt institutions." Payments in arrears amounted to 184,000 florins, so that the commune's total indebtedness, including salaries yet to be paid, amounted to 321,000 florins. Exempt taxpayers such as the King of Portugal accounted for 100,000 florins of the communal debt, this source estimated. The old debts alone amounted to 257,000 florins: this *consulte* charged the new Monte officials to pay creditors one-sixth of this amount in May, and another sixth in September, so that debt that was "old" in 1456 would finally be retired by the end of 1458.[78]

Despite these plans, on 23 November, Niccolò Soderini stated that "the *Monte* is in the worst condition imaginable." Bernardo Gherardi reaffirmed that the *Monte* is "the foundation of liberty, which will defend it always." Francesco di Jacopo Ventura argued that this fact alone meant that "every inconvenience should be borne to improve the situation of the *Monte* for the taxpayers, not to mention the religious and nontaxpayers."[79] Sant'Antonino's *Chronica* makes special mention of Florence's great poverty in 1456 and 1457 not so much because of starvation, but because of scarcity of money.[80]

The fiscal strains and demographic stresses of war and plague were, by the mid-1450s, wreaking havoc on the communal fisc and slightly weakening the hold of the Medici regime. In the years preceding the *parlamento* of 1458, the condition of the *Monte* provided a pretext both for restoring the Medici *balìe* and for the retention of authority by the *Signori e Collegi* over the electoral process. For the Medici side, the prominent lawyer Otto di Niccolini invoked the importance of the *Monte delle Doti* to oppose control of elections by the *Signori e Collegi:*

[He] stood before the Priors and Colleges, and proved with eloquent and elegant argument that nothing is more salutary to cities and republics than that the *Monte* should prosper, since it is the foundation and origin of every public good, if it is properly and wisely managed. If not, the exact opposite will ensue.... The *Mons puellarum,* which confers many public advantages and conserves the patrimony of the city, must not be plundered [by military expenses], so that both old and new investors can be paid.[81]

Legislation passed in 1456 authorized the transfer of money from other sources to the dowry fund.

The debate concerning the performance of the dowry fund is critical to the understanding of two major issues. First, the honor, well-being, indeed, the very survival of the city depended on its ability to honor its commitment to investors in the dowry fund. Secondly, the commune's fiscal emergency deeply compromised its ability to support, or assist taxpayers in supporting, charitable enterprise. The long-term task of courting God's favor all too often had to be sacrificed to the short-term expedients of raising desperately needed funds. At the end of 1456, just a week after the transfer of money to support the dowry fund had been authorized, the consuls of the silk guild again went before the *Signoria* and the Councils to seek additional government subsidy. From 1448 to 1456, the Innocenti's population had grown from 260 to 318, with the result that caring for these children had become proportionately more expensive. Despite the legislation of 1448, and despite the guild's own initiative in taxing its manual workers, the hospital could not meet its expenses. This was largely due to its dependence on interest payments from donors' and testators' credits in the *Monte Comune,* which had been suspended because the *Monte* had fallen so far behind on its payments to taxpaying creditors.

Without something to replace the lost income, argued the consuls, the guild could not continue to support the Innocenti. The consuls therefore petitioned that the hospital be allowed to remain open; otherwise "these infants, chiefly the illegitimate children of slaves and servants . . . would doubtless face death."[82] The consuls also pointed out the honor the hospital brought to the city, making its glory "singular among Christian nations."[83]

In response, the legislative councils granted the petition, giving the Innocenti an amount equal to 10 percent of all prisoners' fines. This 10 percent was not included in the fine, but had to be paid by the prisoner in addition to the full amount of his regular fine. The hospital was entitled to the full amount as soon as it had been paid to the communal treasury. Nonpecuniary condemnations yielded three large florins for the death penalty, and one florin for anyone sentenced to loss of limb. The Innocenti, to assert its claim to this money, had to do no more than brandish a copy of the legislation before the communal treasurer.[84]

In addition to this novel approach to criminal justice, the legislation imposed another gabelle, this time four denarii per pound on "silk, silk-worm threads, doublets, crimsons, indigos, or reds." The gatekeepers were responsible for collecting this amount at the same time they collected other tolls, customs, and taxes. Once a month, the gatekeepers had to "pay the said hospital without complaint, delay, paperwork, or any other formality." Although 53 of 190 votes opposed the legislation, it was renewed in 1463, 1465, 1470, 1475, and 1483. In 1479 the hospital of Santa Maria Nuova benefited from similar legislation, which was passed in 1482, 1486, and 1493.[85]

Yet with the 1456 legislation, the hospital became increasingly dependent on these communally sponsored sources of revenue, which accounted for nearly two-thirds of the hospital's income in 1459. In the case of large money fines, revenues to the hospital could be substantial. In May 1457, a Jewish moneylender from Pisa, Isaac Emmanuel, was sentenced to pay a 7,800 florin fine, of which 780 florins would therefore have gone to the Innocenti. Isaac's first installment was 200 large florins, which at the then-current rate of exchange, yielded the Innocenti 1,080 lire. On 17 April 1458 Isaac paid another 75 large florins, and then another 75 florins on 15 August 1457.[86]

Despite the guild's close involvement in the hospital's administration and the increase in revenues from the guild's own funds, in 1460 the consuls appeared again before the *Signoria,* "because the hospital is in greatest need, and has been for some time, on account of the great number of children who have been abandoned there it will incur great expense for that reason."[87] The provision passed, but one condition of its enactment was the repeal of the 1448 legislation imposing gabelles on merchandise passing through the gates.[88]

In 1462, the guild's other major responsibility, the hospital of San Gallo, merged with the Innocenti. Before the merger, however, the commune stepped in to guarantee the survival of the hospital after the death of its chief patron, Niccolò Guidalorchi, and of his son Bartolomeo. Although the hospital had a prior, Fra Michele di Nanni, it had no effective patronage, even though the Arte della Seta was nominally in charge of it. This is a remarkable example of the direct intervention of municipal government in the practice of charity:

Considering the great importance of the hospital of San Gallo, in order to provide for that establishment so that it does not fall into receivership or into the hands of someone unsuitable to govern it, the Lord Priors of Liberty and the Gonfalonier of Justice of the Florentine people and their legislative Councils, shall be understood to be the true and legitimate protectors and patrons of the said hospital [in the event of the death of Fra Michele di Nanni].[89]

In the event of Fra Michele's death, the *Signoria* was to elect, by a majority of at least thirty-two votes, a new superintendent "who shall be of good character and who cannot be less than forty years of age. The said prior shall wear the insignia of the hospital."[90] The Archbishop of Florence had to confirm his election.

The legislative councils also had a mandate to protect San Gallo from taxation, and to monitor all real-estate transactions, which could not take place without a two-thirds majority vote of the councils. The *Signoria* held complete authority to take care of financial matters at the hospital, so long as money was put to the best use for the hospital's enterprises. In addition, the arms of the commune of Florence were to be placed "in the greater church, the hospital, and on all its possessions and properties."[91] The officials of the hospital were not to remove the coat of arms of the Guidalorchi, however, and Fra Michele di Nanni continued to be the prior, though with no extra compensation.[92] In addition to acquiring the hospital of San Gallo, the hospital of the Innocenti could look forward once again in the early 1460s to receiving payments from its *Monte* credits. The hospital was able to place a hold on its *Monte* credits in 1464, for example, so that it could return a real-estate buyer's deposit by cashing in some of the credits. A *provvisione* of 1463, no longer extant but known by a reference in a later *provvisione*,[93] provided for the commune to repurchase any *Monte* credits offered by a charitable institution at 25 percent of their face value. The institution that realized funds from this sale, however, had to use these funds in its building programs and not on its daily expenditures. In April 1466, the consuls, citing "the intolerable expenses the hospital has to bear,"[94] pleaded that it was impossible to use the money from the sale of its credits for construction. Instead, they asked that the commune grant a waiver so that the Innocenti could use the proceeds to pay its debts. The hospital had an in-house census of 201 males and females, and if the legislation did not pass, they "would begin to lack those things necessary to human life. Nor would they be able to pay the wages of wet nurses holding the infants of the said hospital,"[95] an additional 456 mouths to feed for which the hospital was directly responsible. The situation was reaching the point that "we are beginning not to find enough wet nurses because of the low wage we are paying."[96]

Moreover, argued the consuls, the hospital was so deeply in debt that without an additional subsidy:

> it would be forced to close, which could not happen without great shame, not only to the guild of Por Santa Maria, under whose protection it exists, but also to the entire city . . . an enterprise of such piety should on no account be abandoned.[97]

Even as early as 1465, when the hospital had argued for another extension of the 1456 legislation, the guild officials complained that "[despite the previous extension of this legislation] the hospital is in worse shape than at any of the aforesaid times, and needs more alms because now it has a greater number of children than ever before." The petition presented in 1466 was granted. This gave the hospital four thousand florins to be used in paying its debts.[98]

In addition to extending the reach of its collection activities, the hospital also leased a tavern near the Porta alla Croce called the Albergo Bonsi in the hope of increasing its revenues from the boarders. Between various gabelles and property taxes, however, the hospital was paying the commune five hundred lire per year, more than it could possibly take in through rents from these poor tenants, "so that the hospital derives considerable damage from this arrangement, and the commune is really no better off, because the manager of the inn cannot pay the entire amount."[99] In addition, the guild's officials argued, the hospital now had more than seven hundred mouths, of which four hundred were at wet nurse. Fifty girls were awaiting dowries so they could be married.[100]

The commune's response to this petition conceded the site of the inn to the Innocenti for ten years, during which the hospital would pay an annual fee of three hundred lire in lieu of taxes, whether taxes increased or diminished. The hospital, in turn, could lease the inn to whomever it pleased, but preferably to the highest bidder. The legislation set up a procedure by which the guild could award the contract to the highest bidder, although the ultimate decision concerning who would hold the lease belonged to a unanimous decision of Consuls and *operai*.[101]

Two years later, another piece of communal legislation made it clear that one of the chief obstacles to the Innocenti's solvency was the commune's lax enforcement of its own revenue-producing legislation. The consuls noted in their complaint that:

> many fines are assessed that do not bring money into the treasury. Many condemnations parade under the appellation of declarations so that the said hospital is [constantly] being defrauded and derives little income [from the previous legislation] for the said reason.[102]

The solution was to declare that no matter what they were called, prisoners' fines and:

> privileges, benefits, and emoluments of the said fines granted to the said hospital must, for their effective terms, be observed and enforced by everyone without exception or excuse.[103]

Despite the legislation of 1472, which disposed of the ambiguities in wording that had defrauded the Innocenti, when the guild applied for another extension of the amended law in 1476,[104] guild officials complained that revenues were still not coming in as expected from prisoners' fines. Rather, "the treasurers whose job it is to collect such funds are not faithful either in demanding them or in paying them back to the Innocenti." The guild asked that "such inconvenience proceed no further."[105] The hospital, said the consuls, was in more dire straits than ever, due to not receiving this source of income: "Daily the number of infants grows, and so we have recourse to the clemency of Your Lordships."[106] The legislation established an auditing procedure, according to which the gatekeepers had to be given the account books to review, with a breakdown of how much of the gabelles and fines should go to the *Monte,* how much to the *Camera del Comune,* and how much to the Innocenti. The penalty of twenty-five lire for an official pocketing the fines, however, could hardly have been a serious deterrent to such misanthropes, even if they were brought to account before the guild consuls and the *Conservatores Legum.*[107]

The failure of these penalties was apparent enough eleven years later, in September 1483, when the guild wrote a letter to a communal official:

Your Excellency,

The reason we are writing to you is that we have good evidence that many of your treasurers have in their hands money that belongs to the Hospital of the Innocenti in an amount that concerns the two denarii per lire that has come into their hands from prisoners' fines. The treasurers are these: [The document lists five of them]. We pray you to act in such a way that these [treasurers] will be forced to do their duty to these poor children.

The guild officials received no response to this letter, so they wrote again in January 1484, and once again "he did not reply."[108]

The failure of this once-important source of revenue drove the Innocenti to new expedients. In 1480, the guild consuls petitioned the commune to subsidize the Innocenti with fifty free *staia* of salt each year over the next five years. The petition is as pithy an expression as one finds in official language of the multiple causes of the Innocenti's chronic fiscal crisis:

[This subsidy is sought] because of the multitude of boys and girls who are abandoned there. So great is that number that neither income nor donations suffice to feed and clothe them. Because of war, however, the populace is financially exhausted by endless taxes, so the citizens are not contributing their usual aid to the extent necessary, for which reason the guild is compelled to turn to Your Lordships so that these miserable and abject children may be assisted from public funds.[109]

Hidden in this legislation is an extraordinary sense of desperation not only for the fate of the hospital's children, but also for a sign of some display of cooperation from customs officials. The petition noted that "an accurate count cannot be taken" of money due to the Innocenti "without someone to keep an account of such transactions."[110] No one was willing to keep track of them without extra pay, the very thing that the statutes forbade customs officials to take. The Innocenti therefore asked that this prohibition be waived, so that it could offer the extra payment itself to ensure that the proper amount of money was collected. The petition was granted, so that the Innocenti could offer this extra payment without its being construed as a bribe.[111]

This is an extraordinary departure from legislation at mid-century that demanded full accounting of the hospital's income. Its most astonishing implication is that the Innocenti could not otherwise rely on government officials to be custodians of the institution's fiscal health, or even to refrain from lining their own pockets with the revenues due to the Innocenti.

The causes of this change, if indeed it was a change, are not altogether clear. Perhaps the increasingly desperate search for funds motivated the guild to examine more closely the activities of communal officials. The results, however, were presented starkly in a guild report to the advisory and legislative councils of the government. The report described the hospital in 1483 as "in great debt, even though the Arte della Seta attends to it with great diligence, subventing according to what it can afford without holding anything back."[112] The report also noted that expenditures exceeded revenues by more than three thousand lire annually. Moreover, the hospital had to diminish its patrimony in order to satisfy some of its debts and to buy grain, already in short supply. The choices were simple, according to the guild's report: either provide true public subsidies and finance the hospital publicly, or close it.

The latter alternative was abhorrent, "a matter of grave dishonor, causing many ills." The hospital operated as a haven for infants abandoned at birth, who:

> otherwise would be found dead in rivers, sewers, and ditches. How cruel it would be if in such a famous city and in such a worthy place on which so much money has been spent and to which the public has given its financial support—how cruel that these children should then starve to death, as has already happened. This tragedy cannot, I say, be tolerated by men of such a mild and pious nature as the Florentine people. They could neither tell of such a thing without horror nor hear of it without tears. Yet it is so, and nothing else can be done, because the hospital has contracted so many debts with its wet nurses. When the hospital cannot pay them, they bring the children back and there are too few nurses [in the hospital] to feed them.[113]

At the very least, the consuls hoped for a renewal of previous benefits, as well as for new privileges if they could be granted without great public harm. Again the petitioners trusted "in the compassion of this people and its religion," though not so unconditionally that the consuls could resist a brief homily on the subject of charity:

without which no virtue can bring us to the highest good, because he who is without charity is estranged from God, according to what is found in Holy Scripture. And charity bears all the more fruit the more difficulty and suffering is experienced by he who practices it.[114]

The legislation that resulted from this lament attempted to address the hospital's need in several ways. First, although the hospital was exempt from taxes on estates that passed to it, it was liable for any back taxes that had not been paid. Thus in 1475, hospital officials arranged with the Ufficiali delle Grazie to pay fifty-four florins over a period of five years "for the remaining taxes owed to the commune by Mona Caterina di Santi di Giovanni." The Innocenti had to pay installments twice a year. Nevertheless, the Innocenti continued to accept estates that seemed to have manageable debts, such as the estate of Bartolomeo di Niccolò Guidalorchi, a former patron of San Gallo who died owing seventy-three florins to the commune, and Mona Nanna, widow of Marco di Cintoia, who owed fifty-six florins. By 1484 the burden of these estate taxes was sufficiently heavy that the commune reduced them, and cancelled the hospital's other debts to the communal treasury.[115]

Despite this legislation, ordinances spanning the following twenty years make clear that the Innocenti still had trouble collecting its due from the commune. In October 1495, the government's advisory councils blamed a failure of communication for the Innocenti's failure to receive revenues from condemnations. Communal treasurers, "sometimes because they were unaware of such laws, . . . did not observe them and did not recover the amount owed."[116] The legislation proposed nothing new beyond requiring the officials of each city and town in the *contado* to ensure that the Innocenti received what it was owed.

There can be no doubt that both guild and communal authorities knew of abuses in the transmission of revenues to the Innocenti. For those miscreants who had no inclination to support the Innocenti, however, the legislation was unenforceable. Moreover, those financial expedients in which guild consuls in the mid-fifteenth century had deposited so much hope were clearly exhausted as adequate sources of income. Landucci quoted a provision of 1504 that described the hospitals of the Innocenti and Santa Maria Nuova as "two firm and solid columns supporting the republic and its liberty."[117] Not even patriotism, however, could beget imagination in such extreme circumstances. Even had the hospital been accessible to creative financing, any new source of income would still have had to accommodate the explosion of the hospital's population from 90 in 1446 to 2,150 in 1520. The deceit and greed of the hospital's putative supporters and even patrons was intractable to the most sophisticated and complex accounting systems known to fifteenth-century Florentines. Yet had the guild and commune been able to track down every debtor, every communal official, every guildsman who failed to pay his required share, the hospital would still have the formidable obstacle of depending for its revenue on a government resting on the slippery bedrock of funded debt and military adventure. This inability to maintain coherent social policy precluded the realistic fulfillment of those worthy and grandiose charitable ambitions that would redeem the city in God's sight through the prayers of its children.

The fiscal insolvency of the Innocenti was a product not only of the commune's priorities, but also of the ill-defined relationship between Church and commune, the effects of which shall now be examined. At the heart of this instability was the vexing question of the taxation of clerical property. Leading citizens argued on behalf of the commune that ecclesiastical property was protected by the investment of legitimate taxpayers in the common defense. The opponents of clerical taxation invoked the decrees of the Third and Fourth Lateran Councils in declaring ecclesiastical property exempt from taxation. This exemption was not absolute, however. In times of emergency, laymen could tax the clergy with the bishop's consent. The Fourth Lateran Council narrowed this to require papal consent.[118]

If Florence could not press her claims to clerical taxation as automatically as other states, her need for revenue to support common defense and military adventurism led, in the fifteenth century, to constant pressure on the papacy to grant taxes on the clergy. It has been observed that fully half the Florentine ambassadors to the papal court were lawyers whose chief responsibility it was to press such claims. In the first half of the fifteenth century, the issue did not dominate discussions between ambassadors and the papal court, nor in instructions to ambassadors. Taxation of the clergy surfaced as a major issue in the 1450s, as relations between the commune and the papacy deteriorated over the Monte's decision to suspend interest payments to foreign creditors and *non-sopportanti*. In 1455 a group of Romans, the papal family of the Orsini among them, sued the *Monte* officials for these payments and simultaneously organized papal reprisals, including excommunication.

This pressure effectively turned the discussions in the *Consulte e Pratiche* back to the issue of foreign creditors.[119] For the hospital, the importance of this tangled relationship between commune and Church sprang not only from the hospital's status as a *locus ecclesiasticus* but arose also because the Innocenti's governors cautiously sought clerical guidance and intervention in the hospital's affairs. The legislation of 1430 discussed earlier in this chapter conferred both the advantages and liabilities of a *locus ecclesiasticus*. It did not, unlike the legislation that founded the hospital, rule out taxation by the Church. In those emergency situations in which the commune taxed the clergy or suspended *Monte* payments, the Innocenti had no a priori protection save the global injunctions won by the silk guild in the founding legislation. This was dramatically illustrated during the Innocenti's fiscal crisis of the early 1450s, caused by suspension of interest payments not only to specially exempt and foreign individuals, but also to exempt institutions.

No complete record survives of arguments and counterarguments that moved the Innocenti in the direction of seeking ecclesiastical status when its founders so explicitly eschewed outside interference, especially of the ecclesiastical variety. Certainly the precedents set by hospitals such as Bonifazio Lupi and Santa Maria Nuova were compelling. Of no small importance must have been the need to have some basis for protecting the hospital's legacies from communal taxation. These legacies were the hospital's most important source of income in its early years. Unluckily, the rationalization of the commune's fiscal machinery via the Catasto coincided with the enthusiastic testation and donation of revenue-producing real estate at an accelerated pace.[120] If the commune, not to mention recent historians,[121] suspected that testators hoped to profit from charity by making fictitious donations and arranging with the superintendent to have the donation returned, there is little evidence of their success, and there is substantial evidence that money earmarked for the building program actually financed construction.

Once the communal legislation granting the status of *locus ecclesiasticus* had passed, the guild retroactively sought the advice of the Archbishop of Florence concerning what were the requirements of the Church. The Archbishop specified that a chapel must be built for saying daily masses, with a priest appointed full time as its guardian.[122] I have already discussed the detailed advice given by Pope Eugenius IV concerning the qualifications and election of the superintendent. In the same year, 1439, he exempted the Innocenti not only from all civic tax burdens, but also from any ecclesiastical taxes that might in future be imposed, as well as any interdict, forced loan, or ecclesiastical penalty.

In return, the hospital had to celebrate masses and other divine offices in the chapel, and the guild consuls were to appoint "suitable individuals" as priests who could minister to both men and women, and who would hear confessions, pronounce absolution, and mete out penance. This priest also had to administer the appropriate sacraments, including last rites, to foundlings. Despite the absence of a church building, the hospital should, according to the pope, pay the priest a stipend for performing funeral rites and for burying the dead under the site of the hospital's chapel.[123]

This papal document is notable for several reasons. As can only be expected, it is no precursor of Reformation theology, but rather a reminder of the reciprocities inherent in the act of charitable giving. The piety and compassion of the consuls had its reward in "treasures" and "credits" accumulating in the celestial realm. The ever-precarious balance of debits and credits recalls not only the laypersons' merchant theology of Mazzei and Datini, but also later reminders to the Florentine councils that charity would hasten and encourage the prayers of deceased infants. Thus an apostolic letter issued the same day stated:

> desiring that the acceptable and good works of citizens should return to Our Lord, we extend to the followers of the faithful . . . the following indulgences and remissions of sins, from which they may be more likely to achieve Divine Grace.[124]

This letter noted that the members of the silk guild had undertaken works of charity "mindful of their own salvation, desiring to turn earthly happiness into celestial, and the transitory into the eternal." The indulgences were offered in the hope of making the hospital's chapels centers of devotion, and more importantly, in the hope of stimulating charitable giving to the Innocenti. Those who visited the chapel at least once a year on the feast of the Annunciation would be released from seven years and forty days of penance.[125] The choice of the feast of the Annunciation repeated the motif of civic salvation through charitable giving: Savonarola, for example, would tell Florentines at the end of the century that if they prayed to the Virgin within the Octave of the Annunciation, she would personally intervene to spare the city from God's wrath. The feast of the Annunciation was also associated with *sacre rappresentazioni* that displayed a high order of emotional tenderness and compassion on the part of the Virgin Mary toward the Infant Jesus: "taking Him and adoring Him with the highest devotion and humility, she wept over Him."[126]

Balanced against the power of the reciprocal, the religious, and the symbolic was a sense of the tentativeness of papal authority in the face of lay charitable initiative. Despite the hospital's status as a *locus ecclesiasticus,* it was exempt from papal or ecclesiastical taxation, no interdict or ecclesiastical trial could affect it, and the consuls appointed both the governors and the priests of the Innocenti without seeking any prior ecclesiastical approval. These apostolic letters could not have spoken more explicitly if they had said that ecclesiastical status exchanged tax liability for the price of divine offices and the full-time employment of a cleric. It is no doubt on this firm ground that the guild asked the pope to suggest the most useful procedures for electing the hospital's superintendent.[127]

Such protection from apostolic interference was a guarantee that five other Florentine hospitals in 1445 might well have envied. A letter of instruction written to the Florentine ambassador at the papal court concerned the Pope's plans to inventory the goods of Santa Maria Nuova, the hospital of Lemmo Balducci, the hospital of Messer Bonifazio, the hospital of San Gallo, and the hospital of the *pinzocheri* of San Paolo, for purposes of assessment and taxation. "You know," city officials wrote:

> how necessary and pious [these] places are, and how they are supported and maintained by the patrimonial goods and alms of our citizens. [This plan to tax the hospitals] would result in tremendous inconvenience and scandal to our entire city.[128]

Even more importantly, the plan would damage the fortunes of charitable institutions, all of which had "many more expenses than revenues" and all of which regardless of financial situation had to support "so many needy persons and children with their wet nurses." Their other burdens were too numerous to mention: suffice it to say that "if they were oppressed by a new tax they could not go on without being completely ruined."[129] Citizens would halt alms and pious testaments if they perceived that their gifts might be used to pay taxes and not to succour the poor. Great scandal among donors and those whose ancestors had left their estates to the hospital would arise if they saw those gifts being converted to other uses than the subvention of the poor.

> We therefore wish and command you to go before the Pontiff, and with these reasons and any others that occur to you, to beg His Grace to provide by one of his briefs that the said hospitals not be forced to inventory their goods, nor to pay any tax or impost.[130]

This letter was followed by another the following month saying that:

> the letter of the Cardinal's treasurer in support of the five hospitals has borne little fruit. Messer Paolo [the papal legate in Florence] says he wishes to obey the wishes of the Holy Father. Insofar [as this is true] it benefits you to have either from the Pope or from the Treasurer some brief that would have the effect we desire.[131]

If the commune thus had to act to protect hospitals from papal taxation, clerics also had to intervene to protect ecclesiastical and charitable property from communal taxation. At the end of 1451, as we have already noted, the commune was attempting to address its grave fiscal problems by repudiating its obligations to certain types of creditors. In December 1451 the Signoria and councils decreed that anyone who sold, donated, or alienated property to any person or institution "that does not ordinarily or normally support the burdens of the said city or its contado that its citizens do" had to pay as a gabelle 25 percent of the value of the estate as assessed in the Catasto of 1427. Any unpaid gabelle would invalidate the contract without affecting the commune's right to the gabelle. The legislation specifically exempted goods left in bequests, institutions which had already been granted concessions, and guilds.[132]

The Archbishop of Florence, Sant'Antonino, found these exceptions insufficiently broad, and wrote to the *Signoria* and Councils that:

> the legislation enacted last September [*sic*], which assesses a gabelle of twenty-five percent on sales of property passing from taxpayers to nontaxpayers, is contrary to your salvation and the salvation of those who enacted it, those who support and enforce it, and those who do not work for its repeal.[133]

Antoninus reminded the Lords and Councillors that their oaths of office forbade them to "do anything or enforce anything that might be contrary to the obedience of the church, as true Catholic Christians ... under penalty of excommunication." Antoninus specifically included legislation "against the liberty ... of ecclesiastical persons and charitable institutions." Antoninus proposed as a remedy to this indiscretion that the legislation should declare the definition of *non-sopportanti* to exclude "ecclesiastical persons, churches, and pious places." The Archbishop warned, "as many sessions as are necessary should be held immediately, for anyone who does not work for its repeal or amendment will be excommunicated immediately." The Archbishop's warning was apparently taken to heart, since the legislation was amended to provide for the required exclusions.[134]

A papal bull of 25 June 1454, issued by Nicholas V, addressed a related problem raised by bequests and donations to charitable institutions. As early as 1430, the fate of goods donated by a *commesso* as part of his contract of employment had been a subject of deliberation by the Catasto officials. In the 1430s the Catasto officials had ruled in the Innocenti's favor. In the 1450s, when the influx of children required the presence of wet nurses and permanent staff on the premises, more laymen were likely to seek a *commessione* by which they donated their goods to the hospital in return for employment for life and the usufruct of these goods before their deaths. In the case of monasteries with similar arrangements, the institution could immediately absorb the donation. The Innocenti, however, allowed its *commessi* to live outside the hospital and to continue to use the goods they had donated, a rather more complex legal and fiscal problem. Hence, when Lapo and Dianora Pacini donated their worldly goods to the hospital in 1445, they were required to pay all their back tax obligations as a condition of accepting their *commessione*.[135]

In the early 1450s, the Innocenti's superintendent complained that such requirements afforded the hospital little protection from the commune's forced loans and other forms of taxation. The papal bull pointed out in its preamble that the hospital already met all the criteria of a *locus ecclesiasticus*, even to the point of requiring that its superintendent had to be a cleric:

The care, rule, and administration of the said hospital is not secular but wholly ecclesiastical, designated as such by the aforesaid [communal] authorities, just as is contained in the apostolic letter of my predecessor.[136]

In addition to reissuing this declaration Nicholas also conferred any exemption now extended to ecclesiastical persons or property on *commessi*, even if they were leading citizens of and prolific lenders to the commune. No statute could require these citizens to pay taxes or imposts even if they had failed to seek special exemption, because, Nicholas wrote, hospitals and their charitable work must be able to continue without constant harassment from the commune.[137]

How committed communal government was to charitable enterprise and how successful that commitment was must remain two separate questions. What began in the early fifteenth century, especially around 1420, as an apparently coherent social policy, became increasingly fragmented and even contradictory under pressure of war and military expenditure and, perhaps even more importantly, under the pressure of the unprecedented and unexpected success of the Innocenti's care. Municipal intervention continued to seek collective salvation through charity and compassion to children while increasing the fame of the earthly city through the magnificence and splendor of its charitable works. Yet the practical limitations of this vision were all too clear even before the Innocenti opened its doors in 1445.

In the 1420s, the Innocenti was the beneficiary of numerous and generous private donations. Of the city's economy as a whole in those early years, Giovanni Rucellai would write, "from 1413 to 1423, the commune had few military expenses, and only a few taxes were imposed, so that the land became very wealthy, and had an abundance of money in it." According to Rucellai, the culmination of that prosperity occurred in the years that the Innocenti's foundations were laid: 1418 to 1423, in which time:

> in the New Market and the surrounding streets there were seventy-two banks and money exchanges. I am of the opinion that in cash and merchandise alone the citizens of Florence were worth 2,000,000 florins.[138]

The silk guild's prosperity, and by extension the Innocenti's, also benefited from the introduction of the manufacturing technique of *battiloro*, or weaving metal threads into silk brocades. From 1430 to 1447, annual production of silk jumped from 498 to 2,002 pieces.[139] In the early 1420s leading citizens and guild officials certainly had every right to expect these conditions to combine in favor of virtually unlimited growth and resources. The building program of the Innocenti itself, and the huge sums lavished on it, testify eloquently to the power of this belief. Both the building's magnificence and the broad control granted to the guild in governing the hospital demonstrate the culmination of new directions in philanthropy that had been under way for well over half a century. Despite temporary setbacks to the building program because of lack of funds, even as late as the 1460s contemporary opinion held that the success of the institution in attracting both donations and foundlings was due to the Innocenti's excellent administration.

Even in times of fiscal hardship for the commune, legislators and guildsmen alike sought innovative remedial measures, among which the most frequent were special gabelles collected at the city gates and exemptions from taxes. Legislation requiring prisoners to pay the Innocenti a 10 percent surcharge on their original fines surely represented an attempt to settle the moral imbalance created by the commission of a crime. The consuls of the Arte Por Santa Maria were as aware as any of their contemporaries of the variability of communal fiscal fortunes, and they sought remedies that made the Innocenti less dependent on direct communal subsidy and more dependent on income generated by the silk guild's own expanding commercial market. The commune itself continually sought innovation in charitable practice, even encouraging tradesmen to come to Florence from Bologna not only to revive a lost art but also to do something that would be "to the profit of the poor, who seek with their works and hands a livelihood for themselves."[140]

Finally, the commitment of municipal government to children and to charity is nowhere more clearly manifested than in allowing the children of the Innocenti to receive the benefits of the communal dowry fund. The participation of the hospital's girls in the fund reflected an explicit interest in increasing the city's population. In that respect, the dowry fund placed the Innocenti at the very center of the city's social policy, and placed the preservation of these children's lives as the very cornerstone of the city's survival. The connection that legislative documents made between charity to children and the salvation of the city of Florence was hardly rhetorical posturing.

To affix all the blame for Florence's charitable vacillation on the exorbitant demands of mercenaries misses the point that a commune still defined itself as an association of citizens who on demand pooled their collective resources to provide for common defense. In this respect, no matter how noble or grand the commune's charitable work, that work could not be sustained unless the commune maintained its primary loyalty to itself, i.e., its lenders.

The dependence of the Innocenti on the interest from shares in the common defense, as it were, most of which had been left to it in the relatively prosperous years of the 1420s, proved fatal to the ambitious dream that its very architecture represented.[141] As late as 1446, the guild consuls won a legislative initiative to receive this interest as though the Innocenti had itself loaned money to the commune. Nevertheless, the hospital shared the fate of other noncontributors, and the guild had to petition even to receive dowries in which the hospital's donors had made an investment. At the same time, the hospital was a victim of its own success. Its burgeoning population forced it to operate on a scale that no one could have foreseen and for which guild and gabelle revenues were insufficient.

Although the hospital would survive, and even prosper at times during the sixteenth century, the relationship between commune and hospital underwent considerable alteration. Even as early as 1475, the consuls of the silk guild were writing to Lorenzo de' Medici, petitioning him in the most diplomatic way possible to end the delay in providing for guild elections. These elections must be held, wrote the consuls, "seeing how much it concerns the welfare of our guild and of our hospital, which have many and various serious issues."[142] The guild's appeal to Lorenzo to guard the welfare of the hospital of the Innocenti presaged the close relationship that the grand dukes would have with the hospital's administrators. At the same time, the appeal serves as a convenient marker for the transition from a well-regulated hospital on a small but expanding scale, to an institution whose administrative details and fortunes slipped increasingly out of the control of its governors.

NOTES

1. Archivio di Stato di Firenze (ASF), Provvisioni Registri 87, fols. 295r–296r, 23 October 1398 (for Bonifazio Lupi's hospital of San Giovanni).

2. ASF, Provvisioni Registri, 115, fols. 143v–144v, 30 August 1425 (hospital of Santa Maria Nuova).

3. ASF, Provvisioni Registri 121, fols. 78v–79v, 29 October 1430.

4. ASF, Consulte e Pratiche 51, fols. 86v–87r.

5. ASF, Catasto, 1, fol. 39r, cited in Lauro Martines, *Lawyers and Statecraft in Renaissance Florence* (Princeton, 1968), 173–74.

6. ASF, Provvisioni Registri, 125, fol. 8r, 9 April 1434.

7. ASF, Provvisioni Registri, 142, fol. 216v, 9 December 1451 for the 1451 legislation proposing a 25 percent gabelle on transfers of property from *sopportanti* to *non-sopportanti*. See Martines, *Lawyers and Statecraft,* 177.

8. ASF, Diplomatico, Spedale degli Innocenti, 28 July 1441.

9. ASF, Diplomatico, Spedale degli Innocenti, 22 June 1454.

10. ASF, Provvisioni Registri, 111, fols. 158vff., 10 October 1421.

11. Ibid.

12. Ibid.

13. Ibid.

14. Ibid.

15. Lapo Mazzei, *Lettere di un notaio a uno mercante,* ed. C. Guasti, 2 vols. (Florence, 1880). See Iris Origo, *The Merchant of Prato,* rev. ed. (New York, 1979), 366. As Mazzei's letter (1:211–12) suggests, the Bishop of Pistoia was as likely as not to spend Datini's inheritance "on banquets and horses." The Bishop and Commune of Pistoia engaged in a vitriolic dispute over the mismanagement of two Pistoiese hospitals, the Dolce and the Misericordia.

16. Luigi Passerini, *La storia degli stabilmenti di beneficenza e d'istruzione elementare gratuita della città di Firenze* (Florence, 1853), 844.

17. ASF, Catasto, 844, fol. 6r, *anno* 1427.

18. ASF, Catasto, 293, fol. 16r, *anno* 1429.

19. ASF, Catasto, 293, fol. 16r-17r, *anno* 1433. Bartolomeo's donation appears on fol. 35r. Volume 293 of the Catasto lists property transferred to pious places between 1427 and 1430.

20. ASF, Provvisioni Registri, 121, fols. 78v–79v, 29 October 1430.

21. Ibid.

22. ASF, Provvisioni Registri, 87, fols. 295r–296r, 23 October 1398.

23. Ibid.

24. ASF, Provvisioni Registri 121, fols. 78v–79v, 29 October 1430.

25. Archivio dell'Ospedale degli Innocenti (AOIF), Testamenta et Donationes (IX,1), fol. 71v, 18 January 1430 [modern = 1431].

26. Ibid.

27. ASF, Catasto, 421, fol. 105r, *anno* 1431.

28. Anthony Molho, *Florentine Public Finance in the Early Renaissance* (Cambridge, 1971), 11.

29. Ibid., 13.

30. Ibid., 20.

31. Ibid., 26.

32. Ibid., 27–28.

33. Ibid., 36.

34. Ibid., 42.

35. Ibid., 44.

36. Ibid., 54.

37. Ibid., 157–62.

38. Ibid., 44. For net capital worth of Palla Strozzi and Giovanni di Bicci de' Medici, see Lauro Martines, *The Social World of the Florentine Humanists* (Princeton, 1963), 372.

39. Ibid., 102–4.

40. Ibid., 109, n. 72.

41. ASF, Consulte e Pratiche, 51, fol. 180v, 3 August 1431, cited in Molho, *Public Finance*, 57, n. 75.

42. Lauro Martines, *Lawyers and Statecraft*, 173–74. Cf. Richard Trexler's discussion, "Charity and the Defense of Urban Elites in the Italian Communes," in *The Rich, the Well-born, and the Powerful*, ed. F. Jaher (Urbana, 1973), 64–109.

43. Martines, *Lawyers and Statecraft*, 178.

44. ASF, Signori e Collegi: Deliberazioni Fatte in Forza Ordinaria, 47, fol. 40r, 28 September 1435.

45. ASF, Diplomatico, Spedale degli Innocenti, 28 July 1441.

46. Ibid.

47. Ibid.

48. ASF, Diplomatico, Spedale degli Innocenti, 3 March 1445 [modern = 1446].

49. AOIF, Testamenta et Donationes, (IX,1), fol. 125v, 27 January 1444 [modern = 1445].

50. Martines, *Lawyers and Statecraft*, 175.

51. Ibid.

52. Marvin Becker, *Florence in Transition* (Baltimore, 1968), 2:151–200.

53. Molho, *Public Finance*, 79–87. Molho argues that the purpose of the Catasto was, first, to place the burden of responsibility on individual householders rather than on the *gonfalone* as a whole, the latter having been the basis for previous assessments. Second, the Catasto took into account liquid assets, not just real estate and tangible wealth. Finally, the Catasto was meant to ensure a more equitable distribution of forced loans. Only in the *contado* was it meant as a direct tax. Molho's contention that, "all the Catasti assessed on the urban inhabitants after 1427 . . . were meant to be loans of the citizens to the state" is fully corroborated by the documents of the Ospedale degli Innocenti.

54. Julius Kirshner, "Pursuing Honor While Avoiding Sin: The *Monte delle Doti* of Florence," *Studi Senesi* 89 (1977): 177–258, also published separately in *Quaderni di Studi Senesi* (Milan, 1978), no. 41. Cf. Kirshner and Molho,

"The Dowry Fund and the Marriage Market in Early *Quattrocento* Florence," *Journal of Modern History* 50, no. 3 (1978): 403–38. Also, Alan Morrison, Julius Kirshner, and Anthony Molho, "Life Cycle Events in Fifteenth-Century Florence: Records of the *Monte delle Doti*," *American Journal of Epidemiology* 106, no. 6 (1977): 487–92.

55. ASF, Diplomatico, Riformagioni, 16 February 1445 [modern = 1446].
56. Ibid.
57. ASF, Provvisioni Registri, 139, fol. 46v, 29 April 1448.
58. Ibid.
59. Ibid., fol. 47r.
60. ASF, Consulte e Pratiche, 52, fol. 74r, 16 March 1448 [modern = 1449].
61. ASF, Consulte e Pratiche, 52, fol. 101r, 13 March 1449 [modern = 1450].
62. ASF, Arte della Seta, 246, fol. 101v, 1 May 1451.
63. ASF, Arte della Seta 246, fol. 101r, 10 April 1451.
64. ASF, Provvisioni Registri, 142, fols. 380v–382r, 30 December 1451.
65. ASF, Provvisioni Registri, 81, 12 December 1388; ASF, Provvisioni Registri, 106, 31 December 1415.
66. ASF, Provvisioni Registri, 142, fols. 381v–382r, 30 December 1451.
67. Ibid., fol. 382r.
68. Kirshner, "Pursuing Honor," 27.
69. Giovanni di Pagolo Morelli, *Ricordi*, ed. V. Branca (Florence, 1956), 209, cited in Kirshner, "Pursuing Honor," 7.
70. Kirshner, "Pursuing Honor," 15.
71. ASF, Signori e Collegi: Deliberazioni Fatte in Forza Ordinaria, 47, fol. 91v, 30 October 1435.
72. Kirshner, "Pursuing Honor," 15.
73. Brian Pullan, *Rich and Poor in Renaissance Venice* (Cambridge, 1971), 163.
74. Kirshner and Molho, "Dowry Fund and Marriage Market," 403–9.
75. Ibid.
76. Ibid., 425.
77. ASF, Provvisioni Registri, 142, fols. 468r-469v, 25 February 1451.
78. ASF, Consulte e Pratiche, 54, fol. 53vff., 17 November 1456.
79. Ibid.
80. Sant'Antonino, *Chronica* (Lyons, 1586), pars iii, 557, quoted in Nicolai Rubinstein, *The Government of Florence under the Medici* (Oxford, 1966), 88.
81. ASF, Consulte e Pratiche, 54, fol. 64v, 17 November 1456.
82. ASF, Provvisioni Registri, 147, fol. 169v, 29 December 1456.
83. Ibid.
84. Ibid.

85. Ibid.
86. AOIF, Entrata e Uscita, (CXXII,7), fol. 7r, 15 August 1457.
87. ASF, Provvisioni Registri, 151, fols. 182r–183v, 19 August 1460.
88. Ibid.
89. ASF, Provvisioni Registri, 153, fols. 163v–164v, 27 October 1462.
90. Ibid.
91. Ibid.
92. Ibid.
93. ASF, Provvisioni Registri, 157, fols. 21v–22v, 16 April 1466. This *provvisione* refers to an earlier one enacted 30 January 1462 [modern = 1463].
94. ASF, Provvisioni Registri, 157, fols. 21v–22v, 16 April 1466.
95. Ibid.
96. Ibid.
97. Ibid.
98. ASF, Provvisioni Registri, 156, fols. 13r–14r, 18 April 1465.
99. ASF, Provvisioni Registri, 159, fols. 255v–256r, 21 February 1468 [modern = 1469]. See also Ricordanze A, (XII,1), fol. 135v, 25 February 1468 [modern = 1469].
100. ASF, Provvisioni Registri, 159, fols. 255v–256r, 21 February 1468 [modern = 1469].
101. Ibid.
102. ASF, Provvisioni Registri, 163, fol. 113r–114r, 10 September 1472. See also AOIF, Ricordanze A, (XII,1), fol. 134v, 12 September 1472.
103. ASF, Provvisioni Registri, 163, fol. 113r–114r, 10 September 1472.
104. ASF, Provvisioni Registri, 166, fol. 238v, 16 February 1475 [modern = 1476].
105. Ibid.
106. Ibid.
107. ASF, Arte della Seta, 2, fols. 284r–284v, 16 February 1474 [modern = 1475].
108. AOIF, Ricordanze B, (XII,2), fol. 47r, 27 September 1483.
109. ASF, Provvisioni Registri, 170, fol. 114v–115v, 16 February 1479 [modern = 1480].
110. Ibid.
111. Ibid.
112. ASF, Provvisioni Registri, 175, fols. 160r–162v, 18 February 1483 [modern = 1484].
113. Ibid.
114. Ibid.
115. Ibid.
116. ASF, Provvisioni Registri, 186, fol. 123v–124r, 15 October 1495.

117. Luca Landucci, *A Florentine Diary from 1450 to 1516*, trans. Alice de Rosen Jervis (London, 1927), 272.

118. Martines, *Lawyers and Statecraft*, 251–52.

119. Ibid.

120. ASF, Catasto, 293, fol. 16r, *anno* 1429.

121. Richard Trexler, "Charity and the Defense of Elites," 77.

122. AOIF, Liber Artis Portae Sanctae Mariae (V,1), fol. 43rff., 7 December 1432.

123. ASF, Diplomatico, Spedale degli Innocenti, 8 April 1439.

124. Ibid.

125. Ibid.

126. Richard Trexler, *Public Life in Renaissance Florence* (New York, 1980), 75, 79, 192–94, 477.

127. ASF, Diplomatico, Spedale degli Innocenti, 28 July 1441.

128. ASF, Signori: Carteggi, Missive, Legazioni, e Commissarie, 11, fol. 48r, 20 February 1444 [modern = 1445].

129. Ibid.

130. Ibid.

131. ASF, Signori: Carteggi, Missive, Legazioni, e Commissarie, 11, fol. 49v, 13 March 1444 [modern = 1445].

132. ASF, Provvisioni Registri, 142, fol. 216v, 9 December 1451.

133. ASF, Signori e Collegi: Deliberazioni Fatte in Forza di Autorita Ordinaria 74, fol. 23v, 5 April 1452. The document contains the date 1451. Antonino, however, refers to the offending legislation as having been proposed and passed in 1451. Since April was only two weeks into the Florentine new year, we may, with reasonable safety, assume a scribe's error and date this document 1452.

134. Ibid.

135. AOIF, Testamenta et Donationes, (IX,1), fol. 125r, 27 January 1444 [modern = 1445].

136. ASF, Diplomatico, Spedale degli Innocenti, 22 June 1454.

137. Ibid.

138. Molho, *Public Finance*, 1, 4–5.

139. Gino Corti and J. G. DaSilva, "Une note sur la production de la soie," *Annales: Economie, Société, Civilisations* 20 (1965): 309–11.

140. Umberto Dorini, ed. *Statuti dell'Arte Por Santa Maria* (Florence, 1934), 686.

141. Frederick Hartt, *History of Renaissance Art: Painting, Sculpture, and Architecture* (Englewood Cliffs, N.J., 1969), 115–19.

142. ASF, Archivio Mediceo Avanti il Principato (XXXIII,14), 16 January 1475 [modern = 1476].

Chapter 3

Wills and Testaments

For most of the wills written by testators who left their estates, or part of their estates, to the Ospedale degli Innocenti, collections of personal correspondence do not exist in the splendidly accessible form of Mazzei's letters to Datini. Tuscan wills of the fifteenth century are no less clear on that account; nevertheless, the inferences to be made from them are perforce more cautious and circumspect.

The observations of Philippe Ariès in *L'homme devant la mort* concerning the tremendous conflict between *temporalia* and *aeterna* have considerable relevance to the wills of the Ospedale degli Innocenti.[1] Ariès sees in the premodern testament the resolution of the conflict between an inordinate attachment to friends and possessions, and the soul's salvation. The notion of *usufructus,* the use and enjoyment of goods from an estate, has for Ariès implications more metaphysical than legal. The will permitted the testator to enjoy his possessions during his lifetime; the price paid for such enjoyment was redistribution of his wealth to pious causes after his death. Tied to this is the notion of earthly goods as goods entrusted to the testator by his Creator, and thus to be conceived of and used for the improvement and salvation of the testator's soul.

Yet *temporalia* and *aeterna* were surely more tangled than separate. Just as Datini's legacy expressed his confidence in the ability of municipal and lay institutions to regulate his estate after his death, so were the estates of other testators inexorably and inextricably tangled in the major fiscal institutions of fifteenth-century Florence. Nor was this involvement with *temporalia* and *aeterna* merely political and fiscal. For many testators to the Innocenti, their bequests continued a commitment of their guild and family to the earthly immortality of their charitable work, and to the alleviation of the social problems that made the Ospedale degli Innocenti such a magnet for endowments. A large number of wills and donations, for example, provided capital to be invested in the communal dowry fund on behalf of the girls of the institution.

This surely has its echo in the humanist notion, expressed by Giovanni da Conversano, that "the greatest felicity is, therefore, to be celebrated and honored in this world, and to enjoy eternal beatitude in the next."[2] Similarly Porretane prompts a Dominican monk, in a supposed sermon to a lay audience, to say, "Man must do everything he can in this world to obtain the honor, glory and fame that make him worthy of heaven and that thus lead him to enjoy eternal peace."[3] In one sense, the connection proposed between fame and eternal life marked a radical departure from the medieval position that only by almsgiving could laypersons hope to compensate for the inherent deficiencies of lay status and put themselves on an equal footing with clerics in the race for salvation. Yet in a different sense, the link proposed between earthly fame and eternal life suggests that to Renaissance humanists the idea of a separation between this world and the next was as unfamiliar as it was to their predecessors.[4]

Temporalia and *aeterna* were mixed, too, in the sense that testaments are more usefully understood as being contractual, rather than philanthropic, in nature. At the very least, almost every testament left an obligation to the beneficiary to say weekly masses for the testator's soul. The veritable army of chaplains to be found on the roster of any given charitable institution testifies to the importance of the institution's role as intercessor. Most testaments outlined the severest penalties should the institution fail to honor its obligations to the testator, as the *setaiuolo* Andrea Banchi declared:

> In the event that the superintendent of the said hospital shall neglect to do this (i.e., neglect to have said the *rinovale*), in such case the said hospital from that very moment shall lose the inheritance described herein, and should that occur, he appoints as his universal heir the hospital of Santa Maria Nuova of Florence, with the aforesaid duty of performing the aforesaid office, as above.[5]

What did the institution receive in return? What role did testaments play in the Innocenti's economic life? Although a more detailed analysis will follow in the chapter on the Innocenti's internal administration, a cursory examination of the revenues of the Innocenti from 1448 to 1459 shows that direct income from wills and donations made up a relatively small proportion of total income. In the year from 1 July 1448 to 1 July 1449, for example, the total *entrata* of the hospital was 6,827 lire, 9 soldi, 6 denari, of which only 279 lire, or about 4 percent, came from wills, and 3 percent from donations. In the following year, the percentage of income from wills and donations increased to 20 percent; in 1451–52 the percentage decreased to 12 percent; in the following year the percentage increased again to 19 percent. Every year afterward, until 1460, the percentage of income derived from both wills and donations remained below 10 percent. Table 1 illustrates this phenomenon more clearly.

The value of testaments and donations, then, was largely indirect, and testators and hospital alike had to work through the institutional machinery of the communal funded debt, or *Monte Comune*, even in those cases in which the testator did not directly bequeath shares in those government securities. If a testator or donor did not bequeath *Monte* shares, he or she might donate a parcel of land or an entire estate. The Innocenti and similar institutions were able to double and even triple their real-estate holdings over the course of the fifteenth century.[6] Once the hospital acquired land from a testator or donor, it could exercise several options. By keeping the land, it could (and did) directly use the crops and cattle to meet the nutritional needs of children and staff, in which case its only expenses for feeding them would be for labor and transportation. In a number of cases, sharecroppers divided the fruits of their labor with the Innocenti as they would have with any other landlord. The Innocenti often sold the products grown on its estates as well. The above options were especially useful for those cases in which testators and donors forbade the alienation or sale of the property. It was

TABLE 1. Income from Wills and Donations

Year	Donations	Wills	Total
1448–49	4.1%	2.9%	7.0%
1449–50	0.3	19.7	20.0
1451–52	3.7	8.2	11.9
1452–53	14.0	5.6	19.6
1453–54	3.4	0.0	3.4
1454–55	3.7	0.0	3.7
1455–56	6.3	0.0	6.3
1456–57	5.2	0.2	5.4
1457–58	4.3	1.7	6.0
1458–59	4.0	0.1	4.1

Source: AOIF, Entrata e Uscita (CXXII,1–7), passim.

just as common, however, for testators to bequeath property without restrictions on its sale, and if financial exigencies pressed especially hard, this option proved to be a reliable source of quick funds.

For the purposes of this chapter, I will examine three types of charitable giving to the Innocenti: wills, donations, and annuities. I will begin by examining the question of who these testators were and what were their motivations for giving. What sorts of prior ties bound testators and donors to the institution? I will then present the various types of wills, donations, and annuities to the Innocenti, and then move to the question of the inevitable involvement of these private sources of support with the institutional machinery of the Florentine state. Finally, I will discuss the tremendous obstacles the hospital often had to overcome to lay full claim to the generosity of its benefactors. The evidence for this portion of the study encompasses thirty-five wills and twenty-two donations, the bulk of which the archive of the Ospedale degli Innocenti holds in its first two volumes of testaments and donations. In addition, three volumes of *ricordanze*, or administrative memoranda, supply partial notices of testaments and donations, though rarely within this source do full transcriptions appear. The Archivio di Stato in Florence contains a collection of loose parchments, many of which are the originals of wills and donations left to the Innocenti. The state archives also contain several volumes of notarial protocols in which not only wills reside, but also the seemingly endless litigation that was their inevitable consequence.

Approximately one-third of the thirty-five testators whose wills were drawn up between 1411 and 1484 had easily demonstrable ties to the Arte della Seta during their lifetimes. Of twenty-two donors, among which the Arte della Seta is itself numbered, at least four held either a consulate in the guild, or had some clear tie to the administrative structure of the hospital.[7] As a group, moreover, testators to the Innocenti could boast of considerable wealth. Nearly half of the hospital's testators or their immediate families were listed among the upper six hundred taxpaying families of the 1427 Catasto.[8] Five of the donors could be found on the same list.

Similarly, the upper brackets of the 1403 *prestanza* also contain the names of several donors and testators to the Innocenti.[9] Somewhat atypical of the testators, but an important figure nonetheless in the philanthropic chronicle of the hospital, was Francesco di Lencio di San Miniato. Perhaps better known as the founder of the hospital of Sant'Antonio at Lastra a Signa,[10] he left in his will sufficient discretion to his executors, the consuls of the Arte della Seta, to use part of his bequest to purchase from Rinaldo degli Albizzi the land abutting the Piazza dei Servi on which the hospital would eventually be built.[11] In 1403, Francesco, whose occupation is listed as tailor,[12] was assessed sixteen florins in the *prestanza,* or fifty-seventh highest in the quarter of San Giovanni.[13]

More typical of testators to the Innocenti was Guido di Tommaso Deti, whose testament of 1436 transferred his investment in the *Monte Comune* to the silk guild, on the condition that the interest payments be used every year to provide dowries for poor girls to be named by the guild consuls. Furthermore, if his four sons all failed to accede to the inheritance by the time they reached the age of twenty-five, half his entire estate was willed to the Innocenti.[14] Guido's ties to the guild are well documented. In 1430, Guido himself had been chosen for the office of guild consul; his son, Tommaso, would continue the family tradition as one of the overseers of the Innocenti in 1473.[15] In the 1427 Catasto, Guido listed his taxable assets as 1,819 florins, ranking him 125th in the Santo Spirito quarter.[16]

Guido's wealthier neighbor, Bindo de' Piaciti, provides another example of guild service. In 1430 and 1431 he was a guild consul.[17] His testament of 1439 left three hundred florins to the Innocenti in *Monte Comune* shares, and invited the consuls of the guild to draw upon the interest for the management of the hospital.[18] His 1427 Catasto report placed him as the thirty-fifth wealthiest taxpayer in the quarter of Santo Spirito.[19] In the 1403 *prestanza,* he and his brother Tommaso were together assessed thirty-three florins as their expected contribution to the Florentine treasury, ranking them the eleventh wealthiest household in Santo Spirito.[20]

Some testators to the Innocenti compiled even more spectacular records of guild service, as the cases of Bernardo di Bartolomeo del Benino (1468), Lodovico di Ser Viviano de'Neri (1435), Mariotto di Dinozzo Lippi (1473), and Andrea Banchi (1460) illustrate. Bernardo's father, Bartolomeo di Andrea del Benino, was one of the first overseers of the Innocenti's building program, the year before Brunelleschi, Goro di Stagio Dati, and Francesco della Luna were appointed to the position.[21] Bernardo himself was overseer first in 1439, and went on to hold guild consulates in 1443, 1455, 1457, and 1461.[22] With a net worth in 1427 of 6,785 florins, he ranked forty-fourth in the quarter of Santo Spirito.[23]

Lodovico di Ser Viviano de' Neri served as an *operaio* in 1424, and obtained the office of guild consul in that same year, and again in 1429. In 1431 he served the Innocenti as its treasurer, and served as guild consul again one year before his death in 1436.[24] His declared assets in 1427 placed him among the upper hundred taxpayers of the quarter of Santa Maria Novella.[25]

Mariotto di Dinozzo di Stefano Lippi, whose banking activities are well documented by Florence Edler, was an *operaio* of the Innocenti in 1439, 1443, 1449, 1454, and 1461. In 1461 he was granted lifelong tenure. He also served as consul of the silk guild in 1439, 1441, 1458, and 1470.[26] This record of service had a noticeable impact even on the writer of his obituary. Instead of the usual terse notice, the author of the Innocenti's *ricordanze* wrote:

> I record that on the nineteenth day of October, at 13 hours or so, Mariotto di Dinozzo di Stefano Lippi passed from this life. May God truly pardon him. On the said day his body was buried in the church of San Felice in Piazza with appropriate honors.[27]

Perhaps the most outstanding example of a testator with a long record of service to guild and hospital is that of the renowned *setaiuolo*, Andrea Banchi. Born in 1372, he matriculated into the silk guild at the age of twenty-nine. Between 1414 and 1424, he held the office of guild consul six times. He held this office again in 1425, 1429, 1433, and 1450. In the Catasto of 1427, he was listed as the fourth wealthiest silk manufacturer in the city, with declared assets of 7,441 florins. By 1460, two years before his death, he estimated his fortune to be eighteen thousand florins, not taking into account the value of his house or his villa. He also rendered much service to the Innocenti as one of its *operai* in 1445 and 1450. In 1453, he was granted lifelong tenure in that office, at which time he became a *commesso* of the hospital.[28]

Although he did not leave behind the extensive literary documentation that Datini had, Andrea Banchi's involvement in the project may also have been as personal. His son Piero died childless at the age of twenty-six, and two of Andrea's sons died in infancy. As in Datini's case, he stipulated in his will that all his business partnerships be dissolved within five years after his death. Within the five-year period, his business affairs were to be conducted under the name of the "Commesseria di Andrea di Francesco di Banco." The overseers of the Innocenti were entrusted with seeing that the provisions of the will were carried out.

His partnership, however, fared less well. By the time of its dissolution his partners acknowledged debts to the Innocenti of nearly a thousand florins, which were to be paid back to the hospital at the rate of fifty florins per year.[29]

Although a smaller proportion of donors than testators had demonstrable connections to the hospital or the guild, their commitment was no less striking. Francesco di Lorenzo di Piero Lenzi, for example, held the consulate of the silk guild in 1430, 1431, 1438, 1443, and 1454. In addition, he was treasurer of the hospital in 1425, and his father had been an *operaio* in 1419. Although Francesco was not listed in the upper tax brackets in 1427, his father was ranked thirteenth in the quarter of Santa Maria Novella with assets of 10,940 florins.[30] In 1467 Piero donated 95 florins to be used as capital for dowries in the *Monte delle Doti*.[31] In general, the donors comprised a more varied group than the testators, and even numbered governmental agencies among their ranks. In 1468, the Otto di Guardia, one of the most powerful magistracies of the city, provided a dowry of 50 florins for a young girl of the hospital.[32] The silk guild, in addition to its statutory contributions, also made donations to the Innocenti on occasion, as in 1466, when the guild sent alms of 2 bales of cloth and 206 pairs of red and black shoes for the children of its hospitals of San Gallo and the Innocenti. The consuls who retired at the end of August 1466 also donated 200 lire to be spent on completing the dormitory next to the church.[33]

Occasionally, and perhaps more often than the documents reveal, testators had connections to the hospital that were not necessarily occupational. A female servant of Matteo and Borgo di Rinaldo abandoned her son to the Innocenti in 1445, although a week later Francesco and Dianora Ginori would claim him as a *nipote*.[34] In 1447, Borgo di Rinaldo left six hundred florins of *Monte Comune* to the Innocenti.[35] His guild connections were also occupational: he served as consul in 1440 and 1449, his brother Matteo served as overseer in 1451, and as consul in 1444, 1466, and 1470.[36]

Mariotto Lippi's female servant, Perpetua, abandoned her son, whom she said was hers by a certain Antonio di Donnabuona, to the Innocenti. The abandonment did not take place until the child was two years old.[37] If the silk manufacturers who left large sums to the Innocenti did so to assuage their guilt over the abandonment of their own children, there is scant evidence of it in the Innocenti's archives.[38] Mariotto Lippi appears in the documents more frequently as provider of letters of recommendation for children abandoned at the hospital. In 1472, for example, the scribe wrote of a two-year-old girl who had been sent to the Innocenti: "they say that Mariotto Lippi sent her. Other information we don't have."[39] It is possible, of course, that some important testators were covered under the following rubric, again from 1472: "She had [pinned to her] a note that said she is a child who was born of good blood, and she was sent to this place to avoid scandal." Nevertheless, her mother, a certain Mona Bartolomea di Giovanni di Brescia came to the hospital a short time later and named the father as "Matteo del...," at which point the entry comes to a tantalizing close.[40]

Even if there was no widespread discernible pattern of testators and donors having been beneficiaries of the Innocenti's services, their benefactions could take a very specific and personal form. Francesco di Medillo di Giorgio, of Piancaldoli di Romagna, donated several parcels of land, including his own house, to Maria, one of the Innocenti's foundlings. Francesco promised the prior of the Innocenti that when she came of age, he would "marry her to one of his grandsons."[41]

If testators did not have direct connections to the guild or to the hospital, they were often indirectly connected. Lorenzo di Agnolo Sassoli's medical training in Padua, Bologna, and Ferrara was subsidized in the early years of the fifteenth century by Francesco Datini, and some sixty of his letters are in the Datini collection at Prato.[42] Lorenzo's son left his estate to the Ospedale degli Innocenti in 1477.[43] Bindo de'Piaciti was Datini's agent in Venice.[44] Maso di Sandro, who left half of his estate to the hospital of Bonifazio Lupi and the other half to the Innocenti, was the brother of Pacie di Sandro, prior of the Innocenti in 1458 and who had previously held the post of prior at Bonifazio Lupi's hospital.[45] Other benefactors, such as Matteo di Zanobi Viviani, Domenico Grazianello, and Zanobio di Jacopo, were matriculated in the silk guild, even though they had neither obtained high office there nor served as *operai*. Other testators belonged to minor guilds under the protection of the Arte della Seta: such was the case with Matteo di Lorenzo, a goldsmith who became consul of the silk guild in 1419.[46]

Although the vast majority of testaments and donations was made by laymen, notable exceptions occurred among the ranks of clergy and women. In 1475 the Bishop of Cortona was given permission by the Holy See to add a codicil to his will leaving one quarter of the revenue from several of his farms in the Val di Nievole in aid of the education "of one or several virgin girls to be educated in the said hospital [of the

Innocenti]."[47] Another cleric, Antonio degli Agli, Bishop of Volterra, of whom Vespasiano di Bisticci wrote that "he was learned in Greek and Latin and a man of saintly life," left a house in the Piazza degli Agli to the Innocenti. The proceeds of the sale of the house, which could not be sold for less than twelve hundred florins, were to be used to dower girls at the institution. Vespasiano reports that the Bishop left another nine hundred florins for the same purpose to the girls of the Buondelmonti family.[48]

Three testators of the thirty-five encompassed in this study were women: Mona Caterina, daughter of Alberto di Zanobi; Mona Nanna, daughter of Giovanni di Andrea del Benino; and Mona Cosa, wife of Jacopo Tani. The date of Mona Caterina's demise was not recorded, but the notice that the Innocenti could claim a portion of the inheritance is dated 1469.[49] Her first husband, Pietro Boveregli, had been assessed seven florins in the 1403 *prestanza*. Her second husband, Cristofano Bagniesi, reported assets of 4,067 florins in the Catasto of 1427. Mona Caterina gave five hundred florins to the hospital, which were to be paid after her daughter's death.[50]

Mona Nanna had drawn up her will in 1461, but only in 1470 was the Innocenti notified of its claim. Mona Cosa's husband, Jacopo Tani, was an overseer of the hospital in 1454, and her name appears on the list both of donors and testators.[51] In 1463, for motives of "loving God and from her desire for piety and mercy, and for the salvation of her soul," she donated a farm in the parish of San Pietro in Boscolo, as well as two houses in Florence in the Chiasso Bertinelli to the Innocenti. Her testament of 1467 left "a house located behind the property where the Albergo della Corona used to be, in the street that goes to the hospital of Santa Maria Nuova."[52]

Women were more likely to be donors than testators, however, no doubt because of the peculiar demographic profile of Renaissance Florence: a gap of twenty years between the ages of husband and wife was not unusual. Consequently, a Florentine woman was likely to be widowed at a relatively early age.[53] In many cases, these women either remarried within a short period of time, or took vows. They might also have exercised a third option, that of taking quasi-religious vows at a charitable institution such as the hospital of San Paolo or the Ospedale degli Innocenti. In return for employment, they would agree to leave their estates to the hospital. This practice, by which women would become *commessi* of the Innocenti, was not exclusively or even predominantly feminine, however. Single men and married couples could also undertake such contracts.

The form of donation that was the exclusive domain of women was the sale of annuities. In selling annuities, the hospital agreed to supply specific quantities of grain, olive oil, wine, and other produce for a lifetime in return for donations of cash or property. Goldthwaite and Rearick have already noted the annuity as a steady and reliable source of income for the hospital of San Paolo as well as the hospital of Santa Maria Nuova.[54]

At the Innocenti, this type of arrangement was implicit when a woman was granted the usufruct of a property during her lifetime. Usufruct might extend beyond a single generation, as in the case of Maddalena, the daughter of a certain Mona Caterina.[55] In such a case, the usufruct of the possessions in question defined the limits of the obligation, as was true in the case of Mona Tommasa, wife of Giovanni Barletari of Radda in Chianti. Giovanni, until his death, had governed a small hospice that was under the protection of the Arte della Seta. As a *commesso* of the guild, Giovanni pledged to turn over his estate with the stipulation that his wife could use it if she outlived him. Mona Tommasa did indeed outlive Giovanni, and in September 1444 the hospital of the Innocenti signed an agreement with her at the hospice in Radda, by which the hospital's lawyer, Boccaccio di Niccolò Boccaccio,

> gave and consigned to the above Mona Tommasa, the goods described herein ... to be enjoyed and used as long as she shall live, and not beyond. . . . She promised that having used and enjoyed the fruits of these goods during her lifetime, at her death they shall be restored to the Ospedale degli Innocenti.[56]

These goods included a house and a cluster of buildings in Radda; a long inventory of all household furnishings follows in the original document.

A contract that, more properly speaking, constitutes an annuity was drawn up in September of 1445 between the Innocenti and Mona Lisa, daughter of Lorenzo di Cieco Cione, and widow of Giovanni di Giovanni Grasso, whose father had been one of the first overseers of the Innocenti in 1419. The contract states that Mona Lisa, who lived in the quarter of Santa Maria Novella "has donated freely and for charity, and for the salvation of her soul, fifty silver groats, and has brought to us the said accounts." In return, Lapo di Piero Pacini, the hospital's superintendent, treasurer, and governor, promised to give to Mona Lisa to use at her discretion an annual subsidy of eight barrels of wine, a half *orcio* of good olive oil, and some firewood and kindling, an obligation that would cease at her death.[57]

If annuities were the exclusive preserve of women, contractual arrangements regarding wills extended to both sexes. The hospital's obligations in this regard were so numerous and so extensive that an entire section of the Innocenti's archive is given over to volumes recording them.[58] The necessity for keeping volumes of records was also prompted by the complexity and detail of instructions. Andrea Banchi, for example, entrusted the silk guild, much as Datini had entrusted the Ceppo, not merely with the obligations of its own share of the estate but also with the administration of the entire legacy. Banchi's will makes this quite clear:

> In, however, all other moveable and immoveable property, rights, entitlements, and actions, present and future, in whatever parts of the world, he appointed, constituted, and willed as his universal heir the hospital of Santa Maria degli Innocenti of Florence, with duties and charges as follows: ... that whoever is superintendent of the said hospital at the time is bound to and must execute and totally and effectively fulfill each and every provision as made above by the said testator and each and every thing contained in the said testament.[59]

In addition to seeing that the hospital got two-thirds of his estate, and his descendants one-third, the Innocenti had to say an office for the dead each year in the month of August, for fifty years. The hospital might also be entrusted with external charitable obligations, as happened when Andrea Banchi left five hundred florins to be spent on dowries of thirty florins apiece. He divided the task of appointing the beneficiaries between the hospital and his wife, Dianora. If the hospital failed to carry out its obligations, it would lose the inheritance, a threat that did not extend to Mona Dianora.[60]

Bindo de' Piaciti's will was yet more detailed and explicit. The governors of the Innocenti could receive interest on three hundred florins of *Monte Comune* only if they sent to the Abbey of the Camaldoli four wax plasters for the chapel of Santa Barbara on that saint's feast day. Each wax plaster had to weigh three pounds, and on the day after her feast day the hospital had to send four pounds of wax. Furthermore, eighteen plainsong masses were to be sung in the greater chapel, for which Bindo supplied expenses of eighteen groats.[61]

Lorenzo di Agnolo Sassoli's son, in his testament of 1477, appointed the Florentine hospital of Santa Maria della Scala his universal heir, and the Innocenti as the Scala's successor should the Scala fail to meet its obligations. These obligations included paying the monastery of St. Jerome in Fiesole, the monastery of San Marco in Florence, and the Franciscan monastery next to San Miniato ten florins each. These monastic establishments had to spend the ten florins in appointing twelve "suitable religious men" to celebrate thirty St. Gregory masses for both the testator's soul and the soul of his mother. Not fully confident that his wishes would be carried out, this testator required each monastery to swear an oath before the prior of the Scala that the activities had been performed. If any monastery failed either to swear the oath or to observe it, the Scala was required to withhold the ten florins. What is of interest here is not merely that the multiplication of such obligations by the number of testators must have created an administrative nightmare, but that this testator, as did many others, placed the care of his soul in the hands of lay charitable institutions. If testators required religious men to undertake the intercession, such religious men were subject to the watchful eye of the hospital's administrators, so that "he [i.e., the testator] might have more confidence than he has in the said monasteries that the abovesaid obligations will be carried out."[62]

This confidence also prompted certain donors and testators to burden the Ospedale degli Innocenti with requests that they be allowed to endow chapels. In July 1468, Domenico Bacegli brought a petition before the consuls of the silk guild to be assigned a chapel in the church of the hospital of San Gallo, which in 1463 had merged with the Innocenti. The petition was granted unanimously, allowing him and his descendants "a chapel located in San Gallo on the side where the choir is, on the left hand side as you enter the choir, which is called the altar of the Virgin Mary." Domenico was to be allowed "to make a tablet with his coat of arms and to adorn the altar and said tablet as he pleases." He required the Innocenti to say two masses per week at this altar, and in return Domenico made a donation of thirty florins *di suggiello* and a vineyard in Peretola.[63] In 1484, Matteo di Simone Gondi, in appointing as his heir the Ospedale degli Innocenti, petitioned the guild consuls to have a series of banners made, each with his coat of arms and the figure of a child on it. Ten years after his death, his heirs were granted a chapel in the cathedral of Fiesole, and were allowed to name the chapel San Matteo.[64] More striking are the arrangements made for the chapel. A letter from Giuliano, Bishop of Ostia, confirms that in 1494 an alumnus of the Innocenti, a 23-year old by the name of Alamanno, was appointed deacon and chaplain *in perpetuo.* The letter bore a dispensation from the Pope, Alexander VI, exempting Alamanno from the age requirement for such a post, a requirement established by the Lateran Councils and the Council of Lyons. This dispensation empowered him to administer the sacraments.[65]

Despite the confidence of such testators in the inherent trustworthiness of the Innocenti to carry out their wishes, testaments and donations could just as well become a battleground of conflicting loyalties and emotions. In Pullan's study of sixteenth-century Venice, nearly 40 percent of bequests to the Scuola di San Rocco could be classified as "indirect conditional legacies" in which the Scuola only benefitted from the inheritance should one or more lines of the family die out. Similarly, a testator might threaten to leave his estate to the Scuola if the heirs failed to honor their obligations.[66] This phenomenon was widespread in testaments to the Innocenti as well, which itself could be penalized if it failed to fulfill its terms of the contract.

The more usual alternative to the indirect conditional legacy at the Innocenti was the sort of will in which the testator left a sum of several hundred florins unconditionally to the hospital, and made only the remainder of his estate, usually in land, conditional upon the failure of his heirs to survive. Guido di Tommaso Deti's testament of 1436, which guaranteed the consuls of the silk guild the interest on his two hundred florins of *Monte Comune,* gave to the Innocenti half of his estate only if his four sons all failed to reach the age of twenty-five.[67]

Nevertheless, the indirect conditional legacy was common enough at the Innocenti: nine of the thirty-five wills studied, or 25.7 percent, only left something to the Innocenti once the claims of one or two generations were satisfied. Three examples will suffice to illustrate the tenor of this type of bequest.

In 1465 Guido di Maso Gerini left his estate to an unknown heir, and stipulated that if his possessions in the Mugello were ever sold or alienated "the Innocenti will come into the inheritance." His wife Lucrezia, in drawing up her testament, specified that if her heirs, the friars of the

Servi, did not use some of the proceeds of the estate to celebrate the feast of the Immaculate Conception, then the Innocenti was to accede to enough of the estate to celebrate the feast themselves.[68]

A rather more complex example is the 1452 will of Marco di Jacopo di Mano Caviciulli, otherwise known as Marco della Donzella. The will left one hundred florins each for a dowry to two daughters of Amideo Amidei, his son-in-law, with the stipulation that should the daughters die before reaching marriageable age "he bequeathed, by the laws governing testaments, the said quantity to the hospital of Santa Maria degli Innocenti and its poor children." In 1467 the hospital received notice that one daughter, Marchigiana, had died, and sought legal advice to pry loose the one hundred florins. However:

> we found that Piera [the other daughter] is alive and married, and we cannot receive the hundred florins because the testament is worded so that we have no claim to the money while Piera is still alive.[69]

Marco della Donzella's will is an especially good example of how far down the line of succession to an estate a charitable institution might be. Not only was the hospital unable to collect Marchigiana's dowry; it also had to concede precedence behind Marco's three sons, each of whom had one-third share in the estate, and any of their descendants. Only if Marco's grandsons lack

> any legitimate natural heirs, he leaves as his heir our hospital of the Innocenti. . . . When we are supposed to be notified of the outcome Jacopone d'Andrea di Bonaventura, *nipote* of Piero Ducci, says he will let us know.[70]

In 1480, more than a decade after the testament was drawn up, two of the heirs were dead without issue, but a third was still alive, and the estate had been reduced to one house.[71]

A similar situation existed in the will of Livo di Antonio Mazzoni, and the uncertainty of devolution, coupled with the 95-florin debt Livo owed the hospital at the time of his death, may have contributed to the decision of the consuls and the *operai* to renounce the inheritance in 1469,[72] just as earlier in the century the consuls of the guild had renounced the inheritance of Ceppo di Guido because of its outstanding Catasto obligations.

So strong was the pull of family ties that testators frequently misused donations *ad pias causas* as a way of bequeathing sums to assist their poor relations. The advantage of bequeathing such a fictive sum to charitable institutions was that one could hope to avoid the taxes and debts that might come with a direct bequest.[73] Although in many cases the Innocenti was asked to administer the distribution of an estate, there is no evidence that the sums bequeathed directly to the Innocenti were fictive, and in any case it is clear that until 1484 they were as likely as not to be subject to taxation. Perhaps it was for such tax dodges that the Innocenti renounced inheritances such as that of Francesco di Tommaso Busini, whose testament in 1475 was declared by the *operai* to be "injurious and dishonorable to the hospital."[74]

The Innocenti had every reason to be cautious concerning those estates and donations in which it won the battle in the testator's mind, but lost the war in subsequent litigation with relatives. Even a casual glance at notarial protocols reveals myriad lawsuits over property and cash bequeathed to the Innocenti. Even where no litigation eventually ensued, the hospital could become tremendously entangled in the family affairs of its benefactors, as the following example shows.

Even the most attractive and seemingly certain and reliable of testaments could occasion years of legal wrangling. Such was the case with the testament that Ser Lodovico di Viviano left to the Innocenti on 29 January 1436.[75] As noted earlier, Ser Lodovico had held the offices of *operaio* and consul several times between 1424 and 1434. His father was notary to the Riformagioni during Coluccio Salutati's tenure as chancellor. His father's office carried with it several important ceremonial functions, including that of giving an oration every time someone became a *cavaliere* of the commune. Lodovico's brother, Andrea, was made provost and Apostolic protonotary at Prato in 1409, and his brother Giovanni held several important communal offices in Florence.[76]

Ser Lodovico's testament left his entire estate and all his credits in the *Monte Comune* to the Ospedale degli Innocenti, with the stipulation that his wife, Mona Tita, should enjoy the usufruct of the estate during her lifetime. The first indication that the inheritance might be contested occurs in notarial protocols of 20 July 1440, in which the hospital of the Innocenti, represented by Adamo di Giovanni and Niccolò Bonaiuti, for the guild, and by Boccaccio di Niccolò Boccaccio, the official solicitor for the hospital's superintendent, Tommaso di Maso di Perugia, was described as "heir presumptive with benefit of law and inventory" of Lodovico di Ser Viviano de'Neri. An heir presumptive, in this context, meant simply an heir who had not received the benefits of the inheritance. "Benefit of Law and Inventory" meant first, that the settlement of the estate depended on the legality of the transaction, and secondly, that the assets of the estate outweighed the obligations. The Innocenti was allied with Mona Tita's legal representative, Ser Lorenzo di Francesco di Giovanni di Ser Segno. Bringing the suit against the Innocenti was Giovanni, Lodovico's brother, and the document of 20 July was a *compromessum*, or an agreement to go to arbitration. Even though the centerpiece of the lawsuit was Lodovico's bequest to the Innocenti, the case depended on the interpretation of at least two other testaments: Ser Viviano's, of 1414, which had divided his estate among his sons, and Andrea's (the Apostolic protonotary).

The defendants, Ser Tommaso (the superintendent) and Mona Tita, had three and ten days, respectively, to ratify the agreement to go to arbitration.[77] Two months later, on 16 September 1440, the first two arbitrators were appointed: Piero di Goro del Benino, and Niccolò di Giovanni Carducci.[78] On 15 November Castello di Piero Quaratesi was appointed as the third arbitrator.[79] Four extensions were granted between this date and the decision of the arbitrators. On 1 July 1441 Bernardo di Bartolomeo Gherardi replaced Piero di Goro del Benino and, by that date, Ser Tommaso had been replaced by Piero di Andrea di Piero as the hospital's superintendent. A decision could be reached by agreement of any two of the three arbitrators, whether the third dissented, abstained, or simply failed to participate.[80] After a further six postponements, the arbitrators finally reached a decision on 24 January 1442. The decision ran to eighty-five folios, both sides, and it narrated a long history of all the wills involved and the history of the dispute between Giovanni di Ser Viviano and the Innocenti.[81]

Issues of partiality and potential conflict of interest do not seem to have influenced the selection of arbitrators. Niccolò di Giovanni Carducci had been an *operaio* of the Innocenti in 1431; Piero di Goro del Benino became an *operaio* months after a decision had been handed down, and Bernardo di Bartolomeo Gherardi was an *operaio* in 1440.[82] Only Castello di Quaratesi seems to have had no intimate connection to the hospital, but even the Quaratesi family had close ties to important guildsmen in the Arte della Seta, and to the family of Francesco della Luna.[83] As one often finds in the litigation of late medieval Florence, the arbitrators enlisted the expert opinion of foreigners. In this case, the arbitrators sought advice and counsel from "the Venerable College of outstanding Lord Doctors, Jurists, and Lawyers of the City of Genoa."[84]

In coming to a decision, the arbitrators first reviewed the dispute itself, which centered on Giovanni's claim that much of what Lodovico had bequeathed to the Innocenti was not Lodovico's property, but Andrea's, which through the division made of Viviano's estate, should belong to Giovanni as Andrea's heir. Complicating the issue was Viviano's will of 1414, which bequeathed to four of his sons his house on Borgo SS. Apostoli, with the condition that Francesco, his firstborn, could never dwell there. The house was to be occupied, according to Viviano's will, by Andrea and a servant. Francesco was not to join them because "clerics and laymen do not make good housemates." To Neri, Lodovico, and Giovanni, he left, beyond their share in the estate, a house in Peretola. Viviano's *Monte* credits could not be sold, nor the interest drawn upon them, without the consent of Neri, Lodovico, Giovanni, and Silvestro. His estate itself went to all six sons, and included property located in Sambuco, and in the parishes of San Martino, San Gaudenzio, and Santa Maria di Peretola, as well as Santo Cristofano di Novoli and Santa Maria di Cintoia.

Viviano also proposed in his will that since Andrea was, as protonotary of Prato, comfortably ensconced, he should allow Neri, Lodovico, and Giovanni to receive the profits of his share of the estate, with which the three brothers were to be content until Andrea drew up his last will and testament. When Viviano died, his surviving sons did come into the inheritance, and "the said Andrea, Neri, and Lodovico knew the contents of and arrangements made in Ser Viviano's testament."[85]

Several divisions of property and the sale of eleven shares of *Monte* subsequently took place; finally, Lodovico:

> wishing to come into the division of the homes located in Florence as part of the prebequest to Andrea, Neri, Lodovico, and Giovanni, and this [wish] coming to the notice of Andrea, Andrea wrote a certain letter to Lodovico, and Lodovico wrote back the following: "In the Name of God Amen, 19 March 1417. Late yesterday I received your letter. By this response you are advised that I have begun the division of our houses just as I have already spoken to you about it. For the said reason have faith that you will not come to any harm or diminution of your share.... The reason I am answering you is that my

intention was never, nor is, nor ever shall be, to do what you suspect me of, in this or any other of your accounts. And I am writing to you to let you know that they [Neri and Giovanni] demanded the agreement from me and I answered that I was ready. And I think that we will carry it out without fail, whether by force or by your cooperation. And you know, you must be certain, that I would not do anything against you . . . and let this be said to you forever, that by me neither you nor anyone else will find themselves defrauded, because I would never cheat anyone. I myself have been defrauded, not by you, but by my other relatives, who have troubled me no end and would continue to do this and to cause similar scandals. . . . I believe God will yet repay them. . . . Yours Truly, Lodovico di ser Viviano, in Florence."[86]

After another year and another division of property had passed, this last division presumably being the controversial one, Giovanni wrote to Lodovico that:

The Provost [i.e., Andrea] is staying on in Prato, and there is terrible plague there. He has been written several letters, but he neither comes nor wishes to come to do anything [about the division of property] yet. I think he doesn't want to abandon that concubine of his, Monica.[87]

Andrea died in July of 1419, appointing Giovanni his heir. In 1435, Lodovico died, leaving his estate to the hospital of the Innocenti. In the intervening years, Lodovico paid the Catasto for his portion of the estate and was inscribed as a creditor of the *Monte*. At the same time, however, Giovanni declared in his Catasto return that Lodovico owed him for the share of Andrea's estate he had illegally taken, and which he would later bequeath to the Innocenti.

The notarial protocols then described the specifics of Giovanni's lawsuit, followed by the Innocenti's response, and, finally, the advice of the learned jurists of Genoa. Giovanni's lawsuit sought "that portion of the estate in which the said Andrea was heir to the said Viviano, together with the profits realized from it and restitution of damages and interest from the time of Andrea's death." Giovanni asserted these claims as "heir presumptive of the said Andrea against the heirs and estates of the said Lodovico." In support of his claim Giovanni cited the section of

Viviano's will giving Andrea the property in Florence but its revenues until Andrea's death to the four brothers, and allowing the property to be divided after Andrea's will was drawn up.[88]

The hospital responded that "Giovanni is not entitled to seek or receive anything from the said hospital" because Giovanni and his brothers had all agreed to the divisions that gave Lodovico Andrea's property, and that Giovanni had, in signing those agreements, promised not to contravene them. Moreover, Giovanni had full knowledge of the divisions when they were made, and he knew that it was Andrea's goods that were being conveyed to Lodovico. Nor was Giovanni entitled to the interest on Viviano's *Monte* credits, because according to Viviano's will they could not be exchanged without consent of the four brothers named. Even if Giovanni could seek the *Monte* credits, he could not accede to the property or its revenues, since Lodovico had acceded to the property in good faith. Lodovico never received notice of Andrea's testament, the hospital argued, nor did Giovanni bother to press his claims to the property while Lodovico was still alive.

The hospital argued that even if it were to lose all the above points, the Catasto obligations that Lodovico paid should be subtracted from the revenues from any property that the Innocenti might be compelled to restore. Moreover, the letter from Lodovico to Andrea denying any intention to diminish his share of the estate should not prejudice the hospital's case or its rights to the estate. The other letter brought forth by the plaintiffs hardly suggests that Andrea and Giovanni were on the best of terms.[89]

Despite such earnest pleas from the Innocenti's advocates, the learned jurists of Genoa found decisively against the hospital, ruling that:

> the said real estate that was Andrea's share as heir of the said Viviano that went to Lodovico from the divisions [that the brothers made . . . ought] to be set aside for and belong to the said Ser Giovanni, notwithstanding any opposition from the representatives and attorneys for the said hospital.

The hospital was ordered to make restitution of the property "together with all the profits and revenues realized by the said Lodovico from the time of the said Andrea's death, minus expenses incurred."[90]

The arbitrators also ordered the Innocenti to restore all the interest payments paid out by the *Monte Comune* from Ser Lodovico's account, as well as the money exacted from Ser Viviano's debtors, which should have gone to Andrea but which had ended up in Lodovico's hands. The only Catasto obligations the hospital was allowed to subtract were those that Giovanni would have paid had he come into Andrea's inheritance in 1419. Concerning the revenues realized from Lodovico's estate between 1435 and 1442, the arbitrators ruled that Giovanni had not explicitly sought them.[91]

Less than a month after the arbitrators handed down their decision, the *operai* convened on 12 February 1442.[92] Noting that the hospital had awaited the outcome for some six years already, the *operai* unanimously agreed to return Lodovico's estate only if they were first reimbursed for the expenses of the inheritance itself, and only if two other conditions were met. First, Giovanni had to approve the bequests contained in Lodovico's will to his chapel in SS. Apostoli, which was placed under the stewardship of the guild. Secondly, he had to agree not to file suit against or in any other fashion to proceed against either the bequest to the chapel or the bequest made to Camilla, daughter of Francesco di Ser Viviano, of four hundred florins in the *Monte Comune*.[93] In addition, Giovanni had requested, on 16 February 1442, that the hospital turn over to him a *Monte* credit of 550 florins from Lodovico's estate. This the *operai* refused to do until the expenses of the estate were paid and the other two conditions fulfilled.[94]

This case illustrates that even though Lodovico had clear ties to the guild and to the hospital, the claims of family to the estate overrode Lodovico's right to bequeath what he thought was his patrimony to the hospital of the Innocenti. The case should also stand as a reminder that one cannot rely on wills alone as an indicator of how much funding a charitable institution received from private sources. Between numerous claimants within the family to an estate, the steady erosion of the value of an estate through the tax obligations it incurred, and the amount of time it might take to realize the fruits of an inheritance, the difference between face value and cash value could be enormous. This is countered, nonetheless, by the immediate value that real-estate holdings could have in terms of feeding the resident population or, by the sale of produce, to pay the salaries of wet nurses. The amount of income produced by rents and sales of possessions could fluctuate considerably: in 1445, for example, it accounted for 4.25 percent of the total *entrata*, but the following year, because of the sale of possessions Lapo di Piero Pacini and his wife had donated, such sales accounted for approximately 17 percent of revenue. Most years the amount was less than 10 percent, except in the year 1452, when the sale of the remainder of Lapo di Piero Pacini's estate accounted for 23 percent of the hospital's income for that year. If the totals from table 2 are added to those from table 1, a clearer picture emerges of the real benefit to the institution from benefactions. More importantly, the productive potential of land meant that charitable institutions were hardly passive victims of inflation.

If the interest payments from credits in the *Monte* and revenue from the sale of credits were ultimately due to testamentary generosity rather than government caprice, the importance of private support becomes predominant, at least for the years 1445–1450, when the hospital could count on regular income from the *Monte*. Even these most personal and individual arrangements did not keep the newly acquired patrimony of the Ospedale degli Innocenti from becoming involved in the fiscal machinery of communal government. From the institution's beginnings until mid-century, bequests and donations of *Monte* credits were a popular form of charitable giving. The executors of Francesco di Lencio di San Miniato's testament of 1411, for example, were empowered to liquidate whatever sums his estate was entitled to from the *prestanza* or from forced loans in which he was inscribed as a creditor of the *Monte*. His executors could use these credits as they saw fit.[95] In addition to the seventeen hundred florins used to purchase the construction site for the Innocenti, at least another thousand florins representing interest payments due his estate up to 1422 were paid out in the 1420s and 1430s.[96] This was in addition to the five hundred florins Francesco had bequeathed directly "for the construction of the said hospital for found-

TABLE 2.   Income from Rents and Sales as a Percentage of Total *Entrata*

Year	Rents	Sales	Total
1448–49	4.5%	0.4%	4.9%
1449–50	4.9	8.8	13.7
1451–52	4.9	2.8	7.7
1452–53	5.6	24.0	29.6
1454–55	8.1	0.0	8.1
1455–56	11.1	0.8	11.9
1456–57	10.4	0.7	11.1
1457–58	4.4	0.8	5.2
1458–59	4.6	0.8	5.4

Source: AOIF, Entrata e Uscita (CXXII,1–8).

lings [to be paid] within ten days of the testator's day of death [at the rate of] fifty florins each year."[97]

Other testators were more restrictive. Guido di Tommaso Deti, who left his share of two hundred gold florins of *Monte Comune* to the silk guild in 1436, bequeathed these shares on the condition that once the credit was inscribed under the guild's account, there could be no exchange, sale, or alienation. The guild was authorized to demand the interest payments every January, and the payments were to be spent in providing dowries for poor girls to be named by the consuls. The consuls were not to pay until the actual marriage contracts had been signed, and then "only to the husbands of the said girls."[98] Similarly, the credits of three hundred florins of *Monte* that Bindo de' Piaciti bequeathed to the Innocenti carried the same prohibition, though he did not specify the uses to which the interest payments were to be put.[99] The hospital could also use *Monte* credits as a means of recovering from its debtors, by demanding that the debtor place a *condizione,* or a freeze on payments of dividends to the debtor, so that the dividends would be diverted to the hospital until the debt was satisfied.

The hospital and the *Monte* did not always maintain such a flexible and mutually beneficial relationship. The issue of the tax obligations of Bernardo del Benino, an important guildsman and benefactor, continued to haunt the relationship between commune and hospital from 1471, the date of Bernardo's death, until 1485, when at last the *Signoria,* by special petition, cleared the Innocenti of responsibility for further payment. Bernardo had drawn up his testament in 1468, bequeathing all his *Monte* credits and their dividends, to Piero Neri, Niccolò del Benino, and Leonardo di Piero del Benino.

The four recipients were to arrange for the disbursement of such credits according to "whatever shall be decided by the consuls and officers of the guild of Por Santa Maria." The consuls were charged, with ensuring that when Piero, Neri, Niccolò, and Leonardo withdrew payments from these shares, that the money was turned over directly to the Innocenti, via the guild's treasurer. The Innocenti could only use the dividends to purchase real estate, and the real estate was to be inalienable in perpetuity. Bernardo also willed the remainder of his estate to the Innocenti, and ordered that the proceeds should be used to purchase inalienable property.[100]

The first indication that hospital and commune might come into conflict over this testament came in April of 1471, when Neri del Benino:

> said to me [the scribe of the Innocenti] that if anything happened to damage us concerning the audit of Bartolomeo del Benino in the levy of 1466 ... that he [Neri] had the proof of payment in his possession. [Neri explained that] Bernardo had paid, but failed to bring proof to the auditors' notary, because he didn't want to have to appear in person, on account of his illness preventing him from getting about.[101]

The next step involved an assessment by the *Monte* officials of how the Catasto obligations involved in the estate should be divided among the heirs. Bernardo owed about fourteen florins, and the *Monte* assigned nearly half this debt to the Innocenti. The remaining amount was divided almost equally among five heirs: the two sons of Niccolò d'Andrea del Benino, two nephews, and Bernardo's widow, Bartolomea.

The Innocenti was assigned an even greater share in the division of Bernardo's tax obligations to the *decima*. Out of the thirty-five florins assessed for the entire obligation, the Innocenti was being asked to pay twenty-three florins, or 66 percent of the total. All of the obligations gave the Innocenti the dubious honor of inscription in the quarter of Santo Spirito as the commune's debtor. Once the debt was acknowledged, the *Monte* officials gave permission for the transfer and liquidation of credits, which "must be treated as those of other citizens paying the ordinary taxes of the commune of Florence."[102]

The sources fail to make clear why the transaction should be so complex and involve so many actors. Much that occurred between 1434 and 1470 in the world of Florentine public finance remains to be researched and published. But even in these documents the severe pressure the *Monte* was under in 1470 is evident. It was in this year, after all, that the *Signoria* was moved to call the *Monte*

> the heart of this body which we call city ... [whose] every limb, large and small, must contribute to preserving the heart of this guardian fortress, immovable rock, and enduring certainty of the salvation of the whole body and government of this state.[103]

The elaborate system of proxy and power of attorney that enabled the hospital to realize income from *Monte* shares bequeathed to it appears to have been dictated by a legal requirement that shares could only be paid to "sopportanti."[104] In this respect, the complex activities of guild and hospital seem to have received approval from the Office of Ten, which on 11 April 1472 "decided and declared the *Monte* credits of Bernardo del Benino to be tax-supporting and the powers of attorney conferred to withdraw them to be without intent to defraud."[105] Only in 1484, however, was the issue of Bernardo del Benino's estate fully settled by the *Provvisione* in which the Innocenti was to be held responsible for taxes only for the portion of an estate actually bequeathed to it. Bernardo del Benino's estate was one of three specific instances the consuls complained about to the *Signoria*. These three estates also had tax obligations from the *dispiacente;* two other estates owed a total of forty florins.[106] The back tax obligations were quite substantial: if Bernardo del Benino owed a mere nine florins, Battista di Taccino Bizzini owed 180 florins, a debt the hospital had been paying off at the rate of six florins per year.[107] The 1484 legislation cancelled all these debts.

Another sign of communal fiscal distress in 1470 was legislation of that year, reported in the hospital's *ricordanze,* that three lire per florin of interest payments had to be reloaned to the *Monte*, where the money would be inscribed in the creditor's account to gather more interest:

On that day, 135 florins, 1 lira, 15 soldi, and 2 denarii of the said Bernardo's interest payments, which were still owing to him for his annual interest payments for the year 1470 [and which] according to the law passed that year, gives the *Monte* three lire per florin, or 406 lire. . . . And we sent this amount to the *Monte* in Bernardo's name—it is mixed in among the above-mentioned credits.[108]

Another feature of this same financial crisis, one that can be predated by some twenty years, was an increasing tendency for the distinction between the *Monte* proper and the *Monte delle Doti* to become blurred. In 1441, the government began to transform the *Monte Comune* into a vehicle to satisfy the creditors of the *Monte delle Doti*.[109] Potential investors in the dowry fund were required to deposit their shares from the various old *Monti* in place of cash.[110] Under the Laurentian fiscal regime, the interest owed to creditors of the *Monte delle Doti* was 198,000 florins, surpassing that owed to the *Monte Comune* by some 50,000 florins. The reform of 1470 actively discouraged investment in the *Monte Comune* and made the government's first priority the satisfaction of investors in the dowry fund.[111] This pressure may well explain why three of the purchasers of Bernardo del Benino's *Monte* credits declared their intention to provide dowries with the credits they purchased.

Ten testators of the thirty-five selected for this study made some sort of arrangement for dowering poor girls, as did five of the twenty-two donors. Before the opening of the hospital in 1445, since testators could not provide for the hospital's girls, they either left funds for dowries to be administered by other institutions, or dowered poor girls directly.

Francesco di Lencio di San Miniato, for example, left two hundred florins for dowries to go to the poor girls of the hospital of Santa Maria della Scala in Florence. He left an additional sixty florins to "ten truly poor and needy children" of the parish of Santa Maria Impruneta, to be chosen by the consuls of the silk guild.[112] As had Guido di Tommaso Deti before him, Piero di Maffeo Tedaldi in 1451 earmarked a sum of interest payments on the *Monte Comune* for dowries. Piero's will specified that the consuls of the silk guild who assumed office in January should allocate interest payments from three hundred florins worth of *Monte*.[113]

Matteo di Lorenzo, a goldsmith who left five hundred florins to the Innocenti's building program in 1419, left sixty gold florins to the consuls of the silk guild for "ten truly poor and needy girls from the parish of San Martino a Strada, to be chosen by his executors."[114]

Ceppo di Guido was less specific: he left fifty gold florins to *piis locis* to be used in marrying "virgin poor girls."[115] On a slightly more generous scale, Zanobio di Jacopo, "with the license, permission, and consent of his father," donated 125 gold florins to be given as dowry two years after the donor's death to "five truly poor girls to be nominated by the superintendent of the hospital [of the Innocenti] and the consuls of the guild of Por Santa Maria."[116] In 1419 Domenico Grazianello, a silk-thrower, left all his property to his wife, providing she remained unmarried. If she remarried, she could only receive one hundred florins and her clothes. The remainder of the estate would go to the Innocenti and the proceeds realized from its sale would go to dower poor girls.[117]

The first notice in the hospital's *ricordanze* of a donor's or testator's funds actually being employed as capital in the *Monte delle Doti* occurs in 1458, when an anonymous donor referred to as "una buona persona" invested slightly more than four florins for fifteen-year terms to each of thirty-two inmates of the Innocenti, yielding thirty florins each when the investment came due.[118]

By 1468, eight of the thirty-two girls had died, and the Innocenti recovered the full amount of the capital for each of them. Despite the scribe's earlier notation that the dowries were for fifteen-year terms, the Innocenti collected dowries for the twenty-four remaining girls in 1468.[119] The advantage for the hospital of using the dowry fund was obvious: to have dowered the twenty-four surviving girls directly would have required an outlay of 720 florins. Instead, this amount was paid out by the dowry fund on an initial investment by the hospital of testators' funds of only 150 florins.

Because of the legislative limit on the amount each girl at the Innocenti could receive, it would be fruitless to compare investment patterns of the Innocenti's testators with those of fathers at large. One can compare, however, data on the mortality of girls dowered at the Innocenti with those enrolled in the dowry fund as a whole. For matriculants in the dowry fund, mortality decreased in inverse proportion to the amount of capital invested. The average dowry of girls who married was 417 florins. Girls who became nuns collected an average of 435 florins, and those who died before they were able to collect would only have collected an average of 356 florins at the expiration of their terms. Girls with capital invested below one hundred florins had a mortality rate of 23.7 percent; the mortality of the group of girls whose fathers invested two hundred to eight hundred florins had a mortality rate of only 13 percent.[120] The small sample of thirty-two girls dowered at the Innocenti bears out this level of mortality: eight of thirty-two, or 25 percent, were to die before they could collect. This suggests that once the critical first years of infant mortality had passed in a child's life, the Innocenti provided a level of care for young girls that was comparable to the lower socioeconomic strata of investors in the *Monte delle Doti*. The average age at which girls in Florence were first enrolled in the fund is five years, one month.[121] The girls at the Innocenti were enrolled at four years, ten months, on the average, from the date of their admission, which was usually within three weeks of their birth.

Similar patterns emerge from dowries made by other donors and testators. In 1464 Bernardo di Antonio Scarlatto drew up his testament, in which he left thirty-two florins to the Innocenti to be disbursed over a period of four years. Bernardo was yet another testator who could boast a singular record of service to the guild: he was consul in 1444, 1457, and 1461.[122] Each year after his death, which occurred in 1466, the Innocenti was instructed to dower two girls by investing four florins for each girl, so that eventually each girl would receive a dowry of twenty-five florins. Bernardo also specified that capital returned because of the death of any of the girls was to be reinvested as capital for a new girl.[123] Francesco di Piero di Lorenzo Lenzi donated, in 1467, 92 florins, which were to be distributed as capital in sums of 4 florins, 16 soldi for each of 20 girls. These investments were to be allowed to mature for fifteen-year terms.[124]

Not only individuals, but also institutions found the *Monte delle Doti* an effective way to spend their charitable monies. In May 1468 the Otto di Guardia, or Eight on Security, bought *Monte* credits from Francesco di Bernardo di Piero di Cardinale Rucellai to provide a dowry through the *Monte* of fifty florins for Piera Maria, a foundling of the Innocenti.[125] Mariotto Lippi's will, though a direct bequest to the Innocenti, attempted to inscribe his granddaughter in the *Monte delle Doti,* with the stipulation that if she failed to reach marriageable age, the hospital of the Innocenti and not the girl's father would retrieve the capital. The hospital duly paid the capital into the fund from the proceeds of Mariotto's estate, but the officials of the *Monte* clearly found this to be a highly dubious transaction:

> The abovesaid condition [that the Innocenti should receive the capital in the event of the girl's death] was disallowed because the *Monte* officials did not wish to do it, saying that it is not done, nor in the past has it ever been done. Should it happen that the capital is returned the hospital must claim it from the abovesaid Pagolo Pini [the girl's father and Mariotto's son-in-law], because he must be the one to recover the capital and give it to us.[126]

A striking exception to the normal pattern of waiting until girls had reached the age of five before an investment was made in the *Monte* for them occurs in the 1474 testament of Jacopo di Pagolo Ridolfi, which left enough money to dower fifteen girls in fifteen years, with an expected yield of thirty florins for each one. This testament is another good example of the tendency to use interest from regular *Monte* payments as an investment in the dowry fund as well: the dowries were to be paid from a credit inscribed in the *quartiere* of Santo Spirito. The average amount of time between the entry of these girls into the hospital and their matriculation into the dowry fund was 2.7 years.[127]

The willingness, indeed, the burning desire, of testators to earmark funds for the dowering of girls undermines, as does evidence from the *Monte delle Doti* itself, the hypothesis often advanced that young girls "did not count" in fifteenth-century Florence. Even if they were seen only as a convenient means to the more lofty end of assuring family continuity and survival, it is still incontestable that in this function they were at the very center of the social system. At the same time, if in the society at large dowries were the lubricant of social mobility, by contrast, for the girls at the Innocenti they provided one of several opportunities for reintegration.

The significance of the hospital's involvement in the *Monte Comune* and the *Monte delle Doti* was much deeper than the amount of income realized from those sources. Just as the republic's ability to honor its debts affirmed or tested the faith and commitment of its citizens, so did the city's foremost charitable enterprise depend on the willingness of both leading citizens and the fiscal machinery of government to support the quotidian maintenance of the hospital's operations and to guarantee the honor of the hospital's girls. It is thus not surprising that testators and donors alike found a worthy charitable enterprise in dowries, and in the communal dowry fund a means of supporting the city's finances and the hospital's charitable mission at the same time. The popularity of the dowry fund with investors found its echo in the propensity of donors and testators, both in general and in particular, to provide dowries for impoverished girls. The involvement of these testators and donors suggests that even if the codes of honor and shame were not democratized, wealthy Florentines wished to emphasize their applicability and urgency at every level of the social hierarchy. That testators and communal officials alike encouraged the participation of the girls of the Ospedale degli Innocenti in this fund proved in a very literal and concrete fashion the centrality of the hospital's mission to the maintenance of the Florentine family as a cornerstone of communal survival.

NOTES

1. Philippe Ariès, *The Hour of Our Death,* trans. Helen Weaver (New York, 1981), 190–93.

2. Cited in Ariès, *Hour of Our Death*, 215.

3. Ibid.

4. Ibid. It is important to note, he argues, "the inevitable transition from terrestrial glory to celestial immortality" expressed in Duke Federigo of Urbino's motto "Virtutibus itur ad astra."

5. Archivio dell'Ospedale degli Innocenti di Firenze (AOIF), Testamenta et Donationes (IX,1), fol. 147r.

6. Elio Conti, *La formazione della struttura agraria fiorentina* (Rome, 1965), vol. 3, pt. 3. Conti's figures for the area of Macioli show that in 1427 the *beni non-sopportanti* were all ecclesiastical holdings worth over a thousand florins. By 1498 this property was valued at over 3,200 florins. The three farms owned by the Innocenti amounted to nearly one-third of this amount or, in other words, were equal in 1498 to the value of all ecclesiastical landholdings in that area in 1427.

7. Archivio di Stato, Firenze (ASF), Arte della Seta, 246, fols. 11r–36v, 97r–104r, respectively, list the consuls of the guild and the *operai* of the Innocenti.

8. Lauro Martines, *The Social World of the Florentine Humanists, 1380–1460* (Princeton, 1963), app. 2, tables 5–8, 365–78.

9. Ibid., app. 2, tables 1–4, 353–64.

10. AOIF, Testamenta et Donationes (IX,1), fols. 5v–6r.

11. AOIF, Debitori e Creditori, (CXX,1), fol. 1r.

12. Ibid.

13. Martines, *Social World,* app. 2, table 2, 357.

14. AOIF, Testamenta et Donationes (IX,1), fols. 94v–96r.

15. ASF, Arte della Seta, 246, fol. 16r.

16. Martines, *Social World,* app. 2, table 8, 378.

17. ASF, Arte della Seta, 246, fols. 15v, 16r.

18. AOIF, Testamenta et Donationes (IX,1), fols. 98v–100v, 25 September 1439.

19. Martines, *Social World,* app. 2, table 8, 376.

20. Ibid., app. 2, table 4, 362.

21. ASF, Arte della Seta, 246, fol. 97r.

22. ASF, Arte della Seta, 246, fol. 99v, fols. 22r, 28r, 29r, 30v.

23. Martines, *Social World,* app. 2, table 8, 376.

24. ASF, Arte della Seta, 246, fols. 97v, 98v; fols. 13v, 15v, 17r.

25. Martines, *Social World,* app. 2, table 7, 374.

26. ASF, Arte della Seta, 246, fols. 99v, 100r, 101r, 101v, 102v; fols. 20r, 21r, 29v, 34v.

27. AOIF, Ricordanze A (XII,1), fol. 138r, 19 October 1473.

28. Florence Edler de Roover, "Andrea Banchi, Florentine Silk Manufacturer and Merchant in the Fifteenth Century," in *Studies in Medieval and Renais-*

sance History 3 (1966): 223–85. ASF, Arte della Seta, 246, fols. 13r, 14r, 15v, 17r, 25v; fols. 100v, 101r, 101v.

29. Florence Edler de Roover, "Andrea Banchi," 275–85.

30. ASF, Arte della Seta, 246, fols. 15v, 16r, 19v, 22r, 27v. Martines, *Social World*, app. 2, table 7, 372.

31. AOIF, Ricordanze A (XII,1), fol. 87v, 29 January 1466 [modern = 1467].

32. AOIF, Ricordanze A (XII,1), fol. 105v, 10 May 1468.

33. AOIF, Ricordanze A (XII,1), fol. 78v, 24 May 1466.

34. AOIF, Balie e Bambini A (XVI,1), fol. 22r, 9 September 1445.

35. ASF, Diplomatico, Spedale degli Innocenti, 21 May 1447.

36. ASF, Arte della Seta, 246, fols. 20v, 22r, 25r, 32v, 34v; fol. 101v.

37. AOIF, Balie e Bambini F (XVI,6) fol. 58v, 25 April 1466.

38. See, however, AOIF, Balie e Bambini C (XVI,3), fol. 232r, 16 March 1457 [modern = 1458]: "Adì 6 di marzo in sul ore 16 ci fu rechato e messo nella pilla uno fanciullo maschio e batezatto nel sopradetto nome [Piero e Giovanni] arechò llo Filippo da Datto disse si faciesse chovernare bene e che in pochi dì farano il dovere allo spedale . . . dise era figliuolo della Margherita serva di Mariotto Lippi."

39. AOIF, Balie e Bambini H (XVI, 8), fol. 19r, 8 October 1472. For another example see AOIF, Balie e Bambini D (XVI,4), fol. 44v, 2 December, 1458, in which Mariotto Lippi locates the relatives of a child: "Adì 4 di giugno 1462 si dette detta fanciulla cioè Margerita soprascripta . . . per lectera di Mariotto Lippi a monna Betta d'Antonio d'Andrea sta a chasa a San Felice in Piaza la quale disse era parente di detta fanciulla. . . ."

40. AOIF, Balie e Bambini H (XVI,8), fol. 25r, 4 November 1472: "avea una poliza che diceva e una fanciulla la quale è nata di buono sanghue e per meno scandolo si manda in chotesto luogho et racchomandosi quanto e possibile a tutti e ministri e ministre di chotesto utilissimo luogho che sia data in buone mani et sarete per l'avenire proveduti. Il nome suo e Bartolomea. Veneci Bartolomea di Giovanni da Brescia e dise era sua figliuola e di Mateo del . . ." [end of entry].

41. AOIF, Ricordanze B (XII,2), fol. 26v, 25 June 1483.

42. Iris Origo, *The Merchant of Prato*, rev. ed. (New York, 1979), 300ff.

43. ASF, Diplomatico, Spedale degli Innocenti, 10 September 1477.

44. Supra, 107. See Origo, *Merchant of Prato*, 305.

45. AOIF, Ricordanze A (XII,1) fol. 135r, 20 December 1472.

46. AOIF, Testamenta et Donationes (IX, 1), fol. 27r, 14 July 1419.

47. ASF, Diplomatico, Spedale degli Innocenti, 27 July 1475.

48. ASF, Diplomatico, Spedale degli Innocenti, 18 January 1477 [modern = 1478].

49. AOIF, Ricordanze A (XII, 1), fol. 115v, n.d.

50. Martines, *Social World,* app. 2, table 4, 364; table 5, 366.

51. AOIF, Ricordanze A (XII, 1), fol. 116v, 12 May 1470.

52. AOIF, Ricordanze A (XII, 1), fol. 94v, 26 May 1467.

53. David Herlihy, "Viellir à Florence au quattrocento," *Annales: Economie, Société, Civilisations* 24 (1969): 1341–42. Christiane Klapisch-Zuber, "Fiscalité et demographie en Toscane," *Annales: Economie, Société, Civilisations* 24 (1969): 1327–28.

54. Richard Goldthwaite and W. R. Rearick, "The Ospedale di San Paolo in Florence," *Mitteilungen Des Kunsthistoriches Institut von Florenz* 21, no. 3 (1977): 221–306.

55. AOIF, Ricordanze A (XII, 1), fol. 115v, n.d.

56. ASF, Archivio Notarile Antecosimiano, S 639, fol. 83v, 17 September 1444.

57. AOIF, Ricordanze A (XII,1), fol. 10r, 3 September 1445: "e io Lapo di Piero Pacini spedalingho e ghovernatore di detto spedale prometto per me e per miei sucesori alla detta Mona Lisa per discrezione e per suo susido ongnanno dalle barili otto di vino vermiglio cioè barili quattro daverno e quattro destate e uno mezzo orcio d'olio buono e some sei di lengne grosse e tre some di fraschoni e questo sa fare ognanno mentre chella detta Mona Lisa vive. E dopo La sua morte è libera La chasa di nonavelle a dare più detti vino olio e legne. . . ."

58. AOIF, Obblighi Perpetui e Commessi (LXXVII, 1–5).

59. AOIF, Testamenta et Donationes (IX,1), fol. 147r.

60. Ibid.

61. AOIF, Testamenta et Donationes (IX,1), fols. 98v–100v.

62. ASF, Diplomatico, Spedale degli Innocenti, 10 September 1477.

63. AOIF, Ricordanze A (XII,1), fol. 106v, 27 July 1468.

64. ASF, Diplomatico, Spedale degli Innocenti, 11 September 1492, contains the papal bull of Alexander VI authorizing the construction of the chapel. See AOIF, Ricordanze A (XII,1), fol. 99v, July 1484, for Matteo di Simone Gondi's testament.

65. ASF, Diplomatico, Spedale degli Innocenti, 19 July 1494.

66. Brian Pullan, *Rich and Poor in Renaissance Venice* (Cambridge, Mass., 1971), 159–60.

67. AOIF, Testamenta et Donationes (IX,1), fols. 94v–98r, 29 June 1436.

68. AOIF, Ricordanze A (XII,1), fol. 66v, 6 June 1465.

69. AOIF, Ricordanze A (XII,1), fol. 113r, n.d. The position of this document in the volume suggests early 1469 as the most plausible date.

70. Ibid.

71. Ibid.

72. AOIF, Ricordanze A (XII,1), fol. 113v, 20 July 1469.

73. Richard Trexler, "Death and Testament in the Episcopal Constitutions of Florence (1327)," in *Renaissance Studies in Honor of Hans Baron,* ed. An-

thony Molho and John Tedeschi (De Kalb, 1970), 55–74. Idem, "The Bishop's Portion," *Traditio* 28 (1972): 397–450, and "Charity and the Defense of Urban Elites in the Italian Communes," in *The Rich, the Well-born, and the Powerful*, ed. F. Jaher (Urbana, 1973), 64–109.

74. AOIF, Ricordanze A (XII,1), fol. 148r, 12 August 1475.

75. AOIF, Contratti (X,1), fol. 3r, 29 January 1436.

76. Demetrio Marzi, *La cancelleria della repubblica fiorentina* (Rocca di San Casciano, 1910), 128–32, 161–62, 465.

77. ASF, Archivio Notarile Antecosimiano, S 637, fol. 53r, 20 July 1440.

78. ASF, Archivio Notarile Antecosimiano, S 637, fol. 71r, 16 September 1440.

79. ASF, Archivio Notarile Antecosimiano, S 637, fol. 116r, 15 November 1440.

80. ASF, Archivio Notarile Antecosimiano, S 637, fol. 193r, 1 July 1441.

81. ASF, Archivio Notarile Antecosimiano, S 637, fols. 306r–393v, 24 January 1441 [modern = 1442].

82. ASF, Arte della Seta, 246, fols. 98v, 99v.

83. Martines, *Social World*, 342.

84. ASF, Archivio Notarile Antecosimiano, S 637, fols. 391r–393v, 24 January 1441 [modern = 1442].

85. ASF, Archivio Notarile Antecosimiano, S 637, fols. 379r–380r, 24 January 1441 [modern = 1442].

86. ASF, Archivio Notarile Antecosimiano, S 637, fol. 385r, 24 January 1441 [modern = 1442].

87. ASF, Archivio Notarile Antecosimiano, S 637, fol. 387r, 24 January 1441 [modern = 1442].

88. ASF, Archivio Notarile Antecosimiano, S 637, fol. 387v, 24 January 1441 [modern = 1442].

89. ASF, Archivio Notarile Antecosimiano, S 637, fols. 388r–390v, 24 January 1441 [modern = 1442].

90. ASF, Archivio Notarile Antecosimiano, S 637, fols. 391r–393v, 24 January 1441 [modern = 1442].

91. Ibid.

92. AOIF, Contratti (X,1), fol. 45v, 12 February 1441 [modern = 1442]. The *operai* were Luca di Matteo Panzano, Pagolo di Bernardo Altoviti, and Lodovico di Cece da Verrazano.

93. Ibid.

94. AOIF, Contratti (X,1), fol. 46v, 16 February 1441 [modern = 1442].

95. AOIF, Testamenta et Donationes (IX,1), fol. 4v–7v, 17 June 1411.

96. AOIF, Debitori e Creditori (CXX,1), fols. 10 left–10 right; 167 left–167 right.

97. AOIF, Testamenta et Donationes (IX,1), fol. 4v–7v, 17 June 1411.

98. AOIF, Testamenta et Donationes (IX,1), fols. 94v–98r, 29 June 1436.

99. AOIF, Testamenta et Donationes (IX,1), fols. 98v–99r, 25 September 1439.

100. AOIF, Testamenta et Donationes (IX,1), fols. 169r–170r, 4 April 1468.

101. AOIF, Ricordanze A (XII,1), fol. 121r, 10 April 1471.

102. AOIF, Ricordanze A (XII,1), fol. 122r, 29 April 1471.

103. ASF, Provvisioni Registri, 161, fol. 168r, cited in L. F. Marks, "The Financial Oligarchy in Florence under Lorenzo," in *Renaissance Studies,* ed. E. F. Jacob (London, 1960), 127.

104. ASF, Provvisioni Registri, 142, fols. 380v–382r, 30 December 1451, which petitioned the commune for the hospital's participation in the *Monte delle Doti,* made two references to such legislation: The *Provvisioni* of 12 December 1380 and 31 December 1415. Both these forbade alienation of *Monte* credits or interest to nontaxpaying institutions except by special petition.

105. AOIF, Ricordanze A (XII,1), fol. 130v, 11 April 1472. The notice is mistakenly dated in the original as 1471.

106. ASF, Provvisioni Registri, 175, fols. 160r–162v, 18 February 1483 [modern = 1484].

107. AOIF, Ricordanze B (XII,2), fol. 35r, 18 August 1483.

108. AOIF, Ricordanze A (XII,1), fol. 121r, 10 April 1471.

109. Julius Kirshner and Anthony Molho, "The Dowry Fund and the Marriage Market in Early *Quattrocento* Florence," *Journal of Modern History* 50, no. 3 (1978): 403–38.

110. Other motives besides an attempt to retire the debt of the *Monte Comune* may also have been at stake. One of the grounds on which the theologian Angelo di Chivasso defended the *Monte delle Doti* from the charge of usury was that it was not a loan, but a temporary transfer of rights to *Monte* credits. Kirshner, *Pursuing Honor While Avoiding Sin: the Monte delle Doti of Florence* (Milan, 1978), 48.

111. Marks, "Financial Oligarchy," 130–31.

112. AOIF, Testamenta et Donationes (IX,1), fols. 4v–7v, 17 June 1411.

113. AOIF, Ricordanze A (XII,4), fol. 276v, 27 August 1451.

114. AOIF, Testamenta et Donationes (IX,1), fols. 27r–28v, 14 July 1419.

115. AOIF, Testamenta et Donationes (IX,1), fols. 29r–32v, 19 April 1419.

116. AOIF, Testamenta et Donationes (IX,1), fols. 68v–71r, 15 June 1430.

117. AOIF, Testamenta et Donationes (IX,1), fols. 37r–44r, 23 March 1419 [modern = 1420].

118. AOIF, Ricordanze A (XII,1), fol. 59r, 11 July 1458.

119. AOIF, Ricordanze A (XII,1), fol. 104r, 21 February 1467 [modern = 1468].

120. Kirshner and Molho, "Dowry Fund and Marriage Market," 423.

121. Ibid.

122. ASF, Arte della Seta, 246, fols. 22v, 29r, 30v.

123. AOIF, Ricordanze A (XII,1), fol. 77r, 29 July 1468; fols. 107r–108r, 28 July 1468.

124. AOIF, Ricordanze A (XII,1), fol. 87v, 29 January 1466 [modern = 1467].

125. AOIF, Ricordanze A (XII,1), fol. 105v, 10 May 1468.

126. AOIF, Ricordanze A (XII,1), fol. 144v, 18 August 1474.

127. AOIF, Ricordanze A (XII,1), fol. 140v, 11 January 1473 [modern = 1474]; fol. 146r, 4 April 1475.

Chapter 4

Hospital and Family

Certainly the Innocenti's most distinctive architectural feature is its loggia. Recent studies of domestic architecture cite the *loggie* of houses as evidence of the vitality of the clan and the extended family. These studies differ in their treatment of when these private *loggie* disappear, but to date they all make the assumption that where a loggia is, there is a statement of kin and family solidarity.[1] Yet Alberti's treatise on architecture, written in the 1430s and following Vitruvius closely, notes that in domestic architecture, the line between portico and vestibule divided the private from the public world, with the loggia, or portico, planted firmly in the public world. According to Alberti, the portico is "for the common use of the citizens. Places for walking within the house . . . do not belong at all to the public, but entirely to the inhabitants."[2] In book 3 of his treatise on architecture, Alberti wrote that "just in front of the vestibule nothing can be more noble than a handsome portico, where the youth . . . may employ themselves in all manner of exercise."[3]

Similar principles were in force in Alberti's description of public architecture. In book 8, Alberti invoked Plato's admonition that "in all piazzas there should be spaces left for nurses with their children to meet." Not only did this strengthen children by exposing them to fresh air, it left nurses in sight of each other, "so that they [the nurses] might grow neater and more delicate, and less liable to negligence among so many careful observers in the same business." Such a square would be most suitably adorned by:

a handsome portico, under which the old men may spend the heat of the day or be mutually serviceable to one another. Besides that, the presence of the fathers may deter and restrain the youth . . . from the mischief and folly natural to their age.[4]

141

Alberti recommended that porticoes should be "raised above the level of the ground, one-fifth part of the width, and that their width should be equal to half the height of the columns, including their entablature." These porticoes should be raised precisely because their function is public, a point Alberti reinforces in his discussion of the piazza's potential uses for spectacles, festivals, and displays.[5] Certainly in the late fifteenth century, according to Landucci's diary, the space in front of the Innocenti was the locus of dramatic conversion scenes in which youth renounced their mischief and folly and began at least temporary careers of pious good works on Carnival day.[6]

If Filarete incorporated some ideas from the Innocenti into his design of an ideal city in Milan in the 1450s, he specifically opposed steps that led from the piazza to the portico on the grounds that they encouraged public use of space that should be private.[7] Although the Innocenti's steps were not added until 1457, the original plan for the Innocenti anticipated the steps leading up to the loggia. On 6 August 1420, the Tower officials acted on a petition presented by the *operai* concerning the "new foundling hospital that is being constructed on the Piazza de' Servi of Florence, which Piazza belongs to the aforesaid commune." The *operai* wanted

> to be able to add to the edifice certain steps on the above piazza extending to a height of 3 1/2 *braccia,* and along the entire length of the facade of the said hospital, so that the steps will be in agreement with the loggia of said hospital.[8]

The Tower officials took into consideration not only the "genuine piety" of the enterprise, but also expressed their confidence that such an addition "is becoming to the beauty of the aforesaid city."[9] Only two conditions were imposed: that the steps extend no further out than the roof, and that the Innocenti pay the city for any encroachment of the steps into the piazza.[10]

Thus, from the very beginning of the hospital's construction, the Innocenti's portico was conceived of as public space. Brunelleschi's departure from the building program in the mid-1420s suggests, as Saalman has pointed out, that only the loggia was sufficiently public to require Brunelleschi's depth of talent.[11] The remainder of the hospital could be deduced from the proportions of the loggia, and indeed, only the scale and proportions of the Innocenti's loggia set its ground plan apart from earlier Tuscan hospitals such as Santa Maria Maddalena in Volterra, San Matteo in Florence, and Sant'Antonio a La Lastra a Signa.[12]

Facades such as those of the Innocenti or of the Loggia dei Lanzi held a significance that was crucial to a civic sense of beauty, proportion, and urban design. In this respect it is no mere coincidence that the decision to add a loggia to the hospital of San Paolo in 1455–56 was associated with its elevation to greater civic prominence.[13] The very architecture of the Innocenti's public face, its facade, could be associated with children and their wet nurses, with fathers restraining their adolescent sons. At the same time its interior space as well as organizational structure, suggested just that sense of privacy and family that Alberti's treatise on architecture argued should be enclosed behind the portico.

Yet the internal administrative structure of the Innocenti cannot adequately be described with reference to a single model of organization. Its architectural lexicon mixed familial and monastic metaphors, the loggia with the cloister. The hierarchy required unquestioning obedience and uniformity of dress, yet allowed many dependents to remain married while serving the institution in a full-time capacity. In the sixteenth century, Erasmus would attempt to formulate a humanist conception of community by describing a city as "nothing but a great monastery."[14] Goro Dati's fifteenth-century *Istoria di Firenze* had already noted that the expenses of any of Florence's great hospitals could make it a city in its own right. In the same breath that he noted the magnificence of the city's hospitals, he praised the city's domestic architecture.[15] The fusion in the Florentine imagination between charitable institutions, domesticity, and the civic life supports the assertions of recent scholarship that the boundaries between sacred and secular had undergone rapid alteration in the late fourteenth and early fifteenth centuries. Charity elevated urban, civic, and political life to a level of sanctity that once only the cloister could compel. The organization of the fiscal and administrative life of the hospital of the Innocenti borrowed the techniques and vocabulary of the cloister, the political arena, and the family, if not in equal measure, at least with equal respect.

Other administrative and organizational details bear witness to the notion that the hospital was not only a community or a forum, but also a family. When the Innocenti petitioned for participation in the city's dowry fund in 1451, it asked to have the same claim to a return on its investment that Florentine fathers had.[16] Numerous times, the hospital's personnel referred to the hospital as the "famiglia" or the "brigata."[17]

Husbands of successfully married female foundlings were referred to as "our son-in-law." Just as the institution encouraged its *commessi* to devote their lives to the hospital in pairs, so did certain staff positions assume paternal and maternal roles. The hospital also referred to itself as the "casa," and recorded its expenses as "spesi di casa," house expenses.

Staff at the Ospedale degli Innocenti

The officials responsible for managing the purchase and sale of real estate, as well as for debt management, were the consuls of the silk guild and the *operai,* or trustees, of the Innocenti. As brief as the tenure of these officials may have been, it certainly compared favorably with that of communal officeholders. The consulate changed hands every six months; the *operai,* annually, compared with two to three months for communal officeholders. Both the offices of consul and *operaio* were elective, and both followed the procedures specified for other guild offices.

The role of *operaio,* as opposed to that of guild consul, underwent dramatic changes over the course of the fifteenth century, but throughout the period the *opera* of the Innocenti was more specific and limited than comparable bodies. The Innocenti's *operai* were direct supervisors of the hospital's building program beginning in 1419. In fourteenth- and fifteenth-century Siena, however, the Opera del Duomo was a major corporate participant in the politics of the Sienese commune, as was, to a much lesser extent, the *opera* of Santa Maria del Fiore in Florence. At the Innocenti, *operai* made the major decisions concerning architectural design and the quantity and quality of building materials. As was true with most *operai,* once the building program was largely complete, the office evolved into a sort of trusteeship or guardianship. In 1449 the guild formally marked the transition of the *operai* from overseers of the hospital's construction to guardians of the institution by noting that "the operai were made purveyors and visitors of the hospital, with their sweeping powers restored and renewed."[18]

The Innocenti's *operai,* nevertheless, operated quite independently during the hospital's construction, with guild consuls making decisions only about the allocation of fiscal resources and the hiring of major hospital officials. In the 1440s and 1450s, however, all decisions that required a cooperative effort were made by consuls and *operai* in concert. Indeed, by the 1470s one cannot treat the consuls, the Council of Thirty-Six, and the *operai* as separate entities. By the 1480s, this newly consolidated group not only decided on the larger questions of debt and real estate, but also had to approve the purchase of farm animals and beasts of burden. These deliberative bodies in combination were also minutely involved in the everyday business of hiring and firing the most casual personnel, duties that had previously been delegated to numerous *fattori*, treasurers, superintendents, and other employees.[19] Decisions made during the first phases of the hospital's construction demonstrate most convincingly the independent role the *operai* played in the early 1420s. So involved were *operai* in the artistic decisions affecting the Innocenti that one of their number, Francesco della Luna, continues to be mistaken for an architect. One recent historian has even called Francesco "Brunelleschi's friend and pupil."[20]

Vasari, in the sixteenth century, appears to have begun the tradition of describing Francesco della Luna as an architect. A close reading of fifteenth-century sources, even the ones that Vasari used, does not support the traditional description. Admittedly, one of these sources, Antonio Manetti's biography of Brunelleschi, is itself suspect and its chronology undermined by other, more reliable documentary sources. Manetti, who wrote his version of Brunelleschi's life in the 1460s, was naturally concerned to place his subject in the best possible light, and his portrait of the antagonism between Francesco della Luna and Brunelleschi is doubtless overdrawn. According to Manetti, Brunelleschi "was asked by the guild of Por Santa Maria, the patron who had responsibility, to construct the portico of the Ospedale degli Innocenti." Brunelleschi drew up a plan for the portico, a plan that was still extant in the 1460s and that could be consulted in the guild's headquarters. Brunelleschi, moreover, had issued strict instructions to his craftsmen about how they should proceed in his absence. Upon the architect's return from Pistoia in 1427, according to Manetti, he was aghast at alterations that had been made to the facade. Manetti cited numerous deviations, "one of which can still be seen, where the architrave takes a sharp turn downward to meet the plinth of the loggia."[21]

Manetti himself did not describe a specific encounter between architect and *operaio*. The *Libro di Antonio Billi*, written nearly twenty years later, contains Brunelleschi's famous retort to the allegedly presumptuous *operaio* who claimed in his own defense to have copied the Baptistery: "there is only one mistake in that building, and you have copied and immortalized it." According to the *Libro di Antonio Billi,* Brunelleschi wished the alterations to be destroyed and was dissuaded "only by sweet words from the *operai.*"[22]

However flawed these accounts may have been in their chronology (the alterations to the facade took place at least two years after the infamous encounter), they are more convincing as a portrait of an *operaio* who had a high and perhaps unjustified opinion of his own architectural expertise. According to Manetti, Brunelleschi's original plans were bungled because of "the arrogance of one of the *operai,* who did not want to appear to have less authority than Filippo." These lapses in taste and skill were "nothing less than the presumption of the person who had it built in that manner on his own authority." Lest his readers have any doubts, Manetti elaborated his description of this leading citizen even further in his chronology of the building of the silk guild's headquarters. "One can see," he wrote:

> that the pilaster is not well-placed and that whoever put it there did not clearly understand Filippo's idea and did not take into consideration how the other corners were done. This considerable defect was due to a citizen of good reputation who thought he was a connoisseur and who expended much effort on these matters and thrust himself forward. The deviation from all those arrangements concerning the portico and the facade of the Ospedale degli Innocenti was due to this same man.[23]

The *Libro di Antonio Billi* would positively identify "this same man" as Francesco della Luna, who was "opinionated about architecture."[24]

The most cautious inference from these sources suggests at least that *operai* had strong opinions about architecture and might cite other buildings, however amateurishly, in defense of those opinions. More importantly, whether Manetti's account is accurate or not, *operai* could and did impose their opinions on a project. Account books record payment for "a meal held on the 29th of the past month [June 1427], attended by the consuls, masters, and other merchants." The purpose of this meal was to discuss and celebrate "a certain decision taken concerning the building program." This decision focused on the controversial alterations to the facade, alterations that would not take place for another two years.[25] Although Brunelleschi was not counted as present, Francesco della Luna was, and Antonio di Tuccio Manetti's father, Tuccio di Mara-bottino Manetti, became a guild consul only six months after the meeting took place, and therefore would have been likely to possess enough secondhand knowledge of the meeting to pass down a story of it to his son, Antonio di Tuccio.[26] One can only speculate that Tuccio's account of whatever differences of opinion did exist over the design of the facade might have become deliberately or unconsciously dramatized as a conflict between architect and *operaio*. The last evidence of Brunelleschi's involvement in the project, nevertheless, comes from before this meeting, so that the future of the hospital's building program rested not with him, but with the *operai*.[27] Moreover, at various times during the 1420s, Brunelleschi was not only a consulting engineer, but an *operaio* himself for at least three terms.[28]

One of Francesco della Luna's colleagues on the Works Committee was Goro di Stagio Dati, who also brought to bear on his task considerable knowledge of, and interest in, architecture. Creighton Gilbert has called the last pages of Dati's *Istoria di Firenze,* written in 1423, "the earliest guide to Florentine architecture."[29] In April 1420, Goro di Stagio Dati and Francesco della Luna authorized a payment of seventy-four lire to Jacopo di Giovanni da Montughi to purchase sufficient sand to make the first thousand *braccia* of the hospital's foundations. Recent commentators have seized on this authorization as an indication of Francesco della Luna's creative autonomy, but this document should surely be taken to demonstrate the involvement of *operai* in all phases of a construction project, from design to procurement and finally to completion.[30]

Two extant invitations to competitive bidding in the construction accounts outline quite precisely how the *operai,* or Works Committee, supervised a project and in what decisions the *operai* involved themselves. The first invitation, from 1424, proclaims the decision of the *operai* "to make nine vaults above the portico of the said hospital in front, where the columns are." The *operai* issued minute and detailed specifications. The vaults had to be cross vaults with centered supports, with curving "as such vaults require." The pilasters had to have "ridges that are well-defined, delicate, good and straight." The brick and *intonaco* were to be of the quality and specifications "that shall please the *operai*." The operai had to supply chains and tie-rods, which the contractors were to place under the vaults, starting "from each of the ten columns on the portico, beginning with the bracket above the entablature-plate . . . extending to the wall opposite said columns, so as to make them strong." All this work had to be "fine, neat, well-made, and strong, as is the practice of good master craftsmen."[31] As Baxandall has shown for the Innocenti's commission of Ghirlandaio's *Adoration of the Magi*,[32] the *operai* specified not only criteria of measurement, but also a well-defined set of aesthetic criteria: for the portico the ridges had to be "well-defined and delicate" as well as good and straight.

That the *operai* furnished the materials suggests that they had a thorough knowledge of the quality of materials required. When they found themselves beyond their expertise, they relied on their consultants; in this case, Filippo Brunelleschi. Thus, ironware for the vaults had to be cast in the "shape, length, size, and proportion to be decided by the contractor for the aforesaid Works Committee, Filippo di Ser Brunellesco." The *operai* also set the deadlines for delivery at each stage of a project. In this invitation to bid, all the ironware for the vaults had to arrive between 4 May and 15 August 1424.[33]

The second invitation is similar to the first. It invited applicants to appear before the *operai* or the purveyor "to give their sealed bids in writing concerning what they wish to charge per cubic *braccio* for building the wall," the height of which was not to exceed six *braccia*.[34] *Operai* might act in concert, as in these two invitations to bid, or alone, as Goro di Stagio Dati did when he negotiated a "contract, pact, and agreement" with Lorenzo di Giovanni that the latter would dredge enough gravel within three months to furnish a thousand cubic *braccia* of wall or face a penalty of twenty-five gold florins.[35]

Although a relationship between the office of *operaio* and the position of guild consul is evident, no hard and fast rules seemed to apply to define the nature of that relationship. A comparison of the lists of both groups strongly suggest that they were drawn from separate *borse*. Of the 133 *operai* who held office between 1419 and 1475, only sixteen (12 percent) were never guild consuls during their careers. Eighty-six *operai* (64 percent) held a silk guild consulate prior to their first term as an *operaio* of the hospital. Since the major guild offices changed hands every quarter and the office of *operaio* changed hands annually, guildsmen were much more likely to serve multiple terms as consul than as *operaio*.

Indeed, seventy-eight *operai* (60 percent) served only a single term as *operaio*. Another 28 percent served two terms. Rarely did *operai* serve three or more terms, and only one *operaio* (excluding those made op-

eraio for life) served as many as six terms, as did Salimbene di Lionardo Bartolini between 1420 and 1430. *Operai* were much more likely to hold multiple consulates. Over half of the *operai* held the guild consulate at least three times. Bernardo di Zanobi di ser Zello, for example, held the office of *operaio* three times, but was consul ten times between 1419 and 1452.

Whether or not the guild intentionally organized its officeholding this way, nevertheless the Innocenti could expect a majority of *operai* to have had considerable experience managing guild affairs. This experience, moreover, was managerial rather than strictly fiscal. Only in six cases had *operai* previously held the office of treasurer of the hospital. Indeed, in eleven cases the order was reversed, so that before 1448 most of the hospital's treasurers had experience as an *operaio*.

Four *operai* from 1419 to 1475 had the honor of being appointed overseers for life: Francesco della Luna, in 1433; Andrea Banchi, in 1452; Ser Filippo di Ser Ugolino Peruzzi, in 1438; and Mariotto di Dinozzo Lippi in 1460.[36] The hospital's *ricordanze* and account books chronicle the record of distinguished service of these four men to guild and hospital. Mariotto Lippi, for example, held the guild consulate four times and was an *operaio* of the Innocenti seven times before being appointed *operaio* for life. In 1444 the *balìa* apparently objected to the notion of lifetime terms for *operai,* and Francesco della Luna and Filippo di ser Ugolino Peruzzi lost their offices.[37] Yet in 1452 Andrea Banchi was appointed for life, and Mariotto Lippi's appointment for life came even later than that.[38] In rare instances, a whole group of *operai* might be elected for a second term, as happened in 1428. In 1429, this same group of *operai* was elected to a third term, perhaps because the construction project was in the critical phase of making important decisions about the extension of the facade.[39]

Even more rare than multiple terms as an *operaio* was the concurrence of an individual's tenure as *operaio* with his tenure as consul. In May 1424, for example, Lodovico di ser Viviano Neri became an *operaio,* but renounced his appointment in September to become consul. Likewise, Salimbene di Lionardo Bartolini gave up the office of *operaio* to become consul.[40] Again, however, no hard and fast rules applied, so that in thirteen other cases distributed throughout the period 1419–75 such *operai* as Goro di Stagio Dati (1420), Fruosini di Cece da Verrazzano (1422), Bernardo di Alamanno de' Medici (1444), and Lodovico di Lionardo Boni (1463) held both offices simultaneously.[41]

The endurance of individuals in both guild and hospital offices is eclipsed by the endurance of families. Nearly a quarter of the *operai* between 1419 and 1475 were sons, brothers, or fathers of other *operai*, and a much higher percentage of *operai* had close relatives who served as guild consul. Worth noting, finally, is the presence among the *operai* of figures who were either writers of treatises on the family or "participants" in humanist dialogues on the family. Giannozzo Manetti, who was an *operaio* in 1436, was the author of a treatise on consolation legitimizing the expression of mourning and grief for lost sons.[42] Agnolo Pandolfini, whose sons appear several times in the lists of *operai*, appears himself as an interlocutor in Alberti's other dialogues.[43]

The guild consuls first exercised their power to appoint a superintendent in February 1422, when they elected Ser Lodovico Bertini of Tavernelle. The agreement between Ser Lodovico and the consuls is remarkable not only for its detail in describing the position of superintendent and the nature of the relationship between guild and hospital, but also for its illumination of what the guild perceived its charitable mission to be and the importance of that mission to the spiritual well-being of the polity.

This contract describes the guild as "most powerfully committed to the conservation of those children whose parents...would deny them even nourishment," and the consuls of the guild as

> men embracing, sustaining, and feeding the aforesaid children and exercising their acumen and expertise in this pious work. These are the men whose arms are ceaselessly extended in charitable embrace, and of whom it is written: He sees and is exceedingly glad.[44]

It is the visibility and publicity of "this charitable enterprise that shines in this lovely city," and that dictated that the institution be "well-ruled and healthily governed."[45] The consuls were well aware that upon their efficient and compassionate administration were pinned the city's hopes for worthiness in God's eyes. Moreover, as though divine stewardship were not a sufficiently heavy burden, the faithful of Florence, who entrusted the hospital's administrators with their gifts of alms and property, also required solicitous stewardship, not to mention "the aforesaid children, so completely destitute of help" who depended utterly on good management to be fed and nourished.[46]

Thus, the consuls sought as superintendent someone of "foresight, who is suitable and of good reputation, who has the knowledge, inclination, and aptitude to govern and rule" the Innocenti, and who could distribute properly the revenues of the hospital "in aid of the miserable persons and aforesaid children, as well as in the construction, building, maintenance, and increase of this hospital."[47] In Ser Lodovico Bertini di Maestro Jacopo, Florentine citizen and notary, the consuls felt they had found "a man of good conscience, virtue, honesty, and habits commended by all and concerning whom no sinister background can be presumed to exist." The consuls expressed the hope that through Ser Lodovico's industry, skill, and care, "the hospital would be healthfully ruled, governed, and supported in growth."[48]

The superintendent's term was set to be two years, but he could be recalled at the pleasure and command of the guild and the consuls, who at any time reserved the power "to choose who is to govern the said hospital and to administer its property, business, and legal rights." In more specific terms the superintendent's duties were to "govern, rule, protect, and administer the said hospital and its children, familiars, staff, property, and claims."[49] He was empowered to rent property and to terminate leases, and to hire and fire the labor for that property. It also fell to the superintendent to seek and receive *Monte* credits for the hospital. His powers with respect to governing the hospital were to be considered equal to those of the guild consuls.

Lodovico's first assigned task was to draw up an inventory of the property, possessions, and legal claims of the hospital. He was strictly accountable to the guild consuls for every detail of his administration, and he was instructed that he must turn over all administrative rewards, surpluses or any other revenues at the "request, mandate, and pleasure" of the guild. For his part, Lodovico agreed "to exhibit the proper obedience and deference to the consuls of the said guild," meaning in particular "always to obey the orders of the said consuls," submitting himself to their judgment and voluntarily submitting his resignation should the consuls feel it appropriate, and to "govern wisely and administer the goods of the hospital without damage, fraud, or malice."[50]

Despite, then, the superintendent's heavy responsibilities and his authorization to act on behalf of the guild consuls, the guild was quite anxious to set out explicitly its control over the position and the unquestioning obedience demanded of the superintendent. Here, too, one senses the anxiety that a single superintendent might threaten the guild's control over its enterprise—hence, the guild's emphasis not only on obedience and accountability, but also accessibility of records.

The treasurers of the Innocenti, identified in the account books as *camerlinghi dell'opera*, were elected every year just as the *operai* were. The treasurer of the hospital was also a sort of operations manager. During the priorate of Ser Niccolò di Piero, Lapo di Piero Pacini described himself as "treasurer and governor" of the hospital of the Innocenti.[51] In 1448, the office of treasurer "was placed under the prior" when Lapo di Piero Pacini was removed. In 1449, this decision was found wanting, for on 12 April 1449 "the treasurer was raised to the level of prior. And the prior shall never again appoint the treasurer."[52]

The major effect of this decision on the office of treasurer was to concentrate it in the hands of fewer people. Where the hospital had employed twenty-six successive treasurers between 1422 and 1448, it employed only thirteen between 1449 and 1484. Moreover, from 1472–81, the Innocenti's treasury was in the hands of a single family. From 1472–77, Zanobi Landi held the office alone. Bonaiuto Landi joined him for the two years 1478–79; both were replaced by Jacopo di Jacopo Landi until 1481.

A year after Francesco di Giovanni Tesori became prior in 1483, he assumed the concurrent post of treasurer, doubtless as a result of the pressing and disastrous financial bind in which the Innocenti found itself in 1483 and 1484.[53] Nevertheless, when Francesco di Giovanni agreed to serve at no salary, the guild stipulated that he must "observe the practices of his predecessors."[54]

If the guild was consolidating its authority in the 1440s by making the treasurer more accountable to the guild, other offices in the hospital also underwent a process of compression and consolidation. Thus in 1446 Piero di Andrea di Piero, who had been superintendent in the early 1440s:

> was rehired to apply his person to all the needs and activities of the hospital, and to do all those things that are necessary for the said hospital. He was hired by the Venerable Niccolò di Piero of Florence, prior and superintendent of the abovesaid hospital . . . by seven unanimous affirmative votes.[55]

In addition to the hiring of the treasurer and of men-of-all-trades such as Ser Piero, the women who applied to the hospital of the Innocenti as governesses could also expect to undertake tasks that were beyond strict definition. In August 1449, for example, the Innocenti interviewed and employed a succession of aspiring governesses. Their responsibilities, in addition to watching over the children of the hospital, included the baking of "pane bucati" and "to do honestly" anything else that might be required of them. These governesses worked "for charity" plus reimbursement of out-of-pocket expenses. Mona Nicolosa, the first one hired, was sent away a month later because of her "scandalous behavior." On 25 August 1449 the hospital intended to hire a replacement, but she received no payments, and five days later the hospital employed Mona Druida from Bologna. She stayed for at least five months, receiving a payment of five lire in January 1450.[56] The *commesse* whom the hospital subsequently hired, such as Mona Maddalena, widow of Michele di Francesco, "we hired today . . . to watch over the children." Her charge was "to serve all the poor abandoned children for charity and for the sake of her soul and because of her sins."[57] Women could and did achieve positions considered important in the hospital. In the early 1460s, for example, Mona Smeralda, the wife of Bartolomeo, the hospital's treasurer, held a position called "governess of the *commesse e velate*," (i.e., of the female "third-order" employees). The *Ricordanze* describe her as a *spedalingha*, suggesting that she had complete responsibility for the residents and staff of the women's cloister of the hospital. The hospital called on her, among other things, to bear witness to a document dictating the disposition of the belongings of the *operaio* Mariotto Lippi.[58]

In addition to the women who were hired either to watch over the younger children or to supervise the *commesse*, the hospital contracted skilled artisans to teach the older girls of the hospital. Although weaving was both a male and a female occupation, these contracts specified girls only, perhaps because occupational expectations for boys were higher. In August 1457, the Innocenti hired Mona Apollonia, wife of Piero Lippi from Colpaia, for an annual salary of eleven florins, "because she is a very talented woman in every way, especially at weaving garments. She was hired to teach weaving to our little girls."[59] Here we have yet another example of married couples working for the hospital: her husband Piero was paid in September 1456 for his sixteen months' work as a gardener at the Innocenti.[60]

Although the hospital's educational program comes through clearly in the adoption contracts discussed in the next chapter, the evidence is sparse concerning what, besides weaving, children within the hospital might have been taught between the ages of five and seven, or above the age of seven if they were not fortunate enough to gain an apprenticeship in the trades or household service. The most likely source of instruction during the fifteenth century was the chaplains (sixteenth- and seventeenth-century frescoes clearly document the presence of a master and a classroom in the later period).[61] In 1454, Ser Giovanni di Biagio, a priest, "stayed eight months or so to instruct the children. He also officiated in church" for a total salary for those months of six florins.[62]

Most chaplains, as Pinto has found at the hospital of San Gallo, stayed only a few months at the Innocenti as interns, although longer stays were far from rare. In 1466, for example, Ser Antonio di Giovanni "came to stay here in the House as chaplain in the same way as the other chaplains. We must give him three lire per month as wages." Ser Antonio remained only for two and a half months.[63] Ser Bartolomeo d'Andrea da Volterra, hired in 1464, stayed on for three years and collected a salary of fifty lire per year.[64] Two other chaplains, however, received an annual salary of only thirty-six lire during their two-year stays.[65] At the other extreme of longevity, the consuls and *operai* in 1483 assigned the prior of San Gallo to "our chapel of the Annunziata [in via San Gallo] for the rest of his life without a salary."[66] In July 1482, the consuls and *operai* hired Matteo di Figline to be chaplain "in the chapel of Our Lady located in the cloister" for a salary of forty lire per year plus expenses. This particular appointment had resulted from a specific bequest of Mona Nana, widow of Uccio della Lastra.[67] The Innocenti hired another chaplain, Carlo Jachopo di Maestro Agnolo, on 1 April 1483, "to play the organ and to say mass."[68]

No less important than those who ministered to the souls of children and staff were the doctors and barbers who ministered to their bodies. The records of the Innocenti substantiate Katharine Park's claim concerning the religiosity and charitable devotion of the city's doctors.[69] At no time in the fifteenth century did the Innocenti experience any difficulty procuring the services of physicians to attend to the care of sick children at no salary and rewarded with only tokens of appreciation. The Innocenti from its beginnings had an infirmary in which to isolate the sicker children, and presumably those children with diseases recognized to be contagious.

The first records of physicians date to March 1445, or a month after the Innocenti first opened its doors. Lapo di Piero Pacini:

> the treasurer and governor of the said hospital...hired and confirmed as doctors of the said hospital, for the love of God and the salvation of their souls, without any salary, these venerable and famous doctors of Medicine: Maestro Mariotto di Niccolò and Maestro Lorenzo di Francesco di Domenico. They agreeably accepted out of good will and were quite satisfied. Thus they promised to do what God and the Virgin Mary [would have them do] earning their rewards first on their bodies and then their souls.[70]

On 26 April 1445, Lapo hired a third physician, Maestro Bandino di Maestro Giovanni Banducci, who for motives of love and charity "wishes to become a doctor of this House, and will come here at any hour and for any need to practice medicine for no fee and for the love of God and the salvation of his own soul."[71] In April 1451, however, the prior of the Innocenti rewarded them in terms of their more immediate needs by stipulating that every doctor in the employ of the hospital would receive a capon for All Saints Day and a "chavretto" for Easter.[72] Of the approximately forty physicians practicing their art in Florence in the middle of the fifteenth century, the Innocenti would have been hard-pressed indeed to find three of standing or credentials equal to the three that Lapo di Piero Pacini hired. Maestro Mariotto di Niccolò was a household physician to the Medici and to Piero the Gouty in particular. In addition to Maestro Mariotto's charitable work for the Innocenti, he worked for the hospital of Santa Maria Nuova, to whose library he donated an extensive collection of books.[73] Maestro Lorenzo di Francesco, who had matriculated in the physicians' guild in 1432, was quite well-to-do, apparently from wealth he had earned rather than inherited.[74] Maestro Bandino Banducci was employed by Santa Maria Nuova, as was Maestro Mariotto. Although the Catasto reported a rather modest net worth for him, he was in a relatively high tax bracket.[75] Of the three, only Maestro Bandino was listed in the 1427 Catasto. At that point he was forty-five years old, and would already have been in his early sixties when he agreed to work for the Ospedale degli Innocenti. His father was Francesco Datini's personal physician,[76] and Datini subsidized the younger Banducci's expenses for medical school.[77] Thus, in its early years the hospital of the Innocenti had three reputable physicians in its employ, in comparison to Santa Maria Nuova, which had six.[78]

From the 1450s on, doctors received not only a gift for festive occasions, but also a certain amount of grain per year. Maestro Mariotto, for example, who was rehired in 1458, was to receive twelve *staia* of barley in return for his promise "to come for every need of the House."[79] In 1467 Maestro Piero di Chomino da Novara:

> a Lombard doctor, came to serve the needs of the sick in our hospital
> . . . and at the hospital of San Gallo, with the agreement that for his
> effort he shall receive thirty *staia* of grain for each year he shall serve
> in the hospital. He began on 1 August 1466 with this understanding:
> that he must, in addition to practicing medicine, send us a barber who
> will cut the hair of the *brigata* of the hospital as well as of the hospital
> of San Gallo, that is, those chaplains and laymen who need a haircut.
> If the barber serves at the hospital's expense for four *staia*, then Maes-
> tro Piero [will receive only] twenty-six.

Maestro Piero served until the end of 1468, thus receiving 44 *staia* altogether.[80] In 1482, a Maestro Alberto di Jacopo Borselli from Volterra agreed to "attend with all solicitude possible to the care of our family whenever any illness befalls it." For his trouble he was to receive fifteen *staia* of grain per year, a goose for All Saints and a "chavretto" for Easter.[81] It does not appear that the Innocenti in the fifteenth century set aside a separate area for a pharmacy, but the hospital did rely very much on the services of pharmacists within the city. During Maestro Piero's tenure, for example, the Innocenti bought "an ounce of common pills," as well as almonds and rice from Giovanni di Matteo.[82]

Although Maestro Piero had been instructed to "send us a barber," the hospital more customarily hired its barbers directly. When, in 1482, the hospital gave Maestro Piero di Puccio his back wages of ten *staia* of grain, his title was "barber" but he was described as a "[former] doctor" who was to be given the remainder of his salary for "the time he spent practicing medicine on our family."[83] Until 1384 the statutes of the guild of Doctors, Apothecaries, and Grocers excluded barbers. Only after the failure of the barbers to form their own guild during the Ciompi revolt were they admitted to the doctors' guild. Indeed, in practice, all sorts of claimants to the art of healing who could demonstrate their competence were admitted to the profession. Finally, the confraternity of Santa Maria del Croce al Tempio had both a physician and a barber in its employ to care for prisoners and condemned criminals.[84]

Maestro Piero di Puccio was originally hired in 1449 as both doctor and barber, and the only way in which he seems set apart from his more illustrious colleagues at the Innocenti is by his salary, which was paid for his double duty as barber. "For his effort he shall receive twelve lire per year to shave and adorn the men of the hospital." In addition to practicing medicine, he was to "draw blood whenever it is necessary and to do so, moreover, with diligence and love."[85] When the hospital offered to renew Maestro Piero's contract in 1451, the prior drew up his contract to read that Piero would:

> shave, draw blood, and treat the *famiglia* for no charge ... and he will send a young person every Friday morning to shave the prior and treasurer for 12 lire per year.[86]

In the 1480s the hospital permanently replaced Maestro Piero with another barber who also qualified in medicine, Maestro Vezzano di Giovanni Benvenuti, who was charged to "attend to the care of our family and to heal them, cauterize them, and extract their teeth," all for twenty *staia* of grain per year.[87] When the barber Bartolomeo di Francesco's contract came up for renewal in 1471, it authorized him to shave "our entire staff at San Gallo" and to cauterize the children there "who have need of it." He also did dental work, and "all other things necessary for the House that pertain to his trade," for 14 *staia* of grain per year.[88]

In addition to doctors, the hospital also employed accountants, solicitors and notaries. In the latter case the notary was usually the guild's notary as well. The tenure of the hospital's notaries was commonly quite long: Ser Uberto Martini's career spanned at least two decades, beginning with the hospital's foundation. His assistant, Ser Silvano di Giovanni di Fruosino, replaced him at his death in 1456.[89] Both names appear on the Innocenti's contracts as early as the 1440s. Notaries received twelve florins per year for the post, comparable to the compensation paid to the guild's purveyor.[90]

Solicitors and lawyers are more rarely mentioned in connection with the quotidian administrative life of the hospital, but notarial protocols abound with evidence of lawyers who argued on behalf of the hospital when benefactors' families contested wills or neighbors disputed the boundaries of the hospital's estates. The *Entrata e Uscita*, for example, recorded a payment in March 1456 "to the lawyers of the hospital, in the amount of half [the expenses] of nine lawyers [split] with the guild of Por Santa Maria."[91] Often a guild official would be appointed as a solicitor for the hospital's affairs, as was the case with Marco di Luca di Marco, the guild's purveyor, who was empowered "to do everything concerning matters affecting our hospital."[92]

If the turnover of doctors, lawyers, and notaries was comparatively low, the cooks, gardeners, storekeepers, and millers came and went more frequently and more casually. In August 1449 the Innocenti hired a certain Nanni di Francesco, called "Caprese," whose specialty was making barrels and storing wine in them, and who quite bluntly informed the prior that "he did not want less than four lire per month" for this work.[93] Often the duties of gardeners and storekeepers were indistinguishable. Even more frequently, descriptions of jobs at this level were vague and generalized. Thus in October 1466, "Matteo di Giovanni from Pratovecchio came to stay with us in house to handle matters as they come up ... and to work in the garden at times" for twenty-six lire per year.[94] Similarly, in 1456 Piero d'Antonio Lippi from Volpaia "came to stay with us to do the garden and to take care of the other needs of the hospital ... for L40 per year."[95] In 1484 the hospital appointed Matteo di Antonio di Francesco, from Scarperia, as both storekeeper and gardener for three lire per month plus living expenses.[96]

Arrangements for employees who lived off the premises were more complex. In 1464 the Innocenti renewed its contract with Michele di Giovanni, a *fornaio,* "our tenant at the bakery he rents just outside the San Gallo gate on the road to Bologna." The Innocenti paid his annual rent of forty-four lire plus thirty more lire as an annual wage. In return Michele di Giovanni had "this responsibility: to cook all the roasts needed for the hospital of San Gallo and also all the bread we will need for the brigade at San Gallo as well as at the Innocenti."[97] Meat was not excluded from the diet of either children or staff. The Innocenti drew up a similar contract a few months later, in August 1465, with Galeotto di Finocchio, a miller in Sant'Andrea a Rovezzano, to grind 180 pounds of grain into the same amount of flour. "For each sack he is to be paid s4 for his effort. For sacks weighing less than 180 lbs. he shall be compensated as he and Andrea Pagni [the scribe] shall work out."[98]

Workers on the Innocenti's estates required an entirely separate category of personnel who either labored on or supervised the Innocenti's landholdings. By far the most common arrangement was a modified *mezzadria* contract, which also required the payment of fixed rent. In this sort of arrangement, the Innocenti took one-third to one-half of the produce, or profits from the sale of produce, with the remainder going to the farm's tenants. Thus in 1459, a certain Baldese, "nostro lavoratore," rented a farm from the Innocenti for twenty-four *staia* of grain, or twenty-five lire per year. He was allowed to keep half of the grapes or other crops, but had to pay any expenses incurred in getting the grain to Florence and paying gabelles on it.[99] In January 1466 the Innocenti drew up a similar contract with Francesco, Antonio, and Mariotto, brothers and sons of Carracio from San Piero a Quarachi. This lease ran for five years, during which the brothers had to provide all the cane and willow needed from year to year. They also had to render to the Innocenti half of their wine "as is the custom of good workers."[100]

Another contract from 1466 suggests that the five-year lease was standard. The prior of the Innocenti hired three sons of Chirico di Tuccio to work as *mezzadri* on four farms in Montagnano Val di Pesa. In addition to giving the Innocenti half of their produce, they had to plant all the seeds themselves, and every year give a dozen pairs of capons and several dozen eggs to the hospital.[101]

Sharecropping was not always a simple relationship between a tenant farmer and the hospital. In 1473, for example, the treasurer of the Innocenti, Zanobi Landi, rented out several parcels of land to Ser Giovanni di Filippo, a priest from Albola. The lands in question included a laborers' house and half a farm, both of which, Domenico, a laborer, actually tended. Niccolò di Mino da Pisa and his brothers worked the other half, while Domenico also tended a vineyard in the same parish. Ser Giovanni also rented three more farms: one contiguous to the properties described above, another just outside the walls of the Castello di Volpaia, and the third in Pian d'Albola. In addition to rent, Ser Giovanni also had to account for half of all the wine, oil, and other crops cultivated on these farms, even though he did not work the land himself, but rather subcontracted the work to laborers.[102]

The relationship of all these tenants to the Innocenti differed vastly from the relationship the hospital maintained with its managers and employees in the *contado*. In 1461, the Innocenti hired a priest to be not only a collection agent but also a supervisor of the hospital's estates. His task was "to journey to and oversee all the possessions of the hospital and to provide for any necessities concerning the possessions of the aforesaid hospital."[103] The prior of the Innocenti required this priest to account for all sales of grain, wine, oil, or saffron, as well as to keep careful track of the laborers' accounts and to inventory the "ox, ass, sheep, and pigs belonging to the farms of the aforesaid hospital." Ser Filippo also visited the wet nurses "once or twice a year, as shall please the prior," in order to provide for the needs of children at wet nurse. Ser Filippo's salary, sixteen florins a year, hardly matched the scope of this major undertaking.[104]

Although the tenure of most agents hired to oversee the Innocenti's real estate was not always long, in 1495 a married couple decided to devote the rest of their lives to this endeavour:

> I record that this day, 31 March 1495, Messer Francesco our prior hired Maestro Agnolo di Francesco da Salerno and Mona Nanna his wife to be *fattori* in Pian di Mugnone...to supervise the dovecotes and vineyards. The hospital will pay all their expenses for clothes. They will do this for the rest of their lives, and each party must observe the agreement for the life of the contract.[105]

Some turnover of staff occurred spontaneously, but the practitioners of some occupations, such as carters and construction workers, the Innocenti hired temporarily. In July 1456, for example:

> Giuliano di Giovanni came to the House to stay as follows: Ser Lorenzo, the prior, hired him for a month and agreed to give him one florin *di suggiello* per month. The said Giuliano must go any place we need him to go and transport materials now and in future.

Although the hospital dismissed him on 31 July 1456, the treasurer did not release his wages all at once, but paid him in monthly installments at the end of August, September, and October.[106] The Innocenti did hire some carters at salary, however: in 1483, Francesco della Torre, the prior, hired Michele di Bartolomeo di Dante "to go with the mules, that is, as a carter" for a salary of fifty lire per year.[107] Michele di Bartolomeo stayed only a year. His replacement earned fifty lire his first year and sixty his second.[108]

The construction workers of the Innocenti already have the best documented history of any occupational group in early Renaissance Florence, thanks to the work of F. L. Jochem in 1936 and Richard Goldthwaite in 1980. Both have amply reconstructed from the hospital's building accounts the system the hospital employed in contracting out work.[109] When the hospital opened its doors in 1446, much construction remained to be done. In the year and a quarter between 15 January 1445 and 30 April 1446, for example, the hospital spent nearly eight thousand lire on continued construction; most of this amount paid for wages for masters and manual laborers and reimbursement for materials.[110]

As Mendes and Dallai have documented, major construction continued well into the 1470s.[111] In August 1466, when the Innocenti settled its account with Bene di Chele di Taldo, the hospital's scribe provided an illuminating notation concerning Bene's work history on the project as well as a convenient breakdown of the organization of work on the hospital's building program.

The work in question was actually done at San Gallo shortly after its annexation to the Innocenti. Apparently the contractor, Michele di Michele, had given Bene di Chele some lime as well as digging him a pit the size of 3,000 cubic *braccia* at his farm in Coverciano. To work off his debt of forty lire, Bene was to contribute six and a half working days of his own and nine working days of his manual laborers.

Bene, two other masters, and a manual laborer began work on 20 September 1466:

—On 20 September Taldo did not come to work because he felt ill.
—21 September was a holiday.
—22 September he came to work with Maestro Maso d'Antonio and two laborers.
—On the 23d he came with Maestro Maso d'Antonio and Marco, a laborer.
—On the 24th the abovesaid Maso came with two laborers, Marco and Simone.

These construction workers were most likely working on the roof of the hospital, and in the same month, September 1466, the Innocenti took delivery of "six large building hooks for the building project."[112] The account books for September 1466 also detail the work history of another construction worker, expressed in masters' and laborers' days as well. Jacopo di Martino came on 10 September 1466 "with two workers. On the 11th it rained." 12 September was a holiday, but for three straight days, from the thirteenth through the sixteenth, Maestro Jacopo came with both his laborers. On the seventeenth, he came with just one, and with both laborers again on the 18th. When his account was finally settled in January 1467, the hospital assessed the twelve masters' days at twenty soldi per day. Laborers were assessed at 55 percent of that rate, or eleven soldi per day. Thus the Innocenti paid its contractors in terms of man-days rather than paying workers personally, and the masters, including the contractor, distributed the wages to their laborers.[113]

The same system of payment was also in force in 1467, when the Innocenti agreed to pay Pippo di Lucha:

> master of several trades. He must be paid 4 lire, 15 soldi for the remainder of the fourteen man-hours with which he helped us in several places, and for five laborers' days per our agreement with him on 15 June 1467. Moreover he must be given one lire, fifteen soldi for four drainpipes and three cartloads of stone for walling in a well at Pennone's house in San Gallo.[114]

This system in which the Innocenti contracted with masters, who in turn employed their own laborers, was as predominant at the inception of the hospital's construction in 1419 as it would be through the end of the fifteenth century. Even after the Innocenti had completed its major effort of construction, the *opera* usually supplied its own materials and sometimes reimbursed masters for their purchases.

Wet Nurses and Slaves

In the next chapter I will furnish details concerning the wet nurses and foster families to whom the Innocenti sent its children. In this chapter I will treat only those wet nurses whom the hospital hired to feed and care for the children during their brief stay between abandonment and foster care.

In-hospital wet nurses fell into two major categories: those whom the Innocenti hired, and those whom the Innocenti bought on the local slave market. The methods for recruitment of slaves are much better documented than for in-house wet nurses, although the records for the first in-house wet nurse the Innocenti hired, Mona Chiara di Giovanni from

Dicomano, suggest that the officials of the hospital availed themselves of the same networks as mercantile families. When Mona Chiara left the service of the Innocenti six months after her arrival, she went into the service of Federigho di Federighi.[115] Alessandro di Galeotto's name appears frequently in these transactions, and it would appear that he acted as a broker both in the sale of slaves and servants and in the recruitment of hired wet nurses.[116] Similarly, in the 1460s a certain Mona Pagola, who brought a foundling to the Innocenti, was described as someone "who arranges for wet nurses."[117]

Very few of the women whom the hospital hired as wet nurses in-house came from the city of Florence. Rather, the Innocenti preferred to import them from those parishes and towns in the *contado* to which the hospital sent its infants to be wet-nursed. Towns directly to the east and northeast of Florence, among both the foothills and greater peaks of the Appenines, contributed more than their share. Mona Chiara, for example, the wet nurse above who eventually entered the service of Federigho di Federighi, came from Dicomano, and Mona Fiore, who came into the hospital's service at the end of 1445, came from Popi di Casentino.[118] The Mugello was another popular destination for infants, and this region also supplied a large number of in-house wet nurses.

Several factors might well account for the relative ease with which the Innocenti was able to hire in-house wet nurses. Foremost among these was doubtless wages. Wet nurses who devoted their full-time energies to the hospital and who lived in drew an annual salary of sixty lire, or precisely double what wet nurses caring for infants at home could expect. When the hospital hired an in-house wet nurse, she could bring her own infant to the hospital to be nursed. Mona Chiara "brought one of her children, aged but a few months, whom she was breast-feeding." In return for five lire per month and all the clothes she needed for her own child, she had to "give milk to one boy or girl of our hospital."[119] When Mona Antonia di Domenica brought her son, the hospital supplied clothing, but withheld nineteen lire from her annual salary to recoup the hospital's other expenses in taking care of him.[120] Another wet nurse, Mona Agnola, received only twenty-four lire per year, but the Innocenti supplemented this meager wage by paying not only her living expenses, but those of her seven-year-old daughter.[121] Such liberality on the part of the hospital did not guarantee a happy outcome. When Baroncello Cianchi gave his slave Lucia to the Innocenti, she brought with her a son named Jacopo, who was not kept with her but sent to the wet nurse a month after he and his mother arrived at the Innocenti. Jacopo died not quite a year later at wet nurse.[122]

Wet nurses who were married required their husband's permission to work at the hospital. Unlike the husbands of other staff members, who worked alongside their wives, the husbands of in-house wet nurses remained in the couple's home parish. In June 1446, for example, Mona Francesca, wife of Battista da Rimini "came to stay with us to give milk and to take care of our children . . . and to apply her person to all the needs of our hospital. This she promised to do with the consent of her husband" and in the presence of another witness.[123] An unmarried wet nurse to be hired in-house required her father's permission. Mona Fiore of Popi di Casentino, who stayed at the Innocenti five months, brought her father with her to conclude the agreement with the hospital. When she left the Innocenti's service, her brother not only fetched her home but also received the payment for her services.[124]

In addition to its official role as a foundling hospital, the Innocenti functioned unofficially as a maternity ward for unwed mothers. Not only did unmarried women, especially servants, bring their own infants and older children with them, but also, and especially after 1450, they came pregnant to the Innocenti and gave birth at the hospital. In January 1450, for example:

> Marta, a slave, came to stay as a wet nurse when she was about to give birth. She says she will deliver any day now. When she does deliver, we will write down her salary, as we agreed with Piero di Goro de' Medici. This slave girl belongs to Piero di Chino, who sent her.

A week later, she "gave birth and delivered a beautiful baby boy, who Marta said was the son of her master in Venice." This child's future seemed to be as promising as his appearance at birth: in 1457 he was adopted by someone who agreed to "teach him to read and to write and to make of him an honest man."[125]

The admissions log and wet nurse account books provide an especially outstanding example of a contract with one of these wet nurses, in July 1451:

Let it be recorded, known, and manifest to every person who shall read or hear read this present contract, how today this present day, i.e., 13 July 1451, Mona Maria of Castello San Niccolò di Casentino, who says she is the wife of Agnolo di Matteo from Campi, has made with us a contract and agreement that this present day she came to the hospital to give birth because she is pregnant. And she says that . . . she wishes and promises to stay with us to nurse our children as long as her milk shall last. Her salary will begin as soon as she gives birth, or when she begins to nurse our children. We agree that the child to whom she gives birth shall be sent to wet nurse, and the expenses thus incurred will be deducted from her wages. And Bartolomeo di Matteo, craftsman in the via degli Spedai promises that the aforesaid Maria will observe all the above and that in case she doesn't Bartolomeo will refund to us the expenses of the delivery and every other expense, and in observance of same he pledges his estate and possessions.[126]

In early 1452 the hospital drew up a contract that was similar, but even more restrictive. Antonio di Baschiera, from a parish in Vichio di Mugello, requested the hospital to take on

Mona Buona, daughter of the late Bindo di Cuccio, from the parish of San Michele a Rabia Canina, who is mute and pregnant and wants to have her baby here in the hospital. The aforesaid Mona Buona agrees to stay forever in our service and to fulfill our needs. She will be clothed as she is accustomed to being and shall lack nothing.

Antonio promised to indemnify the hospital if Mona Buona should violate her contract by leaving.[127] Other contracts also specified a period of time to which the wet nurse was bound. Mona Maddalena di Giovanni from Castello San Niccolò agreed to come to the hospital on 22 February 1447 under a one-year contract, for which she was to receive sixty lire.[128] As was true with all the above cases, the hospital hired wet nurses not only to breast-feed but also to attend "to all the other needs of the children" and to "govern the children."[129]

The wet nurses who came to work for the Innocenti were so critical to the first few days of children's lives in the hospital that the prior had to license them annually.[130] In addition, the hospital provided expert medical care to wet nurses of the House who fell ill:

> In June 1453 . . . Caterina came to the hospital and stayed ten days or so. She came with an infection in her breast, so an incision was made in one breast, and it was opened, and the same for the other one. And on account of both she was very ill until 3 July 1453. We treated her, in any case, on the advice of Maestro Mariotto [di Niccolò, the Medici's household physician as well as the Innocenti's]. When she is cured and has a supply of milk sufficient for one child she promised to stay as a wet nurse for as long as her milk lasts for that salary which shall be reasonable and just, that is, Fl [left blank] per year.[131]

Similarly, a slave girl hired by the hospital through Alessandro di Galeotto fell ill a month after her arrival at the Innocenti. Lapo di Piero Pacini, the hospital's treasurer and scribe, recorded that "we sent her ill to Santa Maria Nuova on 16 October 1445. She was sick from fever and pains. She had been treated here until today. She returned to us much improved on 28 October."[132] This expert medical care was only one expression of the esteem in which the hospital held its wet nurses, slave or free. A wet nurse who performed well earned the admiration and respect of hospital administrators, as this obituary from the wet nurse and childrens' account books testifies:

> Then on the third day of November [1449] at about the thirteenth hour it pleased God to call to himself the aforesaid Nastasia. She was sick for about three days and died of plague. Pray God to pardon her soul and to bestow his good will upon her, because in the brief time she was with us she was very good with these infants. . . . We buried her in the pit under the church [with the children].[133]

The distinction between free and slave wet nurses was not particularly sharp at the Innocenti. The hospital paid both for their services unless the parties agreed on other contractual arrangements. Agents recruited both slaves and free wet nurses, and men, either brother, husband, father, or master, had to give their consent before a woman could work as a wet nurse within the hospital. The major difference was that once a slave had begun service at the hospital, she was legally bound to and could not release herself from her contract with the hospital.

Alessandro di Galeotto, as well as being a broker in the slave trade, owned his own slaves as well. When he sold Cicilia to the hospital of the Innocenti, he openly acknowledged his paternity of Cicilia's child, Teologia. Alessandro agreed to pay the hospital for the expense involved in taking care of the child, an unusual gesture toward his slave girl: most other slave girls and wet nurses had child-care expenses deducted directly from their wages.

Contracts for hiring slaves were quite similar to those for wet nurses. When the hospital took on Cicilia, the contract described her as both slave and servant of Alessandro di Galeotto. The hospital paid a salary, although it is not clear to whom. Cicilia's contract was more a lease than an outright purchase. She agreed to stay two years, but if at the end of the first year she wished to return to Alessandro's service, the superintendent was to return her to him.[134]

Some contracts with slaves specified even shorter tenures. Thus, in April 1447 "we took from Messer Giuliano Benini a wet nurse whose name is Margarita. She is the slave of Niccolò Benini." For the six months she was to stay, the hospital agreed to pay sixteen lire.[135] Even purchase contracts, however, often set a limit on the number of years to be served. In November 1451:

I, Lapo di Piero Pacini, with the permission of the guild consuls, bought a thirty-three year old slave by the name of Maria from Guglielmo di Giovanni, a stationer in the parish of San Jacopo tra le Fosse, for four years, which will terminate on 24 November 1455, to give milk for the price of twenty-nine florins *di suggiello,* which I paid for her to the bank account of Giovanni Teghiacci. And he promised us that if she does not stay for the full four years, or it turns out that she was not legally his . . . that he will refund the said twenty-nine florins.

Two days later Maria agreed to stay another year beyond the original four "for charity and for the sake of her soul . . . in order to serve the hospital and the children."[136] In August 1448, the prior of the Innocenti, Messer Andrea di Giuliano, lent 196 lire to the hospital's treasury to buy a slave "for nursing the children who lack a wet nurse." In this case the hospital paid nine lire to a broker to arrange the transaction.[137]

Slaves might leave the service of the hospital in several ways. In August 1449, for example, Bernardo di Lionardo Baroncelli, the hospital's treasurer, sold Caterina, one of the hospital's slaves, for sixty-three gold pieces, on the advice of one of the hospital's *operai* and of the hospital's notary: "it was done for the sake of the poor and nothing more could be done."[138] In 1451, Lorenzo di Giovanni Orlandini "bought from the hospital a slave by the name of Lucia for the price of thirty-four florins for a period of six years." If he did not adhere to certain conditions of the contract "we may sell her as we please, without any exception."[139] A slave not sold might escape. Thus in December 1449 a certain Maria "who stayed in-house" returned an overpayment that she took "when she fled the hospital."[140]

Slaves who endured might enjoy a happier end to their tenure. In 1456, Lorenzo di Fruosino, the Innocenti's prior, discovered that Masa, a slave girl, had been in the service of the hospital "for some time" and that she "gave us good service and always bore herself well while she was here." The prior ordered that Masa:

> be free and be allowed to stay in whatever place she likes with this condition: that she stay two more years in the hospital. And the said ser Lorenzo, prior, did this to make peace with his conscience and to do his duty toward the aforesaid Masa. . . . I, Lorenzo, priest and prior aforesaid am content with and will do as much as is said above, i.e., that the abovesaid Masa be free starting two years from this date. This I do out of reasons of clear conscience.[141]

This rather anecdotal glance at personnel records suggests relatively high staff turnover at all levels and makes it nearly impossible to plot changes in staff-to-patient ratios over time. In the 1480s, however, the hospital's new prior, Messer Francesco della Torre, undertook administrative reorganization, at least part of which was to begin publishing in the *Ricordanze* an annual census.[142] On 17 January 1483 "we have numbered our family currently in residence: i.e., at our hospital in Florence." This census makes explicit the familial model on which the hospital was organized. In addition to listing "Messer Francesco, our prior," the census also listed "Mona Agatha, our prioress." In addition, two women, Mona Mea and Mona Tita, were listed as "the doorkeepers" who stood at the wheel and the font where the infants were first abandoned. The census identified three more women, Mona Buona,

Mona Fruosina, and Mona Sandra, as service personnel. The first of these was the same Mona Buona hired thirty years previously because she was "mute and pregnant." In addition to these women the Innocenti had fourteen wet nurses in residence as well as four men: Giovanni, a chaplain; Giorgio, a collection agent; Ser Francesco, "the prior's clerk"; and Ser Piero, the gardener and storekeeper. The total in-house staff, then, numbered twenty-five.[143]

When this census was taken, 118 girls were also resident in the hospital, of whom 6 were ill in the infirmary. Only 33 boys resided in the hospital at the same time, a disproportion much greater than that reflected by the admissions statistics. In addition to the 151 children who had been weaned, the fourteen wet nurses in-house were breast-feeding another 20 children. Six were boys, and 14 girls. Altogether the resident staff-to-patient ratio was 25 staff to 171 children.[144]

Less than nine months later the prior conducted a recount of the staff and children of the hospital of the Innocenti, but this time he included the children of San Gallo.[145] Since San Gallo was reserved for the admission of older children, the census broke them down by age. The largest contingent was a group of eighteen older girls: sixteen to eighteen years of age and, therefore, of marriageable age. Three girls aged six to ten and three servant women completed the contingent of women at San Gallo. The San Gallo portion of the census also lists eleven men, seven of whom were patients, three chaplains, and one unidentified. Again the domestic model prevailed. Mona Margherita was the prioress at San Gallo, and a married couple, Mariotto di Jacopo Soldi and his wife Mona Nanna, were *commessi* at San Gallo.[146]

At the Innocenti itself, the staff census over the first nine months of 1483 remained fairly constant. The prior's clerk had left, but the hospital had hired "Gabriello, who goes out begging with the children."[147] The number of wet nurses had decreased from fourteen to nine. The prior either created a new position or perhaps reactivated a vacant one: Mona Sandra di Biancho, who "supervises the wet nurses."[148] Thus eight staff women and five men, as well as nine wet nurses, served 138 girls and 41 boys. The nine wet nurses were responsible for feeding 15 infants. Thus in nine months the census of the hospital's resident children had gone from 171 to 194, but the staff was reduced from twenty-five to twenty-two. At San Gallo, however, twelve staff members supervised only 22 older children.[149]

In both places, staff often brought their own children to work with them. At San Gallo, for example, both Bartolomeo di Dante and his son were listed in the census. At the Innocenti, Piero, the gardener and storekeeper, had his daughter Lorenza listed among the children in-house.[150] In October 1483 when the consuls and *operai* made several personnel decisions, they declared specifically that "Bartolomeo di Dante and Michele, his son, starting the beginning of October, will no longer be welcome in our hospital, either in Florence [i.e., the Innocenti] or at San Gallo."[151]

The *Ricordanze* of 1483 provide further evidence that both the consuls and the prior had undertaken a major administrative reorganization. The consuls terminated the employment of two chaplains, and decided that several people either had to remain at San Gallo or accept a transfer there "to keep it open." In addition to the chaplains already stationed there, two alumni of the Innocenti were to stay there as clerks. San Gallo was to keep its storekeeper and its carter, and Mona Margherita was to remain its prioress. Mona Tita, however, found herself transplanted from her post as doorkeeper at the Innocenti to a post at San Gallo.[152]

In addition to keeping better track of the census, Francesco di Martino also kept a detailed account in 1483 of how much food the staff and children of the Innocenti consumed (table 3). On Thursday, 23 October 1423, for example, seventy-five children sat "at the children's table." Although boys and girls maintained separate living quarters and separate cloisters within the hospital, they ate together at table. This table required eighteen loaves of bread, weighing thirty-two pounds altogether, so that each child had a ration of 5.12 ounces of bread at the morning meal. A somewhat larger ration went to the twenty-four children in the infirmary: seven loaves amounting to thirty-two pounds. The hospital set aside another fourteen loaves "for the boys and girls who are out at the shops all day," which gave each of these children 21 ounces for the entire day. Among the thirteen wet nurses who sat at the children's table, sixteen loaves of bread were allotted, amounting to a ration of nearly 26 ounces. Another forty loaves were set aside "for the women of the refectory, who number eighty-one mouths." Since this seems to be an extraordinarily high number for employees, this group must have included older girls of marriageable age who still resided at the Innocenti. Finally the chaplains, each of whom had a ration of a half loaf, had their own refectory.

A child's portion of breakfast consisted of one-quarter of a two-pound loaf—an adult's portion twice that. Just for the morning meal, then, the hospital required 106 loaves. The total number of loaves distributed for the day was 195. At lunchtime, only the healthy children at the large table of seventy-five ate. The children in the infirmary, the infirmary staff, and the older women did not eat lunch. Thus the seventy-five children in question were most likely between the ages of two and six, as weaning took place at twenty-four months, and the six-year-olds and older children were out "working in the shops." All were reunited at the evening meal, but with individual rations of bread slighty reduced.

Although bread was the major component of the children's diet, it was not the only one (table 4). This day also saw the consumption of 16.5 quarts of wine for breakfast and another half barrel for the evening meal. The next day's solid foods were rather more varied. They included

TABLE 3.   Bread Rations at the Ospedale degli Innocenti, 27 October to 18 November 1483

Date	Loaves *(coppie)*	Pounds *(libbre)*
27 October	147.0	286.5
28 October	209.0	400.5
29 October	214.0	395.0
30 October	185.0	309.5
31 October	204.5	304.0
1 November	200.5	402.0
2 November	185.0	345.5
3 November	188.0	328.5
4 November	177.5	373.5
5 November	189.5	388.5
6 November	167.5	367.0
7 November	175.0	391.5
8 November	162.5	365.5
9 November	180.5	396.5
10 November	196.5	386.0
11 November	201.0	384.5
12 November	214.0	390.0
13 November	188.0	387.5
14 November	159.5	332.0
15 November	200.0	369.0
16 November	246.0	405.5
17 November	221.0	391.0
18 November	231.0	402.0

Source: AOIF, Ricordanze B (XII,2), fols. 51v–66r, 27 October to 18 November 1483

Note: A Florentine *libbra* weighed 0.339 kg, compared to 0.454 kg for a modern British or American pound. In the measurement of silk, 1 *coppia* = 2 *libbre,* but the weight of the *coppia* for bread, as can be seen from the table, is variable. See Ronald Zupko, *Italian Weights and Measures from the Middle Ages to the Nineteenth Century* (Philadelphia, 1981), 133. It is also worth noting that the *libbra* was divided into twelve, not sixteen *oncie,* or ounces, so that a Florentine *oncia* is for all intents and purposes the same as a British or American ounce. See Zupko, *Italian Weights and Measures,* 74.

two blocks of cheese, totaling eight pounds, "oil for cooking and for salad," and 18.5 quarts of wine for a snack and for dinner.[153] Further variations were rare, although about twice a week the fare included two or three pounds of dried, salted meat. There is no way to discover among whom or how the meat was distributed, but each day 1–2 quarts of oil were consumed in cooking. The menus mention salad at least once a week, though again its distribution remains unknown.[154] Salad may have gone only to those who were allotted a measure of oil "because they don't eat meat."[155]

It is clear from an analysis of the diet of staff and children at the Innocenti from 23 October through 18 November 1483 that even the economic conditions of the later fifteenth century were not so severe as to make it impossible for the Innocenti to feed all its older children.

When a petition presented only three months later spoke of children

TABLE 4.   Cheese, Wine, Oil, and Meat Rations at the Ospedale degli Innocenti, 27 October to 18 November 1483

Date	Cheese (lb.)	Wine (barrel)	Oil (qt.)	Meat (lb.)
27 October	3.0	1.5	3.5	
28 October		1.5	2.0	3.0
29 October	7.5	1.5	2.0	
30 October		1.5		1.0
31 October		1.5	3.0	
1 November	12.0	1.5	3.0	
2 November		1.5	1.0	
3 November		1.5	2.0	1.0
4 November		1.5	1.0	
5 November	7.0	1.5	2.0	
6 November		1.5	1.0	
7 November	6.5	1.5	3.0	
8 November	1.0	1.5	2.0	
9 November		1.0	1.0	1.0
10 November	6.0	1.0	3.0	14.0
11 November		5.0		
12 November	6.0	1.5	2.0	
13 November		1.0		1.5
14 November	6.5	1.0	3.0	
15 November		1.5	3.0	
16 November		1.0		54.0a
17 November	8.0	1.0	2.0	17.0
18 November		1.5	2.0	55.0b

Source: AOIF, Ricordanze B (XII,2), fols. 51v–66r, 27 October to 18 November 1483

Note: Menus for November 16 and 17 also include "una pollastra per l'infermi."

a50 pounds of *carne di bechaio* (fresh meat) and 4 pounds of *carne secche* (dried meats).

b53 pounds of "charne di bechaio" including "bue e porcho e chastrone" and 2 pounds of *charne secche.*

dying of hunger,[156] it meant infants: both those who could not be placed with wet nurses and those who had been placed with wet nurses to whom the Innocenti made its payments in arrears. Children who escaped death in the first two years might expect a varied and adequate diet once they returned from the wet nurse, and certainly the overwhelming preponderance of infant over child mortality at the Innocenti bears this out. The presence of legumes, meat, and cheese in the hospital's diet supports recent scholarship on the improved composition of the European diet after the Black Death. Not insignificant was the presence of the tenant whose job it was to "cook all the roasts" for the hospital of San Gallo.[157]

A meal at the Innocenti typically fed two hundred or more people by the 1480s. Their daily ration of bread varied from 1.5 to 2 Florentine pounds. Total daily amounts varied from 286 pounds to 405 pounds, but the mean was 365 pounds of bread to feed 200 people each day, or 21.9 U.S. ounces per person per day.[158] Even the seventy-five children ranging in age from two to six had 95 pounds on average, or well over a pound each. Just as important as the quantitative information these sources yield is the qualitative flavor they give of enormous gatherings of adults and children at each mealtime. The Innocenti combined the monastic vocabulary of the refectory with the familial setting of small boys and girls eating at the same table.

Also supportive of this sense of family was the major instrument of pious devotion for married couples known as *commessione*. Although this legal term embraced anyone, including clerics,[159] who committed themselves and their possessions to the hospital, the *commessi* of the Innocenti were preponderantly, though not exclusively, married couples who took quasi-monastic vows to serve the institution and its children for life. The property of *commessi* was an important issue in the contract of *commessione*. At the very least, *commessi* had to remember the Innocenti in their wills or in donations inter vivos. Unlike the employees of the hospital of Santa Maria Nuova,[160] the *commessi* of the Innocenti enjoyed the usufruct of their properties until the properties reverted at death to the hospital. This form of lay piety, though impressive, was not new. The practice of dedication, commission, and donation was a possible, even common, expression of lay piety as early as the twelfth century.[161]

In Florence, quasi-monastic rules governed all the employees of the hospital of Santa Maria Nuova. The statutes of 1374 prohibited not only the superintendent, but also "the *conversi, oblati,* familiars, and servants" from owning property. Those who came to work for Santa Maria Nuova, within three months of their appointment, had to turn over their property to the hospital "so that it can be converted to support the sick poor of the hospital." Accentuating this monastic sensibility were numerous restrictions on the mobility of *conversi*. They could not leave the hospital's grounds without the superintendent's permission. The superintendent himself could not go out alone, nor stay overnight anywhere "without a legitimate reason."[162]

A third-order group known as the *pinzocheri* governed and operated the hospital of San Paolo in Florence during the fifteenth century. The architecture of the hospital, across the piazza from the church of Santa Maria Novella, was consciously derivative of the loggia of the Innocenti, and Michelozzo's designs were part of larger efforts of rebuilding and organizational reform, both of which the hospital of San Paolo required desperately.[163] *Commessi*, therefore, had ample precedent in Continental lay devotion. The Innocenti's contribution to this form of lay piety was its conscious approbation of domesticity and the prevalence of couples who, in addition to carrying out their quotidian tasks, served as familial models for the children in their care.

Even before there was enough of a physical structure at the Innocenti to harbor communal life, the hospital began accepting *commessi*. In 1422, Bartolomeo di Matteo di Chele, in the presence of Goro di Stagio Dati and other witnesses, signed an agreement in the guild's headquarters with Ser Lodovico Bertini, the superintendent of the hospital:

> On account of the reverence Bartolomeo says he has toward the new hospital, and also on behalf of the salvation of his soul and for the remedy of his sins and for the love of God . . . he offered and dedicated himself and his person for the entire remainder of his life, to serve with obedience and reverence. . . . He promised to show due and eternal obedience to the said hospital, to the said Lord consuls, and their successors, as his true superiors and betters. He must do and perform everything in the said hospital that he is required to do and as such *commessi* are accustomed to do. Also, the superintendent and the aforesaid consuls humbly and devoutly accepted and received the said Bartolomeo in the service of the said hospital, and they promise that he shall be kindly treated.[164]

Surprisingly, *commessi* did not have to be childless to enter into this arrangement. Bartolomeo di Matteo di Chele was allowed in his will to pass part of his estate to his son, Piero.

These possessions included farms, vineyards, and houses in Scandicci, Greve, and Cerreto Guidi. The usufruct of these properties, with which the Catasto officials had specifically taken issue, were "eternally safe and reserved to him for the remainder of his life." The dowry of his wife, Mona Tommasa, enjoyed a similar protection. Should she survive him, she was to continue to enjoy the usufruct of their possessions and retain her dowry until her death, providing "she does not remarry, and pursues an honest life."[165]

Mona Tommasa did not herself become a *commessa* of the Innocenti. In 1425, however, the married couple who governed one of the guild's other hospitals, Sant'Antonio a La Lastra a Signa, committed themselves to lifelong service to the Ospedale degli Innocenti. Lucia, the wife of Francesco Giusti, and Francesco himself drew up separate contracts. Lucia's contract specified, nonetheless, that she had obtained her husband's consent, and Francesco, as was standard Florentine practice, acted as her representative, or *mundualdo*.[166]

If Lucia and Francesco left a hospital to serve the Innocenti, another *commesso*, Giovanni di Barlettari from Radda in Chianti, devoted himself to the Innocenti:

> considering that he is getting on in years and is without sons and daughters, he donated to us a house and a farm with two houses in Radda. The superintendent of the Innocenti must see to it that a hospital be constructed to receive poor pilgrims and other poor and miserable persons. There must be at least six beds, and the hospital must be supplied with everything necessary for housing the poor, namely, four beds for men and two for women. The said superintendent must... maintain the said hospice properly without neglecting anything it needs.[167]

Giovanni intended that this hospital, to be called the hospital of Santa Maria della Misericordia, should be a branch of the hospital of the Innocenti. The officers of the Innocenti and the silk guild he named as the hospital's protectors, and its management must not fall "to anyone else, especially not to any ecclesiastical person or place, but rather shall be a lay institution."[168] The officers of the Innocenti and of the silk guild enjoyed full authority both to elect and, if necessary, to remove a superintendent.

At Giovanni's death in January 1445, Maffeo di Francesco and his wife made known to the guild consuls their wish to become governors of the new hospital of Santa Maria della Misericordia.[169] Just days later, the most illustrious of the Innocenti's *commessi*, Lapo di Piero Pacini and his wife, Dianora, began their tenure barely two weeks before the Innocenti opened its doors to foundlings.

Lapo's and Dianora's acts of dedication convey a sense not only of grandeur and formality, but also of the hospital as a community for the first time. Their dedication took place not only in the presence of the hospital's superintendent, but also in the presence of the guild's consuls and of the *operai*. Lapo:

> considering at present that he is an old man and without sons or daughters as well as beyond hope for having any, pledged to serve under the rule and habit of the said hospital, on bended knee, and with his hands joined... offered and dedicated himself, his person, and all his worldly goods, present and future. [He is to obey the superintendent, and] to serve God, the Virgin Mary, and all the children abandoned there, just as the rule and life of the said hospital shall demand. And so he swore on God's Holy Gospel in the presence of the said Lord Consuls and also in the presence of me, Uberto [di ser Martino] the notary, with Lapo's hands touching the scriptures and with himself kneeling before the missal. The aforesaid superintendent, taking the said Lapo by his right hand, humbly, kindly, and devoutly admitted and received Lapo as a *commesso*. He promised to govern him and feed him unto death, as is customary when one is in obedience to the rule and habit of the said hospital.[170]

Lapo also transferred all his possessions, houses, and *Monte* credits to the Innocenti, and promised not to revoke the donation nor to proceed in any way against the hospital. Lapo's wife, Dianora, became a *commessa* the same day. The motivations and formulas invoked were the same as her husband's. If Lapo and Dianora drew up separate contracts, the copy of their *commessione* in the Innocenti's archives clearly recognized that their former status as lay, married persons would continue within the life of the hospital. The bottom of the page has a drawing of Lapo and Dianora assuming the traditional stance of donors, kneeling with their arms crossed. Their attention and adoration, however, is focused on the Christ child standing resplendent between them, and printed through the top of the drawing is the inscription: "OMNES SANCTI INNOCENTES ORATE PRO NOBIS": "All Holy Innocents, pray for us."[171]

Not only the guild and the hospital, but also the Signory of Florence took an interest in this particular act of dedication, from both a ceremonial standpoint, in approving and encouraging it, and also a fiscal and legal standpoint by granting Lapo and Dianora permission to turn over their worldly goods to the hospital and to settle the issue of their taxes. This permission was granted and confirmed in January 1445.[172] By March the guild's notaries had completed their inventory of all the possessions Lapo and Dianora had given to the hospital, as well as their real estate and furniture in Castelfiorentino and Pontormo. These inventories provide the best information about who this couple was and by what path they might have come to serve the Innocenti.[173]

Both Lapo and his father were members of the Arte della Seta, and it is likely that Lapo took over his father's silk business in Castelfiorentino. Lapo himself, however, never appeared in lists of the guild consuls or of the hospital's trustees. He was first appointed treasurer and director of operations in 1445. His duties included keeping the *Ricordanze* and the hospital's record of admissions. His distinctive and elegant hand graces nearly every internal document written between 1445 and 1450, with intervals of absence already documented earlier in the chapter.[174]

During one of those absences from May to September 1448, Lapo was one of the captains of the Company of San Zanobio. If his membership in that confraternity reflected in any way the direction of his spirituality, his choice was appropriate.[175] One of Florence's oldest confraternities, San Zanobio ran schools to teach children how to sing *laude*. Although Lapo himself was childless, the membership of the confraternity was predominantly married (77 percent) and predominantly fathers (65 percent), by contrast to the membership of the confraternity of San Paolo, 42 percent of which was married and 40 percent were fathers.

The ethos of this confraternity mixed a high level of spirituality with laic and civic concerns for the active life, justice, and good works. The confraternity's cult objects, the Virgin Mary and, specifically, the Annunciation, formed part of Lapo's inventory as well. This confraternity, moreover, represented an unparalleled example of civic spirituality. Its meeting place in the Duomo was decorated with large shields depicting *popolo* and *comune,* while the company's ballot urn displayed the arms of the Florentine republic.[176]

The guild's inventory suggests that Lapo and Dianora gave up a considerable worldly fortune to work for the Innocenti. The enumeration of their possessions runs to six folios, both sides, two columns to a side. Their wealth was largely in fine cloths and linens: endless tablecloths, coats, copes, capes, pillows, towels, and pillowcases. Hardly less impressive was their collection of jewelry and fine accessories: several belts "with buckles and holes enameled and filled with silver." The inventory also lists "a sapphire in a setting of gold . . . worth ten florins" and "a garnet in a gold setting." Although childless, Lapo and Dianora had several items for children, including a child's bedspread and small bed.[177]

Lapo's and Dianora's luxurious material life did not efface their spiritual devotion. The inventory lists several religious objects: "A crown of Our Lady," a relief of the Annunciation, and "an altarpiece of Our Lady with little windows and Lapo's coat of arms." In addition to this altarpiece donated to the Innocenti, Lapo also had one in his silk manufactory in Castelfiorentino. In his residence at Pontormo he also had a paper drawing of the Virgin Mary.[178]

Perhaps most revealing is his library, which he donated to the Innocenti when the inventory was first drawn up. This library included a small book of the Mass with a calendar, and the epistles and gospels copied in Lapo's own hand. His study, or *scriptoio,* contained "several quantities of books of the fathers . . . and some writing paper." Lapo's literary tastes included Giovanni Villani's chronicle, "a Dante in *carta banbagia* and bound . . . with two locks," and a letter of Saint Bernard concerning the solitary life. Lapo had also copied in his own hand some of the works of Saint Francis, and "a book of sayings from the Bible."[179] One may safely assume that later and older generations of children would find these books in the Innocenti's library.

Lapo's inventory also included several large chests and strongboxes, which were opened upon his death in 1452 and found to contain 200 florins.[180] The sale of some of his real estate brought in another 340 florins. Indeed, nearly 40 percent of the hospital's revenue for the year 1452 came from the sale of what was only a small portion of Lapo's estate.[181]

Lapo and Dianora Pacini represent only the best-documented example of the role of lay piety in the life of the Innocenti during the first few years the hospital was open. These pious lay men and women became, in effect, foster grandparents. Not only did these arrangements ensure a dedicated staff to care for children; they also provided a means of replicating an extended family setting within the walls, in which people at both extremes of age could participate in a communal and familiar setting. The next chapter will explore not only the role of children within this setting, but also the way in which these children, though abandoned by their parents, were trained and educated to participate in the wider civic world of Renaissance Florence.

NOTES

1. Richard Goldthwaite, "The Florentine Palace as Domestic Architecture," *American Historical Review* 77 (1972): 997–98. See idem, *Private Wealth in Renaissance Florence* (Princeton, 1968), passim. F. W. Kent, "The Rucellai Family and its Loggia," *Journal of the Warburg and Courtauld Institutes* 35 (1972): 397–401, and idem, *Household and Lineage in Renaissance Florence* (Princeton, 1977), passim.

2. Leon Battista Alberti, *Ten Books on Architecture,* trans. James Leoni (London,1955), 84. For purposes of quotation, I have modified Leoni's eighteenth-century translation.

3. Ibid., 85.

4. Ibid., 173.

5. Ibid.

6. Luca Landucci, *Diario fiorentino dal 1450 al 1516* (Florence, 1883), 125–30.

7. Richard Goldthwaite and W. R. Rearick, "Michelozzo and the Ospedale of San Paolo," *Mitteilungen des Kunsthistorisches Institut von Florenz* 21, no. 3 (1977): 280.

8. Archivio dell'Ospedale degli Innocenti di Firenze (AOIF), Testamenta et Donationes (IX,1), fol. 21r, 6 August 1420.

9. Ibid.

10. Ibid.

11. Antonio Manetti, *Vita di Brunelleschi,* trans. Howard Saalman (University Park, Pa., 1970), 142.

12. Goldthwaite and Rearick, "Michelozzo," 269.

13. Ibid.

14. Natalie Davis, "Poor Relief, Humanism, and Heresy: The Case of Lyons," *Studies in Medieval and Renaissance History* 5 (1968): 217–69.

15. Creighton Gilbert, "The Earliest Guide to Florentine Architecture," *Mitteilungen des Kunsthistorisches Institut von Florenz* 14 (1969): 33–46.

16. Archivio di Stato, Firenze (ASF), Provvisioni Registri, 142, fols 380r–382v, 29 December 1451. See also AOIF, Ricordanze A (XII,1), fol. 157r, 28 April 1479: "e pero apartengono [i soldi] al nostro spedale chome al padre di detta fanciulla."

17. Fifteenth-century Florentines used the term *brigata* interchangeably with *famiglia,* almost in the sense of "our gang." See Alessandra Strozzi's letter in *Lettere di una gentildonna fiorentina,* ed. C. Guasti (Milan, 1877), letter 35, 314: "Marco e la brigata sono per ancora a Firenze, che ci è escarso dove andare: che per le ville ne muore."

18. ASF, Arte della Seta, 246, fol. 101r, 23 April 1449.

19. AOIF, Ricordanze B (XII,2), fol. 49r, 21 October 1483.

20. Attilio Piccini, *L'Ospedale degli Innocenti ed il suo museo* (Florence, 1977), 5.

21. Manetti, *Vita,* 94–95.

22. *Il libro di Antonio Billi,* ed. Cornelius von Fabriczy (London, 1891), reprinted from *Archivio Storico Italiano* 7, no. 5 (1891): 299–368.

23. Manetti, *Vita,* 100.

24. *Il libro di Antonio Billi,* 317.

25. AOIF, Debitori e Creditori (CXX,1), fol. 146 left, 15 July 1427.

26. ASF, Arte della Seta, 246, fol. 14v, 1 January 1427 [modern = 1428].

27. AOIF, Debitori e Creditori (CXX,1), fol. 146 left, 29 January 1426 [modern = 1427].

28. ASF, Arte della Seta, 246, fol. 97r, 1 May 1421; fol. 98r, 1 May 1426.

29. Creighton Gilbert, "Florentine Architecture," 33ff.

30. Manuel Mendes and Giovanni Dallai, "Nuove indagini sullo spedale degli Innocenti a Firenze," *Commentari* 17, nos. 1–3 (1966): 85.

31. AOIF, Libro delle Muraglie A (VII,1), loose folio, n.d., *anno* 1424.

32. Michael Baxandall, *Painting and Experience in Fifteenth-century Italy* (Oxford, 1972), 6–7.

33. AOIF, Libro delle Muraglie A (VII,1), loose folio, n.d., *anno* 1424.

34. AOIF, Libro delle Muraglie A (VII,1), loose folio, 17 April 1428.

35. AOIF, Libro delle Muraglie A (VII,1), fol. 11r, 13 November 1419.

36. ASF, Arte della Seta, 246, fols. 11r–103v, 1 May 1419–1 May 1476.

37. ASF, Arte della Seta, 246, fol. 100r, 4 June 1464.

38. ASF, Arte della Seta, 246, fol. 101v, 17 December 1453, and fol. 102v, 1 July 1461.

39. ASF, Arte della Seta, 246, fol. 98r, 1 May 1428 and 1 May 1429.

40. ASF, Arte della Seta, 246, fol. 13v, 1 May 1424.

41. ASF, Arte della Seta, 246, fols. 11r, 12v, 22v, 31r (consuls); fols. 97r, 97v, 100r, 103r (operai).

42. ASF, Arte della Seta, 246, fol. 99r, 1 May 1436. See James Banker, "Mourning a Son: Childhood and Paternal Love in the *Consolateria* of Giannozzo Manetti," *History of Childhood Quarterly* 3, no. 3 (1976): 351–62.

43. The treatise once attributed to Pandolfini, the *Trattato dello governo della famiglia,* was recognized in the mid-nineteenth century as book 3 of Alberti's *Della famiglia.*

44. AOIF, Testamenta et Donationes (IX,1), fol. 35r, 13 February 1421 [modern = 1422].

45. Ibid.

46. Ibid.

47. Ibid.

48. Ibid.

49. Ibid.

50. Ibid.

51. ASF, Arte della Seta, 246, fol. 101r, 1 May 1448.

52. ASF, Arte della Seta, 246, fol. 101r, 23 April 1449.

53. ASF, Arte della Seta, 246, fols. 97r–103v, 1419–1476.

54. AOIF, Ricordanze B (XII,2), fol. 97v, 28 June 1484.

55. AOIF, Ricordanze A (XII,1), fol. 20r, 11 January 1445 [modern = 1446].

56. AOIF, Balie e Bambini A (XVI,1), fol. 205r, 8, 24, and 30 August 1449.

57. AOIF, Ricordanze A (XII,1), fol. 10v, 3 November 1449; AOIF, Balie e Bambini A (XVI,1), fol. 219v, 3 November 1449.

58. AOIF, Ricordanze A (XII,1), fol. 62r, 17 November 1461.

59. AOIF, Ricordanze A (XII,4), fol. 175r, 17 November 1457.

60. AOIF, Ricordanze A (XII,4), fol. 142r, 8 September 1456.

61. Piccini, *Lo Spedale degli Innocenti,* 13.

62. AOIF, Ricordanze A (XII,4), fol. 56r, 15 August 1454.

63. AOIF, Ricordanze A (XII,1), fol. 90r, 22 January 1466 [modern = 1467].

64. AOIF, Ricordanze A (XII,1), fol. 90r, 13 April 1464.

65. AOIF, Ricordanze A (XII,1), fol. 90r, 10 June and 15 December 1465.

66. AOIF, Ricordanze B (XII,2), fol. 34r, 12 August 1483.

67. AOIF, Ricordanze A (XII,4), fol. 170r, 1 July 1482.

68. AOIF, Ricordanze B (XII,2), fol. 18v, 1 April 1483.

69. Katharine Park, *Doctors and Medicine in Renaissance Florence* (Princeton, 1985), 141.

70. AOIF, Ricordanze A (XII,1), fol. 3v, 8 March 1444 [modern = 1445].

71. AOIF, Ricordanze A (XII,1), fol. 3v, 28 April 1445.

72. AOIF, Ricordanze A (XII,1), fol. 3v, 27 April 1445.

73. Park, *Doctors and Medicine,* 114, 196.

74. Ibid., 182, 183.

75. Ibid., 105, 141.

76. Ibid., appendix 3, 249.

77. I wish to thank Katharine Park for this information.

78. Park, *Doctors and Medicine*, 106.

79. AOIF, Ricordanze A (XII,4), fol. 222v, 2 September 1458.

80. AOIF, Ricordanze A (XII,1), fol. 100r, 18 October 1457.

81. AOIF, Ricordanze A (XII,1), fol. 174r, 1 November 1482.

82. AOIF, Giornale D (XIII,1), fol. 17v, 19 February 1467 [modern = 1458].

83. AOIF, Ricordanze A (XII,1), fol. 173r, 2 October 1482.

84. Park, *Doctors and Medicine*, 8, 47, 107.

85. AOIF, Ricordanze A (XII,4), fol. 3v, 1 April 1449.

86. AOIF, Ricordanze A (XII,4), fol. 14r, 1 August 1451.

87. AOIF, Ricordanze A (XII,1), fol. 171v, 19 November 1483.

88. AOIF, Ricordanze A, (XII,1), fol. 129r, 1 February 1471 [modern = 1472].

89. ASF, Arte della Seta, 246, fol. 28r, 19 April 1456.

90. AOIF, Entrata e Uscita (CXXII,3), fol. 75r, 25 October 1451; vol. 7, fol. 43v, 18 April 1457.

91. AOIF, Entrata e Uscita (CXXII,2), fol. 64r, 27 March 1456.

92. AOIF, Ricordanze A (XII,1), fol. 164r, 27 April 1482.

93. AOIF, Ricordanze A (XII,1), fol. 9r, 1 August 1449.

94. AOIF, Ricordanze A (XII,1), fol. 84v, 19 September 1466.

95. AOIF, Ricordanze A (XII,1), fol. 142r, 8 September 1456.

96. AOIF, Ricordanze B (XII,2), fol. 96v, 20 April 1484.

97. AOIF, Ricordanze A (XII,1), fol. 68v, 17 April 1464.

98. AOIF, Ricordanze A (XII,1), fol. 70r, 27 August 1465.

99. AOIF, Ricordanze A (XII,4), fol. 256v, 21 August 1459.

100. AOIF, Ricordanze A (XII,1), fol. 72r, 25 January 1465 [modern = 1466].

101. AOIF, Ricordanze A (XII,1), fol. 79r, 21 June 1466.

102. AOIF, Ricordanze A (XII,1), fol. 141r, 17 November 1473.

103. AOIF, Ricordanze A (XII,4), fol. 268v, 19 June, 1461.

104. AOIF, Ricordanze B (XII,2), fol. 10v, 1 January 1482 [modern = 1483].

105. AOIF, Ricordanze B (XII,2), fol. 127r, 31 March 1495.

106. AOIF, Ricordanze A (XII,4), fol. 99r, 1 July 1456.

107. AOIF, Ricordanze B (XII,2), fol. 20r, 18 April 1483.

108. AOIF, Ricordanze B (XII,2), fol. 95v, 18 May 1484.

109. Frederick Jochem, "The Libri dello Spedale," (Ph.D. diss., University of Wisconsin, 1936). Goldthwaite, *The Building of Renaissance Florence* (Baltimore, 1981), 132–70.

110. AOIF, Quaderno del Camarlingo (CXXVI, 1), fol. 24r, 3 April 1446.

111. Mendes and Dallai, "Nuove indagini," 89ff.

112. AOIF, Ricordanze A (XII,1), fol. 84r, 17 September 1466.

113. AOIF, Ricordanze A (XII,1), fol. 85r, 9 October 1466.

114. AOIF, Ricordanze A (XII,1), fol. 95r, 15 June 1467.

115. AOIF, Balie e Bambini A (XVI,1), fol. 3r, 1 February 1444 [modern = 1445].

116. AOIF, Ricordanze A (XII,1), fol. 10v, 15 September 1445; AOIF, Balie e Bambini A (XVI,1), fol. 194v, 6 March 1446 [modern = 1447].

117. AOIF, Balie e Bambini F (XVI,6), fol. 70r, 18 June 1466.

118. AOIF, Balie e Bambini A (XVI,1), fol. 31v, 1 December 1445.

119. AOIF, Balie e Bambini A (XVI,1), fol. 3r, 1 February 1444 [modern = 1445].

120. AOIF, Balie e Bambini A (XVI,1), fol. 55r, 11 July 1446.

121. AOIF, Balie e Bambini A (XVI,1), fol. 47r, 10 May 1446.

122. AOIF, Balie e Bambini A (XVI,1), fol. 216v, 3 September 1449.

123. AOIF, Balie e Bambini A (XVI,1), fol. 51v, 28 June 1446.

124. AOIF, Balie e Bambini A (XVI,1), fol. 31v, 1 December 1445.

125. AOIF, Balie e Bambini A (XVI,1), fol. 223v, fol. 227v, 11 January 1449 [modern = 1450].

126. AOIF, Balie e Bambini B (XVI,2), fol. 38r, 13 July 1451.

127. AOIF, Balie e Bambini B (XVI,2), fol. 64v, 26 February 1451 [modern = 1452].

128. AOIF, Balie e Bambini A (XVI,1), fol. 194r, 22 February 1446 [modern = 1447]: "Mona Maddalena di Giovanni da Chastello Sancto Niccolò s'achorda ogi in questo dì 22 febraio 1446 per balia in chasa a dare la poppa e a fanciulli e tutti li altri servigi che bisongna iterno a fanciulli et anchora a ffare tutti li altri servigi che lli fuissi chomandati che bisognasse per chasa. E obblighassi di stare uno anno et per suo salario l'anno lire sesanta che viene il mese lire cinque——L 60. A dì 15 novembre si partì la sopra detta balia."

129. AOIF, Balie e Bambini A (XVI,1), fols. 55r–55v, 11 July 1446.

130. AOIF, Balie e Bambini A (XVI,1), fol. 47r, 23 May 1456.

131. AOIF, Balie e Bambini B (XVI,2), fol. 135r, 3 July 1453.

132. AOIF, Ricordanze A (XII,1), fol. 10v, 16 October 1445.

133. AOIF, Balie e Bambini A (XVI,1), fol. 47r, 23 May 1456.

134. AOIF, Ricordanze A (XII,1), fol. 10v, 16 October 1445.

135. AOIF, Ricordanze A (XII,1), fol. 37r, 20 April 1447.

136. AOIF, Ricordanze A (XII,1), fol. 50r, 24 November 1451.

137. AOIF, Entrata e Uscita (CXXII,2), fols. 3r, 111r, 28 August 1448.

138. AOIF, Entrata e Uscita (CXXII,2), fol. 13v, 1 August 1449: "rechò Bernardo di Lionardo Baroncelli chama[rlingho] in sugiello di x per cento s'ebi pezi 63 d'oro e s. 59 piccioli. I quali denarii sono pregio di Caterina nostra schiava gli vendemo di chonsiglio di Mariotto Lippi nostro operaio e di ser

Uberto Martini. E tutto si fecie per grande bisognio de' poveri e non si pote più a libro bianco S[egnatura] A a 97.——Fl. 70."

139. AOIF, Balie e Bambini D (XVI,4), fol. 13r, 12 May 1451.

140. AOIF, Entrata e Uscita (CXXII,2), fol. 15v, 18 December 1449.

141. AOIF, Ricordanze A (XII,4), fol. 101v, 18 July 1456.

142. AOIF, Ricordanze B (XII,2), fol. 5v, 17 January 1482 [modern = 1483].

143. Ibid.

144. Ibid.

145. AOIF, Ricordanze B (XII,2), fol. 45r, 17 September 1483.

146. Ibid.

147. Ibid.

148. Ibid.

149. Ibid.

150. Ibid.

151. AOIF, Ricordanze B (XII,2), fol. 49r, 21 October 1483.

152. AOIF, Ricordanze B (XII,2), fol. 55v, 4 November 1483.

153. AOIF, Ricordanze B (XII,2), fol. 50r, 23 October 1483. For some sample daily menus, see the appendix.

154. AOIF, Ricordanze B (XII,2), fols. 50v–66r, 23 October–18 November 1483.

155. AOIF, Ricordanze B (XII,2), fol. 60v, 10 November 1483.

156. ASF, Provvisioni Registri, 175, fols. 160rff., 18 February 1483 [modern = 1484].

157. AOIF, Ricordanze A (XII,1), fol. 67r, 6 July 1465.

158. See table 3.

159. AOIF, Entrata e Uscita (CXXII,1), fol. 159v, 7 October 1447.

160. These 1374 statutes from the hospital of Santa Maria Nuova can be found in Luigi Passerini, *Storia degli stabilmenti di beneficenza e d'istruzione elementare gratuita della città di Firenze* (Florence, 1853), 840.

161. In twelfth-century Toulouse, couples might dedicate themselves to a particular monastery, as Bernardus de Maso and his wife Petrona did for the Cistercian monastery at Grandselve. This pious couple also enjoyed the usufruct of their endowment until death. Even before they dedicated themselves to the monastery, Bernardus and Petrona had operated their home as a hospice, and in this respect differed from the majority of the *commessi* at the Innocenti. See John H. Mundy, "Charity and Social Work in Toulouse," *Traditio* 22 (1966): 213–14.

162. Passerini, *Storia degli stabilmenti di beneficenza,* 840–46.

163. Goldthwaite and Rearick, "Michelozzo," 224–26.

164. AOIF, Testamenta et Donationes (IX,1), fol. 49v, 10 June 1427.

165. AOIF, Testamenta et Donationes (IX,1), fol. 71rff., 18 January 1430 [modern = 1431].

166. AOIF, Testamenta et Donationes (IX,1), fol. 54v–55v, 13 November 1425.

167. AOIF, Testamenta et Donationes (IX,1), fol. 126rff., 15 April 1438.

168. Ibid.

169. AOIF, Testamenta et Donationes (IX,1), fol. 120r, 7 January 1444 [modern = 1445].

170. AOIF, Testamenta et Donationes (IX,1), fol. 123r–125v, 11–27 January 1444 [modern = 1445].

171. Ibid.

172. Ibid.

173. AOIF, Entrata e Uscita (CXXII,2), fols. 2r–6r, 22 March 1444 [modern = 1445].

174. ASF, Arte della Seta, 246, fols. 11r–103v, 1 May 1419–1 May 1476.

175. ASF, Compagnie Soppressi, San Zanobi, 2170, fol. 106v, 1 May–1 September 1448. I wish to thank Elaine Rosenthal for this reference.

176. Ronald Weissman, *Ritual Brotherhood in Renaissance Florence* (New York, 1982), 49, 63, 85.

177. AOIF, Entrata e Uscita (CXXII,2), fols. 2r–6r, 22 March 1444 [modern = 1445].

178. Ibid.

179. Ibid.

180. Ibid.

181. AOIF, Entrata e Uscita (CXXII,5), fol. 4r, 4 March 1452 [modern = 1453].

Chapter 5

Omnes Sancti Innocentes

Although the hospital's own statutes of 1451, as well as that year's legislation granting the hospital's participation in the communal dowry fund, specified that hospital employees should number each child as it came into the hospital, the hospital had been keeping records of wet nurses and children since the hospital's opening in January 1445.[1] From the resulting series of *Balie e Bambini,* it is not at all difficult to reconstruct the moment of abandonment, by turns poignant or horrifying, nor is it difficult to identify the range of motives that led parents to abandon their children in the first place. The historian owes no small debt to the scribes and doorkeepers of the Innocenti, who, if the child's bearer did not flee, assiduously extracted as much information as possible about the circumstances of abandonment. The frequency with which bearers said "they didn't want to say who the father was" suggests that hospital employees probed and prodded to find the respondents' thresholds of discretion. Although the economic interest of the questioners was clear enough, since the hospital tried to encourage abandoning parents to assume at least the expense if not the responsibility of caring for the children they abandoned, the frankness of many of the answers suggests the profound ambivalence parents often felt at the moment of abandonment.

The first question an abandoning parent who lingered would face was: had the child been baptized? If not, and the child was healthy, the hospital would, within the first two days, bring the child to the baptistery of San Giovanni to be baptized. If the child was seriously ill, baptism would take place immediately.[2] If parents were not in a position to divulge this most precious piece of information, they often left salt with the child, a token that the child required baptism.[3] The parentage and provenance of the child followed as the next two most important questions, and included in this part of the deposition was some indication, more often than not misleading, of whether the parent intended to re-claim a child. If a parent was diffident, he or she might leave a counter-sign to identify the child in the event of reclamation. This countersign might be an object, or a drawing on the note pinned to the child's clothing. The *Balie e Bambini* have several examples of countersigns the scribe copied both from the objects and from drawings.[4] Medieval litera-ture concerning abandonment as well as recent studies of eighteenth-century hospitals suggest that both salt as a sign of need for baptism and countersigns as tokens of reclamation were traditional means of commu-nication for at least a millennium.[5] Finally, the scribe attempted to get as detailed a history as possible of the circumstances surrounding the abandonment.

Before the Innocenti assigned a child a wet nurse, the scribe took down, in addition to other information from parents or bearers, the date and hour of admission, the condition of the child, and the extent and condition of the child's clothing. Only children who were newborns and who had then been rushed to the hospital came without clothes at all, and even this was exceptional. Even if the child's wrappings were little more than rags, abandoning parents took pains to ensure the warmth of the infants abandoned to the care of the hospital. Thus the second child admitted to the Innocenti, Alessandra Smeralda, had a "straciuolo ro-magnuolo" or strip of very rough cloth that the scribe characterized as "little and torn." She also had with her "a strip of a small piece of cloth and a little swaddling band made from a shirt ripped into three pieces."[6] When she went to wet nurse twelve days later the hospital supplied the wet nurse with "a piece of new wool, new swaddling clothes, eight pieces of good cloth, and an old cloak."[7] Infant boys came to the hospital in similar wrappings: Niccolò Salvestro, born of the slave girl of the *li-naiuolo* Antonio di Taddeo, came with "a piece of old red wool, and two little pieces of cloth, a sad-looking swaddling band . . . and he had a sack of salt as a sign that he was not baptized."[8] Even when a child is de-scribed as "nude" he or she might actually have been "wrapped only in a little piece of rags." Jacopa Anna, the daughter of a slave girl, was brought to the Innocenti "in the nude covered only with a wretched little piece of torn cloth."[9]

Children, about 90 percent of whom were between three hours and three weeks old on admission, were first fed by the staff of resident wet nurses, who numbered about fifteen, before being sent to the country-side for wet-nursing. The average waiting period between admission and the journey to wet nurse was six to twelve days, but might range from a few hours to a few months. Infants usually stayed with the same wet nurse until it was time to be weaned, between the ages of eighteen and twenty-four months. They returned to the hospital for a very brief period to await the assignment of foster parents. Children usually returned to the Innocenti to take up full-time residence for two to four years at the age of four. In 1449, for example, the income and expenditure journals of the hospital record elaborate preparations for "the return of the *fanciulli*," who were the survivors from the first cohort of children admitted in early 1445.[10]

Within two years of returning from foster care, boys were put up for adoption, usually as apprentices. Hospital officials just as eagerly sought placement for girls not only as household and domestic servants, but as workers in various tasks associated with silk production, such as washing and weaving cloths. The hospital farmed both boys and girls out during the day for some apprenticeships, and fed them an evening meal upon their return. Adoption and apprenticeship contracts, at least for boys, showed as much interest in an education in reading and manners as they did in teaching the mechanics of trade and artisanry.

This rudimentary outline of the organization of care at the Innocenti demonstrates how difficult it is to compare this fifteenth-century hospital and institutions of later centuries. A child abandoned at the Innocenti in the fifteenth century might spend as little as two of his or her seven years under the hospital's care actually on the premises of the hospital. Even late in the fifteenth century, when admissions rose to two hundred per year, the census of children remained at or below a hundred at any given time. This is in marked contrast to the sixteenth century, when the institution under the grand dukes assumed more of a residential character on the "Boys' Town" model. Vincenzo Borghini, a collaborator of Vasari and superintendent of the Innocenti in the sixteenth century, wrote a treatise that considered alternatives to marriage or monachation of the girls of the hospital who were of marriageable age.[11] Either a cause or a symptom of this institutional change must have been an increase in the hospital's population during the early sixteenth century, an increase that no doubt signified a decrease in the demand for adopted children.

The converse of this statement illuminates, finally, the role of this charitable institution in fifteenth-century Florence. The hospital took in abandoned children and tried, practically from the moment of admission, to propel them into a family setting. Adoption and apprenticeship contracts, drawn up for the most part when children were older, stipulated that the children must be treated as if they were the adoptive parents' own sons and daughters. In households and small business enterprises where the depopulation caused by recurring plague threatened their very survival, the children of the Innocenti must have been economically as well as emotionally valuable. Even the most formal contracts abound with expressions of affection for adopted children, and the scarcity of children made abandonment itself a highly ambivalent experience for the parents with whom the Innocenti had daily contact.

How, then, did such affection manifest itself? In 1445, Antonia Ginevra, one of the first children abandoned at the Innocenti, was abandoned with a note. The Innocenti's porter wrote:

> a boy brought her [Antonia] . . . and he would not say what her name was or whose daughter she was. He left a note, which says that her name is Antonia Ginevra, and that she has a mother and a father who will provide well for her. They recommend her for love of God and the Virgin Mary.[12]

Similarly, on 23 May 1445 the bearer of Piera Domenica:

> said she was born Wednesday last [four days ago]. He brought a letter with him [that said] Vespasiano di ser Jachopo [said] his father is in jail. He commends her highly, saying in the said letter that she should be well-treated and that the father will come back for her and give us what he owes us.[13]

Despite this promise, nevertheless, his daughter was still unclaimed at the Innocenti five years later.

Some abandonments resulted from a teenage, or at least premarital, pregnancy. In October 1445, Lucia Innocente, who had come from Pozzolatico nude except for a lone piece of rag, was, according to the child's grandfather, who was bearer and informant:

> born that very morning of one of his daughters, whose name is Liperata, and Giovanni di Duccio his neighbor from Pozzolaticho—she [Lucia] was born from her [Liperata's] love for the said Giovanni.[14]

Not all bearers were so voluble or loquacious, even if their children were—it is interesting to note here what criteria the Innocenti used to judge this child's age:

> Brigida Innocente is six months old or more, since she has begun to talk. We will never know whose she is, or who placed her there, since we did not see them. They think she belongs to one of the poor who go begging or who stay at the Servi. She was on our doorstep for two hours [before] she was heard crying and brought in by Branco di Noe, our stonecutter.[15]

Yet others who we might think would have reason to hide their origins did not. Giovanna Caterina, abandoned in December 1445, was the daughter of "Ser Agnolo," a priest and "chaplain in Santa Maria del Fiore of Florence."[16] In 1457, when a female child was brought to the Innocenti, the woman who brought her said "she is the daughter of a priest who was a *pievano*, but she would not say where he was from. She was born in Florence and the mother is not married."[17]

Parents might abandon children because of the illness or death of a spouse. In mid-March 1446 Girolamo Ambrogio was anonymously abandoned at the Innocenti:

> Then, on the twentieth of the said month a woman came to us who said she had left the boy. She also said that the mother of the boy was dead and that the boy was the son of Michele di Benvenuto, a *spadaio* from the parish of Santa Felicita in Florence.[18]

Although Michele left no indication that he would ever return, eight years later, in 1454, he did come back to the Innocenti and reclaim the boy. In 1448, another father, who is not named, "brought a female infant and placed her on the font. [He] brought her because the mother is said to be ill at the hospital of Messer Bonifazio."[19] This father, however, had second thoughts, and the Innocenti returned his daughter to him the same day. In 1452, the daughter of a carter:

> was placed on the font and baptized with the name Andrea. She was about ten months old or more. She is the daughter of Giorgio, a carter

who lives by the Porte alla Croce, and his wife, Mona Margherita. Giorgio sent his daughter to us because his wife is ill and was sent to [the hospital of] Santa Maria Nuova. She is very ill, and a poor person.

The following year, however, Andrea's mother recovered and returned to the Innocenti to claim her.[20]

These cases raise a number of questions. Fathers seemed incapable of, or ill suited to, the task of raising children in the mother's absence. Certainly the late weaning of children (eighteen months to two years) may have made Florentine fathers fear starvation for children. Yet this still begs the question of the absence of support from any kind of extended family structure. No grandparents or aunts came to the rescue. Certainly the low status of the fathers' occupations may have made a wet nurse difficult to afford. Yet a father did come to reclaim his son the same day and to undertake single-handedly the task of child-rearing.

More serious was the situation in which both parents became ill. In November 1452, when Girolamo Bartolomeo, age two, was left at the Innocenti, the scrap of paper attached to him gave his name and noted that his parents and two of their other children were patients at the hospital of Santa Maria Nuova. This child stayed with the same foster parents, who had renamed him "Friano," for ten years before returning to the Innocenti at the age of thirteen. His father had died, but his mother returned to the Innocenti for him.[21] In all cases where the remaining parent or parents were poor, the Innocenti waived the usual demands for the support payments required to reclaim the child.

In plague years the hospital of Santa Maria Nuova might admit entire families. Thus Angelico and his family were admitted there, dying of plague, in 1457. When the remainder of his family had died, an official from Santa Maria Nuova brought Angelico to the Innocenti, where he died a week later.[22] In another case a mother abandoned her child because the father had died. The child, who was left at the Innocenti in 1462, was named Giovanni da Scotia, "John of Scotland":

She said that he had been born from her and her legitimate husband who had died at Santa Maria Nuova.... She said that they were from Scotland and that the boy was one year to fourteen months old—at least as far as we could understand, since we could not understand her language very well.[23]

Most of the abandonments due to the death or illness of a spouse seem to have been intended as short stays. Mothers for whom the burden of taking care of children was too heavy turned to the Innocenti when their husbands fell ill. When a priest's laborer from Calcinaia brought Antonia Giovanna to the Innocenti in early 1465, he reported that she was the daughter of a laborer who was ill and whose wife had no milk. Only three days later Antonia's mother returned to the Innocenti to claim her.[24]

A boy was abandoned at Camaldoli in 1465 at the age of ten months because his mother was ill and "his father is a weaver. He lives in Camaldoli ... in his house with one of his two sons who are heralds in the palace."[25] The father promised to pay the child's expenses, and in this case the hospital directed the wet nurse straight to the child's father for payment. He spent about six weeks away before being reunited with his parents. Similarly:

On 23 May 1457, a female infant was left on the font and baptized. She had a note saying that her name was Lisabetta di Matteo d'Andrea. Her mother brought her and said she was ill and for that reason could not breast-feed her. She seemed to be about three months old. On 30 May the aforesaid girl was returned to her mother, who came and waited for her.[26]

More common was a mother's decision to abandon her child because she had been widowed and was remarrying. Simona, a child of thirteen months, was brought to the Innocenti by an unidentified man from Orbatello:

He says she is the daughter of a woman called Mona Rosa, today the wife of a German who lives in Camaldoli. He says that the woman's husband does not want her in the house because she is a daughter from her first marriage.[27]

Similarly, in 1465, concerning another abandoned girl:

the person who brought her said that she is legitimate and that she is born of Berto di Papi di Niccolò di Berto, parish of Sant'Andrea a Mosciano ... and of Mona Felice his legitimate wife. The said Berto died and the mother remarried. The father's brother and [therefore] the child's uncle is Niccolò di Papi di Berto di Niccolò. She [the child] was brought in very bad condition.[28]

Three months later this child died at wet nurse. In this case the availability of extended family was not at issue. An uncle existed but did not step forward to take the child. In another case, the lack of outside support from an aunt moved the mother to take her child back in spite of having remarried:

This 20th day of June [1472] Mona Carmellina, wife of Pagolo Bocherini was here. She said the girl belonged to her and that she will soon be married to the said Pagolo, and that she wanted to raise her herself, since the child's aunt did not wish to.... She swore an oath...that the child was hers.[29]

Some abandonments were more hard-hearted. Certainly the hospital bestowed the name "Margherita bella, pazza, e mutola" with more affection than the parents who had abandoned her because of her stammer:

On 18 September 1452 at the thirteenth hour a female child was brought and placed on the font. She was about eighteen months old, and the person who brought her fled and did not wish to say whose she was or what her name was. She brought with her a note that said she had her tongue-string cut because she stammered, and that afterwards she spoke badly. The abovesaid child is mute and crazy and therefore the wet nurse will be given thirty-five soldi per month.[30]

In at least two cases, porters discovered children battered beyond hope or recognition on the doorstep of the Innocenti. In September 1449:

When the call for dinner came, an old man brought a child. The old man was a poor person. He knocked with the hammer, and as soon as he was answered, he fled. He [the child] was about four months old by the looks of him. He had been found with a slash between the ribs. On 18 September he died and went to Paradise. May God bless him and pardon his father and mother.[31]

The hospital named this boy "Sanza Rimedio." Similarly, in 1452:

> a dead baby girl was left on the font. She had been beaten in several places on the head and in the face so that her nose was squashed to the sides of her mouth. She was a dark thing to see, all livid and black. It could not be seen who brought her nor will we ever know.

So moved were the staff of the Innocenti by this sight that the *commessi* prepared her for burial, which was attended by:

> Dianora, my wife; Mona Agnola di Maso, our *commessa;* Mona Caterina di Mona Masa; Mona Antonio di Casino di Casentino; Maria and Masa, our slaves, and Mona Maddalena di Giovanni Banchi; all our wet nurses in-house: Big Maddalena, Lionarda, Lucia, Agatha, and several of our little girls in house saw to it that she was buried. May God bless her.[32]

At the other end of the affective scale were the parents or relatives who attached notes to the children they abandoned. "Do not take a fancy to this little girl" one note read:

> We are waiting for her father to return from Rome soon. [In the meantime] see that she is well provided for. We believe that if it be God's pleasure the hospital will lose nothing by it. Christ be your guardian.[33]

Promises to pay child support were not in short supply in these notes. Another note, this one from 1456, promised that "the hospital will be well provided for and should see to it that he is well brought up."[34] Some notes elaborated this theme even further: "she is the daughter of a person of means and the hospital will do well by him and it should treat her well."[35]

Indeed, countersigns could serve both as an indication that the writer's intention was reclamation and restitution of the hospital's expenses, and as a sign of baptism:

On the 24th of May in the evening at the 23rd hour a little girl was placed on the font. A slave brought her and the little girl had a note and a little coin around her neck. The note said that the little girl was to be recommended. She was born at ten o'clock in the morning. Give her the name Zanobia Maria. The object around her neck is a sign that we had her baptized and therefore that you are to give her the said names.[36]

From a purely functional perspective, notes pinned to children served as letters of introduction and recommendation, just as a note slipped in the pages of the *Balie e Bambini* might recommend an adult: "Lator est amicus et bonus homo. Te recomicto fideliter."[37]

Although it was not by any means rare for girls to come warmly recommended to the hospital by their parents, boys more often arrived with a sign or token that would make them recognizable if and when they were reclaimed. Thus, in December 1461, an infant came with a note that said:

I record today this ninth day of December 1461: "To Messer Giro-lamo di San Gimignano, at present superintendent of the hospital of the Innocenti in the Piazza dei Servi: [Here is] a baby who has the name Ambruogio Miniato. He is baptized and has around his neck a Pisan halfpenny as a sign so that he is recommended to you, because he is the son of a person of means, one of our Florentine citizens who will do his duty toward you. Make a note of the day he came and of his expenses, and everything will be repaid."[38]

This infant died soon after in the hospital.

A child with such a countersign often was sent out to wet nurse later than most children were. Although these delays were primarily among male children, parents of female children often left explicit instructions for the hospital not to give the child away to wet nurse:

Friday 11 June 1462 at one-thirty in the morning the aforesaid little girl, Caterina Lucretia was brought to the font. And her bearer brought a note to this effect: "I swear that the said infant girl has the name Caterina Lucretia, who is born of a very wealthy person. And thus it is begged of you, the prior . . . to keep this countersign and see that she is not given to others. Keep it marked, and when we are able we will do our duty. We recommend her to God's love today, Saint Barnabas's day, and as a countersign a thread from her clothes and half a Bolognese groat is inserted in this note."[39]

A countersign, although it was supposed to protect the child from the malfeasance of incompetent wet nurses, did not necessarily mean that the hospital actually screened the wet nurses for these special children more carefully. Less than a month later, on 7 July, the hospital heard "from a person worthy of faith that Caterina was dying of hunger and that [the wet nurse] did not have milk." The prior ordered Caterina's immediate return, but not until 28 September did the wet nurse actually return her, "sick unto death, badly kept, and badly cared for."[40] Fears of such horrors led another parent to write:

I recommend to you this little girl. Have her baptized and give her the name Provegha Maddalena. She is the daughter of Piero di Gualtiero, a butcher from Mattonaia. Do not send her outside the hospital.

Despite this explicit instruction the hospital loaned her to Giovanni di Quirico, presumably to stimulate or relieve his servant's milk supply, and then hospital officials sent her twice to wet nurse, where she died two years later.[41]

Notes pinned to children might also express affection for the hospital itself:

Dearly Beloved of the Hospital of the Innocenti: I send you a baby boy born this day [26 December 1462] whose name is Giovanfrancesco di Tommaso, whom I pray you make sure is carefully raised, because I am most faithful and devoted to this house. I send you as a countersign this on *cartapecora*... which I will redeem. I am happy to pay the wet nurse month by month as you will see from experience. Christ save all of you.[42]

Both these notes and the depositions left with porters suggest the importance of noneconomic motives between 1440 and 1500.[43] Indeed, in almost every case, children who came with a countersign had fathers who were "persons of means." If, on one hand, notes indicating motives of poverty became more frequent in the 1460s, on the other, abandonments for other, sometimes obscure motives continued unabated, as this note from 1472 suggests:

> she was born of good blood, and she was brought to avoid scandal. She is commended to you as much as possible and to all the administrators and personnel of this most useful institution, that she may be placed in good hands and will be well provided for in future. Bartolomea di Giovanni from Brescia came and said she was the daughter of Matteo and her.[44]

A somewhat earlier note, from 1463, begins:

> + Most Reverend in Christ: He [Antonio Lorenzo] was born of my slave . . . at ten o'clock. He was sent to you with his little cloak and in swaddling clothes. The father . . . is Jacopo di Viterbo, who was an official with the captain. His mother's name is Caterina, my slave. Do not send her to wet nurse for long periods of time.[45]

Others were even less reticent about hope for a good wet nurse:

> On 23 March we sent you an infant boy. He is the son of Giovanni Tavolacino of the Signory and of Monna Maria. Send him to wet nurse and the father will reimburse you. Give him to a good wet nurse because the father will do his duty by providing well for you.[46]

At the other end of the economic and social scale, tremendous economic pressure sometimes came to bear on a family's decision to abandon. In January 1464 a note attached to a three-year-old boy said that:

> he was brought here because it was not possible to bear the expense of having him. [His mother], a widow, was dying of hunger and could not feed him. She has a girl eighteen years of age and an old man of eighty to care for. One of her guests took everything in the house. He [the child] has no father or mother.[47]

Another note described similar circumstances:

On 3 April 1464 Domenica Francesca was brought to the hospital of the Innocenti. She is the daughter of Simone di Domenico from Piombino, who sent her here because he will not be at home, but in the galleys. She was brought here because her mother is poor and cannot keep her any longer.[48]

A preponderance of notes to the Innocenti promised some form of remuneration. A variety of motives stood behind these promises. Some parents, or donors on behalf of parents, viewed the support of a child as a charitable donation. One could "sponsor" a child, often that of a friend or relative, but one could also sponsor a designated child with no demonstrable relationship to the donor. Many other notes promised to defray all the expenses of wet-nursing, and attempted to induce the hospital to keep the child with in-house wet nurses with promises to pay and to redeem the child within a short time. Finally, if parents wished to have the child they had abandoned returned to them, the Innocenti expected reimbursement. In the 1460s, as the hospital's fiscal crisis took on tragic proportions, administrators perceived that the likelihood was small of parents having accumulated enough money over several years to pay for reclamation, and no longer accepted a vague commitment when the child was abandoned. Thus in the 1460s written promises became more common, along with payment schedules and the right to seize the property of parental debtors. Driven by the pressure of an increasing in-house population and mounting expenses, the Innocenti did not resist the move toward becoming a fee-for-service institution, although even in the worst economic times the hospital's administrators would waive payment requirements for parents who were poor, especially widowers and widows. Nor is there evidence that the hospital ever turned away children, except to send them to San Gallo if they were too old for the Innocenti, and even this stopped with the merger of the two hospitals in 1463.

The range and variety of motives cited above might even coexist in the same person: a young person who wished not to give his name gave two florins for his son's wet nurse.

He gave them to us for charity and for these poor little ones because [nearly a year ago] on 5 May 1449 we returned to him his abovesaid child.[49]

A similar combination of motives induced the silk merchant Antonio di Simone to give the hospital, six lire "for charity, or rather for the nourishment given to his two children, kept here at our expense."[50] Some children had anonymous sponsors. In 1456 the hospital received "from a good man, five lire to subsidize an infant girl."[51] Another anonymous source gave fifteen soldi "for alms for an infant boy who was in the hospital."[52] In another case, an uncle agreed to pay the expenses of his brother's child by paying the wet nurse directly, but backed out when he discovered the child was not his brother's.[53]

Nor was sponsorship restricted to men. In 1454 the hospital accepted ten lire, two soldi from "a good woman of means [who] gave us two large florins for the feeding of Francesca Tommasa."[54] And in 1468, a priest, Ser Marsilio di Antonio, rector of the chapel of the Annunziata in Poggibonsi, agreed to pay seven florins in support of his nephew Piero Pulliciano.[55] In 1467, Ser Antonio di Jacopo da Prato, "a priest and a scholar living in Florence, who at present officiates in San Michele," promised to pay semiannually twelve and a half lire in support of the *fanciulla* Maria Barbara.[56]

The question of whether or not a parent would pay child support was often a pressing one. Even as early as the mid-1450s, parents went so far in their notes as to give a detailed accounting of their net worth. On 8 June 1454 one such father instructed the bearer of his child to tell hospital officials that the father "would under oath give an accounting of how much he is worth, i.e., four thousand florins, so make sure the child stays well, since the father is quite rich."[57] Parents also hoped that such a display of wealth would constitute sufficient evidence that they intended to reclaim the child. In January 1455, Cristofano di maestro Antonio, a hosier from Conigliano, abandoned Quaraddo Zacheria:

> The said Cristofano wishes that you promise to keep him in the hospital so he will stay well, and he will pay whatever the prior wishes as a gift so that the hospital will not lose anything. In addition he will give the hospital fifty soldi a month for a wet nurse.[58]

If to modern eyes these exhortations come perilously close to bribery, they do indicate not only strong fatherly concern, but also serious ambivalence and well-founded fear on the part of fathers about the act of abandonment.

In the case cited above, the Innocenti's officials did respond by keeping the child in the hospital several extra days before finally sending the child to wet nurse. Yet despite strong parental sentiment and the lingering, perhaps illusory hope the hospital had that this parent would bestow large sums of money, the hospital was unable to screen this boy's wet nurse. The wet nurse's husband came in late December 1455 seeking payment, which the hospital refused since:

> on 16 December his neighbor told us the infant was dead. We don't want to pay the *balio* until he brings back the baby's clothes, because we are not sure just when the baby died.[59]

Fathers responded to their own fears and ambivalence in several ways. Some hoped, often vainly, that the promise of large sums of money would encourage the hospital to monitor their children more closely. A grandparent in 1459 took a more direct and practical approach by paying the hospital for an in-house wet nurse: "Giovanni Cavigiani owes us for the twenty days he kept Agnesa, our wet nurse, to provide milk for one of his sons."[60] Still other fathers did not end their involvement with their infant children at the moment of abandonment, but followed their progress by making payments directly to the wet nurse. In May 1457, for example: "Brancazia Cardinalesca was brought by an old woman who said nothing except that the father wanted her back when he was able." The hospital did not give her to a wet nurse for another six weeks. Six months later:

> on 25 November 1457 Mona Margherita [the wet nurse] gave the child to Mona Maria di Simone del Pancione da Campi. The father of the said little girl wanted her given to another wet nurse because, he said, Mona Margherita was not doing a good job of keeping her.

The Innocenti, perhaps precursor of the modern bureaucracy, told this father that he was henceforth to arrange the *balia* himself, because he had failed to seek the hospital's permission for the change.[61]

Indeed, so frequently did parents pay wet nurses directly that it is difficult to avoid the conclusion that the Innocenti acted as a referral service for wealthy families to recruit their own good wet nurses. The infant boy Piero di Bartolomeo, abandoned at the Innocenti:

was born this very hour, and he came half dead and all ashen and foaming at the mouth. We baptized him and conferred on him the aforesaid names. On 5 April 1445 we gave the aforesaid Piero Bartolomeo to Alamanno Salviati, who came on behalf of Vieri Davanzati with the wet nurse and her husband, with whom he had made arrangements. He gave us twenty-three silver groats as alms.[62]

Yet not only the wealthy used this arrangement to stay involved with their abandoned children. In 1465, a certain Giovanni and his wife abandoned their son Giovanbattista "because Mona Anna [his mother] is ill and cannot care for her son and went to the hospital." Giovanni was a weaver with two sons who were heralds in the Palazzo Vecchio.

He promised to pay month-by-month the salary of the wet nurse. . . . Take note that when the wet nurse and her husband come for the money that the father has promised to pay. . . . Note [16 June 1465] that the wet nurse says she is content with what she has been paid and that she returned the boy to his father.[63]

Nor were slaves immune to the emotional tug of their children whom their *padrone* had abandoned. A broker for wet nurses left the infant boy Donato Bartolomeo at the Innocenti, and she identified the parents as Bartolomeo di Lodovico di Cece da Verrazzano and the slave-girl Margherita. Thirteen months later Margherita:

went to the wet nurse's house and stole the said boy. On 6 August [Margherita] was in my office saying that she had not received . . . the baby's clothes from the wet nurse. She gave us five large florins incurred as expenses in feeding the said child.[64]

Naturally, parents who arranged the wet-nursing of their children through the hospital and then paid the wet nurses directly left the hospital vulnerable to parents who might make the arrangements and then attempt to retrieve the child without paying expenses. This partially explains the increasing use on the part of the hospital of written contracts to replace verbal agreements with parents who had promised to pay. In March 1467, for example: Giovanni di Domenicho, a hosier from San Frediano, set up a repayment agreement with the Innocenti for the forty-four lire he had promised to pay for the wet-nursing of his daughter. In this agreement he was given two years to pay in annual installments of twenty-two lire, and his estate and possessions could be attached for failure to pay on time.[65] Although the hospital was most likely to draw up these contracts when a parent returned to claim a child, hospital administrators also insisted on more formal promises and procedures when a child was first admitted. In 1466, a father abandoned his daughter because her mother had died. Thus, he said, "he wanted to pay all expenses incurred in wet-nursing, weaning, and feeding her. He agreed to hold the hospital harmless" and to allow his property and possessions to be attached if necessary to satisfy the debt.[66]

The Innocenti did attempt maximum flexibility when dealing with parents whose resources were limited. In September 1462, for example:

> Giovanni d'Antonio di Ghuarlone...and his wife Mona Lena, [the parents] of Urbano Innocente, promised Messer Girolamo, acting on behalf of our hospital as superintendent, to give to said hospital four barrels of wine per year until he has satisfied all the hospital's expenses in bringing up and feeding his son, Urbano.[67]

In the five years between 1457 and 1462 that Urbano stayed at the Ospedale degli Innocenti, he had run up a bill of ninety-six lire. The Innocenti released Urbano to his parents as soon as they had put their signatures to the above contract. When Maestro Rafaello, a scholar, abandoned Niccolò Salvestro in 1445 but returned for him six weeks later, he paid the Innocenti sixteen lire to cover the three-quarters of the expenses his son had incurred at wet nurse. To affirm his pledge to pay the remainder, he gave the prior "a grammar book that the prior said he had [always] wanted to read."[68]

Children could also be redeemed by their parents for less than it had cost the hospital to feed them. Thus one of Pagholo Pagholi's slaves, Giuliana, was allowed to take back her child Lorenzo in 1459 by promising to pay by the month for twenty-five months half of the fifty lire the hospital had spent on her son's care.[69] Similarly, payments could be spread out without interest charges or could be paid in kind.[70] If the parents' poverty was sufficiently severe the hospital might return the child free of charge:

On 4 September at 17 hours a small boy about two years old was brought and placed on the font. He was brought by a woman who said he was the son of Bartolomeo, and his mother was named Mona Brigida. She said that the father was dying and the mother was ill in the hospital. The boy was wearing a shirt, a pair of new shoes, and a cloth skirt.... On 25 June the wet nurse came here to tell us that she was giving the child back because his father wanted him and that they would do their duty to the House, but that they have no more money. On 24 July 1456 the aforesaid boy was sent back to us with all his clothes. He is in-house. On 25 July 1456 we gave the boy to his father without charge because he is a poor person and because Francesco Masini knows him.[71]

In 1453 the hospital offered the same clemency to the parents of ten-month-old Andrea because the child's father was a carter: "she was returned to her mother without cost for charity and because of their poverty."[72] If poverty was the usual reason for waiving the cost of up-keep, it was not the only reason. In April 1456 the Innocenti returned a boy who had stayed only four days "gladly to the person who sent him, because we understand he was a good father to the aforesaid boy," a perception no doubt reinforced by the father's subsequent donation of four silver groats.[73]

In a 1452 census drawn up by Lapo di Piero Pacini, which covered the years 1445–52, 6.3 percent of 534 children were returned to their parents, at the rate of about 10 percent of the boys and 3 percent of the girls. Along with some of the more concrete evidence cited earlier, this suggests that one of the hospital's social services was to provide temporary and respite care for children whose parents were ill or otherwise burdened with family cares. This was especially true for the wealthy whose slaves had borne children. Indeed, they were twice as likely as other abandoning parents to reclaim their illegitimate children. The sex ratios of this 1452 census strongly suggest that male infants were more likely to be returned than female. Of the thirty-four children in the 1452 census who had been returned to their parents, only nine were female, although both sexes were otherwise accounted for (table 5).

Thus the hospital served, in addition to its resident constituency of genuinely poor parents and children, two functions not normally associated with foundling hospitals. First, hospital administrators at times were little more than a referral service for wealthy families who were trying to find good wet nurses. Second, another important service the Innocenti offered its wealthier clients, but which was also extremely beneficial to its abandoned children, was to loan children to maintain the milk supply of domestic servants and slaves. Luca Innocente was loaned to "Bernardo Adimari for the use of one of his slaves. He brought her back on 14 September 1445."[74] On one occasion the hospital lost track of a loaned child:

> She is the daughter of Piero di Jacopo da Popi. Giulio d'Antonio da Romena brought her and said she was born 24 February [two weeks ago]. The prior lent her in May and says that he doesn't remember to whom she was lent. He told me nothing at the time. [When she was returned to the hospital] still nothing was said to me.[75]

None of these loan arrangements either cost or yielded the hospital anything, even if the child was loaned for months or to a *persona da bene*.[76]

Most children the Innocenti loaned only once. Agnola Innocente, who was loaned three times before her death in July 1446, was born to:

> Federigho di Giovanni dalla Magnia [*sic*] who stays with Messer Giovanni Boscholi . . . she is the daughter of Caterina, a slave of the said

TABLE 5. Status of Children by Sex According to 1452 Census

Status	Male	Female	Total
In-house	15	24	39
On Loan	4	5	9
"Missing"	16	20	36
Redeemed	25	9	34
Adopted	3	6	9
Subtotal	63	64	127
(Died)	102	139	241
(Nursing)	79	90	169
Total	244	293	537

Sources: AOIF, Ricordanze A (XII,1), fols. 53r–55v, 6 May 1452; numbers in parentheses: AOIF, Balie e Bambini A–B (XVI,1–2).

Note: Tables 5–19 cover twenty-two years of data from 1445 to 1466. Two problems in the sources prevent further exploration for the fifteenth century: the *Balie e Bambini*, which record admissions and deaths, show a gap between 1484 and 1520. Second, beginning in 1466, three years after the merger of the hospitals of San Gallo and the Innocenti, scribes only rarely recorded the age of children on admission, rendering calculations of infant mortality from 1467 to 1484 unreliable. Certainly the qualitative evidence suggests that mortality continued to increase over the course of the fifteenth century, as chapter 2 of this study shows.

Messer Giovanni. We lent her to Carlo di Francesco di Messer Palla [degli Strozzi] on 15 October 1445. Then we lent her to Simone Bartolo Strada for one of his wife's wet nurses. On 18 November we lent [her] to Niccolò di Brancazio Rucellai; on 16 April 1446 I sent her to Campi to the residence of Domenico Borghini. On 10 June we had her back.

In addition to all this the Innocenti also sent her to paid wet nurses in the same year.[77]

Mortality among these children was much lower than among either those children who remained in the hospital or who were sent directly to wet nurse. Thus "we lent the said child to Luca di Buonaccorso Pitti who said he wanted him for one of his wet nurses who lives in Peretola. . . . We have him back very well cared for."[78] Similarly Nastasia Innocente returned from being loaned on 24 March 1451 "fat and fresh."[79] The reason for this low mortality was undoubtedly the better material circumstances of these noble families as well as greater motivation for the enterprise to succeed: "On 23 March we lent the aforesaid boy to Antonio Martelli for ten or twelve days to maintain his wet nurse's milk until his wife gives birth."[80] Of the first hundred children admitted to the Innocenti, thirteen were loaned. None came back "badly treated" and only one died while on loan. Clearly, improved material circumstances drastically increased children's chances for survival. Moreover, children were loaned either within the city or within a few miles of the city, rather then traveling thirty miles to the Casentino to be nursed.

What other constituencies did the hospital serve? Of the first hundred admissions to the Innocenti, forty-one bearers told where either the child or its father or mother came from. Only 34 percent of this group came from Florence itself, although we may safely presume that Florentines might be less likely than people from remote locations to identify themselves. Most of the remaining 66 percent came from the Florentine *contado*, and even more precisely, 12 percent came from the Mugello, directly to the north of Florence. Also well represented were the mountainous areas to the east of Florence: Poppi di Casentino and Castello San Niccolò. Towns in the Val d'Arno between Florence and Arezzo accounted for 7.3 percent, and the remainder from the Florentine dominions came from small towns to the south of Florence: Pozzolaticho, Bagno di Ripoli, Certosa, and Antella. Another 10 percent were "foreigners" from Siena, Genoa, Venice, France, and Scotland. Very few of these first admissions came from west of Florence, perhaps because a large number of charitable institutions in Prato, Pistoia, Pescia, and Lucca already served this population.

These first hundred cases show a close correlation between social status and geography. Nearly all the admissions from the city of Florence mentioned the name of a wealthy Florentine family. Names such as Martelli, Pitti, Davanzati, and Salviati grace the first volume of admissions to the Innocenti. Nearly all of these were children of these scions and their slaves. In only one case out of the fourteen where Florence was identified as the origin of the child was the father's occupation mentioned: he was a baker in the Mercato Vecchio. Most foreigners were also sons and daughters of high rank as well: two outstanding examples were Francesco Contarini of Venice and Messer Agnolo di Tura of Siena. Children brought to the Innocenti from the countryside, however, tended to be children of laborers, artisans, and craftsmen.[81] Thus the father of Mattea Nicolosa was a sawyer from Castello San Niccolò.

The petition of 1448 asking for a municipal subsidy of some sort for the hospital also viewed the social class of abandoning parents from a Florentine, rather than a rural, perspective. This petition blamed the hospital's overcrowding on "the greater than usual number of household servants in the city."[82] The *Balie e Bambini* document the parentage of 55 percent of the first few years' admissions to the Innocenti. Of this documented group, 60 percent were the offspring of liaisons between masters and servants. Although males made up only 48 percent of the hospital's first hundred admissions, 62 percent of them could count slave girls as mothers. The comparable figure for girls was 57 percent.[83]

Recent studies of Florentine social and economic history support the notion that in many cases motives other than poverty compelled parents to abandon children.[84] Two observations of the patterns of admissions to the Innocenti give substantial credence to this hypothesis. If poverty were widespread, one would expect that the proportion of children of slaves in the population of admitted children would decrease, and this indeed does happen in the mid-1460s. Second, one would expect a high ratio of admissions to baptisms, of which an extreme example was eighteenth- and nineteenth-century France, where nearly a third of all baptized children were abandoned to foundling hospitals.[85]

Admissions to the Innocenti remained below a hundred per year during its first decade, and between one hundred and two hundred per year in the following two decades (table 6).[86] In scale alone, this is in stark contrast to institutions in Northern Europe in the eighteenth and nineteenth centuries, or even to the Innocenti itself during the seventeenth and eighteenth centuries. The data in table 7 show that the annual admissions to the Innocenti as a percentage of baptisms at San Giovanni rose from 4.8 percent in 1451 to 8.9 percent in 1465.[87] This surge, moreover, took place during a period of rapidly rising grain prices. Baptisms remained quite steady in the early 1460s while both grain prices and admissions to the Innocenti increased dramatically. Even at 10 percent, double the level of 1451, the Innocenti did not approach the figures of 30 percent that were documented for eighteenth-century Paris.[88] In the seventeenth century, the Innocenti took in only 13.7 percent of the region's children,[89] but by the nineteenth century, when Dr. Francesco Bruni was writing his massive two-volume history of the Innocenti, the hospital was taking in nearly 40 percent of all baptisms at San Giovanni.[90] Thus, one reason the Innocenti did not suffer the staggering mortality of these more recent institutions was that it was caring for one twenty-fifth rather than one-third of the city's children.

Another approach to the issue of motivations for abandonment would be to compare the curve of hospital admissions with grain prices. For eighteenth-century Limoges and Rouen, recent studies have discerned a very strong correlation between grain prices and admissions, suggesting the predominance of economic motives for abandonment in those two towns.[91] In mid-fifteenth-century Florence, the correlation is not only weak, but practically nonexistent until the early 1460s. The data in table 8 show that, from year to year, admissions fluctuated wildly while grain prices remained nearly constant.[92]

From 1450 to 1453 grain prices rose more sharply as admissions to the Innocenti declined and then rose again. The sharp increase in grain prices between 1455 and 1457 was followed by only a very small increase in admissions. From 1458 to 1461 grain prices plummeted to their lowest level in the entire twenty-two year period, yet admissions continued to climb. Only between 1461 and 1465, when grain prices rose very suddenly, did admissions to the Innocenti experience a similar rise. The low prices of 1460–62 may well have made the sudden increase of 1462–65 more psychologically and economically devastating, resulting in the quantum leap from 125 admissions in 1461 to 202 in 1465. Documentary evidence strongly supports this conclusion, as the *Balie e Bambini* report a sharp increase in the number of children wet nurses brought back "distended and dying of hunger." More common in the early 1460s, too, was the lament of abandoning parents that they could no longer suppport another mouth to feed.[93]

Some interesting patterns of seasonality of admissions emerge from table 9, especially when cross-tabulated with plague and famine years. If the 2,567 admissions to the Innocenti had been evenly distributed, about 214 would have occured for each month over the total twenty-two years, or 9.7 per month each year. February, June, September, and November were the months closest to the mean. March was the month during which babies were most likely to be abandoned, perhaps because it was such a vulnerable month in the food cycle, and December the least likely, suggesting that perhaps sexual abstinence during Lent reduced births in November and December. Years of economic hardship exaggerated rather than contradicted this pattern, although months that were usually "quiet" also became busy in the 1460s. Most striking is the admission of twenty-three children in November of 1464, suggesting

TABLE 6.   Annual Admissions to the Ospedale degli Innocenti, 1445–66

Year	Male	Female	Total
1445	26	36	62
1446	36	30	66
1447	42	45	87
1448	34	38	72
1449	34	56	90
1450	23	45	68
1451	47	47	94
1452	40	50	90
1453	34	52	86
1454	46	52	98
1455	44	68	112
1456	52	63	115
1457	49	65	114
1458	49	79	128
1459	55	88	143
1460	69	80	149
1461	57	68	125
1462	61	67	128
1463	63	93	156
1464	74	115	189
1465	92	110	202
1466	93	100	193
Total	1,119	1,447	2,567
Percentage	43.6%	56.4%	

Source: AOIF, Balie e Bambini A-F (XVI,1–6).

that perhaps either an unusually cold winter or severe food shortage had made its effect felt earlier than usual that year. Admissions during plague years tended to be lower than in other years, and drastically lower during the traditional plague months of August, September, and October, perhaps because in 1449 and 1456 the wealthy families that supplied the Innocenti with its foundlings had fled to the *contado,* and the poorer families from the *contado* preferred to stay there when plague raged in the city.[94]

More important than seasonality was the sex of the child being abandoned. Parents were more likely to abandon girls than boys to the Innocenti. Only in 1446 and 1451 did the number of boys nearly equal or exceed the number of girls admitted. As admissions climbed, so did the preponderance of girls.[95] Although the ratio of boys to girls at baptism in the records of San Giovanni was 104 to 100, 56.4 percent of the hospital's admissions were girls and 43.6 percent boys, out of the 2,567 admissions between 1445 and 1466. The preponderance of female admissions, especially during difficult economic times when the disproportion of the sexes in admissions was even greater, indicates not traditional Mediterranean misogyny, but more immediate and compelling economic

TABLE 7.   Number of Baptisms in the City of Florence and Admissions under the Age of One Year to the Ospedale degli Innocenti, 1451–66

Year	Baptisms	Admissions	Percentage of Admissions to Baptisms
1451	1,847	89	4.8
1452	2,132	86	4.0
1453	2,046	83	4.1
1454	2,100	94	4.5
1455	2,100	107	5.1
1456	2,207	111	5.0
1457	1,882	110	5.8
1458	1,781	125	7.0
1459	2,058	138	6.7
1460	2,105	145	6.9
1461	2,206	120	5.4
1462	2,206	124	5.6
1463	2,191	152	6.9
1464	2,039	180	8.8
1465	2,180	195	8.9
1466	2,111	188	8.9

Sources: for baptisms, Marco Lastri, *Ricerche sull'antica e moderna popolazione della città di Firenze per mezzo dei registri del battistero di San Giovanni dal 1451 al 1774* (Florence, 1775), 33–34; for admissions, AOIF, Balie e Bambini A-F (XVI,1–6).

issues, viz., dowry. This would certainly explain the reluctance of abandoning parents, despite explicit statements of their intentions to the contrary, to clamor for the return of their infant girls, which in turn distorted the sex ratios of the children under the care of the hospital even further. Yet this disparity did not hold when it came to adoption, despite the universal requirement that a person adopting a girl had to provide a dowry, although admittedly not a very large one. Of greater importance, if statistics can illuminate how widespread certain practices and attitudes were, they cannot convey the range of behavior possible in a culture nor the emotional weight and importance of "minority" behavior in a culture. This is not simply a failure of statistics to bear the weight of a particular point of view—rather, if statistical analysis alone could drive a very complex view of culture, how does it fail to account for the

TABLE 8. Grain Prices in Florence and Admissions to the Ospedale degli Innocenti, 1445–66

Year	Price[a]	Index	Admissions	Index
1445	15.0	81.5	62	53.4
1446	15.5	84.2	66	56.4
1447	15.5	84.2	87	74.4
1448	16.0	87.0	72	61.5
1449	16.0	87.0	90	76.9
1450	16.0	87.0	68	58.1
1451	17.5	95.1	94	80.3
1452	19.0	103.3	90	76.9
1453	20.0	108.7	86	73.5
1454	18.0	97.8	98	83.8
1455	21.0	114.1	112	95.7
1456	33.0	179.3	115	98.3
1457	30.0	163.0	114	97.4
1458	20.0	108.7	128	109.4
1459	12.0	65.2	143	122.2
1460	10.0	54.3	149	127.4
1461	10.0	54.3	125	106.8
1462	11.0	59.8	128	109.4
1463	16.0	87.0	156	133.3
1464	25.0	135.8	189	161.5
1465	29.0	157.6	202	172.6
1466	20.0	108.7	193	165.0

Source for grain prices: Richard Goldthwaite, "I prezzi del grano a Firenze dal XIV al XVI secolo," *Quaderni Storici* 28 (1975): 5–36; idem, *The Building of Renaissance Florence* (Baltimore, 1981), 29–66.

Note: Indices: 100 = Mean Price of a Staio of Grain 1445–66; 100 = Mean Number of Admissions, 1445–66.

[a]In *soldi della lira di piccioli.* The mean price of grain for the years 1445–66 was 18.4; the average number of admissions for that period was 116.6.

centrality in Florentine political, spiritual, and economic life of the commune's dowry fund?

The Innocenti's statistics concerning the likelihood of mortality within the first few years of life also manifest a disproportion by gender. Although female infants made up 56.4 percent of admissions to the Innocenti they accounted for 60.4 percent of deaths within a year of admission. Female "infant" mortality thus averaged 522 per thousand admissions, while male "infant" mortality was 443 per thousand admissions. On the basis of a preliminary study of the years 1445–52, in a study that yielded similar figures, Richard Trexler has argued that the hospital encouraged infanticide in general and selective female infanticide in particular (table 10). If more boys died in hospital but more girls died at wet nurse, either the institution encouraged female infanticide by sending a greater proportion of girls to wet nurse, or, if the distribution of sexes was equal in wet-nursing, the wet nurses themselves were guilty of bias against females.[96]

TABLE 9.   Admissions by Month to the Ospedale degli Innocenti, 1445–66

	Jan.	Feb.	Mar.	Apr.	May	Jun.	Jul.	Aug.	Sept.	Oct.	Nov.	Dec.
Year												
1445	1	10	5	5	6	4	4	4	6	7	7	3
1446	5	5	5	9	8	4	5	7	5	6	3	4
1447	8	10	12	9	7	8	6	5	5	5	4	8
1448	8	4	6	4	10	8	7	9	3	3	5	5
1449	6	9	15	8	10	8	8	4	8	6	4	4
1450	8	3	10	6	6	5	8	4	4	6	5	3
1451	6	5	6	9	11	13	12	6	5	4	9	8
1452	2	11	5	3	7	13	12	6	7	8	9	7
1453	4	11	13	10	9	6	7	4	4	7	8	3
1454	6	11	11	13	8	11	8	3	5	10	10	2
1455	14	7	14	8	15	7	6	3	8	11	11	8
1456	6	9	13	10	9	12	12	13	7	7	9	8
1457	9	8	19	12	13	8	7	7	9	9	8	5
1458	7	11	14	11	15	4	13	10	13	10	11	9
1459	13	10	20	10	15	14	9	13	5	17	8	9
1460	10	16	13	19	13	12	11	13	14	7	12	9
1461	11	5	15	14	15	8	11	10	8	13	8	7
1462	11	9	14	9	7	14	7	11	15	8	17	6
1463	20	14	15	11	8	13	12	12	19	12	10	10
1464	13	16	14	21	13	11	16	16	19	15	23	12
1465	14	12	21	12	26	13	20	18	21	14	14	17
1466	14	17	23	15	13	15	20	10	17	15	13	21
Total	196	213	283	228	244	211	221	188	207	200	208	168

Source: AOIF, Balie e Bambini A-F (XVI,1–6)

The first hypothesis presumes an awareness on the part of hospital officials of the dynamics of differential mortality by gender, an awareness that prima facie is highly unlikely and totally unsupported. Moreover, all children who were brought to the Innocenti and not returned to their parents within a few days were sent to wet nurse, most of them within two weeks, regardless of sex, which brings us to the second hypothesis. As we have seen, abandoning parents attempted to influence the choice of wet nurse by promising large sums of money, but the hospital was no more successful than with other children in ensuring their safety. Most importantly, however, the location of a child's death is a most unreliable guide as to who should accept responsibility for the death of the child. The death of children who arrived at the Innocenti already too weak to stand much chance of survival unfairly caused blame to fall on the hospital. The deaths of children who in winter might have to survive a day's journey to the Casentino would unfairly cause blame to fall on the wet nurse, and children who were mistreated or neglected by wet nurses would arrive at the hospital's doorstep on the point of death. Thus if boys were dying in greater numbers within the hospital itself, one might justly attach blame to the wet nurses and argue that they preferred the survival of female infants. Since Trexler does not

TABLE 10.   Infant Deaths by Sex and Place of Death, 1452–66

Year	Hospital		Wet Nurse		Total	
	M	F	M	F	M	F
1452	10	15	7	8	17	23
1453	8	3	9	15	17	18
1454	6	6	10	15	16	21
1455	6	11	10	23	16	34
1456	13	14	20	22	33	36
1457	12	10	11	25	23	35
1458	7	14	8	29	15	43
1459	10	17	11(1)	31	22	48
1460	10	13	16	33(2)	26	48
1461	9	5	10	24	19	29
1462	6	8	10	16	24	24
1463	13	26	13	18(1)	26	45
1464	9	29	16	35	35	64
1465	24	26	24	33	49	59
1466	28	37	23(1)	30	51	67
Total	181	234	198(2)	357(3)	381	594

Sources: AOIF, Balie e Bambini A–F (XVI,1–6); Richard Trexler, "Infanticide in Florence: New Sources and First Results," *History of Childhood Quarterly* 1 (1974): 101.

Note: Numbers in parentheses represent deaths of babies on loan.

distinguish between in-hospital deaths before wet-nursing and in-hospital deaths after a few months at wet nurse, one might even argue that wet nurses were more fearful of sanctions if they allowed male infants to die instead of bringing them back ill when they were supposed to. If wet nurses felt fewer sanctions would apply to the death of a female at the wet nurse's, they might have not rushed to bring an ill female child back to the Innocenti, which would exaggerate any sense of disparity of treatment by gender.

Another approach might be to ask whether the sheer weight of numbers would explain differential mortality. According to this model, within the hospital female children might be less well-cared for because, segregated from males but in quarters of roughly the same proportions, they were more vulnerable to overcrowding and communicable diseases. At wet nurse, if boys were monitored separately from girls, the smaller number of boys might allow for more careful monitoring. Tables 11 and 12 report the results of testing this hypothesis, results that are of mixed usefulness at best. Certainly, in 1451, the year that female infants comprised the highest proportion of admissions, female mortality was the third highest during the twenty-two-year period. The effect seems even more pronounced on the cohort arriving a year later, 63.6 percent of whom died within the first year of life. Two years that produced a high proportion of female admissions, 1449 and 1450, were followed by two years, 1450 and 1451, where female morbidity was impressively high. Yet in 1457 and 1464 female abandonment was very high, but female mortality, though high, was not much higher than male mortality. Conversely, 1466, a year in which nearly 70 percent of female admissions died, was also a year they made up barely a majority of admissions. Years in which girls were a minority of admissions sometimes were years in which morbidity was low, but often enough low female admissions are paired with very high female morbidity.

There is a stronger link between years of high male admissions and years of high male mortality (table 12). Thus, 1448, 1451, and 1466 are the years of the highest number of male admissions and also the years of highest male mortality. Yet in 1446 and 1447, two years of very high male admissions, male mortality was extremely low.

Finally, a simple comparison of mortality by gender (table 13) is misleading, since about 10 percent of boys were returned to their parents and only 3 percent of girls were. Table 14 shows how figures adjusted to reflect differing rates of return would look. Although accounting for different rates of return reduces the disparity in mortality by gender, it does not eliminate it (except to reverse it for 1452 so that males had higher mortality). Even without accounting for the disparity in rates of return, mortality could occasionally be higher among the boys, as it was in the years 1447, 1448, 1449, 1453, and 1456. In 1447 this could partially be explained by the preponderance of boys admitted in 1446, an explanation that might hold for 1448 as well. Plague explains the higher mortality for boys in 1449 and 1456, but there is no explanation I can find for the higher male mortality rate in 1453.

None of these hypotheses, however, can diminish the importance of the social and cultural phenomenon of the girls' domination of the admissions statistics, a cultural phenomenon reinforced by the greater ambivalence abandoning parents had about placing boys permanently with

TABLE 11. Comparison of Percentage of Female Infants Admitted to the Ospedale degli Innocenti and Percentage of Female Infants Dying within First Year of Life

Year	Admissions	% Female Admissions[a]	% Female Deaths[b]
1445	60	58.4	37.2 +
1446	64	45.3 +	37.9 +
1447	84	52.4 +	29.6 +
1448	70	52.9	48.6
1449	86	61.7*	50.9
1450	64	65.7*	63.4*
1451	89	49.5 +	63.6*
1452	86	55.8	47.9
1453	83	60.2	36.0 +
1454	94	53.2	42.0
1455	107	61.7*	51.5
1456	111	55.0	59.0*
1457	130	63.8*	55.6
1458	125	61.6*	55.8
1459	135	60.7*	56.5
1460	155	56.8	61.5*
1461	120	54.2	44.6
1462	124	55.6	36.9 +
1463	151	39.6 +	49.5
1464	180	61.7*	57.7
1465	195	54.4	55.6
1466	188	51.6 +	69.1*

Source: AOIF, Balie e Bambini A-F (XVI,1–6).
[a]Calculated as percentage of female admissions to total admissions each year
[b]Calculated as percentage of female deaths to female admissions each year
*Five highest values in each column
+ Five lowest values in each column

the institution, and the comparative unwillingness of parents to redeem girls within a short period of time.

Just as imprecise, given the nature of the data, is the notion of "infant" mortality. Traditionally defined as mortality occurring before a child's first birthday, infant mortality is quite difficult to specify when not all of the Innocenti's bearers gave the child's age or date and hour of birth. About 96 percent of children for whom we do have ages were admitted to the hospital less than three weeks old, but even in the 1440s and 1450s only about a quarter of the respondents gave the exact age of the child. Yet precision would be critical in establishing just how statistically significant disparities in female and male deaths were. If parents favored males, for example, and waited a month or two before abandoning them, this fact alone would reduce male infant mortality by 50 percent, the current estimate in the literature of the percentage of

TABLE 12. Comparison of Percentage of Male Infants Admitted to the Ospedale degli Innocenti and Percentage of Male Infants Dying within First Year of Life

Year	Admissions	% Male Admissions[a]	% Male Deaths[b]
1445	60	41.6	12.0 +
1446	64	54.7*	19.9 +
1447	84	47.6*	35.0 +
1448	70	47.1*	57.6*
1449	86	38.3 +	54.6
1450	64	34.3 +	43.5
1451	89	50.5*	57.8*
1452	86	44.2	44.8
1453	83	39.8	51.6
1454	94	46.8	36.4
1455	107	38.3 +	39.0
1456	111	45.0	66.0*
1457	130	36.2 +	48.9
1458	125	38.4 +	31.3 +
1459	135	39.3	41.5
1460	155	43.2	38.8
1461	120	45.8	34.6
1462	124	44.4	27.1 +
1463	151	40.4	42.6
1464	180	38.3	50.7
1465	195	45.6	55.0*
1466	188	48.4*	56.0*

Source: AOIF, Balie e Bambini A-F (XVI, 1–6).

[a]Calculated as percentage of male admissions to total admissions each year

[b]Calculated as percentage of male deaths to female admissions each year

*Five highest values in each column

+ Five lowest values in each column

newborn (defined as less than one month old) mortality to infant mortality.[97] If parents were abandoning one-month-old male infants but newborn female infants, this would explain away much of the apparent gender disparity in mortality rates. Unfortunately, as the fifteenth century progressed, scribes were even less meticulous about recording the exact age of the child on admission, and the Innocenti's merger in 1463 with the hospital of San Gallo, which traditionally accepted only older children, marks the point at which scribes only rarely indicated the age of the child.

The Innocenti's first few years of operation indicate that mortality was at very low levels for a premodern foundling institution. The years 1445, 1446, and 1447 yielded infant mortality rates at the Innocenti of 27 percent, 28 percent, and 32 percent, respectively. The plague of 1449, however, had a devastating effect on the cohort admitted in 1448, 53 percent of whom died within the year. Perhaps because of the suspension

TABLE 13.   Infant Mortality at the Ospedale degli Innocenti, 1445–66

	Deaths			Rates		
Year	Male	Female	Total	Male[a]	Female[b]	Total[c]
1445	3	13	16	120.0	371.5	271.2
1446	7	11	18	200.0	379.3	281.3
1447	14	13	27	350.0	295.5	321.4
1448	19	18	37	575.8	486.4	528.6
1449	18	27	45	545.5	509.4	523.3
1450	10	26	36	434.8	634.1	562.5
1451	26	28	54	577.8	636.4	606.7
1452	17	23	40	447.4	479.1	465.1
1453	17	18	35	515.2	360.0	421.6
1454	16	21	37	363.6	420.0	393.6
1455	16	34	40	390.2	515.1	467.3
1456	33	36	69	660.0	590.2	621.6
1457	23	35	58	489.4	555.6	527.3
1458	15	43	58	312.5	558.4	464.0
1459	22	48	70	415.1	564.7	507.2
1460	26	48	74	388.1	615.4	510.3
1461	19	29	48	345.5	446.2	400.0
1462	16	24	40	271.2	369.2	322.6
1463	26	45	71	426.2	494.5	467.1
1464	35	64	99	507.2	576.6	550.0
1465	49	59	108	550.1	556.6	553.8
1466	28	37	75	560.4	690.7	627.7

Source: AOIF, Balie e Bambini A-F (XVI,1–6).
[a]Male mortality rates: male infant deaths per thousand male infant admissions
[b]Female mortality rates: female infant deaths per thousand female admissions
[c]Total mortality rates: total infant deaths per thousand total infant admissions

of *Monte* payments,[98] mortality rates did not improve from 1450 through 1452. The years 1452 through 1455 represent a modest surcease, but in 1456, the year the Innocenti petitioned for its communal subsidy of prisoners' fines, mortality rose to 62 percent, presaging the plague year of 1457. Although the death rates dropped only slightly during the following two years, in 1460 and 1461 they plunged to levels reminiscent of the hospital's opening years. During the years 1462–66 the rise in infant mortality coincided with both rapidly increasing admissions and sharply rising grain prices.[99]

If a child survived its first year of life under institutional care, its chances of surviving several more years greatly improved. The highest rate of child mortality was concentrated in the first year of life (tables 15 and 16). Rates dropped off dramatically after that point, even during

TABLE 14.   Infant Mortality at the Ospedale degli Innocenti, 1445–66, Adjusted to Reflect Different Rates at Which Children Were Returned to Their Parents

Year	Male Death Rate	Female Death Rate
1445	166.7	406.3
1446	222.8	391.3
1447	390.0	304.8
1448	641.3	501.9
1449	607.7	525.6
1450	484.4	654.1
1451	643.7	668.8
1452	498.4	494.2
1453	483.5	364.0
1454	341.3	424.6
1455	366.1	520.8
1456	619.4	596.7
1457	459.3	561.7
1458	293.3	564.5
1459	389.7	570.9
1460	364.2	622.2
1451	324.3	451.1
1462	254.5	373.3
1463	400.0	499.9
1464	476.0	598.9
1465	516.3	562.8
1466	525.9	698.4

Source: AOIF, Balie e Bambini A-F (XVI, 1–6).

Note: Rates for 1445–46 reflect actual percentages of children returned to their parents that year. All other figures are based on the 1452 census, using return rates from 1445–52 (10 percent for boys, 3 percent for girls) to cover 1453–66. The assumption, somewhat unlikely, that rates remained constant rules the calculations for the latter set of dates in the table.

plague years. Only in 1456 and in 1462 did the level of first-year mortality to total mortality drop below 50 percent.

The pattern for girls differed to some extent from the pattern for boys. In years of relatively low mortality for girls quite a high proportion of them died under the age of one year. Before 1460, years of high mortality for girls showed a smaller concentration of deaths among those less than a year old. After 1460, just the opposite occurred: girls under one year old during years of high female mortality became especially vulnerable, as was the case for boys. Mortality of girls corresponded more to years in which more of them were admitted than to years of high mortality for boys, though again in the early 1460s, mortality became more equalized between the sexes. Finally, all of these data for girls are consistent with Molho and Kirshner's findings that mortality for girls enrolled in the dowry fund was much higher during the first year of life, despite the tendency of their parents to postpone their enrollment until they were a few months old.[100]

Since such a high proportion of the hospital's infants were at wet nurse, the Innocenti was often hard-pressed to specify causes of death. Most such entries simply say "morì," "morta," or "morto." Those infants who died in-house, however, occasionally had a cause of death recorded for them. For the period 1445–50, the twenty-three deaths due to identifiable causes are listed in table 17. *Mal maestro,* in addition to

TABLE 15.   Distribution of Male Mortality by Age, 1452–66

Year	Age in Years							
	0-1	1-2	2-3	3-4	4-5	5-10	10-15	Total
1451	18	6	2	0	0	1	0	27
1452	17	1	1	1	0	0	0	20
1453	17	2	0	0	1	1	0	21
1454	16	2	3	1	4	0	0	29
1455	16	4	1	0	1	0	0	22
1456	33	1	1	0	0	0	0	35
1457	23	3	1	0	0	0	0	27
1458	15	2	2	0	2	0	0	21
1459	22	2	1	2	2	1	0	30
1460	26	5	1	2	3	0	0	37
1461	19	2	0	2	0	5	0	28
1462	16	10	5	3	0	1	0	35
1463	26	3	5	3	1	1	0	39
1464	35	6	3	0	0	0	0	44
1465	49	3	4	0	0	1	0	57
1466	51	2	1	0	1	0	0	55

Source: AOIF, Balie e Bambini A-F (XVI, 1–6).

its meaning of epileptic convulsions, was undoubtedly applied to convulsions of any sort, of which those stemming from infections and fever were probably the most common. Every child's death, in those instances where the cause of death was listed, was followed by "May God bless him (or her)." Thus Pietro Paolo, who was not baptized before being abandoned at the Innocenti, died in June 1445: "May God bless him. He died of the *male male* that seized him."[101] Similarly, Filippo Innocente, who had come highly recommended by his father, died on 28 June 1445. "He was buried in the hospital."[102] Martino Innocente, who died of plague on 14 October 1449, had two large swellings, "one under his ear, and one under his arm."[103] If the malfeasance of a wet nurse was suspected, "May God pardon the wet nurse" inevitably followed the entry, but this was more commonly an issue with the wet nurses outside the hospital. Only rarely did the Innocenti record incidents such as the following:

> On 23 March 1452 on Friday at the nineteenth hour or so a male child was brought to us, unbaptized. A servant, or rather wet nurse of Andrea Masini brought him and said that he was the son of one of Andrea's slaves.... On 23 March we lent the aforesaid infant boy to Antonio Martegli for ten or twelve days to maintain the milk supply

TABLE 16.   Distribution of Female Mortality by Age, 1451–66

Year	Age in Years							
	0-1	1-2	2-3	3-4	4-5	5-10	10-15	Total
1451	19	0	1	0	0	0	0	20
1452	23	1	0	1	0	1	0	26
1453	18	3	3	3	2	0	2	31
1454	21	3	5	3	1	4	1	38
1455	34	7	4	0	0	2	0	47
1456	36	8	1	0	0	1	0	46
1457	25	3	2	3	1	2	1	47
1458	43	4	2	0	3	3	0	55
1459	48	0	0	4	5	3	1	70
1460	48	3	0	2	1	1	0	56
1461	29	3	2	3	0	3	0	40
1462	24	8	3	3	3	2	0	43
1463	44	12	6	2	0	1	0	65
1464	64	8	2	3	0	0	0	77
1465	59	8	4	0	1	1	2	75
1466	67	5	2	0	2	1	0	77

Source: AOIF, Balie e Bambini A-F (XVI, 1–6).

of Anna, his wet nurse, until his wife gave birth. . . . He died 17 June [1453] Saturday night or early Sunday morning. He was found dead at the side of the wet nurse. May God forgive her and bless him.[104]

Wet nurses did not come under suspicion when children had recognizable signs of communicable disease. The Innocenti cited at least two cases of smallpox: in 1451 "the aforesaid infant boy, Potenziano, died of smallpox and fevers. The wet nurse's husband brought him back dead and he was buried here in-house."[105] Bernardina Innocente, who was brought from a hospital near the Certosa, died a month before Potenziano "because she was full of smallpox. She died in the hospital here, God bless her."[106]

Intestinal diseases such as dysentery and symptoms such as diarrhea appear frequently in the Innocenti records. Nor were bacteria the only intestinal hazards. In May 1451, a two-year-old girl by the name of Nanna was abandoned at the Innocenti.

An old man brought her and said that she had no father or mother. We told him that we only take in children who are not yet weaned, but he fled saying he could not carry her any more. We placed her in-house and she is with the other children. On 16 May the aforesaid girl died in house here. She was full of worms: so many that they killed her. May God bless her. We buried her under the [hospital's] church where the other children are [buried].[107]

Accidental deaths also happened to children, usually in foster care or at wet nurse. A three-year-old boy, Domenico Cristofano "fell into the fire and burned himself to such an extent that he died,"[108] as the wet nurse's husband reported. Another child, probably in her mid-teens,

TABLE 17.   Causes of Death, 1445–50

mal maestro (convulsions)	8
segnio, or *morbo* (plague)	9
suffocation (overlaying)	1
vaiuolo (smallpox)	2
mignatti (worms)	1
accidents	2
Total	23

Source: AOIF, Balie e Bambini A-B (XVI,1–2), 1445–50.

"drawing water at the well where the clothes are washed caught herself on the pulley, which took and threw her into the well, where she drowned."[109]

Unfortunately, no widely available studies of fifteenth-century foundling hospitals exist to put mortality at the Innocenti into its context. Nor are data sufficient to do more than suggest what mortality rates outside the institution might have been. By comparison with seventeenth- and eighteenth-century institutions, however, both in Italy and elsewhere in Europe, the Innocenti's mortality figures were impressively low. Of the Innocenti's successors in Europe, only Christ's Hospital in London had mortality figures lower than the Innocenti's.[110] Christ's Hospital's enviable record, moreover, was related more to the age composition of its admissions than to its standard of care. Only a seventh of the infants under one of year of age admitted to Christ's in the sixteenth century was under a month old—moreover, only 282 out 772 admissions to Christ's between 1563 and 1583 were infants under the age of one year.[111] By comparison, at least 2,450 of the Innocenti's 2,567 admissions between 1445 and 1466 were under a year old. Christ's Hospital only admitted fourteen infants and twenty-five older children per year, on the average, and therefore served a much smaller constituency and would not, in theory at least, suffer the injustices and demands of instant popularity.

Charity toward children in eighteenth-century Reims was altogether a different question, however. The Hôtel-Dieu, from 1779 to 1789 accepted eight hundred abandoned children, of which 735, or 92 percent, were under a year old. The organization of care at Reims was quite different, moreover. Expectant mothers came to the Hôtel-Dieu to give birth to their out-of-wedlock children, who were then placed with wet nurses. Thirty-eight percent of infant deaths occurred within the first month of an infant's arrival at the Hôtel-Dieu, and of those, 63 percent died within the first two weeks. Average mortality at the Hôtel-Dieu was quite comparable to mortality at the Innocenti: 460 infant deaths per thousand infant admissions.[112]

The decade prior to the French Revolution brought even higher mortality to the abandoned infants of Rouen, whose hospitals assisted 3,558 children between 1782 and 1789. Charity on such a massive scale had its fruit in equally massive mortality: 86.4 percent of all children admitted to institutions died under their care. Newborns were even more vulnerable. Of 833 newborns admitted between 1783 and 1789, 756 (91 percent), died before their first birthday. Of these, nearly 70 percent died within the first month of life. Hospital administrators blamed this extraordinary mortality on the lack of good wet nurses and the disturbing effects of the long carriage ride from the hospital to the countryside. Although the institution had attempted to remedy the former by bottle-feeding and the latter by the provision of more comfortable carriages, mortality continued its devastation.[113] The importance of scale seems important in prerevolutionary Paris also, whose foundling hospitals admitted from four thousand to six thousand children each year, and where mortality in the first month of life reached 82 percent.[114]

Outside Western Europe at the end of the eighteenth century the fatal association between institutionalization and infant death persisted. Catherine the Great of Russia initiated foundling hospitals in Moscow and St. Petersburg. The designers of these hospitals planned for the education of unwanted foundlings according to the principles of the French Enlightenment. According to the original scheme, the hospitals would accept children only after they had been weaned, hoping to mold them into "an altogether new class of enlightened, free urban dwellers."[115] Moved apparently by humanitarian considerations, the Moscow designer lifted the prohibition of younger infants, resulting in an overwhelming influx of babies. In the Moscow foundling home, a smallpox epidemic in 1767 was superimposed on normal mortality to produce a mortality rate of 98 percent of the children admitted that year. By the end of the eighteenth century, these two foundling homes were each receiving between 1,500 and 2,000 infants and children per year. At the end of the nineteenth century, the Moscow home alone was receiving 16,000 to 18,000 infants annually and sending 10,000 of them to village foster parents. This program of village fosterage reduced mortality within the walls of the institutions, but institutional and village fosterage mortality remained at a level of about 75 percent.[116]

Italian hospital mortality, especially in Florence, may have reached similar proportions in the nineteenth century. During the eighteenth century, the Ospedale degli Innocenti, for example, took in between six hundred and a thousand children per year. Mortality during the first year after admission (not *infant* mortality) varied from a low of 378 per thousand in 1763 to a high of 595 per thousand in 1756. Moreover, there was no clear relationship between the number of admissions in a given year and mortality for that year. In 1756, the year of the highest mortality, there were 699 admissions, compared to 753 in the year of the lowest mortality. In 1766 the Innocenti admitted 944 children but recorded only 408 deaths that year from that group of children. This suggests remarkable resilience for an institution its size: the Innocenti in the eighteenth century took in more than ten times the number of children than the Hôtel-Dieu in Reims, yet mortality was only slightly higher.[117]

More recent studies, however, suggest much higher mortality rates at the Innocenti during certain years in the eighteenth and nineteenth centuries.[118] In the years 1700–1702, when the Innocenti was assisting children at the rate of about five hundred per year, the infant mortality rate was 684 per thousand. From 1792–94 the toll was higher yet: 738 per thousand. By 1841, mortality for children at all ages admitted to the Innocenti had dropped to 53 percent, and infant mortality to 30 percent. Some of this decrease may have been related to parents' willingness to reclaim abandoned children. During the years 1700–1702, only 2.1 percent of parents chose to do so. In 1792–94, this proportion was 5 percent, but in 1841 it was 24 percent. Indeed, the fifteenth-century mortality figures bear out this sort of relationship—infant mortality in institutions rose and fell in inverse proportion to the percentage of children reclaimed.[119]

Yet the explanation of larger issues is rather more complex. Large urban foundling hospitals in eighteenth-century Europe that pursued an open-admissions policy courted infant mortality rates that virtually constituted the sanctioning of infanticide. Even in instances where the data are ample and their interpretation not suspect, mortality levels of 80 to 90 percent were not uncommon. Those studies able to make comparisons between mortality within and without institutions have consistently shown that outside infant mortality rarely rose above 20 percent.[120] Even those institutions that tried to make mortality rates acceptable by restricting admissions, such as the foundling hospital of London, still had mortality rates that reached 70 percent.

The records of twentieth-century institutions were no better in this regard. As René Spitz observed in 1945, one of the premier foundling homes in Germany at the turn of the century had an infant mortality rate of 71.5 percent. In 1915, American foundling hospitals reported infant death rates ranging from 31.7 percent to 75 percent. In Baltimore the rate may have been closer to 90 percent.[121]

The explanation for such staggering mortality rates resides only partly in the quality and scale of care institutions attempted to provide. Just as critical in the difference between the Innocenti in the fifteenth century and an American hospital in 1915 is the organization of care. Specifically, these later hospitals were often organized on a residential model of care, rather than the Innocenti's foster model. When Spitz studied a foundling home in the United States in the early 1940s, his work made it clear that neither lack of antibiotics nor lack of hygiene lay at the heart of the morbidity of children:

> The children in foundling home showed all the manifestations of hospitalism, both physical and mental. In spite of the fact that hygiene and precautions against contagion were impeccable, the children showed, from the third month on, extreme susceptibility to infection and illness of any kind. There was hardly a child in whose case history we did not find reference to *otitis media,* or *morbilli,* or *varicella,* or *eczema,* or intestinal disease of one kind or another.... During my stay an epidemic of measles swept the institution, with staggeringly high mortality figures, notwithstanding liberal administration of convalescent serum and globulins, as well as excellent hygienic conditions. Of a total of 88 children up to the age of 2 1/2, 23 died.... The significance of these figures becomes apparent when we realize that mortality from measles during the first year of life in the community in question outside the institution was less than 1/2 percent.[122]

The comparatively low mortality of the Innocenti's foundlings compared to foundling institutions in the late eighteenth through twentieth centuries is attributable first to questions of scale: the larger institutions in northern France were caring for as many as 40 percent of children of their cities and surrounding towns; the Innocenti, only 4–10 percent. The question of scale obscures a deeper question. In eighteenth-century London, Thomas Coram faced considerable opposition to the foundling hospital he proposed to build. Londoners argued that the presence of a foundling hospital would only serve to sanction illegitimacy, and would only increase parents' incentive to abandon. Certainly the second of those two fears was well founded, and successful eighteenth-century hospitals found that soon they could not hope to cope with their own success.[123] The Innocenti in the fifteenth century faced this problem as well, but in a much more limited way. If a petition of 1446 boasted that the hospital was becoming overcrowded because people felt that children sent there would be "well-governed and well-cared-for," the Innocenti quickly found the limits of its resources in caring for the 2,567 children that passed through its doors between 1445 and 1466. Nevertheless, high infant mortality due to recurrent plague in Florence, the high proportion of truncated and atomized households, and a relative shortage both of labor and of children, combined to make children valuable and less vulnerable to abandonment. This is why Alberti's *Della Famiglia* encourages young men to take a wife and to renew families; this is why Alessandra Strozzi's letters to her sons are obsessed with arranging and celebrating marriages and marriage alliances.

Yet the organization of care at the Innocenti must also have accounted for the success it did achieve. As the hospital within the walls grew over the course of the fifteenth and sixteenth centuries, its character became more residential, and adoption and apprenticeship accounted for a smaller share of the disposition of children. Most important, as eighteenth- and nineteenth-century institutions replaced wet nurses with bottle-feeding, the dangers of hospitalism and the failures of babies' immune systems when babies had less physical and human contact than they had with wet nurses, must have made them more vulnerable to infection. In eighteenth- and nineteenth-century Russia, for example, village fosterage was reintroduced in an attempt to reduce mortality rates, though with limited success. In twentieth-century America, studies such as René Spitz's were crucial in making the final transition from institutional to foster care for unwanted children.[124]

Just as foster care today is not immune from criticism of standards and quality of care, and the incidence of child abuse by foster parents receives widespread attention, so in the fifteenth century wet nurses were the focus of intense scrutiny on the part of their neighbors and hospital administrators alike. In the early years of the hospital's operation, hospital administrators were reasonably successful in screening wet nurses and in attracting good ones. By the 1460s, however, the hospital's fiscal problems were so severe that payments to wet nurses were made either in arrears, or not at all.[125] Indeed, when cash reserves ran out, wet nurses were often paid in kind, as the hospital's *Giornali* from 1467 and 1468 demonstrate.[126] Since the early 1460s coincided with a quantum leap in admissions, the Innocenti was unable to choose its wet nurses with as much discrimination as it had exercised in less pressing times.

If it is not clear how the hospital determined that a wet nurse was not giving the required standard of care, it is clear that such determinations were frequent. Nurses who were not meeting the standard could expect timely requests that the child be returned to the hospital. In October

1445, for example, the hospital demanded that a wet nurse from Ponte alla Badia bring Andrea Francesco back to the hospital "because she was not doing a good job of caring for him."[127] The hospital demanded the return of another infant, Antonio Domenico, who was returned "badly treated and battered." This child's next wet nurse was offered an incentive for not repeating this child's experience. Mona Rosa di Jacopo, from Castello San Niccolò di Casentino, would receive two lire, fifteen soldi for nursing Antonio, or "if she cares for him well, three soldi per month." Other wet nurses, such as Mona Mea d'Agnolo di Castello San Niccolò, required no such incentives. Her husband was so taken with Andrea Francesco that Mea told a hospital official "that he doesn't want to give him back."[128]

Wet nurses the Innocenti used came predominantly from the countryside, and predominantly those areas of the *contado* that abandoned infants came from. Of the first hundred services by 130 wet nurses, fifty-six different place names were mentioned. Two surprises emerged from the data (table 18). First, Castello San Niccolò di Casentino was mentioned by twenty-four separate wet nurses, suggesting that the Innocenti either developed a network of contacts in that village or exploited an already existing network. Indeed, popular lyrics frequently cited the association between the Casentino and wet-nursing.[129] Moreover, although the documents do not themselves suggest that women who were the Innocenti's wet nurses also abandoned their own children there, such a high concentration of wet nurses in one village strongly suggests a microeconomy based on wet-nursing that might have made abandonment profitable, and that might explain the reticence of some porters to identify the parents of children they were abandoning.

Secondly, even though one traditionally associates wet nurses with the countryside, the second most frequently mentioned place name for the provenance of wet nurses was Florence. Florentine wet nurses practiced their art in via San Gallo, San Lorenzo, San Pier Maggiore, and the Porta alla Croce, among many other sites. In the *contado,* towns to the north, northeast, and east predominated, with some towns to the south of Florence represented, and very few to the west. Children might be sent as far away as Borgo San Lorenzo and Firenzuola, thirty to forty miles away, or as close as a mile from the hospital itself.[130]

One might well ask why children were sent as far away as thirty or forty miles, and the statutes of 1415, which prescribed pay scales for "domestic servants and nurses," suggest that variable costs played a major role. Caretakers for boys and girls within a house had to be given food and drink, as well as a salary of no more than fifteen florins annually. For wet nurses employed to nurse boys or girls outside the house, pay scales decreased as distance from the center of Florence increased. Wet nurses within the city of Florence or within the jurisdiction of San Giovanni outside the walls could earn four lire per month. Nurses who lived outside this central area up to twelve miles out could only earn a maximum of three lire per month, and nurses from twelve to twenty-four miles out could earn a maximum of only two lire, ten soldi per month, which was the standard wage the Innocenti paid most of its wet nurses.[131]

The high concentration of wet nurses in Castello San Niccolò also permits us to examine Trexler's claim that wet-nursing fed on death.[132] Did wet nurses have an economic incentive either to "overlay" an infant

TABLE 18.   Provenance of Wet Nurses, 1445–46

Town	Number of Times Mentioned
Castello San Niccolò	28
Firenze	15
Barberino di Mugello	6
Prato	5
Antella	5
Vichio di Mugello	4
Montespertoli	4
Pieve/Bagno/Badia a Ripoli	3
San Casciano	3
Cascia	3
Borgo San Lorenzo	3
Pontassieve	3
Montereggi	3
Dicomano	2
San Piero a Varlungho	2
La Lastra/Montughi	2
Pozzolatico	2
San Donato in Poggio	2
Radda	2
Pontormo	2

Source: AOIF, Balie e Bambini A (XVI,1), 1445–46

Note: The following towns were mentioned once: Castello Fiorentino, La Lastra, Badia degli Calzi, Volpaia, Castello Castaprato, Barberino Val d'Elsa, Ponte alla Badia di Fiesole, San Salvi, San Andrea a Rovezzano, Empoli, Tavernelle Val di Pesa, Pratovecchio, San Godenzo, Greve, Coverciano, Puliciano Val di Pesa, San Giovanni Val d'Arno, Badia di Fiesole, Carpineto, Torri di Val di Pesa, Carmignano, Galluzzo, Firenzuola, Pian di Mugnone, San Martino alla Strada, S. Piero a Sieve, and San Brancazio Val di Pesa.

or to take on more infants than she could feed? If a wet nurse had her own infant to feed, for example, would she tend to take two more children to her breast, since she was being paid by the head? Obviously we cannot account for any children she took in from families. But of the twenty-eight mentions of the town of Castello San Niccolò during the first two years of the hospital's operation, twenty-four were for separate wet nurses. In no case, however, did the Innocenti send two unweaned children to the same wet nurse. In the four cases where wet nurses are mentioned twice, only one of the Innocenti's children was at the same pair of breasts at one time. The Innocenti even separated twins to ensure that they would not go to the same wet nurse. Nor did wet-nursing need to "feed on death," as Francesco Datini implied,[133] or twins in premodern (or preformula) society would have been impossible. Most important, from the perspective of the hospital's administrators, there was no alternative to wet-nursing. Even if the hospital had been able to recruit scores of in-house wet nurses, children would have been extremely vulnerable to mortality from contagious disease. The prior of the Innocenti recognized this when he returned Guidotto to a wet nurse whom he had previously refused to pay:

> for reason of a fraud she perpetrated against the hospital concerning the said boy. We returned him to her for a good reason, because of the high mortality [in house].

In this case, the prior's instincts were sound. Guidotto survived the fraudulent wet nurse at least long enough to be adopted.[134]

The pay scales for wet nurses also reflected the hospital's view, and undoubtedly also the prevailing view elsewhere, that since young children were the most difficult to care for, and since the *balia* was the only source of nutrition for these infants, wet nurses who took care of children until weaning should receive higher pay. Salaries for wet nurses at the Innocenti throughout the fifteenth century ranged from two lire, five soldi per month to three lire for children *a popa*. To draw comparisons with other categories of Florentine workers is difficult, because most wage rates for those workers are expressed in daily wages, and the number of days worked per month could vary widely. Nonetheless, it does appear that the Innocenti paid its wet nurses from 62.5 to 75 percent of the average monthly wage of the Innocenti's lowest-paid manual workers, its carters, who were paid four lire per month.[135] When weaning took place, at the age of eighteen to twenty-four months, the wet nurse had to return the child to the hospital, which then arranged foster care at half the prevailing rates wet nurses received. In addition to noting the reduction in the wet nurse's salary, the hospital's accountant noted what clothes accompanied the children to their new foster-care arrangements. The hospital, as we have seen, might require the return of a child well before weaning took place. In some cases, this was due to the malfeasance of the wet nurse. In other cases, a wet nurse would return an infant voluntarily because she could no longer care for it. Thus the Innocenti's second admission, Alessandra Smeralda, was returned by her wet nurse to the institution "because the wet nurse has a fever and an infection in her breast."[136]

Although the hospital had formal licensing procedures for in-house wet nurses, hospital administrators relied on a system of scheduled and surprise inspections to monitor its wet nurses outside the walls. In 1461, for example, when the hospital hired Ser Antonio di Filippo as the hospital's chaplain to supervise its real estate, he also had the charge to "provide for the needs of the children who are at wet nurse, and to visit the children at least once or twice a year as shall please the prior."[137] The hospital sometimes sent someone informally as well. Bardo Altoviti, a kinsman of Ridolfo Altoviti, one of the silk guild's consuls, requested an infant for the wife of one of his laborers. But when Bardo "went to visit our children, he found that she was dead."[138]

Hapless parents sometimes discovered fraud themselves:

On 10 September 1455 we gave the aforesaid Maddalena for fourteen months at fifty soldi per month and then [she was weaned] and we gave her at half price to Mona Francesca di Giacomo [from the] *popolo* di San Piero a Piemonte a Palazzuolo. Do not give her money because the father of the said girl wants her brought back to the hospital. This record was made 20 October 1455. The said girl is the daughter of Alderotto Pitti. He wants to speak with the wet nurse's husband. We were told that she was dead. We want to know the truth.[139]

Nevertheless, neighbors rather than inspectors discovered and reported the vast majority of deaths, mistreatment, and neglect. Neighbors often traveled long distances at their own expense to make personal representations to the prior about the activities of Innocenti wet nurses. The most common abuse was the wet nurse's failure to report the death of a child and to continue collecting payments:

> On 21 June 1457 [the wet nurse] came to us and said [the child] was dead and that she had put her arm in the fire. She doesn't know when she died and didn't bring her clothes back.[140]

Yet the record of payments shows that she was paid until just three days before she notified the hospital.

In 1456 a neighbor performed a similar service on behalf of one of the Innocenti's children:

> On 1 February we returned Gherardesca Innocente to wet nurse at fifty soldi per month, and [when she is weaned, the amount will be reduced to] twenty-five soldi per month. [The hospital recorded four payments to her, the last of which was made October 1457]. On 17 December 1457 a good person came to us and said the aforesaid Gherardesca was dead. In either April or May 1457, as can be seen, [the wet nurse] came to us afterward and collected payments. We need to know the truth.[141]

Similarly, in 1455, a male infant was sent to wet nurse, and not long afterward a "buona persona" came to tell the hospital that the child had died.

> We want to know if this is true, and [if it is] she is to be given no more money. She [the wet nurse] took the money and did not tell us he was dead. On 28 March 1458 she brought us the *fede* saying that he died on 11 November 1457.[142]

The *fede*, or written oath sworn in the presence of, and usually written by, the local parish priest, was the only formal control the Innocenti could use to protect itself against this sort of fraud. The *fede* served two purposes. First, it allowed the priest to collect burial expenses:

> On 3 July the said Andrea died and we got all her things back. And [the wet nurse] brought the oath of the priest that he buried her, which said that he is owed fifteen soldi for her burial.[143]

The second purpose was to keep wet nurses honest and to certify a date of death so the hospital could perform any necessary adjustments to the wet nurse's payments:

The aforesaid girl died on 30 November 1445, according to the *fede* we had in the handwriting of Ser Nicholaio di Ser Jacopo, the priest at San Vito a Sofignano di Mugello.[144]

Often the hospital withheld payment until the nurse produced the *fede*. In 1461, the husband of Mona Lisa, a wet nurse from Impruneta "brought back the clothes but not the oath from the priest. We want to know how and when she died."[145] The hospital expressed moral outrage, yet was reluctant to press charges or levy penalties. Hence in 1457, the hospital expressed its hope that a certain wet nurse "will do her duty to the House, [or face] that shame she deserves."[146]

The hospital's sense of outrage was even less muted, though no more effective, in cases that involved easily proven abuse and neglect. In March 1452, Alessandra, ten months old, returned from the wet nurse to the hospital, and:

she remains in the hospital. We do not want to give the wet nurse any more money because she treated her like a beast and cared for her badly, or so say the women of the hospital.[147]

Similarly, when an infant named Giovanni was returned by the wet nurse with all his clothes, hospital officials wrote:

They [the wet nurse and her husband] are wicked to behave this way. On 2 August 1456 the aforesaid boy, Giovanni, died, and was buried in the church with the other children. He died in House.[148]

Similarly, in 1458, another wet nurse "brought back the aforesaid child to us with his supplies. He is on the point of death, badly looked after and sick in such a way that the wet nurse deserves nothing. We do not want to pay her."[149] Another infant boy was returned "ill, on the brink of death, in such a way that the wet nurse would deserve much punishment."[150]

Wet nurses might also, instead of collecting payments after a child had died, engage in a more insidious and deadly form of abuse and neglect by keeping the child even after their milk supply had run out, either because of their own increasingly precarious nutrition, because of untreated mastitis, or most frequently and most importantly, because of pregnancy. This form of neglect became especially serious beginning in the late 1450s, reflecting not only precarious nutritional circumstances but also a precarious economic standard of living. Especially deadly was the hospital's resort to widows as wet nurses, not because popular suspicions of widows necessarily were true, but because fifty soldi per month was not the living wage in the 1460s it had been two decades earlier. It was, rather, a supplementary wage that required the presence of someone else in the household bringing in income. Typical of entries from this period is the following one:

On 7 July 1462 we gave the aforesaid infant girl to nurse with Mona Nanna di Benedetto of the parish of Santa Lucia of Terranuova for thirteen months at fifty soldi per month.... We want her back now because she is being badly treated. We understand from a person worthy of faith that she is dying of hunger and does not have milk. On 28 September 1462 the wet nurse brought the child back on the brink of death, badly treated and cared for. On 1 October the aforesaid girl died here in-house and was buried with the others.[151]

In another 1462 entry, one wet nurse who had lost her breast milk because of mastitis maintained a seven-month old infant on bread only. This wet nurse's sister finally took the infant and instructed an acquaintance to notify the hospital. The child, surprisingly, did survive.[152]

A 1463 entry also makes it clear that the hospital expected wet nurses to return children who took ill to the hospital forthwith:

The wet nurse brought back the child so badly cared for that she could not be worse. We do not want to give the wet nurse anything because the child is about to die, due to the fact that she was sick and the wet nurse kept trying to breast-feed her, instead of bringing her back right away.[153]

Wet nurses and their husbands were not averse even to clumsy lying to cover up, if hospital officials in the following case were right: "On 24 May, Guido, the wet nurse's husband, was here. He came for his money and said he brought back the girl on May 16th. We instead believe that she is dead."[154] Nor were more violent forms of abuse unknown: a female child came back "very badly neglected, as badly as could be. She had her arm broken."[155]

In reaction to such cases the hospital might even threaten punishments of some kind, but rarely, if ever, did such sanctions go beyond the withholding of salary:

> On 20 June 1463 [Mona Bartolomea of Borgo San Lorenzo] brought Piera Domenica back to us. The child was very badly neglected and ill nearly to the point of death. She did not have milk and she deserves to be forced to give back the cost of her services.... She received 27 August two lire, ten soldi for the remainder of what we owe her, by agreement with her husband.[156]

As the number of admissions multiplied beginning in the late 1450s, it became difficult even to recruit, never mind to monitor wet nurses. Indeed, as in the case above, more and more frequently the hospital would resolve to withhold wages and then continue to pay the wet nurses. Thus "on 7 January 1457 [modern = 1458], a good person came to us and said Agnolla Maria was being very badly cared for and therefore the wet nurse should not be given money."[157] Yet the very same page in the record documents payments to the wet nurse of forty lire over the following ten months. Not until a year and a half later did the wet nurse return the child, "who is very ill." A month after being returned the child died in the hospital. Similarly, Lazzerina Lisabetta, abandoned in November 1463, was brought by a man:

> who said his name was Lazzero Antonio. He did not wish to say anything else except that her father would like her back.... On 7 December 1463 we gave the said infant girl to wet nurse for fourteen months, at fifty soldi per month, and then at twenty-five soldi per month to ... Mona Ginevra, widow, wife of the late Jacopo d'Antonio di Maso ... from Pontassieve. [Here the hospital recorded payments through 28 April 1464 totaling fourteen lire.] On 23 June 1464 we paid her son in the expenditures book, page 148, three lire. And we were told that she was being badly treated and cared for. On 9 July 1464, she brought back the said girl all distended and dying of hunger, badly cared for and looked-after, almost dead from hunger and mistreatment.[158]

Some cases were without doubt more sinister. In the first twenty-two years of the hospital's operation, two accusations of infanticide caught the attention of hospital officials. The first case involved neglect without intention to defraud. The wet nurse's husband was paid only for the two months the child was alive at wet nurse:

> We were told how the said girl was dead and how she was found dead during the night at the wet nurse's side, where she was suffocated. The wet nurse treated her very badly, and used to go out for straw in the morning and left the baby the entire day without feeding her.[159]

The records are silent concerning the identity of the informant and how the information was acquired. Nor did the hospital pursue any sort of legal recourse or sanctions.

In the second accusation, the victim was an infant girl who had come to the hospital with effusive recommendations from her father promising the hospital reimbursement of all expenses incurred in her feeding. A week and a half later, Giovanna Innocente was sent to a widowed wet nurse in San Felice a Ema. Here is the entire case history:

> She had with her a note that said: "In the name of God the 9th day of August 1463. This girl has the name Giovanna. Hold on to this note so that whoever comes for her can tell which one she is. She is most highly recommended to you." ... On 22 August 1463 we gave the said girl to wet nurse for fourteen months at fifty soldi per month, and then at half the rate to ... Mona Cosa, wife of the late Nardo di Francesco ... *popolo* di San Felice a Ema, a laborer of Antonio called "the gouty" who used to sell wine.... She had 15 November 1463 one large florin and a new set of swaddling clothes. On 20 February that crude bitch, the aforesaid wet nurse, brought back the abovesaid little girl weak and dying of starvation, on the very brink of death, scarcely able to breathe. And she brought her back because it was said to us by several persons that the child was being mistreated. We even sent someone to tell her to bring back the child ... because she wouldn't do it herself. And when several of her neighbors told her to bring the child back, she said she wanted the money first and then she would bring her back. We were also told that the child was left unwatched in the tower all day to starve and die, the poor little thing. On 23 February the said girl died in the hospital from the privations

she endured, too weak even to take the breast. She was buried under the church with the other children.[160]

Despite this harsh condemnation no record of prosecution survives. Yet it is clear that hospital administrators were far from emotionally indifferent to the plight even of an infant girl, and that their charity was not just a vehicle for their own salvation but also a mirror of deeply felt compassion for helpless infants.

Some foster parents the Innocenti employed, however, responded with obvious affection for their charges, even if the affection was not shared by both foster parents. Alesso Biagio, who had returned from wet nurse in Montereggi because the husband "did not want to keep him any more," was returned to this nurse for a day "because she said she wanted to celebrate Carnival with him, and that she would bring him back for the first day of Lent."[161] Nor did wet nurses confine their affection to boys: in 1470, when Maria Girolama was eight years old, one of her former caretakers asked for her back temporarily "for her own consolation."[162] The Innocenti sent a seven-year old girl, Colonetta Margherita "to Mariotto di ser Pagolo. She was sent by permission of the prior. He said he wanted to keep her for his contentment until the September fair."[163] Pasqua Innocente was given "to the nurse's husband for two months without cost because he wanted her for his contentment."[164]

Similarly, Francesco di Medillo di Giorgio, from Sant'Andrea a Piancaldoli took an interest in Maria, whom his wife had nursed. Not only did he adopt her, but also bequeathed to her "the house with furnishings where he now lives, a piece of vineyard with land and crops, about eight or nine *staiora,*" and "several pieces of arable land." Francesco "promised the prior that when it will be time for her to be married, he will marry her to one of his grandchildren."[165] Children whom a foster family did not adopt might still come back "fat and fresh," or "molto bella."[166] Even if foster parents did not wear their hearts on their sleeves, the adoption of children by their foster parents was by no means rare. In 1447 a nurse and her husband adopted Giuliana Ginevra "because she is a good and beautiful girl. I am informed by the neighbors that she was well-treated."[167] In some cases the nurse and her husband had to agree to a long contract, especially if the child to be adopted was a girl. When Zanobi from Rovezzano wanted to adopt a child he and his wife had had in foster care, "because he has no children," he had to be prodded to part with his promised deposit in the communal dowry fund.[168] When

Nello di Nanni of Castello San Niccolò adopted Benvenuto Piero, however, he had only to promise to "make him prosper and not to accept
any more salary."[169]

Even caretakers of infants who were loaned to families of noble reputation to maintain the milk of their domestic servants wished to adopt
infants. Francesco, who was the son of Giovanni, a German staying with
Niccolò di Stefano di ser Piero, was abandoned by Niccolò at the Innocenti. The hospital:

> lent the said boy to the said Niccolò di Stefano di ser Piero on 21
> February 1444 [modern = 1445] to maintain the milk of Mona
> Margherita his wet nurse. I cancelled the aforesaid entry because
> Niccolò is keeping him and doesn't want to bring him back.[170]

How did the foundlings of the Innocenti fare by comparison to their
peers within Florentine families? Studies of fifteenth-century family
memoirs and diaries suggest that among children of wealthy Florentine
families mortality at wet nurse was under 20 percent, in striking contrast
to the much higher mortality figures for children the Innocenti sent to
wet nurse.[171] Other patterns of mortality are also strikingly different. In
Klapisch-Zuber's studies of Florentine families, infant mortality among
boys sent to wet nurse was higher than that for girls (18.1 percent for
boys, 15.8 percent for girls).[172] Even more surprising was the high rate
of reported smothering among wet nurses of these Florentine families.
Out of 356 child deaths studied over the course of the fourteenth and
fifteenth centuries, sixty-two (15 percent) died as a result of admitted
suffocation by the wet nurse.[173] Either Florentine fathers were more
suspicious than hospital officials, or hospital officials assumed as a
matter of course that a death at the wet nurse's was deliberate, so that
the frequency of infanticide in the Innocenti records should not be meas-
ured by how often smothering is explicitly mentioned, but by how often
the scribe writes: "May God forgive the wet nurse."

Indeed, neither the records of these Florentine families nor the records
of the Innocenti shed much helpful light on the issue of "smothering"
by wet nurses. The popularity of "the family bed" in recent times suggests just how difficult it is for such death to be accidental. Yet what
motivations would a wet nurse have for smothering an infant? Surely,
since Klapisch-Zuber could not find one instance of a wet nurse holding
more than one child, such smothering could not have been profitable.

The disparity between the mentions of smothering in the Innocenti records (where mention is rare) and the more frequent mentions of smothering in diaries suggests that distraught Florentine fathers may have been more likely to ascribe to smothering what may have been death from natural causes. A *balio* of Andrea Minerbetti, for example, refused to be paid after a baby girl entrusted to him was "smothered" by his wife. Certainly, as relatively powerless persons in an emotionally charged situation, the husbands of wet nurses might well accept their employers' interpretations of events. Either wet nurses cared about the children they accepted, in which case they would have avoided both accidental and deliberate smothering, or they were indifferent to the fate of children and viewed them as only a means of survival and profit, in which case why would they risk their clients' good will and chances of future employment through negligence or malice? The traditional portrait of the murderous wet nurse that Florentine fathers painted with harsh words in their *ricordanze* and that subsequent historians have echoed, makes less sense as a description of what actually happened than as a reflection of both intense grief and rampant misogyny. In this respect it is worthy of note that of the nine cases that Klapisch-Zuber studied in some detail, only one suffocation was ascribed to the wet nurse's husband. Moreover, the percentage of "smothering" to overall causes of death is not incompatible with what we would think of as an expected rate of "crib death," or Sudden Infant Death Syndrome.[174]

Even wealthy Florentines operated under the same constraints as did the officials of the Innocenti. The geographical distribution of wet nurses these Florentine families used, for example, was strikingly similar to the location of the children the Innocenti had farmed out. Indeed, the Innocenti distributed its infants between city and countryside in exactly the same proportions as did Florentine families, with 13 percent sent out within the city of Florence. Unlike the infants of wealthy families, however, the foundlings of the Innocenti remained with their Florentine wet nurses as long as those placed with wet nurses in the countryside. Just as the Innocenti did, the families whose diaries Klapisch-Zuber studied showed a strong preference for the Mugello and the Casentino; however, the Innocenti, whether consciously or not, shunned the plain between Florence and Prato, which was a popular destination for the infants of wealthy families.

This congruence between the practices of Florentine families and those of the hospital of the Innocenti continued as the infant matured.

Children at the Innocenti were likely to have more than one wet nurse before being weaned, and the average age of children at weaning was 18.7 months for the children of Florentine families, followed by their return home at an average of 20.4 months. Although the exact age of children on admission is not always clear at the Innocenti, weaning inevitably occurred between the ages of eighteen and twenty-four months for the hospital's charges as well. This too was followed by their return to the hospital. Although most Florentine families made this return home permanent for their children, the Innocenti nearly without fail then arranged for some sort of foster care for its foundlings, at rates exactly half of those for wet nurses, rates that also prevailed for Florentine families. The similarities between the practices of Florentine families and those of hospital officials also had a more mundane and practical common source: Piero Puro, described in the Innocenti documents as "nostro commesso," was an agent who found wet nurses not only for the Innocenti, but also for a number of wealthy Florentines. Indeed, much of the source material for our knowledge of wet-nursing comes from his *ricordanze*, which comprised part of the estate he left to the Innocenti as a condition of his permanent employment.[175]

Comparisons that are striking enough in the aggregate become even more so in the particular. The *ricordanze* of Giuliano di Giovencho de' Medici and his children and grandchildren are mixed in, as one would expect, with the wool accounts of the family business from which Florence Edler de Roover extracted her exhaustive glossary of medieval business terms. Unlike Francesco Datini, who began every page "in the name of God and profit," this branch of the Medici preferred the more circumspect and verbose "In the name of God and of His Mother the Virgin Mary: grant us a good beginning and good fortune, and our salvation, and the salvation of those born of us."[176] Giuliano di Giovencho de' Medici, recording the birth of a son in 1421, relied on a formula that is strikingly similar to the first entries of information for abandoned children at the Innocenti:

I Giovencho di Giuliano de' Medici shall keep a record that in the name of God on 22 September 1421 an infant boy was born to me, to whom we gave the name Giuliano Matteo. He was born to us between the hours of sixteen and seventeen. I baptized him on the twenty-third of the said month.[177]

In the 1420s, Giovencho was more precise about the date and hour of his sons' births than of his daughters'. When his son Giuliano recorded the births of his children in the 1440s and 1450s, however, this distinction disappeared. Moreover, for this younger generation of merchant Medici, explicit mention of a wife in the invocations and formulae of the accounts suggests a greater recognition of the central role of women in the family: "In the name of God and of my salvation and hers."[178]

Even in this wealthy mercantile family, the mortality of infants and children was high, especially during plague years. The sense of human life as literally "borrowed time," a sense that pervaded popular preaching as well as personal letters, found its expression with respect to the fragility of childhood in the notion that one's children were borrowed from God, or lent by God. Giuliano di Giovencho de' Medici wrote of "the children God has lent to me and to my wife Lionarda." The Medici baptized all the children mentioned in their *ricordanze* at San Giovanni. The Adimari family frequently stood in as godparents, but nearly as often the witnesses and sponsors might be "a poor woman who was at San Giovanni." Girls and boys were baptized with equal haste, usually within two days. Of his children of both sexes Giuliano customarily wrote "God lend them good fortune." Both the infant boys and girls who died, moreover, were buried in the family tomb "under the step at San Giovanni," unless they died at wet nurse, in which case they were buried in the wet nurse's parish church. Table 19 records, insofar as the evidence allows, the lifespans of the fifteen children that Lionarda di Guido Deti bore Giuliano di Giovencho de' Medici.[179]

Giuliano sent all these children, except the male twins born in June 1456, to wet nurse. The female twins, Bartolomea and Francesca, were each sent to a wet nurse. Both children died there:

> I, Giuliano de' Giovencho de' Medici aforesaid record that on 11 February 1451 [modern = 1452] a female infant was born to me at fourteen hours. I baptized her the said day and gave her the name Bartolomea. I sent her to wet nurse in Calenzano. She died 23 July 1452 and was buried at San Piero a Ponte. In the name of God and of salvation, hers and mine: I, Giuliano di Giovencho de' Medici record that on 11 February 1451 [modern = 1452] a female infant was born to me at 14 hours, whom I baptized on the said day. A poor man sponsored her at Santo Stefano, and we gave her the name Bartolomea Francesca, whom I sent to wet nurse at Piero di Piero from

Artimino. She died 20 August 1453 and was buried in the parish church of Artimino.[180]

The pay scales of Medici wet nurses, not surprisingly, were nearly double what the Innocenti paid. The Medici could both afford and find wet nurses who were sufficiently close to the city to be paid the statutory four lire per day. Giuliano even paid 4 lire, 10 soldi for the wet-nursing of his son Antonio. Antonio stayed unweaned at the same wet nurse until 20 January 1452, when the wet nurse and her husband "came to Florence and said the wet nurse was pregnant and therefore they weaned him." Giuliano and the *balio* agreed to have Antonio stay on at the reduced rate of two lire per month.[181]

Yet even at the higher rate of pay, the Medici were on occasion no more fortunate than the Innocenti in the quest for good wet nurses:

> I, Giuliano di Giovencho de' Medici, record how I gave to wet nurse Bartolomea, the daughter of Lionarda and myself, to... Mona Mea from the parish of San Martino on 5 March 1452 for four lire per month. On 31 March she brought her back very ill and therefore was paid nothing.

TABLE 19.   The Children of Lionarda di Guido Deti and Giuliano di Giovencho de' Medici

Name	Date of Birth (day/month/year)	Age at Death
Antonio Giovanni	3/5/1449	41
Francesco Romolo	29/10/1450	?
Bartolomea Romola	11/2/1452	5.5 months
Bartolomea Francesca	11/2/1452	6.5 months
Giovencho Biagio	2/2/1454	?
Guido Giovanni	11/6/1455	10 years
Giovanni Domenico	6/6/1456	5 days
No name	6/6/1456	5 days
Averardo Domenico	4/6/1457	26
Bartolomea Anna	22/6/1458	13.5 months
Piero Mario	19/2/1460	31
Tommaso Bartolo	3/3/1463	30
Nanna Mattea	28/3/1466	?
Guido Barnaba	10/6/1468	2
Bernardo Nofri	10/6/1468	2

Source: Harvard University, Baker Library of Graduate Business Administration, Medici Collection, vols. 491 and 500.

Given to another wet nurse, the wife of Cione from San Piero a Ponte, Bartolomea "died on 23 July 1452 and was buried...at San Piero a Ponte. We paid the wet nurse nothing."[182] The other twin, Bartolomea Francesca, lived a year longer, but the Medici suspected no malfeasance on the part of her wet nurse, who was paid the equivalent of forty-three lire in gold florins.[183]

Apart from Bartolomea's unfortunate treatment at the hands of her wet nurses, the Medici experienced considerably more reliability at the hands of wet nurses than did the foundlings of the Innocenti. Only two children of thirteen died there, and only one of them due to discernible neglect by the wet nurse. What is clear is that individual wealthy families had the luxury of time to choose and fewer numbers to arrange care for. A Medici child, on the average, was bounced from wet nurse to wet nurse fewer times than the average Innocenti child. None of the children of Lionarda and Giuliano had more than three nurses, wet or "dry."

The prevalence of wet-nursing in medieval Tuscan culture raises some interesting and difficult issues. If the officials of the Innocenti were constrained by a simple lack of alternatives, wealthy and noble Florentine families deliberately chose wet-nursing over maternal breast-feeding for their children. Since mothers transmit immunities and antibodies through colostrum in the vital first few days of feeding, it is not unreasonable to speculate that the institution of wet-nursing itself contributed to very high infant mortality. Moreover, even wealthy Florentines and moralists believed colostrum to be milk that was very thin and therefore polluted, so that if a wet nurse was not immediately available they would not have been inclined to supplement with maternal breast-feeding.[184]

Moralists highly recommended mother's milk, but "conceded" that it weakened the mother, turned her prematurely gray, and made her unfit for further childbearing. Animal milk, apart from its genuine inadvisability (even now physicians prefer infant formula to animal milk in the child's first year), was shunned even more by fifteenth-century Florentines, who believed that the child would grow up with the characteristics of whatever animal it had received its milk from. A child fed on animal milk, wrote Paolo di Certaldo, "doesn't have perfect wits like one fed on women's milk, but always looks stupid and vacant and not quite right in the head."[185]

More importantly, perhaps, the institution of wet-nursing for Tuscan families distanced them emotionally and geographically from the painful facts of infant mortality. Medici children who died at wet nurse, for example, were buried in the parish where they died, not in the family tomb. In *Della Famiglia*, Alberti assigned the care of children under two years of age to women.[186] Emotions surrounding the mortality of children were far more complex than alleged lack of affection. As we have already seen, parents abandoned even the children of their servants and slaves reluctantly and with considerable ambivalence. Parents returned frequently to claim children within a few days, in some cases, or within a few years, in others. Even where girls were involved, the memory of the child a parent had abandoned often lingered. Parents followed their child's progress not only through wet nurse, but even after adoption.

Indeed, it is in the Innocenti's adoption records that the affection of Florentines for children and their hopes even for abandoned children leave no room for doubt that fifteenth-century Florence was, in a profoundly religious way, a child-centered culture. The Innocenti's success in rescuing its surviving children from the margins of the community and restoring them to what one historian has called "the charismatic center"[187] had its practical expression for boys in combining adoption and apprenticeship, and for girls in combining adoption and household service. In some cases, girls, too, were apprenticed. In any case, the hospital went to considerable lengths to ensure that adoptive parents of female foundlings provided a dowry and arranged a suitable marriage, as the hospital itself provided for the girls who remained residents until they were of marriageable age. When the hospital described itself and its children as "tutta la famiglia," it was engaging not in a mechanical exercise of rhetorical bombast; rather, hospital administrators acted both legally and actually as parents, consciously aiming to develop the participation of children in both civic and domestic life.

Moreover, the pattern of adoption by gender stands in striking contrast to the lopsided figures for infant mortality and for the reclamation of children by their parents. The hospital's 1452 census recorded nine adoptions from its first cohort of admissions: six were girls, three were boys.[188] In 1460, the hospital took another census, this time of all children adopted in the years 1459 and 1460. Of 126 children adopted in those two years, exactly one-half were girls. Although this falls short of the percentage of girls available for adoption, it is still quite remarkable, especially considering the conditions and restrictions the Innocenti imposed on the adoptive parents of a girl. Adoption figures are, moreover, artificially depressed for girls for those two years because what prompted the hospital's census in the first place was a temporary explosion of apprenticeships for boys.[189]

Less clear than the adoptive parents' contractual obligations is the process, if any, by which they were screened. A certain Mona Andrea, for example, had only to write to the prior that she wanted "an adopted son."[190] When Mona Zanobia wished to adopt Caterina Lucia, the hospital agreed to the placement "because she has no children and wants to give her a dowry."[191] In both cases, however, the guild consuls and *operai* gave their approval, so that it is at least clear that neither guild nor hospital treated the issue of adoption casually.

Within a year of the hospital's first wave of adoptions in 1451, the guild's consuls and the hospital's trustees formulated the beginnings of a policy. On 28 May 1453, for example, hospital officials set certain conditions on the adoption of Veronica Innocente by Monna Antonia di Francesco di Piero. Similarly, the adoptive parents of a boy had to:

> teach him a trade and good moral habits, on those terms to be declared by the wise and prudent men, Bernardo Gherardi, Carlo Gondi, and Lodovico Galilei, at present the *operai* and governors of the said children, according to whose [terms] it shall be done.[192]

Mona Mea di Luca could adopt Dorotea Innocente "as her own daughter to be married as our consuls shall declare. . . . She promised to have her married at the proper time and to raise her well and honestly. Let her conscience be so burdened." By September 1453, the consuls had issued a policy rather than guidelines, for both Ricca Castellana and Bartolomea were adopted at the age of six on the condition that their adoptive parents "give her a dowry, as our consuls and trustees have ordered."[193] Not until 1483, however, did the policy again become the subject of guild deliberations: The *operai* and Council of Thirty-Six decreed that those who adopted or apprenticed girls had to guarantee that they would be married by the age of twenty, with a dowry of at least twenty florins. Moreover, the adoptive parents had to swear an oath to the consuls and *operai* "so that they will be satisfied she will be well-kept and honestly treated."[194]

Despite the tardiness with which hospital officials made the dowry requirement statutory, as early as 1455 a wet nurse adopting a child agreed to pay a dowry "according the procedure and custom of the guild."[195] Nevertheless:

> Not by virtue of the *balio* was the dowry paid. A good person came to us and said that this man had told him he didn't want to pay the dowry. On 14 March 1460 [modern = 1461] we remain in agreement with the aforesaid Zanobio di Cristofano called "The Beard" from Rovezzano that to subsidize the dowry he shall give us 16 lire: eight this year and eight the next.[196]

Similarly, in 1470, the silk guild's consuls ordered a wool guildsman, Francesco di Guccio, to pay the silk guild's treasurer thirty florins, as he had agreed to do in installments, but had failed to do. In addition, Francesco was required to turn over to the treasurer of the Innocenti several articles of clothing that were to form part of the dowry of a girl he had taken into his household service.[197] Some time between 1455 and 1456 the hospital summoned Dorotea Innocente from her first adoptive parents "because they made little effort to make a deposit in the dowry fund."[198] When Angiola Innocente was adopted the hospital gave her:

> to Domenico d'Andrea Porcellani and his wife Mona Pipa, who take her on the following terms: that they wish to raise her as their own daughter, and to teach her all good manners and that trade at which she would be adept, in such a way as to lead her to honor. When it will be time for her to be married they shall give the hospital 120 lire: 80 in cash and 40 in gifts, and anything more their conscience will permit. When she reaches the age of sixteen years, and if before that time, i.e. the sixteenth year, the said girl shall die, the aforesaid Domenico must give the hospital one half the aforesaid dowry: i.e., seventy [*sic*] lire. And for the sake of clarity concerning these points the said Domenico will sign below in his own hand.[199]

Another adoptive parent agreed to raise Agatha Maddalena "as his own daughter so that in all things she shall be of modest and good moral character, as all good men must do."[200]

Although dowries for boys were not required, they were not unknown. In May 1454, the hospital of the Innocenti gave Niccolò Lorenzo, aged eight:

to Pagolo di Cecco d'Agnolo from Quercietto di Bibbiena di Casentino. We gave him for an adoptive son in this way: that within a year or two he will have deposited six florins in the dowry fund. Giuilano di Francesco . . . promised to do this if he defaults.[201]

In December 1454 the hospital gave another boy to a broker, who agreed to "take Lorenzo Giovanni as his adopted son and provide for him a dowry of 50 florins, through the *Monte delle Doti*."[202]

Parents who adopted boys were customarily expected to provide apprenticeship at a trade. An important part of these adoption and apprenticeship contracts was the stipulation that boys learn to read, write, and use the abacus. In November 1451:

> The consuls of the silk guild agreed to give Venturo, called Venturino, a six-year old boy from our hospital, to Giovanni di Fruosino, a cutler who lives . . . in Florence, because the said Giovanni has no children. He promised to keep him and treat him just as if he were his own son, and to have him learn to read and write, and to do sums on the abacus, and then to place him at whatever trade he likes.[203]

Similarly, a silk guildsman who lived behind Santa Croce promised to take a boy from the Innocenti and to "make him learn to read and write, and [to use] the abacus and thus to have him learn his trade. And he promised to treat him as if he were his own son."[204] A Florentine citizen living in Pisa promised to treat Isforzo Niccolò "as if he were his own son in feeding him and making him a man of means, as good fathers do for their children."[205] Thus hospital officials sought fathers who could teach boys the basic skills required by a trade, and for this reason deferred adoption until boys were five or six years old. A rare exception, however, set forth the hopes that hospital administrators placed in both the adoptive parents and the child, in this case an infant:

> On Monday 3 February 1465 the said boy [Biagio Mariano] was brought to the font at San Gallo at about 14 hours. A woman brought him and said he was the son of one of Messer Dietisalvi di Nerone's slaves. He had with him two rather sad-looking pieces of cloth and a grey and tattered woolen. On 16 February 1465 by consent and license of Messer Girolamo di Niccolò our prior of the said hospital, the said Biagio was given to Manuello di Michele, a Roman merchant

from Aragon and Mona Maria his wife, the daughter of Alfonso of Sicily, for their adopted son. And the said Manuello and Maria together, and each one separately, and each speaking for both, promised to the said Messer Girolamo as well as to me, Stefano d'Antonio treasurer of the said hospital on behalf of Messer Girolamo superintendent, representing the said Biagio Mariano, [that they must] have, hold, raise, and nourish him as if he were their own son and born of them, to treat him with care and diligence, and not otherwise except as a son with diligence, charity, and love. And at the end of their lives, at their deaths, each one shall institute the said Biagio as their universal heir, as if he were any of their children. And if they bear other, legitimate children they must institute him as heir in equal portions with the other children. And they promised to pay attention to and to observe the said things fully to me, Ser Stefano, representing the aforesaid Biagio as above, without exception. And therefore they obligate themselves and each one of them, their present and future wealth and renounce any rights, etc. And each of them swore an oath by touching physically the Scriptures, to the saints and to God's Holy Gospel . . . to pay attention to and observe in every respect everything written above, with full and pure knowledge, without fraud, stain, fiction, or deceit of any kind. And the following are witnesses to all the aforesaid things.[206]

Some hospital administrators took so seriously the task of restoring abandoned children to the mainstream of civil life that they adopted the children of the Innocenti themselves. A *commessa* of the Innocenti, Mona Antonia di Guido, adopted a girl named Francesca, who had been abandoned to the Innocenti at the age of six, "because she wanted to raise her and take care of her for the sake of her soul. And so she was given by the prior [Messer Niccolò di Piero] on 20 May 1446."[207] In 1450 the hospital gave to Ser Silvano di Giovanni di Fruosino, the hospital's notary, another girl:

on these terms: the said Ser Silvano vowed that he would raise her as his own daughter in all things that pertain to modesty and good character as all good men must do. At the end of eighteen or twenty years he must have her married and provide her with a dowry of at least forty florins.

Agatha stayed with Ser Silvano for only two years, however, returning to the Innocenti in March 1454.[208]

A superintendent's adoption of Maddalena Giovanna proved to be more enduring. This governor of the guild's hospital in Radda adopted a girl "because he said he wanted a girl at home to raise because he would raise her as a daughter."[209] The superintendent of the guild's hospital of Sant'Antonio a Lastra a Signa adopted Marietta Margherita in 1452 on the same terms and with the approval of the guild consuls.[210]

If most adoptions of boys aged five through ten specified permanent apprenticeships as part of the contract, the hospital made contracts with some local merchants for temporary placement. Thus, the hospital placed Domenico with a cloth weaver named Simone di Giovanni. Simone was to pay Domenico a total of seventeen florins over the course of three years, beginning with four florins for the first year, with annual increases for the subsequent years. Simone also agreed to teach Domenico the trade and to "treat him with responsible discretion as is customary for masters." This contract did not specify that Domenico was to be taught to read and write, and in fact Simone di Giovanni himself was unlettered.[211] Similarly, in 1478, Giovanni di Biagio d'Agnolo, a tailor in Or San Michele "took our boy Baldassare for a period of two years beginning 15 May. For his salary...he must have twenty-eight lire." After this period of time was over, however, he was hired by Giovanni di Biagio for another three years beginning in October 1483, at a considerably higher salary: 18 florins *di suggiello*, "just as he is accustomed to pay the apprentices who work at this trade."[212]

These examples of temporary apprenticeships were rare variations of the more common practice of combining adoption and apprenticeship of boys. Thus, in 1482, "we gave Lippo, our boy, to Piero di Simone Bastiere. He must keep him at home and in the shop and teach him the skills pertaining to his trade. For the time he has him, he must clothe him."[213] Similarly, of another boy the hospital's scribe wrote that Simone da Righo, a weaver, "who at present lives in the Canto alla Marina, promised to teach him his trade and treat him as a son. He must support and clothe him."[214]

Boys did not always serve out their full contracts. In some cases their own discontent impelled them to seek work elsewhere. In 1483, the hospital placed Giovanni with a tradesman who lived in Borgo San Niccolò, and who agreed to take him for five years, paying him three large florins a year, and to teach him how to make eyeglasses. By 28 October

1484, a little over a year into this arrangement, Giovanni reported to the hospital that Smeraldo had left some time ago, and that "he didn't have a clear idea of his whereabouts but thinks he went to Rome."[215]

Some apprenticeships, for both boys and girls, involved working at the shop for the day but coming back to the hospital to dine and to sleep. Hence in October 1483, the hospital reserved fourteen places at the dinner table "for the girls and boys who go to the shop for the day."[216]

The hospital rarely, if ever, combined adoption of girls with trade apprenticeships, and the apprenticeships officials did arrange for girls were therefore temporary. Within the silk industry, however, the Innocenti found ample opportunities for girls to experience temporary employment that was equivalent in length, if not in salary, to apprenticeships for boys:

> Record of how today this first day of January 1451 I Lapo di Piero Pacini, treasurer and governor of the hospital of the Innocenti placed three of our girls for two years beginning on the said day and ending as follows—the girls are these: Antonia, Tita and Zanobia [who were placed] with Mona Tita and with Michele di Cino her husband, who is a furrier. They live in Piazza San Marco. He must teach them to wash and to put *sirocchetti* into crude silk. We agree that he must give each girl eight lire for the first year and sixteen for the second. They must pay these salaries every six months. In case one of the said girls should die or not stay with them, they are not obligated to pay except for the time she stayed with or served them. They promised to teach these girls everything pertaining to the said trade.[217]

Starting in January 1452, Lapo di Piero Pacini apprenticed three more girls for a period of two years. He sent Pacie, Dorotea, and Giovanna to Mona Maria, the wife of Jacopo di Santi, a cloth-cropper who lived in a lane "off the Via Larga. She must teach them to cleanse silk and wind it onto reels, and the whole trade." The wages for these girls were also meager: eight lire the first year and sixteen the second.[218] On the same day Lapo also placed Piera, Brigida, and Ramposa with Mona Sandra di Giorgio, who in her home near the headquarters of the guild, would teach the three girls "to throw silk, spin it on to reels, and cleanse it."[219] The hospital's accounts make it clear that the girls themselves were not entrusted with the sums they earned, although the boys were. What they do not make clear is whether these sums were ever returned to the girls or if, perhaps, they went into a general fund to subvent dowries.[220] By 1469, the salaries for these girls had risen: thus when Mona Caterina in that year took on Simona, Sandra, and Maria to teach them how to throw crude silk, she paid the hospital forty lire per year.[221]

The hospital also hired women to stay *in casa* to teach girls various tasks associated with cloth. In 1457, the hospital hired Mona Apolonia, the wife of Piero Lippi from Colpaia, "because she is a very skilled woman in every respect. She was hired to teach weaving to the girls in the hospital."[222] Those girls not serving apprenticeships stood an excellent chance, as we have seen, of being adopted. In early 1452 Lapo di Piero Pacini drew up an especially specific contract according to which Costanza Innocente could be adopted by:

> Guglielmo di Francesco, who lives as a waiter in Cosimo's house, and to Mona Giovanna his wife. Costanza is three years old, and I have given her freely because they promised to marry her . . . when she has reached the age of fifteen, and to put in a deposit for her into the dowry fund. [They also promised] to treat her like a daughter and in each and every instance with good and pure love. She [the adoptive mother] has no other children, and in her will she will make a sizeable donation to our hospital . . . for the salvation of their souls.[223]

At issue in the salvation of this couple's souls was not the adoption but the donation. One may well ask why, if girls were such a liability in the household setting that they were abandoned well out of proportion to their numbers, were adoptive parents such as the above couple so anxious to take them? What did they receive in return?

Apart from the affection for girls that played a major role in these contracts, they also allowed couples of modest means to employ household help. Thus Anellina, given to a broker who agreed to pay her dowry "didn't want her because she seemed small and not suited to the needs of his household."[224] Another adoptive parent raised the issue even more explicitly:

> I record how this day 8 December 1464 Messer Girolamo di Niccolò, our prior, gave to Piero di Rossi a girl of ours who is named Fiammetta, on these terms and conditions: the said Piero must keep her at home in his service for eleven years, and feed and clothe her at his

expense. And he now must put a deposit in the dowry fund by the end of April 1465, so that once eleven years have passed Fiammetta will have a dowry.

Nevertheless, Fiammetta returned to the hospital within a very short time, and the agreement was cancelled, suggesting either that girls, too, had some latitude in their decision about whether to stay, or more likely, that the adoptive parents had had second thoughts about keeping her.[225]

Indeed, when one follows the adoptions of both boys and girls beyond their first few years away from the hospital, the impermanence of adoptions is striking. Girls were especially vulnerable to the sort of exploitation in which they might be returned after only a short period of time and the adoptive parents could avoid the more burdensome obligations occurring when it was time to marry their adopted daughters off to someone. Undoubtedly this is why the Innocenti, from the early 1450s, began to insist that the promise of dowries be underwritten by a hasty deposit in the dowry fund. The first set of adoptive parents of Dorotea Innocente, for example, returned her when she was still only seven years old because "she seemed tired." Twice more she was sent out—once she was returned with no explanation, the second time because the adoptive parent "did not want her in the house."[226] This could happen to boys as well: thus Luca Innocente was returned to the hospital after being kept for over a year by Antonio di Pagolo, a laborer, because "he did not satisfy the needs of the said Antonio."[227]

The hospital did its best to suppress the exploitation of its children by instituting a trial period during which either the adoptive parents or the adoptive child could sever the newly formed family ties informally. Thus on 8 September 1463:

> by license and consent of the prior, Margherita was given for a one-month trial to Arigo di Piero, a *famiglio* of the guild of Por Santa Maria. Arigo promised both the prior, and me, Stefano the notary, representing as a public person both the prior and the girl, that if the said girl pleases him he will make a deposit in the dowry fund.[228]

On 24 June 1461, a girl named Ventura was given to Meo Graselli:

> with these terms and conditions: that the said Meo must keep her two months, and if he likes her he must [since she already has a deposit

in the dowry fund] provide a dowry for one of the other girls in-house, whom it shall please the prior to choose.[229]

Two months was an unusually long period of time for a trial to run; more commonly fifteen to thirty days passed before an adoptive parent either had to return the child or make a deposit in the dowry fund. That the trial period was a response to earlier problems is clearly suggested by the case of Dimitella in October 1463, which was set "according to the regulations of the hospital."[230]

If this trial period gave adoptive parents a certain freedom of choice, the hospital was also surprisingly generous toward children who no longer liked their placement. Luca Innocenti, for example, who did not satisfy the needs of his first adoptive parent, was adopted three more times before the hospital thought it had finally found a suitable match for him. A year after the third disgruntled adoptive parent had returned him to the hospital, two weavers, a team of husband and wife, adopted him. They "promised to teach him the art of weaving." But Luca "did not want to stay, so he is back in the hospital."[231] The Innocenti also held firmly to the principle espoused in humanist pedagogical literature that boys should be allowed to choose the occupation that suited them. At the Innocenti this latitude extended to the choice of a master. The hospital arranged a placement for Giovanni Innocenti, for example, with Francesco di Giuliano Benintendi for three years, with progressive salary increases of six, nine, and twelve lire for each year. "The said Giovanni," however, "did not wish to stay, and so the contract is cancelled."[232] The priest Ser Tommaso di Rosso promised to teach Natale di Stefano "and to make him a priest, insofar as the boy wants to become a priest... and insofar as it is the right choice for him." Natale Stefano's aptitude for the priesthood must not have been all it could be, however, since Ser Tommaso "didn't want him and sent him back to the hospital."[233] Another boy, placed in 1483 with Piero di Antonio di Giovanni Grasso, "returned to the hospital because he didn't want to stay."[234] In 1484, two other boys returned to the hospital: one had stayed with his adoptive parent for only a few days, another came back to Florence from Pisa "because he didn't want to stay."[235]

Yet for those boys whose endurance of the eccentricities of their employers was more steadfast, the rewards could be considerable. In 1460, the hospital conducted a review of all the children who had been adopted in the previous two years.[236] Undoubtedly, one of the major reasons for this census was that in 1458 and 1459, Ser Cristoforo di Malvicino of Viterbo, during his tenure as Capitano del Popolo of Florence, not only encouraged Florentine merchants to bask in the more favorable economic climate of Viterbo, but also actively sponsored the transfer of boys from the Innocenti to both native and Florentine merchants in the city of Viterbo.[237] Of sixty-three boys adopted in the years 1458 and 1459, nineteen went to Viterbo. Both the man who made this possible and the phenomenon itself deserve closer examination.

Saint Antoninus, in his Florentine *Chronica,* wrote that:

> In the year of our Lord 1456–57 there was great poverty in the city not so much from lack of food as from scarcity of money, because those accustomed to living from the labor of their own hands were not working at their own trade but had left the trade for various business reasons.[238]

Even before Ser Cristoforo assumed the position of Capitano del Popolo, he must have been actively recruiting Florentine merchants, and certainly was recruiting boys from the Innocenti to serve as apprentices. Described by a much later antiquarian as "one of the greatest boosters of the city" of Viterbo,[239] and by the Innocenti's scribe as a "dottore" of Viterbo, Ser Cristoforo adopted Francesco Carlo in 1457. "He says he will make him wealthy. He went through the good offices of Vieri Bartoli, a Florentine citizen and merchant."[240] On 26 June 1459 Ser Cristoforo adopted Giuilio Martino,[241] and the good captain also assisted in the return of the foundling Federigo Andrea to his parents:

> On 16 August 1463, by the will and permission of Messer Girolamo our prior, the said Federigo Andrea was given to Ser Napolione di Viterbo, a cavalier of Messer Cristofano Malvicini from Viterbo, the *podesta* of Florence, to bring him back.[242]

Other merchants from Viterbo were also adopting children from the Innocenti as early as 1457. In April of that year, Tommaso Guccio was "given to a relative of Maestro Piero di Domenico di Maestro Petruccio from Viterbo." Although mostly boys went to Viterbo, on 20 October 1461 Giovanni di Nicola Conciliati adopted Crescita and "promised to give her a dowry and treat her as a daughter."[243] The opportunity to go to Viterbo, however, seemed to be a signal honor usually reserved to boys:

> On 24 November [1483] we sent Brancazio Antonio to Maestro Antonio d'Alberto from Bologna, prior of the church of Santa Maria de' Servi, who says he is worth sending to Viterbo, to Ser Lesso, a notary who is also a trustee of the Church of the Virgin Mary . . . in Viterbo. He says Ser Lesso will keep him for a son because he has no natural children.[244]

Ser Cristoforo himself appeared to have made his reputation as Viterbo's greatest civic booster by his role as papal ambassador. Not only did he actively lobby for the canonization of a local saint, Santa Rosa, but together with Jacomo di Nicolasso, acquired papal bulls of pardon "for every crime committed since Messer Princivalle died, until 17 February [1457]." In addition, every citizen of Viterbo who had fled, except rebels of the commune, "could return safe and sound."[245] Such was the factionalism and fatuity of the good citizens of Viterbo, wrote their chronicler Niccola della Tuccia, that even as late as 1460 they found themselves "almost undone" by shortages of food and materials.[246]

Although the chronicler credits Ser Cristoforo and his papal connections with bringing some calm to the city, it seems highly likely that Ser Cristoforo's connections with the papal curia also brought a certain measure of prosperity to Viterbo, making it a center of clerical and papally sponsored humanism. Beginning in 1460, the city of Viterbo began "to regain its prosperity, to improve its condition, and to increase its population."[247] Citizens began to build palaces and great houses with fountains of mineral waters. "And several Florentine gentlemen and merchants of every trade and craft came to live in Viterbo; chiefly Florentines, Sienese," and people from the Marches and the Romagana came with their households, with quite a few merchants, traders, builders, and master craftsmen in wood:

> For which reason Viterbo infinitely increased its population, and held studies in grammar, logic, and other areas of knowledge. Because of this up to today there have been many quite young people who have returned to Viterbo with honor, doctors of civil law, and learned men

in several areas of expertise, and quite a few of them are in Rome staying in the houses of Lord Cardinals to improve their condition.[248]

Even if only a small number of the Innocenti's adoptees might aspire to such dizzying heights, the hospital expressed considerable concern for its alumnae and alumni by tracking their progress even after they had been adopted:

> On 31 July 1454, one of our girls was given to Giovanni di Niccolò d'Aringo. Her name is Francesca Domenica and she was abandoned at the hospital 13 May 1446, as appears in the book of wet nurses, page 80. Then he gave her some time ago to Giovanni his relative, who kept her a certain time, and then had her married.[249]

The hospital then noted to whom she was married, and the amount of her dowry. Not only compassion, therefore, but also vigilance over adoptive parents motivated the hospital to make sure it knew the whereabouts of its girls and whether the adoptive parents were fulfilling their obligations in the contracts.

Hospital officials even sought the return of adopted children who were subjected to neglect or mistreatment:

> We gave on 25 April 1456, the aforesaid Anellina to Mona Antonia, wife of the late Giuliano di Giovanni, a carder of the parish of San Friano [i.e., San Frediano] in Florence. She said she wanted her for her adopted daughter and that she wished to make a deposit in the dowry fund as is customary with the other girls.... We sent for her because it was said to us that she neglected her.[250]

Similarly, Mona Costanza, who, as we have seen, adopted Ventura Innocente, promised:

> to get her married when the time comes, and if she has a dowry in the dowry fund, to provide a dowry for someone else in the hospital.... On 24 May 1461 the said Ventura was brought back. She was being ill-treated by the aforesaid Mona Costanza.[251]

Like some infants who died at wet nurse, adopted children who died in the custody of their adoptive parents were returned to the Innocenti for burial:

> The said Gino died on 11 June 1467 and was buried with the other children in our cemetery because he was brought back dead to us on the same day. The person to whom we had given him treated him very well and with tremendous love.[252]

By the 1480s, the hospital had incorporated into its standard adoption contract the stipulation that officials could demand the return of an adopted child as they saw fit:

> On this day 2 April 1483, I record that we placed Batista, our boy, with Maestro Antonio di Domenico di Graziano from Castelfiorentino [who lives] in Viterbo and promises to keep him in his house. If the boy does not succeed in his intentions, he promises to send him back here to the hospital and not to send him away. In case we do not like the way he is being treated, he promised to return him whenever we wish.[253]

A more general sense of obligation, in addition to specific examples of tracking, quickens the spirit of even the earliest adoption contracts for boys. Indeed, none of Lapo di Piero Pacini's successors matched his enthusiasm or eloquence in expressing the shared features of mercantile and humanist pedagogy:

> Memorandum written by me Lapo di Piero Pacini treasurer of the hospital of Santa Maria degli Innocenti by license of the consuls of the guild of Por Santa Maria [concerning how] I gave Matteo Dicomano, one of our boys of the said hospital, to Francesco Pecori. [Matteo] is about 7 years old. We gave him to Francesco because he promised us that he would take him for his adopted son, because he has no children of his own. He promised to teach him to read and write, to use the abacus, and also [to teach him] grammar in such a way that he would become a gentleman, or truly a religious doctor, but in any case would not fail to make him a merchant. [Francesco promised] that after his death he would leave him rich and in a good position.[254]

In 1458, the hospital gave Agnolo Innocenti to:

Stefano d'Agnolo . . . from Orte on this side of Rome. We gave Agnolo
to him for his adopted son. He said he would make him a man of
means and teach him virtue. We have good information that he is a
good person and that [Agnolo] was well-placed.[255]

Adoptive parents were expected to provide well for their adopted
sons:

On 23 November we gave Fruosino Francesco as an adopted son to
Piero Cholla [*sic*] chancellor of Cardinal Orsini. They think that the
boy will succeed because Piero Cholla will make him a great master,
i.e., give him benefices, and if he is taken, to make him a priest. . . .
Lorenzo the Prior and Niccolò Anselmi gave the boy to him because
it seemed to us that he would be in a good place. Thus may it please
God to make him good through his grace.[256]

The hospital's adoption policies and practices clearly hoped to bring
these foundlings back from the margins of Florentine society, and even
in the hospital's most trying years during the fifteenth century, hospital
administrators committed themselves personally as well as charitably to
this task. In 1484, for example, a sixteen-year-old foundling named
Giorgio was described as a "clerk" when "we placed him with Francesco
di Martino della Torre, who used to be our prior. He left our hospital
in February 1483 [modern = 1484]."[257] During that same decade the
guild sought and received a papal dispensation for Alamanno, a foundling of the Innocenti, to serve as chaplain for the Gondi chapel in the
cathedral of Fiesole despite his tender age.[258] Most boys could expect, if
they were adopted, to acquire basic literacy, mercantile skills, and
proficiency at a trade or craft. A select few could aspire to the best
humanistic education available to make them "gentlemen" and "men of
virtue," or even, in Lapo Pacini's words, "religious doctors."

If the hospital's educational program for girls was much less ambitious from a learned and scholarly point of view, adoption and apprenticeship of girls not only taught them various menial tasks associated
with weaving and silk manufacturing, but also consciously recognized
the centrality of women and their dowries in Florentine hopes for family
survival, progeny, and personal immortality. For those girls who never

were adopted and dowered, the hospital set aside funds and sought, as assiduously as Alessandra Strozzi, suitable marriage partners. In the legislation allowing the hospital to invest in and benefit from the *Monte delle Doti,* the institution was to be treated "as the girls' true and legitimate father."[259] Not only legislation but practice consecrated the hospital thus. If both the natural parents of a girl foundling died, the dowry reverted to the hospital. Thus in 1479, the natural parents of Alessandra Lena died without leaving any other children: "Because the father died before the mother ... we are expecting her mother's dowry, [which belongs] to the said hospital as father of the said girl."[260]

In marriage contracts as well the hospital acted as its girls' legal father. In 1470, for example, Alessandra, whose father died and whose relatives committed her to the Innocenti:

> is therefore the hospital's daughter. On this day, as is said above, Messer Pacie, our prior, married her to Francesco Galighaio from the parish of Santo Stefano a Ponte.[261]

When the prior married Margherita to Filippo di Tommaso d'Antonio, the hospital gave him a 100 lire dowry:

> because this girl has her dowry in the communal dowry fund.... Our aforesaid son-in-law goes by the name Filippo di Tommaso d'Antonio, from the parish of San Niccolò a Pisignano, commune of San Casciano. He is now one of our creditors in the Red Book G, page 68.[262]

Filippo, described also in a subsequent document as "our son-in-law," brought an associate from San Casciano to offer him:

> as a husband for one of our girls. He used to have a wife, and he is now 45 years old. He has no children or other relatives except for one brother, Domenico di Tamburino. He lives by himself and rents a house. There seemed to be no need for him and therefore nothing was concluded.[263]

Whom did the girls of the Innocenti marry? Most of the hospital's sons-in-law were farm laborers and millers, some of them on the Innocenti's own properties. In 1471, for example, Archangela Innocenti "married Benci di Michele, our laborer."[264] On 22 November 1472, "Francesco di Ristoro Schiattesi [a sharecropper in our vineyard at Peretola] married our girl Maddalena, who used to be Bernardo del Benino's slave."[265] The protocols left by the hospital's notaries, Ser Uberto di Martino and Ser Silvano di Giovanni, also record marriages such as those of the two girls married on 14 September 1464: one to a "laborator terrarum," another to a miller.[266] In the Pellegrinaio frescoes of the hospital of Santa Maria della Scala of Siena, there is a representation of the *sposalizio* of two of the hospital's foundlings,[267] although I could find no instance during the fifteenth century that this occurred at the Innocenti.

Both the dowries paid by the hospital and the social status of its sons-in-law suggest that girls had little hope of improving their social status as dramatically as boys could. Nevertheless, at least the hospital's girls got married in the fifteenth century—in contrast to the sixteenth century in which the marriage prospects of the hospital's girls seemed very bleak indeed. The hospital's dowries were slightly above the statutory minimum, amounting in some cases to thirty florins, with perhaps five to six florins in gifts and clothes rather than cash.[268] In 1468, when one of the girls of the Innocenti was married, the groom acknowledged receipt of twenty florins, plus capes, shirts, towels, handkerchiefs, a mirror, and a comb.[269] The mission of the Ospedale degli Innocenti, then, was to refashion the lives of the children under its care into the structure of the Florentine family. Both legally and organizationally, the hospital was a parent to its children, with the same high hopes and expectations that Florentine families had for their sons and the same sense of the centrality of marriage and dowry to the material and spiritual survival of the state that Florentine families had for their daughters.

NOTES

1. Archivio dell'Ospedale degli Innocenti di Firenze (AOIF), Filza d'Archivio (LXII,16), fol. 15r–16v, rubric 12, *anno* 1451. Archivio di Stato di Firenze (ASF), Provvisioni Registri, 142, fol. 381v, 30 December 1451.

2. AOIF, Balie e Bambini A (XVI,1), fol. 33v, 2 January 1445 [modern = 1446].

3. Richard Trexler, "The Foundlings of Florence, 1395–1455," *History of Childhood Quarterly* 1 (1973): 259–84. AOIF, Balie e Bambini A (XVI, 1), fol. 32v, 5 February 1445 [modern = 1446].

4. AOIF, Balie e Bambini A (XVI,1), fol. 9r, 28 March 1445. For another example of a countersign cf. fol. 25v, 15 October 1445: "per segnio rechò uno agnus deo chon un breve."

5. Some fine examples of eighteenth-century countersigns are still extant in the museum of the London Foundling Hospital. See Ruth McClure, *Coram's Children: The London Foundling Hospital in the Eighteenth Century* (New Haven, 1981).

6. AOIF, Balie e Bambini A (XVI,1), fol. 2v, 6 February 1444 [modern = 1445].

7. AOIF, Balie e Bambini A (XVI,1), fol. 2v, 18 February 1444 [modern = 1445].

8. AOIF, Balie e Bambini A (XVI,1), fol. 32v, 5 February 1445 [modern = 1446].

9. AOIF, Balie e Bambini A (XVI,1), fol. 19r, 5 February 1445 [modern = 1446], and fol. 26r, 21 October 1445.

10. AOIF, Entrata e Uscita (CXXII,2), fol. 174r, 25 October 1449, records the purchase of eighty-one pairs of children's shoes at sixteen soldi per pair.

11. Vincenzo Borghini, *Considerazioni sopra l'allogare le donne delli Innocenti fuori del maritare o monacare,* ed. Gaetano Bruscoli (Florence, 1901).

12. AOIF, Balie e Bambini A (XVI,1), fols. 4v, 142v, 13 February 1444 [modern = 1445].

13. AOIF, Balie e Bambini A (XVI,1), fol.13v, 23 May 1445.

14. AOIF, Balie e Bambini A (XVI,1), fol.26r, 23 May 1445.

15. AOIF, Balie e Bambini A (XVI,1), fol. 29v, 4 November 1445.

16. AOIF, Balie e Bambini A (XVI,1), fol. 32v, 8 December 1445.

17. AOIF, Balie e Bambini C (XVI,3), fol. 193r, 28 July 1457.

18. AOIF, Balie e Bambini A (XVI,1), fol. 40r, 14 March 1445 [modern = 1446].

19. AOIF, Balie e Bambini A (XVI,1), fol. 121r, 16 January 1447 [modern = 1448].

20. AOIF, Balie e Bambini B (XVI,2), fols. 71v, 144v, 24 May 1452, 30 December 1453.

21. AOIF, Balie e Bambini B (XVI,2), fol. 96v, 4 November 1452: "ci fu rechato e messo nella pila el sopradetto d'eta d'anni due o circha e chi llo rechò lasciò chonesso una poliza che diceva avea nome Girolamo di Bartolomeo di Polo il Chardassiere, e ch'el padre e lla moglie et i suoi figluoli erano alo spedale di Santa Maria N^a."

22. AOIF, Balie e Bambini C (XVI,3), fol. 199r, 11 September 1457.

23. AOIF, Balie e Bambini E (XVI,5), fol. 110v, 23 March 1462 [modern = 1463].

24. AOIF, Balie e Bambini E (XVI,5), fol. 275r, 10 March 1464 [modern = 1465]: "Domenicha a dì 10 di marzo e a ore circha 19 ci fu rechata e messa

nella pila detta fanciulla. Et recòlla Domenicho . . . di Matteo della Noratta pop. di Sct. [left blank] a Chalcinaia comune di Gangalandi lavoratore del prete di detto popolo. E disse chè detta fanciulla era figliuolo [*sic*] di Piero di Giovanni lavoratore di Iacopo Ciacchi e di monna Maria sua donna ligietima e che detto Piero era malato e detta sua donna non aveva latte e che sono molti poveri e che detta fanciulla era batezata in detto nome et che essa nata dì xi. . . . A dì 13 di marzo 1464 si rende a la madre."

25. AOIF, Balie e Bambini E (XVI,5), fol. 292r, 9 May 1465.

26. AOIF, Balie e Bambini C (XVI,3), fol. 182v, 23 May 1457.

27. AOIF, Balie e Bambini A (XVI,1), fol. 234v, 9 April 1450.

28. AOIF, Balie e Bambini F (XVI,6), fol. 36v, 18 February 1465 [modern = 1466]. Christiane Klapisch-Zuber, in her article, "Maternité, veuvage, et dot à Florence," *Annales: Economie, Société, Civilisations* 38, no. 5 (1983): 1097–1109, documents this phenomenon extensively. Children belonged to the father's lineage, so that when widows remarried, second husbands assumed the role of stepfather only rarely, and even then with considerable reluctance and often only on a provisional basis. Such widows customarily would be torn between the demands of their kin for remarriage and the subsequent necessity that their dowries be transferred to the families of the second husband, leaving the children of the first husband effectively without support. Cf. Giovanni Gherardo da Prato, *Il Paradiso degli Alberti,* ed. A. Lanza (Rome, 1975), 179–84 (cited in Klapisch-Zuber, 1109): "Since women cannot take their children, nor keep them with them, and they cannot remain alone without harm, nor remain without masculine protection, it is almost perforce that mothers see themselves constrained to choose the best compromise. But it is not to be doubted that they think constantly of their children and remain strongly attached to them in spite of this separation."

29. AOIF, Balie e Bambini H (XVI,2), fol. 2r, 19 June 1472.

30. AOIF, Balie e Bambini B (XVI,2), fol. 90v, 19 September 1452. In the seventeenth century, parents or nurses cut the tongue strings of children to make it easier for them to nurse; David Hunt, *Parents and Children in History* (New York, 1970), 113–14.

31. AOIF, Balie e Bambini A (XVI,1), fol. 213r, 18 September 1449.

32. AOIF, Balie e Bambini B (XVI,2), fol. 68r, 5 April 1452.

33. AOIF, Balie e Bambini A (XVI,1), fol. 233v, 23 March 1449 [modern = 1450].

34. AOIF, Balie e Bambini C (XVI,3), fol. 161r, 15 March 1466 [modern = 1467].

35. AOIF, Balie e Bambini C (XVI,3), fol. 203r, 7 October 1457.

36. AOIF, Balie e Bambini D (XVI,4), fol. 85v, 24 May 1459.

37. AOIF, Balie e Bambini A (XVI,1), loose scrap, n.d.

38. AOIF, Balie e Bambini E (XVI,5), fol. 21r, 9 December 1461.

39. AOIF, Balie e Bambini E (XVI,5), fol. 50v, 11 June 1462.

40. Ibid.

41. AOIF, Balie e Bambini E (XVI,5), fol. 56v, 13 July 1462.

42. AOIF, Balie e Bambini E (XVI,5), fol. 80v, 27 December 1462.

43. My first impulse was to treat these as motives of social shame. Judith Brown, however, has pointed out to me that as far as fathers were concerned, the acknowledgment of illegitimate children in family diaries was commonplace and unperturbed in the fifteenth century. Moreover, not until the very late fifteenth century did the Innocenti itself make a distinction between legitimate and illegitimate children. Yet the notes do specifically mention the avoidance of scandal and that fathers were wealthy men who promised to reclaim their abandoned children. It is also possible that the notes lie; that social importance might be falsely claimed in order to increase the chances that hospital officials would send the child to a good wet nurse. If social shame was not a motive, the jealousy of wives might well be and might, perhaps, explain much of the ambivalence these parents showed concerning abandonment. Certainly this would be the situation in households in which the marriage was infertile and the husband's extramarital involvements would be a source of intense pain, as in the case of Francesco and Margherita Datini. See Iris Origo, *The Merchant of Prato*, 2d ed. (New York, 1979), 168–71.

44. AOIF, Balie e Bambini H (XVI,8), fol. 25r, 4 November 1472.

45. AOIF, Balie e Bambini E (XVI,5), fol. 161v, 9 December 1463.

46. AOIF, Balie e Bambini F (XVI,6), fol. 50r, 23 March 1465 [modern = 1466].

47. AOIF, Balie e Bambini E (XVI,5), fol. 167r, 24 January 1463 [modern = 1464].

48. AOIF, Balie e Bambini E (XVI,3), fol. 187v, 3 April 1464.

49. AOIF, Entrata e Uscita (CXXII,2), fol. 18v, 4 April 1450.

50. AOIF, Entrata e Uscita (CXXII,2), fol. 18v, 27 April 1450.

51. AOIF, Entrata e Uscita (CXXII,6), fol. 16r–16v, 23 April 1456.

52. Ibid.

53. AOIF, Balie e Bambini D (XVI,3), fol. 190v, 10 November 1459: "Adì 10 di novembre ore [left blank] ci fu messo nella pila 1º fanciullo batezzato. Chi llo recò disse era d'un suo fratello che pagherebbe il balio. Recò 6 peze line e lane e 1ª facia era batezato in detto nome.

Adì 11 di novembre demo il sopradetto fanciullo a latte a mª Fiore donna fu Giovanni di Domenicho da Dicomano per soldi cinquanta cinque el mese. No ci metto el numero di mese perche dicie el fanciullo lo paga. E fornimenti sua sono questi: 12 pezze line 3 lane e fascie e uno mantellino foderato verde.

Adì 14 di marzo 1462 ci fu detta monna Fiore balia di detto fanciullo . . .

. . . detto Antonio non voleva pagare per detta balia perche disse avea trovato il fanciullo non esser di suo fratello e voleva noi la paghesimo."

54. AOIF, Entrata e Uscita (CXXII,6), fol. 7v, 1 March 1454 [modern = 1455].

55. AOIF, Ricordanze A (XII,1), fol. 110r, 1 October 1468.

56. AOIF, Ricordanze A (XII,1), fol. 99v, 17 October 1457.

57. AOIF, Balie e Bambini B (XVI,2), fol. 189v, 8 June 1454.

58. AOIF, Balie e Bambini C (XVI,3), fol. 3v, 8 January 1454 [modern = 1455].

59. Ibid.

60. AOIF, Ricordanze A (XII,4), fol. 256v, n.d., *anno* 1459.

61. AOIF, Balie e Bambini C (XVI,3), fol. 179v, 25 November 1457.

62. AOIF, Balie e Bambini A (XVI,1), fol. 5r, 5 April 1445.

63. AOIF, Balie e Bambini E (XVI,5), fol. 292v, 16 June 1465.

64. AOIF, Balie e Bambini F (XVI,6), fol. 70r, 18 June 1466.

65. AOIF, Ricordanze A (XII,1), fol. 89v, 6 March 1466 [modern = 1467]: Giovanni di Domenicho chalzolaio di San Friano disse stava a chasa in sul Chanto della Chocholia de dare adì vi di marzo 1466 L quarantaquatro sono per baliato d'un suo figliuolo ci mandò il quale a nome Francesco e Giovanni. E abia glieli alle voto e facto notrire mesi xii a llate a soldi l il mese e mesi xi a nutrichare a soldi xxv il mese chome appare a libro nero dalle balie S[egnatura] A a 280. Il quale Giovanni sopradetti renderci e soddisfare indrietto esopra ditti denari, cioè L xliii per dì qui a dì vi di marzo 1468 paghandoci detta quantita in due paghe cioè per dì qui a dì vi di marzo 1467 L 22 e chosi per dì vi di marzo 1468 L xxii e per cio oservare obligha se e sua rede e bene e nominatemente la meta d'una sue chase posto in via Chiara dal chanto alla Chocholia da primo via Chiara da 1/1 1/3 1/4 Lionardo d'Ipolito la quale prometa nonne a pigionare senza nostra licenzia o farci prometere la pigione di deta."

66. AOIF, Balie e Bambini F (XVI,6), fol. 37r, 22 February 1465 [modern = 1466].

67. AOIF, Ricordanze A (XII,1), fol. 97r, 8 September 1463.

68. AOIF, Balie e Bambini A (XVI,1), fol. 32v, 5 February 1445 [modern = 1446].

69. AOIF, Ricordanze A (XII,4), fol. 254r, 3 May 1459.

70. AOIF, Ricordanze A (XII,1), fol. 106r, 17 July 1468: "Richordo chome ogi questo dì xvii di luglio di licenzia di messer Pace nostro priore noi abiamo renduto uno de'nostri fanciulli il quale a nome Benedetto e Innocente. Venne a nostro spedale infino a dì xxiiii di marzo 1455. A Bartolomeo di Pagholo fabro il quale disse deto fanciullo era suo nipote e ch'era figluolo di Giovanni di Tinacio fabro. E veduta la spesa se futa per allevare e nutrichare deto fanciullo chome appare a libro nero S[egnatura] E 83 siamo rimasi d'achordo chon sopradeto Bartolomeo di Pagholo che s'obrigha darci barili quaranta di vino, cioè in quatro anni barili x per anno chomenciando il primo anno per presente anno 1468. Per chiareza di cio sisochrivera qui dapie voleva oservare a quanto di sopra

e schrito . . . A dì xv di setembre 1468 di chomesione e volonta di messer Pacie nostro priore si rende alla madre il sopra deto Benedeto."

71. AOIF, Balie e Bambini C (XVI,3), fol. 46r, 4 September 1455.

72. AOIF, Balie e Bambini A (XVI,1), fol. 141v, 25 July 1456.

73. AOIF, Balie e Bambini C (XVI,3), fol. 86v, 19 April 1456.

74. AOIF, Balie e Bambini A (XVI,1), fol. 18r, 3 September 1445.

75. AOIF, Balie e Bambini A (XVI,1), fol. 38v, 5 March 1445 [modern = 1446].

76. AOIF, Balie e Bambini A (XVI,1), fol. 40v, 14 March 1445 [modern = 1446].

77. AOIF, Balie e Bambini A (XVI,1), fol. 25r, 13 October 1445.

78. AOIF, Balie e Bambini B (XVI,2), fols. 10r, 134r, 202r, 25 March 1451.

79. AOIF, Balie e Bambini B (XVI,2), fol. 6r, 24 March 1450 [modern = 1451].

80. AOIF, Balie e Bambini B (XVI,2), fol. 116v, 23 March 1452 [modern = 1453].

81. AOIF, Balie e Bambini A (XVI,1), fols. 2r–53r, 25 January 1444 [modern = 1445] to 2 July 1446.

82. ASF, Provvisioni Registri, 139, fols. 46v–47v, 29 April 1448.

83. AOIF, Balie e Bambini A (XVI,1), fols. 2r–53r, 25 January 1444 [modern = 1445] to 2 July 1446.

84. Richard Goldthwaite, "I prezzi del grano a Firenze dal XIV al XVI secolo" *Quaderni Storici* 28 (1975): 5–36; idem, *The Building of Renaissance Florence* (Baltimore, 1981), 29–66.

85. Claude Delasselle, "Les enfants abandonées à Paris au XVIIIᵉ siècle," *Annales: Economie, Société, Civilisations* 30 (1975): 187–218.

86. AOIF, Balie e Bambini A-F (XVI, 1–6), 1445–66.

87. Marco Lastri, *Ricerche sull'antica popolazione della città di Firenze per mezzo dei registri del battistero di San Giovanni dal 1451 al 1774* (Florence, 1775), 34–39.

88. Delasselle, "Enfants abandonées," 213.

89. Carlo Corsini, "Materiali per lo studio della famiglia in Toscana dei secoli XVII–XIX," *Quaderni Storici* 33 (1976): 1039.

90. Ibid.

91. Jean-Claude Peyronnet, "Les enfants abandonées et leurs nourrices à Limoges au XVIIIᵉ siècle," *Revue d'histoire moderne et contemporaine* 23 (1976): 418–41.

92. Goldthwaite, "Prezzi del grano," passim; idem, *Building*, 318–19.

93. AOIF, Balie e Bambini F (XVI,6), fol. 128r, 2 November 1463.

94. AOIF, Balie e Bambini A-F (XVI,1–6), 1445–66.

95. AOIF, Balie e Bambini A-F (XVI,1–6), 1445–66.

96. Richard Trexler, "Infanticide in Florence: New Sources and First Results," *History of Childhood Quarterly* 1 (1974): 98–116.

97. Carole Cunningham and R. S. Schofield have estimated that half of infants dying during their first year died in their first month of life. See Cunningham, "Christ's Hospital: Infant and Child Mortality in the Sixteenth Century," *Local Population Studies* 18 (1977): 38; and R. S. Schofield's correspondence in *Local Population Studies* 9 (1972): 50.

98. ASF, Provvisioni Registri, 142, fols. 468v–469v, 25 February 1451 [modern = 1452].

99. Richard Goldthwaite, "Prezzi del grano," 5–36; idem, *Building*, 29–66.

100. Alan S. Morrison, Julius Kirshner, and Anthony Molho, "Epidemics in Renaissance Florence," *American Journal of Public Health* 75, no. 5 (1985): 531–32.

101. AOIF, Balie e Bambini A (XVI,1), fol. 15r, 14 June 1445.

102. AOIF, Balie e Bambini A (XVI,1), fol. 16v, 21 and 28 June 1445.

103. AOIF, Balie e Bambini A (XVI,1), fol. 18v, 14 October 1449.

104. AOIF, Balie e Bambini B (XVI,2), fol. 116r, 17 June 1463.

105. AOIF, Balie e Bambini B (XVI,2), fol. 3r, 26 July 1451.

106. AOIF, Balie e Bambini B (XVI,2), fol. 15r, 8 June 1451.

107. AOIF, Balie e Bambini B (XVI,2), fol. 21v, 16 May 1451.

108. AOIF, Balie e Bambini B (XVI,2), fol. 182v, 15 December 1454.

109. AOIF, Balie e Bambini B (XVI,2), fol. 15r, 8 June 1451.

110. Carole Cunningham, "Christ's Hospital," 37–40.

111. Ibid., 39.

112. Annette Chamoux, "L'enfance abandonées a Reims à la fin du XVIIIe siècle," *Annales de Demographie Historique* (1973): 263–301.

113. Jean-Pierre Bardet, "Enfants abandonées et assistés à Rouen," in *Sur la population francaises a XVIIe au XVIIIe siècles: Homages à Marcel Reinhard* (Paris, 1973), 19–47.

114. Delasselle, "Les enfants abandonées à Paris," 187–218.

115. David Ransel, "Abandoned children of Imperial Russia: Village Fosterage," *Bulletin of the History of Medicine* 50 (1976): 501–10.

116. Ibid.

117. Gaetano Bruscoli, *La storia dello Spedale degli Innocenti* (Florence, 1900), 290–91. Of 15,847 admissions to the Innocenti between 1755 and 1774, 11,074 children died between those two dates, although Bruscoli's figures cannot give even an approximate indication of *infant* mortality in that period.

118. Corsini, "Materiali," 1039.

119. Ibid.

120. Bardet, "Enfants abandonées à Rouen," 27.

121. René Spitz, "Hospitalism: An Inquiry into the Genesis of Psychiatric

Conditions in Early Childhood," *The Psychoanalytic Study of the Child* 1 (1945): 53.

122. Ibid., 59. See Sally Provence and Rose C. Lipton, *Infants in Institutions* (New York, 1962), passim, which catalogs motor and sensory deficits of institutionalized children.

123. See McClure, *Coram's Children*, chap. 1. One of the major objections to the building of the London Foundling Hospital was that it would sanction illegitimacy.

124. Spitz, "Hospitalism," 54.

125. ASF, Provvisioni Registri, 157, fols. 21v–22v, 16 April 1466.

126. AOIF, Giornale D (XIII,1), fol. 6v–8r, 25 January 1467 [modern = 1468].

127. AOIF, Balie e Bambini A (XVI,1), fol. 6r, 9 October 1445.

128. AOIF, Balie e Bambini A (XVI,1), fol. 6r, 20 April 1447.

129. *Canti carnascialeschi del Rinascimento*, Charles Singleton, ed., (Bari, 1936), nos. 29, 39, and 94; Christiane Klapisch-Zuber, "Blood Parents and Milk Parents: Wet-nursing in Florence 1300–1530," in *Women, Family, and Ritual in Renaissance Italy* (Chicago, 1985), 137.

130. AOIF, Balie e Bambini A (XVI,1), passim.

131. G. Masi, ed., *Statuti populi et communis Florentiae anno salutis MCCCCXV* (Freiburg, 1778–80), vol. 2, rubric 149, 268.

132. Trexler, "Infanticide," 100.

133. Klapisch-Zuber, "Blood Parents and Milk Parents," 137, also notes the unwillingness of Florentines to encourage the nursing by the same wet nurse of more than one child at a time. See Iris Origo, *The Merchant of Prato*, rev. ed. (New York, 1979), 214ff.

134. AOIF, Balie e Bambini C (XVI,3), fol. 97r, 5 June 1456.

135. See the discussion of construction workers' wages in chap. 4, pp. 160–62.

136. AOIF, Balie e Bambini A (XVI,1), fol. 2r, 6 February 1444 [modern = 1445].

137. AOIF, Ricordanze A (XII,4), fol. 266v, 19 June 1461.

138. AOIF, Balie e Bambini B (XVI,2), fol. 100r, 26 November 1452.

139. AOIF, Balie e Bambini C (XVI,3), fol. 42r, 11 July, 10 September, and 20 October 1455.

140. AOIF, Balie e Bambini B (XVI,2), fol. 227v, 21 June 1457.

141. AOIF, Balie e Bambini C (XVI,3), fol. 50v, 1 February 1456 [modern = 1457].

142. AOIF, Balie e Bambini C (XVI,3), fol. 75v, 28 March 1458.

143. AOIF, Balie e Bambini A (XVI,1), fol. 25v, 13 October 1445.

144. AOIF, Balie e Bambini A (XVI,1), fol. 26r, 21 October 1445.

145. AOIF, Balie e Bambini D (XVI,4), fol. 221v, 27 April 1461.

146. AOIF, Balie e Bambini C (XVI,3), fol. 192r, 18 July 1457.

147. AOIF, Balie e Bambini B (XVI,2), fol. 28v, 1 March 1451 [modern = 1452].

148. AOIF, Balie e Bambini C (XVI,3), fol. 90r, 28 April and 8 July 1456.

149. AOIF, Balie e Bambini C (XVI,3), fol. 152r, 2 June 1458.

150. AOIF, Balie e Bambini D (XVI,4), fol. 62v, 3 July 1459.

151. AOIF, Balie e Bambini E (XVI,5), fol. 50v, 11 June 1462.

152. AOIF, Balie e Bambini E (XVI,5), fol. 54v, 30 June 1462.

153. AOIF, Balie e Bambini H (XVI,8), fol. 37v, 13 May 1473.

154. AOIF, Balie e Bambini H (XVI,8), fol. 39v, 24 May 1473.

155. AOIF, Balie e Bambini H (XVI,8), fol. 50r, 2 August 1473.

156. AOIF, Balie e Bambini E (XVI,5), fol. 84v, 20 June 1463.

157. AOIF, Balie e Bambini C (XVI,3), fol. 198r, 7 January 1457.

158. AOIF, Balie e Bambini E (XVI,5), fol. 157v, 7 December 1463, 23 June and 9 July 1464.

159. AOIF, Balie e Bambini E (XVI,5), fol. 40r, 24 March 1461 [modern = 1462].

160. AOIF, Balie e Bambini E (XVI,5), fol. 135v, 20 February 1463 [modern = 1464].

161. AOIF, Balie e Bambini A (XVI,1), fols. 3v, 172r, 10 February 1450 [modern = 1451].

162. AOIF, Balie e Bambini F (XVI,6), fol. 48r and 160v, 16 August 1467 and 1 July 1470.

163. AOIF, Balie e Bambini E (XVI,5), fol. 72r, 3 October 1453.

164. AOIF, Balie e Bambini B (XVI,2), fol. 61v, 6 June 1450.

165. AOIF, Ricordanze B (XII,2), fol. 23r, 25 June 1483.

166. AOIF, Balie e Bambini B (XVI,2), fol. 6r, 25 December 1450; C (XVI,3), fol. 11r, 15 February 1454 [modern = 1455].

167. AOIF, Balie e Bambini A (XVI,1), fol. 123r, 257r, 11 February 1447 [modern = 1448]

168. AOIF, Balie e Bambini C (XVI,2), fol. 184v, 3 June 1457.

169. AOIF, Balie e Bambini C (XVI,3), fol. 11r, 15 February 1454 [modern = 1455].

170. AOIF, Balie e Bambini A (XVI,1), fol. 5v, 21 February 1444 [modern = 1445].

171. Klapisch-Zuber, "Blood Parents and Milk Parents," 146–50.

172. Ibid., 151 n. 66.

173. Ibid., 146–47 n. 51.

174. Ibid., 147 n. 52. Recent studies of the epidemiology of Sudden Infant Death Syndrome (SIDS) have explicitly noted the correspondence between mortality attributed to smothering and mortality from SIDS. T. L. Savitt's work noted a remarkable similarity in the age distribution of 226 infants who were

"smothered" in Virginia between 1853 and 1860 and the distribution of SIDS in King County, Washington State, in the mid-1960s. SIDS is the leading cause of death in the two-to-six-months age group. Although its frequency in most modern populations is 2.3 to 3 infant deaths per thousand live births, in third world countries with economic conditions similar to those of the premodern world, the incidence is as high as 6.56 per thousand live births. Despite conclusive experiments conducted in the mid-1940s that showed the near impossibility of accidental smothering by blanket or by overlaying, in some parts of the United States as late the early 1970s the legal community continued to prosecute parents. The plight of these parents is movingly described by Abraham Bergman, *The "Discovery" of Sudden Infant Death Syndrome: Lessons in the Practice of Political Medicine* (New York, 1986), passim. See also T. L. Savitt, "Smothering and Overlaying of Virginia Slave-children: A Suggested Explanation," *Bulletin of the History of Medicine* 49 (1975): 400–404. On the epidemiology of SIDS, see Bernard Knight, *Sudden Death in Infancy* (London, 1983), 15–42.

175. Klapisch-Zuber, "Blood Parents and Milk Parents," 163. Piero Puro's role as "nostro commesso" at the Innocenti is documented in the inventory of his possessions drawn up at his death: AOIF, Ricordanze A (XII,1), fol. 74v, 24 April 1466.

176. Baker Library, Harvard Business School, Medici mss. (hereafter referred to as Baker-Medici), 491, fol. 13r, 22 September 1421.

177. Baker-Medici, 491, fol. 13v, 22 September 1421.

178. Baker-Medici, 500, fols. 41r–45v, 3 May 1449–10 May 1468.

179. Ibid.

180. Baker-Medici, 500, fol. 41r, 11 February 1451 [modern = 1452].

181. Baker-Medici, 500, fol. 45r, 28 January 1452 [modern = 1453].

182. Baker-Medici, 500, fol. 45v, 5 March 1451 [modern = 1452].

183. Ibid.

184. Klapisch-Zuber, "Blood Parents and Milk Parents," 137 n. 19.

185. James Bruce Ross, "The Middle Class Child in Urban Italy," in *The History of Childhood,* ed. Lloyd de Mause (New York, 1974), 187.

186. Leon Battista Alberti, *Della Famiglia,* trans. Rene Watkins as *The Family in Renaissance Florence* (Columbia, S.C., 1969), 49–50.

187. Richard Trexler, *Public Life in Renaissance Florence* (New York, 1980), 419.

188. AOIF, Ricordanze A (XII, 1), fols. 53r–55v, 6 May 1452.

189. See Ricordanze A (XII, 1), fols. 181r–186r, for the 1459–1460 census. See infra, 253–55, for details of adoptions to Florentine merchants in Viterbo.

190. AOIF, Balie e Bambini A (XVI,1), loose folio, n.d.

191. AOIF, Balie e Bambini C (XVI,3), fol. 184v, 3 July 1467.

192. AOIF, Balie e Bambini B (XVI,2), fol. 130r, 28 May 1453.

193. AOIF, Balie e Bambini B (XVI,2), fol. 130r, 14 June 1467.

194. AOIF, Ricordanze B (XII,2), fol. 72r, 22 December 1483: "Che chonsoli et operai per sette fave nere possino porre chon altrii delle fanciulle dello spedale chon questo: che chi ne vorra prima le chari dello spedale debba promettere et sodere doverle maritare prima che passino anni venti e di darle di dote Fl venticinque di suggiello per ciaschuno et debbino giurare e chonsoli et operai che chredino che quella le terra l'abbi a ttratare bene et tenerle onestamente."

195. AOIF, Balie e Bambini A (XVI,1), fol. 38v, 9 January 1454 [modern = 1455].

196. AOIF, Balie e Bambini C (XVI,3), fol. 184v, 14 March 1461.

197. AOIF, Ricordanze A (XII,1), fol. 116r, 5 June 1470: "Richordo questo dì 5 di giugno 1470 e chonsoli dell'arte di Por zanta Maria dichiarono et chondamono Francesco di Ghuccio detto Rossi lanaiuolo dovere paghare nelle mani del chamarlingho di detta arte fl xxx di suggiello per le chagioni che nello partito si chontiene che non fa bisogno dirle qui. I quali denarii debbe paghare la meta per tutto giugno 1470 et l'altra meta per tutto luglio 1470. E anche lo chondamorono fra detto tempo dovere paghare in mano del chamarlingo dello spedale degli Innocenti una ghamurra da donna da tenere per ongni dì et una ghamurra buona da tenere pel di delle feste e 1ª cioppa bigiella da donna per chasa e 1ª cioppa nera buona per di delle feste e 1ª chamicia da donna e asciughatoi e fazoletti quanti e chome si richiede. Avea una fanciulla e tutte le dette chose ... vogliono che il sopradetto Francesco ne' sopradetti modi paghi perche tutto sia per dote della Bene nostra fanciulla di chasa ... la quale è stata più anni sono passati in chasa il sopradetto Francesco a suo servigio e al presente è qui nello spedale."

198. AOIF, Balie e Bambini A (XVI,1), fols. 45r and 152r, 13 June 1453.

199. AOIF, Balie e Bambini A (XVI,1), fols. 12v and 260r, 5 December 1450.

200. AOIF, Balie e Bambini A (XVI,1), fols. 35r and 163r, 28 January 1452 [modern = 1453].

201. AOIF, Balie e Bambini A (XVI,1), fols. 38r and 188v, 13 May 1454.

202. AOIF, Balie e Bambini B (XVI,2), fol. 11v, 26 January 1454 [modern = 1455].

203. AOIF, Ricordanze A (XII,1), fol. 50v, 1 January 1451 [modern = 1452].

204. AOIF, Ricordanze A (XII,1), fol. 52v, 6 May 1452: "Jachopo die Ser Marco a Francesco di Mariano Simoni fu setaiuolo sta di rimpetto a Santa Crocie e promisse di fallo inparare a legiere e scrivere e l'abacho e fallo imparare arte e promisse tratallo bene e con diligenza proprio chome se fosse suo figluolo."

205. AOIF, Balie e Bambini D, (XVI,4), fol. 19v, 11 October 1463: "Adì xi d'ottobre 1463 di licentia e volonta di messer Girolamo di Nichilo spedalingho e priore dello spedale si e dato a Chimenti di Biagio Borromei cittadino fiorentino habitante a Pisa nella chapella di Santo Martino ... el quale Chimenti

lo tolse e promisse a detto priore presente per detto Sforza come s'egli fusse figluolo in alimentallo e insegli a lui et fargli quello di bene che fano i boni padri a' figliuoli."

206. AOIF, Balie e Bambini F (XVI,6), fol. 31v, 3 February 1465 [modern = 1466].

207. AOIF, Balie e Bambini A (XVI,1), fol. 31r, 20 May 1446.

208. AOIF, Balie e Bambini A (XVI,1), fol. 35r, 163r, 20 January 1463 [modern = 1464]. See also AOIF, Ricordanze A (XII,2), fol. 52r, (same date).

209. AOIF, Balie e Bambini A (XVI,1), fol. 53r, 21 February 1450 [modern = 1451].

210. AOIF, Balie e Bambini A (XVI,1), fol. 254v, 6 May 1452.

211. AOIF, Ricordanze A (XII,1), fol. 103r, 2 February 1467 [modern = 1468].

212. AOIF, Balie e Bambini A (XVI,1), fol. 169r, 15 May 1481; AOIF, Ricordanze B (XII,2), fol. 37v, 26 August 1483.

213. AOIF, Ricordanze A (XII,1), fol. 168r, 6 July 1482.

214. AOIF, Ricordanze A (XII,1), fol. 168v, 15 July 1482.

215. AOIF, Ricordanze B (XII,2), fol. 36v, 18 October 1484.

216. AOIF, Ricordanze B (XII,2), fol. 50r, 23 October 1463.

217. AOIF, Ricordanze A (XII,1), fol. 50v, 1 January 1451 [modern = 1452].

218. AOIF, Ricordanze A (XII,1), fol. 51r, 1 January 1451 [modern = 1452].

219. Ibid.

220. AOIF, Entrata e Uscita (CXXII,3), fol. 14v, 6 August 1452.

221. AOIF, Ricordanze A (XII,1), fol. 52v, 1 January 1451 [modern = 1452].

222. AOIF, Ricordanze A (XII,1), fol. 175r, 17 November 1457.

223. AOIF, Ricordanze A (XII,1), fol. 51v, 1 January 1451 [modern = 1452].

224. AOIF, Balie e Bambini A (XVI,1), fol. 82v, 30 September 1445.

225. AOIF, Ricordanze A (XII,1), fol. 66r, 8 December 1464.

226. AOIF, Balie e Bambini A (XVI,1), fols. 45r and 152r, 14 June 1453.

227. AOIF, Balie e Bambini A (XVI,1), fol. 18r and 116v, 8 November 1453.

228. AOIF, Balie e Bambini D (XVI,4), fol. 109r, 8 September 1463.

229. AOIF, Balie e Bambini C (XVI,3), fol. 95r, 26 June 1461.

230. AOIF, Balie e Bambini D (XVI,4), fol. 143r, 23 October 1463.

231. AOIF, Balie e Bambini A (XVI,1), fols. 18r and 116v, 17 November 1455.

232. AOIF, Ricordanze B (XII,2), fol. 15r, 10 March 1482 [modern = 1483].

233. AOIF, Balie e Bambini A (XVI,1), fols. 65r and 145v, 13 July 1456.

234. AOIF, Ricordanze B (XII,2), fol. 19r, 11 November 1483.

235. AOIF, Ricordanze B (XII,2), fol. 96v, 23 June 1484.

236. See Ricordanze A (XII, 1), fols. 181r–186r, for the 1459–60 census.

237. Ignazio Ciampi, ed., *Cronache e Statuti della città di Viterbo: Cronache di Nicola della Tuccia* (Florence, 1872), 65, 110, 252.

238. Sant'Antonino, *Chronica* (Lyons, 1586), pars 3, 557, cited in Nicolai Rubinstein, *The Government of Florence under the Medici* (Oxford, 1966), 88.

239. Cesare Pinzi, *Storia di Viterbo* (Rome, 1887–89), vol. 4: 147, 171–72.

240. AOIF, Balie e Bambini A (XVI,1), fol. 253r, 27 April 1457.

241. AOIF, Balie e Bambini C (XVI,3), fol. 93r, 26 June 1459.

242. AOIF, Balie e Bambini B (XVI,2), fols. 3r and 116r, 11 November 1450 and 26 June 1459.

243. AOIF, Balie e Bambini B (XVI,2), fol. 190v, 28 October 1461.

244. AOIF, Ricordanze B (XII,2), fol. 68v, 24 November 1483.

245. Ciampi, *Cronache e Statuti,* 65.

246. Ibid., 110.

247. Ibid.

248. Ibid., 252.

249. AOIF, Ricordanze A (XII,1), fol. 177r, 31 July 1454.

250. AOIF, Balie e Bambini A (XVI,1), fol. 82v, 25 April 1456.

251. AOIF, Balie e Bambini C (XVI,3), fol. 95r, 17 May 1456 and 26 June 1461.

252. AOIF, Balie e Bambini D (XVI,4), fol. 31r, 11 June 1467.

253. AOIF, Ricordanze B (XII,2), fols. 16v and 18r, 2 April 1483.

254. AOIF, Ricordanze A (XII,1), fol. 50v, 10 August 1451.

255. AOIF, Balie e Bambini A (XVI,1), fol. 41r, 25 June 1458.

256. AOIF, Balie e Bambini A (XVI,1), fols. 62v and 266v, 23 November 1453.

257. AOIF, Ricordanze B (XII,2), fol. 79v, February 1483 [modern = 1484].

258. ASF, Diplomatico, Spedale degli Innocenti, 11 September 1492.

259. ASF, Provvisioni Registri, 142, fols. 380v–382r, 30 December 1451.

260. AOIF, Ricordanze A (XII,1), fol. 157r, 28 April 1479.

261. AOIF, Ricordanze A (XII,1), fol. 119v, 15 November 1470.

262. AOIF, Ricordanze B (XII,2), fol. 72r, 22 December 1483.

263. AOIF, Ricordanze B (XII,2), fol. 92r, 11 May 1484.

264. AOIF, Balie e Bambini B (XVI,2), fol. 29r, 21 June 1451 and 23 February 1470 [modern = 1471].

265. AOIF, Ricordanze A (XII,2), fol. 134v, 22 November 1472.

266. ASF, Archivio Notarile, S 648, fols. 227r–228r, 24 September 1464.

267. Daniela Gallavotti, "Gli affreschi quattrocenteschi della Sala del Pellegrinaio nello spedale di Santa Maria della Scala in Siena," *Storia dell'Arte* (1972): 1–42; Augustus C. Brown, "The Eight Surviving Pellegrinaio Frescoes at the Ospedale della Scala and their Social and Visual Sources," Ph.D. diss., University of Pittsburgh, 1976.

268. AOIF, Balie e Bambini D (XVI,4), fol. 263r, 10 August 1460.

269. AOIF, Ricordanze A (XII,2), fol. 112r, 12 November 1468.

Chapter 6
_____

Orate pro Nobis

Renaissance Florentines perceived that charity, tenderness, and compassion toward children were crucial to personal immortality, the survival of families, and the salvation of the State. The foundling hospital of the Innocenti was without doubt the vehicle for that appealing vision. The hospital's founders and testators, as well as guild and communal officials, stressed that alms themselves were insufficient to secure God's favor. Such alms, rather, had to result in direct benefit to their intended recipients. Just as one discovers the intellectual background to shifts in the uses of wealth and the direction of charitable giving in the humanists' renunciation of the worthiness of voluntary poverty, so do the ideas of both merchants and humanists find their echo in the adoption contracts of the hospital of the Innocenti. Humanist pedagogy, as best realized by the works of Leon Battista Alberti and Matteo Palmieri, took its models from antiquity: children learn moral and political behavior by the force of love, reason, and example, and not by the application of coercion and physical force.

Recent historians have cited a wealth of examples, many of them Victorian, to show that moralists viewed children as creatures of naturally evil disposition: bent rods in need of straightening.[1] By contrast, fifteenth-century "self-help" treatises on childhood, pedagogy, and family life observed the behavior of children with a keen eye for detail and a finely nuanced sensitivity to the subtle psychology of children's behavior. Alberti, for example, in *Della Famiglia,* believed children, especially sons, to have naturally good dispositions. Both modeling and positive reinforcement were at the heart of humanist and mercantile education of children. *Della Famiglia* itself used the technique of dialogue and exemplum to impart these values to its lay audience.

Yet, one might argue, the distance between the advice of Alberti and Palmieri and the childhoods experienced by the foundlings of the Inno-

273

centi was vast. Even Alberti's expressions of the ideal of family cohesion were a sorry comparison indeed to the reality of his own upbringing. What connection could possibly obtain between the scions of patrician families whom Alberti hoped to instruct, and the infants of slaves and servants abandoned to the Innocenti? Even taking for granted the vast charitable resources directed at the foundlings of the Innocenti by the most wealthy merchants of the city of Florence, what relevance did humanist pedagogy have to to the silk guild's administration of a large charitable enterprise?

This final chapter will demonstrate that these are, in the end, *questions malposées*. The work of Lauro Martines has placed the Italian humanists in their social context;[2] Gene Brucker has demonstrated the liveliness of humanist sensibilities and the models of classical antiquity in the practical debates of the Florentine Councils.[3] Finally, Christian Bec has noted how the milieu of Florentine private merchant diaries was derivative of humanist culture.[4] Although Bec stresses the opposition between a practical education for mercantile occupations and a rhetorical education for young civic humanists, a close reading of Alberti's *Della Famiglia* and of Matteo Palmieri's *Della vita civile* makes it clear that these humanists appropriated the models of classical culture in the service of offering practical advice as well as in articulating a laic vision that addressed the difficult issues of how to employ one's own intellect and reason in the service of outwitting and conquering the vicissitudes of fortune. On a more practical plane, the humanists treated issues of household management and the upbringing of children, but without losing their grasp of the notion that the family and child-rearing were the private rehearsal for the public performance of civic obligation and political power.

Although the more profound issues of influence and audience are ably treated by intellectual historians, several phenomena connect the charitable enterprise of the Innocenti to humanist pedagogy. One can certainly dismiss out of hand the view that the great merchants of Florence did not find the works of humanists to be of value: Giovanni Rucellai, in his *Zibaldone Quaresimale,* appropriated entire sentences concerning the care of young children verbatim from Matteo Palmieri's *Della vita civile.* Matteo Strozzi lent Francesco Barbaro's *De re uxoria* to Matteo Castellani, who praised Barbaro's treatise in personal correspondence. Similarly, the humanist Guarino da Verona dedicated a treatise to the Florentine merchant Corbinelli, in which he praised Corbinelli for the care and solicitude he brought to the education of his own children.[5]

Connections between humanists and the welfare of the Innocenti's foundlings were even more direct. The priors of the Innocenti, in half a century of *ricordanze,* marked the death of only one public figure: Matteo Palmieri, on 12 April 1475.[6] In 1436 and again in 1441, Giannozzo Manetti served as one of the Innocenti's trustees, or *operai.* Finally, the eventual disposition of the hospital's children, and the education prescribed in their adoption contracts, makes clear that the officials of the Innocenti viewed the education of the hospital's foundlings as both practical and moral.

Not only were the pedagogical principles of Renaissance humanism shared by merchants and by the *operai* of the Innocenti, but also by stern Dominican clerics such as Giovanni Dominici. If the writings of classical antiquity, with which all three estates of thinkers were familiar, guided the sensibility of the new pedagogy, these works also reveal that for both humanists and merchant pedagogues, the experience of infant mortality engendered extreme and contradictory responses. One might expect, as Lawrence Stone has suggested, that high infant mortality numbed the affections of parents for their very young children: yet not only at the Innocenti did parents manifest ambivalence. If wet-nursing allowed Florentine parents to distance themselves emotionally from their children during the precarious first year of life, nevertheless, the pedagogical and hortatory literature of the early Italian Renaissance directly confronted the experience of the death of children, expressing and legitimizing the stages of parental grief. Florentines drew consolation and wisdom from the last words of their dying children and from dreams in which their dead children appeared offering not only forgiveness but the promise of favorable divine intervention in their earthly fortunes. Writers as far apart as Alberti and Savonarola emphasized the simplicity and innocence of children. Such innocence was not only to the delight of parents, but also a key to the role of children in the city's ritual life, in which the children of the Innocenti clearly participated well into the fifteenth century.[7]

Several important features of the "new pedagogy" shed enormous light on the special and exalted place of children in the culture of early Renaissance Florence. These features include the celebration of marriage and children in the perpetuation of the individual within the family, and of greater importance, the role of family and kin as corporations within the larger political community, and the intense emotional and intellectual investment of fathers in the upbringing of their children.

Alberti's *Della Famiglia* treats marriage as insurance against a family's decline into poverty and oblivion. As an incentive for young men to take wives, Alberti argues that one should speak to sons "of the delights of this primary and natural companionship of marriage."[8] Children, according to Alberti, are "the pledges of marital love and kindness," on whom all a man's hopes and desires are focused. If the man who acquires wealth and lands has no heirs, his labor has been in vain. In contrast, a man who leaves heirs never dies: his children "keep his own position and his true image in the family," as Dido wished to have a little Aeneas to preserve the image of her lost love and "to provide consolation in her grief and anguish." Likewise, "our children are our comfort and are apt at every age to give us great joys and satisfactions."[9] Indeed, the relationship between fathers and sons quintessentially defined the relationship of *humanitas* and *divinitas*. Just as Man expressed the image and likeness of the heavenly father, so does a father "take delight in seeing [his children] express his very image and likeness." Alberti pursues the theme of the immortality conferred by children even further: in the same manner as the writer, the poet, and the painter, "every man loves his own works.... All try to make their works widely pleasing, to win praise and to gain as much immortality as they can."[10]

Matteo Palmieri's *Della vita civile* makes explicit the relationship between love for children and the salvation of the *civitas:*

> it is a useful thing to have had children, having increased the population and given citizens to the *patria,* providing they are accustomed to living well, and useful both inside and outside the city in matters of war and peace relating to the common weal.[11]

After children are esteemed grandchildren who, by making possible marriage and kinship alliances among great families and *consorterie,* initiate mutual aid and proffer advice, favors, patronage, and help.

For Alberti, the raw, unrestrained appetites of men undermine the defense not only of republics, principalities, and kingdoms, but also of families. Conversely, reason, learning, and the study of books are directed to the goal of making "your civil life shine by your splendid character."[12] For this reason, "the old cannot more appropriately acquire, increase and conserve great authority than by caring for the young. They must draw them toward virtue and make them every day more learned and more charming, more loved and more valued."[13]

Not even such conservative clerics as Giovanni Dominici lost the connection between the education of the young and the ideal of *civiltà*. Not only does Dominici strongly discourage partisanship, he also suggests that children be punished for allowing themselves to be swayed by "love, words, gifts, or fear," so that they will not learn:

> to corrupt justice which today is banished from the world by similar defects from the whole world where justice is nothing else than gain, force, money, friendship, or relations, and all other books of law may be burned.[14]

Even more specifically, Dominici wrote that children should learn grammar, history, and law to enable them to undertake careers in public service. The future demands of public office require that children "be solicitous, neither neglectful nor too cautious," virtues they could acquire by serving in the sacristy. In the study of law, children should cultivate a love for the defense of the city "for which charity is a better defense than any other sweet saying; whereas without charity, nothing else prevails."[15] True defenders of the *civitas,* Dominici argues, should so love justice that they undertake:

> the defense of the oppressed, such as the poor, prisoners, strangers, widows, and orphans.... [Children] must be raised lovers of justice, zealous for the State, servants of God, and prayerful always.[16]

For Dominici, in short, states are run by paternosters, and children should be taught to pray and recite psalms for the State. In this respect, Dominici makes what seems to us the unlikely connection between humanist pedagogy and millenial enthusiasm. Children, in any event, are the key to both. As is the case with Alberti's and Palmieri's treatises on the family, Dominici finds the aims of education to be twofold: by virtue and reason, children learn how to conquer fortune, and in so doing, learn how to govern the State.

In a culture in which education was tied to the fortunes of chief political actors, who were male, the upbringing of children was in theory the primary responsibility of fathers, though for demographic reasons the care Alessandra Strozzi took in the education of her sons was perhaps more reflective of actual practice. Yet the compassion of fathers of abandoned children at the Innocenti often led them to follow the progress of their children through wet-nursing and even after adoption, and Christiane Klapisch-Zuber has noted that fathers were the chief negotiators of contracts with the husbands of wet nurses.[17] So widespread was the cultural ideal, at any rate, that John Demos has even noted the importance of emotionally involved fatherhood in colonial Plymouth, Massachusetts.[18] Not only did fathers undertake the burden of responsibility for the future of the *patria* in the education of their sons, but also, at least in the literature of exhortation, were presumed to be intellectually and emotionally attuned to every detail of their children's dispositions and characters. Fatherhood, as idealized by Adovardo in Alberti's *Della Famiglia*, was an experience of unrestrained emotional commitment: "Who would believe, except by the experience of his own feelings, how great and intense is the love of a father toward his children?" Men have been known to risk all for their friends, "but I am sure that no love is more unshakable, more constant, more complete, or more vast than the love which a father bears towards his children."[19]

Indeed, in the eyes of Alberti's contemporaries, if Florentine fathers were vulnerable to any vice, it was overindulgence rather than excessive harshness. Just as children who have excellent character "are a proof of the diligence of the father and an honor to him," so those whose characters are poor:

> must be a terrible sorrow to any father who is not insensible and utterly foolish. Not only will the ugly and disgusting acts of the son be distasteful to him, but, as everyone knows, every errant child in many ways brings shame on his father.[20]

Matteo Palmieri warns against accustoming an infant's tongue to sweets, for fear that the child will become so accustomed to such delicacies that he or she will constantly demand them.[21]

Assuming that fathers have surmounted the dangers of overindulging their children, Alberti defines the duties of paternal love as unceasing watchfulness over the moral welfare of the family:

> The duty of a father is not only, as they say, to stock the cupboard and the cradle. He ought far more to watch over and guard the family from outsiders, to check over and consider the whole company, to

examine the practices of every member, inside and outside the house, and to correct and improve every bad habit. He ought preferably to use reasonable rather than indignant words, authority rather than power.... He ought in every thought always to put first the peace and the tranquillity of his entire family. This should be the kind of goal toward which he, using his intelligence and experience, guides the whole family with virtue and honor.[22]

Thus the relationship between fathers and sons depended on the Mediterranean public values of honor and shame. "I see too well," says Adovardo, "that your reasoning will lead to the conclusion that it is only negligent fathers who have many causes of grief."[23] In *Della vita civile,* Palmieri asserts, "the father to whom a son is born, before every other consideration, must have perfect hope for him and inspire him to succeed in being virtuous and worthy among men."[24]

If fathers shouldered the awesome burden of maintaining the family's public position, they also had to devote considerable attention to every detail of the child's upbringing. Despite his advice that children should remain under the care of women until they are weaned, Alberti took great pains in *Della Famiglia* to guide fathers in their choice of a wet nurse. Indeed, long before the father could enjoy the laughter and solace of his children, the ordeal of choosing a good wet nurse occasioned sorrow and tears. Matteo Palmieri's *Della vita civile* devoted space even to the subject of prenatal care. Both Alberti and Palmieri expressed in humanistic terms views that we might consider more characteristic of the late nineteenth and early twentieth centuries: the earliest years of a child's life determine how successfully one will fulfill the potential of *humanitas*. According to Palmieri, even the mother's ingestion of certain foods during pregnancy will affect her child's future character and fortune.[25]

It is hardly unknown that fifteenth-century moralists preferred maternal breast-feeding to wet nurses. The practice of wet-nursing was sufficiently prevalent, nevertheless, that both Alberti and Palmieri spent considerable ink on assisting the father in choosing one. Indeed, Palmieri's very objections to wet-nursing explain why the choice of a wet nurse was so important: "thus it follows that nourishment from any source rather than that which one's own mother gives, does not act as well to preserve the virtue of little children."[26] The child who has genetically acquired a good disposition from the father is put at risk "through the malice and corruption of the wet nurse, [and is] depraved and likely to become full of vice." Deformities of complexion and character both come from wet nurses who "are loose, dissolute, . . . full of putrid and noxious humors, to whom rash fathers who give the matter no thought, send to feed at the breast their noble and well-born sons."[27] It is in this passage that Palmieri reveals with no shortage of perceptiveness why maternal breast-feeding was so idealized:

> From this [i.e., wet-nursing] the expert philosophers say often follows the diminution of the natural bond of maternal love, since the child's desired love-object, which must be united only with his mother, is not fulfilled.[28]

The very objections that Paolo da Certaldo had to animal milk, that it made children look "stupid, vacant, and not quite right in the head,"[29] applied with equal force to the character of wet nurses. Not content merely to assault our senses with a description of the wet nurses' putrid and noxious humors, Palmieri dwelt at length on the "bestial" Tartar slaves and servants to whom Florentines entrusted the future of their State. For both Palmieri and Alberti, wet nurses had to be chosen carefully to conserve the child's natural *humanitas*. Just as nature made:

> birds to fly, horses to run, and the savage beasts to be cruel, so nature has made men desirous of and suitable for learning, and ready to exercise the mind in subtle and worthy pursuits.[30]

Similarly, both authors concerned themselves with the speech of both wet nurses and parents. Precision in speech was critical in making certain that children did not fail to acquire those rhetorical skills so essential to the service of the State.

Once the child returned from the wet nurse, the father learned from Alberti and Palmieri how to acquire and exercise a very different range of paternal skills. Nature, wrote Alberti:

> did not give to children such hidden and dark ways of action, nor to fathers such callow and inexpert judgment that they could not, from a variety of evidence, learn the direction of their sons' interests.[31]

Indeed, said doctors, fathers can tell by an infant's reaction to snapping the fingers whether "his temperament will be suited to manly exercises or arms," or, if the infant prefers songs and being rocked to sleep, "he is born for a life of contemplation and leisure filled with letters and science." Thus "a diligent father learns from day to day" and "thoughtfully interprets every little action, word, and gesture." Certainly fathers have the innocent natures of children to assist them, since the art of determining a man's vices with a glance is all the more easily practiced "with children than with those who are older in years and in malice. Children do not know how to cover up nicely with lies or with some kind of disguise."[32]

Such heavy burdens of observation were not without their rewards. The age following the wet nurse:

> is full of delight and is accompanied by general laughter. The child begins to make known his wishes and partly to express them in words. The whole family listens and the whole neighborhood repeats his sayings ... already there seems to be a sparkle and promise in the child's face, manner, and words. On his ways infinite hopes are founded, wonderful evidence is seen of subtle intelligence and keen memory.[33]

Palmieri's observations of early childhood behavior are equally acute. As soon as a child has left the wet nurse:

> he will begin to be good at expressing every voice.... In the first part of childhood, he likes to tease with little jokes, and he laughs very happily and changes a thousand times per hour.[34]

From this impressionable period of childhood it was already important that fathers watch carefully the types of associations their sons had with other children.

Palmieri also expected fathers to be involved in a very detailed and time-consuming way with the education of their young sons. Immediately upon return from the wet nurse, fathers should teach children letters, as long as children are not burdened in such a way "that they develop a hatred for them and never will approach them with delight." Palmieri suggested forming letters in fruit, cookies, and other baby foods. Then, "once you have the child excited promise to give him one if he recognizes it." Such diligence by fathers, according to Palmieri, should result in children staying two years ahead of the progress of their peers, and thus to reach the age of reason sooner, so that "the mind and natural intelligence is elevated to provide that as little as possible is lost."[35]

Just as was true for the moralists of antiquity whom Palmieri had read, he argues that the force of parental example drives character, for better or worse. Fathers must be careful that their families see only the best examples of behavior: "always in the house one speaks of a good and honest subject, and even in the tales of women [to find] admonitions to honest living."[36] Conversely:

those whose parents' speech is dissolute and ugly will have the worst tongues, and parents allow dissolute words that cry out to be punished [by rewarding] children with laughter and kisses [when they utter them]. What an outrage it is to teach the child to put his thumb between his closest fingers, and then to teach him to show it to his own mother ... then parents wonder why their children turned out so badly.[37]

Alberti's *Della Famiglia* makes a virtue of positive example. Fathers could learn not only to observe their children's behavior in minute detail, but also to teach them not with force, but by modeling and encouragement:

Usually in a naturally good disposition, any excellence increases with the encouragement of praise.... A father may be allowed to overestimate the virtues of his sons; nor will I be called unwise, if, to encourage them in the love of virtue, I show in their presence how much it delights me and how pleased I would be to see them achieve excellence.[38]

In the pursuit of good parenting Lorenzo, one of the interlocutors of *Della Famiglia,* claims to have:

always applied my efforts and my intellect ... to make myself loved by all more than feared. I have never wished to appear as a master to those who viewed me as a father. So these children have always been voluntarily obedient and respectful, and have listened to my words and followed my commands.[39]

Elaborating this theme, Lionardo says that "a father must act like a father, not odious but dignified," remembering that power achieved and maintained by force is:

> less stable than authority maintained by love.... Kindness, the more easy and free of harshness it is, the more it wins love and acceptance.... A noble mind by nature resents being treated like a slave, instead of a son.[40]

This moderation in reprimands and discipline, although it did not always spare the rod, appropriated the father's natural skills of observation in the service of choosing a trade or an occupation for his son. Just as fathers could tell if their sons were hiding vices, so too could fathers discern from their sons' behavior what occupations sons would pursue with the most pleasure and benefit. According to Lionardo in *Della Famiglia*, a watchful father "will discover without too much difficulty what sort of work fits his son's inclinations, and what sort of achievements lie within his scope."[41]

Again, the congruence of humanists and clerics is apparent in Giovanni Dominici's advice. Dominici also argues the natural inclinations of children should be examined in terms of what the child does best:

> Thus if each one heeded his own station in the mystical Body and did not, neglecting his own, attempt to occupy that of another, countries would be well-governed, commerce would be honestly carried on, the arts would advance, and the Republic would enjoy peace and great abundance, happy in all its activities.[42]

As we have seen, the Osepdale degli Innocenti also allowed children and adoptive parents considerable flexibility in the choice of an occupation.

What links these diverse strands of advice on education and the planning of careers is an unmistakable recognition of the special nature of childhood, the importance of affection for children, and, finally, the importance of the individuality of each child.

Merchant pedagogy was equally attentive to the individuality of children. Thus Giovanni di Pagolo Morelli noted that his father, despite being ignored by his parents, still exhibited an excellent disposition. Paolo da Certaldo also assigned to fathers the essential role in directing and forming children. If Paolo recommended blows as discipline for young children, he argued that blows delivered to adolescents were already useless, and that they should be trusted to follow the natural inclinations of their reason.[43] Christian Bec has noted a shift that occurred over the course of the fifteenth century from emphasis on corporal punishment to an emphasis on the force of example, a shift for which Giovanni di Pagolo Morelli was himself partly responsible.[44] Morelli argued that excessive punishment was contrary to the proper development of children, and berated himself for the demands he had placed on his own son and for the affection he had failed to bestow.[45] Paolo da Certaldo also wrote that children should be placed in various occupations according to their natural inclinations and abilities, while Giovanni di Pagolo Morelli wrote that the father must shape his child "by reason and example."[46]

Equally important to the pedagogy of merchants was the political nature of education. Merchants' sons, according to Morelli, should learn music, singing, and dance to develop the virtues of sociability and *civiltà*. Morelli viewed the socialization of adolescents as a sort of apprenticeship for adulthood.[47]

The connection between humanist and merchant pedagogy is nowhere clearer than in Giovanni Rucellai's *Zibaldone Quaresimale*. Rucellai's advice on child-rearing echoes Palmieri's *Della vita civile,* albeit in condensed form.[48] "Don't laugh at [your son] when he says some dishonest thing or when he puts his thumb between his two nearest fingers."[49] Rucellai also suggested, as had Palmieri, the method of teaching children their letters at an early age by using puerile foods. Similarly, Rucellai advises strongly against the use of corporal punishment: "beating them causes only a brief pain and they have but a brief memory of it and think that the wrong has been righted immediately," whereas strong verbal criticism will augment the importance of the transgression without necessarily inciting the resentment of the transgressor.[50]

There is perhaps no better source for exploring the dimensions of the cult of childhood in Renaissance Florence than in the letters of Alessandra Strozzi to her sons. In them there is no shortage of instruction and moralizing, it is true, but there is also the more immediate reaction to important events in the relationship between parents and children, as well as examples of the practical applications of the ethos of family life that diarists and pedagogues tended to treat theoretically. More importantly, Alessandra Strozzi's letters are a useful corrective to the viewpoints of Alberti and Palmieri, whose emphasis on the roles of fathers reflected a cultural idealization that would have been demographically impossible for many Florentine families. Herlihy and Klapisch-Zuber have noted the significance in the 1427 Catasto of truncated families whose fathers had died, leaving their widows to supervise the upbringing of young children. Alessandra Strozzi's husband had died before their sons were fully grown; Guasti's collection of letters begins when Matteo, the youngest, was eleven years old. As in the case of Alberti and Palmieri, sons in Alessandra Strozzi's letters are the major focus of parental and familial concern. Unlike the works of Alberti and Palmieri, Alessandra Strozzi's letters make explicit the impact and importance of daughters, dowries, and marriage alliances in furthering the political and material fortunes of great Florentine families.

Alessandra Strozzi's acquaintance with the consuls and *operai* of the Innocenti, moreover, were far more than casual. Marco Parenti, who married Alessandra's daughter Caterina, was the son of one of the consuls of the silk guild, and Marco himself became a consul in 1475. Alessandra describes the death of Francesco della Luna, one of the better-known *operai* of the Innocenti, as a "great blow."[51] Francesco was, in fact, a Strozzi kinsman to Alessandro di Filippo di Messer Lionardo Strozzi by marriage. Finally, when Alessandra's favorite son Matteo died at the age of twenty-three, she wrote to her son Filippo in Naples that "I have had today from the kindness of Messer Giannozzo Manetti a letter from which I have taken quite some comfort, seeing the affection and love he bears you, and with how much charity and how many examples he encouraged me to have patience."[52]

The Strozzi letters also provide as clear an example as any in fifteenth-century literature of the importance of children to family structure. Hardly a letter passed from Alessandra in Florence to her son Filippo in Naples without some mention of the importance of marriage in her plans for her children. The importance of marriage as an economic and political structure, and the impersonality, materialism, and ambition that surrounded the institutions of kinship and dowry have led some modern historians to assume that such structures were hostile to companionship and affection.[53] Alessandra Strozzi, for example, wrote to Filippo that:

it is true that my desire would be to see both of you married, as other times I have told you; that even on my deathbed I fear I might not have the opportunity of experiencing what every mother desires: to see her sons wifed ... so that what you have expended effort and toil on acquiring over a long period of time your children will be able to enjoy. I have concentrated on maintaining what little I have had, so I can leave it to someone for the sake of our souls and of the souls of our ancestors. Through the hope that you take a wife so you can have children, I am content that I have done so.[54]

Yet one only has to compare these anxieties and concerns with the current popular slogan "we're spending our kids' inheritance" to realize that the preservation of family honor and patrimony in fifteenth-century Florence represented the highest order of concern, compassion, and affection for children. Even more striking is that as family-centered and lineage-centered as she was, Alessandra Strozzi still recognized how important the Florentine household system was to the survival of the State:

Of the young men who are in the territory [of Florence], there are some who gladly do not take a wife, and the land is in bad condition because of it, since the expense is always on the woman's back, as is the present custom. It is not such a wonderful dowry, if, when a girl gets married, it is with all that she owns.[55]

The marriage of Alessandra's elder daughter Caterina to Marco Parenti illustrates beautifully the coexistence of impersonality and affection in marriage arrangements. Alessandra's letter of 24 August 1447 to her son Filippo in Naples is a sudden plunge into the chilly waters of human supply and demand. "If I had not accepted this match," Alessandra wrote:

she would not have been married this year. Who wants a wife wants cash, and I couldn't find anyone who wanted to wait until 1448 or 1450 [for her deposit in the dowry fund to mature].[56]

Since Caterina, at the ripe old age of sixteen, was losing her value in the marriage market as a potential spouse, a dowry of 1,400 or 1,500 florins would have been required "to marry her to someone of greater status and nobility."[57] Caterina could have found a better partner, in other words, if Alessandra had been able to afford a higher dowry. Similarly, Alessandra doubted that Caterina would be pleased with the match, since with Marco's status "there are no benefits and there are considerable burdens."[58] Both Caterina's and Alessandra's disappointment were mitigated, however, by Marco Parenti's lavish gifts.

Yet Caterina, despite the burdens imposed by being female, would, according to her mother, "be as well off as any Florentine girl; she has a mother-in-law and father-in-law who are so happy about it they can think of nothing else but her happiness." Of Caterina herself, Alessandra wrote to Filippo, "she is beautiful . . . so that in truth there is no one in Florence more beautiful than she. She has both kinds of beauty, in the opinion of many: May God grant her health and grace for a long time, as I desire."[59]

Alessandra Strozzi's affection and concern extended to her female grandchildren as well, about one of whom, Filippo's daughter, she wrote in 1469: "She is a beautiful child, and a double of [her mother] Fiammetta: white like her, and with all her features. She is bigger than Alfonso was. May God lend her a long life."[60] Nor was this solely the affection of a grandmother; Marco Parenti also wrote to Filippo as well in Naples to describe Filippo's new daughter:

> It seems to me that since you already have a boy, and seeing how grand he is, that you should be no less joyful about this one being a girl, than if she were male, because you will begin to draw fruit earlier than if she were a boy, i.e., you will be able to make a good alliance faster [because girls marry at an earlier age]. Today she was baptized. May God make her as good as she is beautiful and still more.[61]

Filippo's wife Fiammetta, however, seems to have harbored the most disappointment about the sex of the child, when she wrote that Ginevra "gave birth to a beautiful baby boy. Because she carried him for a year, and he is a boy, there is nothing bad to say about it." The remainder of Fiammetta's letter is devoted to their son Alfonso, with no mention of the female infant she had just borne.[62]

The importance of kinship alliances, nevertheless, kept children of both sexes at the very center of attention and hope for the future. Such alliances, cemented by dowry and gifts, formalized and extended networks of mutual aid, patronage, and reciprocity. When the Parenti and Strozzi families agreed on the matter of dowry, Marco Parenti, Filippo's prospective brother-in-law, wrote to Filippo that:

I could not possibly be more well-disposed nor more affectionate toward you than I am. For which I have to say that, in anything that should happen to you in which you think I might be of help, do not hesitate to ask me, because no effort on your behalf or concerning your affairs would be a burden.[63]

Certainly the vulnerability of widows with small children made kinship alliances crucial to individual survival. Alessandra scolded Filippo to render thanks to his patron and kinsman Niccolò di Lionardo degli Strozzi: "Keep in mind what Niccolò has done for you, so that you are worthy to kiss the ground where he has walked ... you are more obligated to him than to your father or mother."[64] Niccolò and Filippo both received the appeal of Isabella, the widow of Soldo degli Strozzi, to provide protection and care:

there are no children more undone and more endangered by the death of their father than are these children ... chiefly, two big girls ready to be married, who have no principal invested in the dowry fund.[65]

It is in Alessandra's treatment of her three sons, however, that the features of this child-centered culture most clearly stand out: "I have no other wealth in this world," she wrote, "except you, my three sons."[66] In 1448 Filippo was in Naples and Lorenzo in Bruges, and as early as 1447 Filippo had suggested that his mother send their younger brother Matteo, age eight, to Naples. To compensate for his mother's possible loss, Filippo wrote, rather insensitively, perhaps, "take in a child of some poor person ... see if you can do without Matteo. He will prosper with us ... God has given him the grace of a good disposition."[67] Alessandra must have replied as she did in August of 1447, that:

as far as sending Matteo away is concerned, I don't want to for now, because he is still little and I am a widow. I cannot do without him, especially since Caterina is getting married, and after that I would be too much alone. ... I have taken him from the study of the abacus, and he is learning to write; and I will place him at the bank, where he will stay this winter. Then we shall see what he wants to do.[68]

By July 1449, however, Filippo's entreaties had moved his mother to write that:

I will be content to do your will and Niccolò's, seeing your great desire to have Matteo and to make something of him, looking not to my own happiness but to your will. And so I will do to the very end, if I live long enough.... I raised Matteo believing that only death would sever him from me.... I have decided not to think about the fact that of my three sons none shall I have for my needs, but rather, to think only of your welfare.[69]

Just as Alessandra had taken this decision, plague and weather intervened to forestall Matteo's departure. Kin, neighbors, and clergy alike strongly advised against sending him until conditions had improved, all with expressions of outrage that Alessandra should even consider such neglect of her son.

In anticipation of Matteo's departure, however, Marco Parenti wrote to Filippo Strozzi in Naples that Matteo, at this point eleven years old, "is possessed of a naturally good disposition." Moreover, Matteo was an apt and willing pupil. Marco Parenti warned Filippo not to be overenthusiastic about having him do more than he was able: "suffer to teach him not everything you want him to know all at once when the task requires trial and error." Marco reminded his brother-in-law that no reproof was less cheerfully endured than that of an elder brother. Since Matteo will guard jealously his sense of liberty and equal footing, as a master "it does not pay to remonstrate either with shouting or blows, because you would only cause him to disdain learning and to turn out badly."[70]

Alessandra Strozzi was also liberal with advice on the treatment of her youngest son. "When you answer Matteo's letters, do not criticize him, so that this exercise will profit him."[71] In 1450 she wrote to Filippo again:

Do not give him blows. Be discreet and patient with him. He does, it seems to me, have a good disposition. When he does make a mistake, reprove him sweetly and you will be more successful this way than with blows.... He has written me many letters, as well as to Antonio and Marco, which are well-written and dictated so that they would suffice for a grown man's. This gives me a certain amount of comfort about him, so that I want him near me.[72]

In still another letter, she exhorted Filippo to give Matteo "caresses and endearments, and make sure he is washed and clean. He still needs to be reminded about it."[73] Alessandra's son in Bruges also had to be reminded, occasionally, of his mother's high hopes. What is striking is that concern for her children, so clear in childhood and adolescence, extended into Lorenzo's early adulthood. She wrote to him in 1453:

> You are not of an age when one can put your errors down to igno-
> rance . . . if you are such a brain that you know good from evil, espe-
> cially when you are reproved by your superiors . . . [why are you not]
> behaving as I would wish? I derive a great deal of displeasure from it
> and I am fearful lest one day a great ruin should befall you. . . . Re-
> member not to throw my reproof over your shoulders, which reproof
> is made with love and with tears.[74]

With grandchildren Alessandra was full of leniency and forbearance. Her grandson Alfonso she described as "a dangerous boy who goes beyond himself and is rather thin, though strong."[75] Even in the same letter that Alessandra discussed whether to send Alfonso back to wet nurse, she wrote to Filippo, "Don't be surprised if Alfonso is so ahead of his age that I am teaching him to read. I tell you, if you saw him, you would notice even more than I can say." There was no need to tell Alfonso anything more than once, she wrote: "he was prompted, and repeated 'banbo a Napoli': and so he does with everything, which is a sign he has a good memory. . . . On the other hand I get pleasure and comfort from it."[76] Despite all her delight and consolation in children, Alessandra Strozzi's letters also reveal a constant, anxious preoccupation with her children's health and her unceasing fears of their premature death.

The psychological reaction of Florentine parents to their very young children was a complex one. The extreme vulnerability of this age group to mortality, especially in plague years, caused the interlocutors of *Della Famiglia* to ponder the mixed blessings of parenthood. Far from engendering indifference, high infant mortality provoked anxiety, compassion, and concern. Such feelings were not always conscious, as when Lionardo suggested in *Della Famiglia* that the care of children under the age of two properly belonged to women, who were the only sex equipped to handle children with sufficient gentleness to keep them from breaking.

Lionardo betrays his real wish for protection from infant mortality when he elaborates on the fragility of babies:

> At that age the least thing can strain or twist those tender little bones. One can hardly squeeze or handle them without the greatest gentleness, lest a limb be thrown out of joint, as a result of which some are left twisted and crooked.[77]

After Lionardo enumerated the delights and joys of having children, Adovardo argued that "you can quickly realize that from their birth children not only bring joy and laughter to their affectionate father, but also sorrow and tears." Fathers not only had to find wet nurses of exemplary character, but also had greater and more pressing concerns:

> Consider, you who hate to see them cry when they fall and hit their heads, how much anguish it is to a father to think that more children perish at this age than at any other. [Every time children fall ill, fathers must wait in] agonized fear of losing so great a happiness.

Not only does the father suffer from fear of childhood diseases, but also from seeing his children suffer from pains "they are unable to explain to you. Every little sickness becomes a major illness to you.... Even the little pains of children keep the soul of the father in agony."[78]

Lionardo then takes the position of the Stoic first, that illnesses in children appear much worse than they really are, and second, that the good father must understand that his children are mortal. As in the case of the diaries of Giovanni and Giovencho de' Medici, the Stoic position held that children were God's loans to parents, and that even when a child dies parents should render thanks to God because of the joys and delights they were able to experience.

In the dialogue, Adovardo rejects this position in favor of the argument that fathers cannot help worrying about the mortality of their children:

> You should hardly judge me mad, however, for all that I cannot frequently help worrying about my children. If you do, you must consider all fathers utterly foolish, for you cannot find one who does not struggle mightily and who is not filled with fear at the threat of losing those who are dearest to him.[79]

Alberti's discussion of the Stoic position was part of a distinguished tradition of humanist consolation reaching back to Salutati and even Petrarch.[80] Giannozzo Manetti's dialogue on consolation states the anti-Stoic position with even more force. Manetti married in 1429 and was the father of six or seven children, three of them sons. In 1438, two years after Manetti's first term as an *operaio* of the Ospedale degli Innocenti, his son Antonio died. In the dialogue, Manetti answered the Stoic position, expressed in the dialogue by Agnolo Acciaiuoli, that because of Manetti's great learning and wisdom, he should have anticipated and prepared for the eventuality of his son's sudden death.[81] Manetti responded that:

> It is not possible that fathers for the loss of their sons not grieve at least lightly because I do not understand what can be to fathers more gentle, more dear, more sweet, than the healthy life of their nurtured sons, the deprivation of which cannot occur in any way without emotional torment.[82]

Just as moralists feared that nursing from animal milk might make future men bestial, so did Manetti in this dialogue caricature the Stoic position by having Agnolo argue that rearing children was no different than taking care of pets.[83] When Agnolo fused the Stoic and Christian positions he argued that Manetti's grief was selfish, because he would, if possible, deprive his son of the opportunity to escape the grief and cares of this world, and keep from him the joys of heaven.[84] Manetti nevertheless argued on behalf of the importance of the psychological and phenomenological experience of grief, and the Prior of Certosa, in accepting Manetti's argument as the superior one, reconciled this experience of grief with the possibilities of Christian consolation. Finally, Giannozzo appealed to his dead son to intercede for him on his behalf. Thus on an individual level Manetti expressed the connection between charity and children that sustained the Ospedale degli Innocenti: he justified his request by noting that he had taken especially good care of his son while he was still alive.[85]

Again, other sources provide clear evidence that the avenues of consolation explored by Manetti were not theoretical, but rather were the means that Renaissance parents used to come to terms with their own deprivation and grief. Alessandra Strozzi, when her son died at the age of twenty-three from tertian fever was, of course, consoled by one of

Manetti's own letters. More importantly, in the actual resolution of grief, Florentines uttered Stoic commonplaces in the same breath as cries of emotional pain. Alessandra Strozzi wrote that "one must bear such losses patiently, because God does everything for the good of our souls."[86] Yet despite her bravest intention not to think about the irremediable, even though she knew that Matteo had lacked nothing, "I still have pain over it."[87] Only a few days after Matteo's death, she wrote that, "there's no doubt, in my view, that I received enough harm from it, and still more, because my injury is for maternal love, which is to say the most ample possible." In the same letter, she comforted herself with the Christian consolation that "the sooner we depart this miserable life, the lighter is the bundle of sins we carry with us."[88] More than a half-century earlier, Lapo Mazzei had availed himself also of this form of consolation. Concerning the death of three of his sons, Mazzei wrote: "while we are in this flesh, or prison, we are caged in by false things," from which death is liberation.[89] In August 1394, when his son was very ill, Mazzei wrote to Datini that "rather I should say he is very well, because he is escaping the craziness and tangles and dreams of this world rather than being caught in them."[90]

Alessandra Strozzi found comfort not only in the Christian perspective of death, but also in her son's demeanor on his deathbed. A certain Neapolitian friar, Fra Domenico, who had been at Matteo's side, wrote to Alessandra at some length about her son's last hours: "he confessed him, and step-by-step told me how he behaved to that extreme point. That is what gives me pleasure and mitigates my sorrow a little."[91]

Not only adult children could provide by their deathbed demeanor the consolation their bereaved parents so eagerly sought. Lapo Mazzei's letter to Datini of 31 July 1400 described the devastating toll of plague on his household:

I have proved [that the world is a prison of falsehood] for the third day in a row. I have seen two of my sons die in my arms in just a few hours. God knows how much hope I had of the first, who already was a companion to me and a father to the others; and how quickly he had advanced at Messer Ardingo's bank, where he placed himself in everyone's good graces and all eyes were upon him. God only knows for how many years he did not fail, morning and evening, to say his prayers on his knees in his room. How often I pitied him, kneeling there through hot and cold! God knows and witnessed what he did on the point of death, and what counsels he gave, and how he showed us that he had been called to judgment, and how he was disposed to obey He who required it.[92]

If Ser Lapo did not tell us of what his son's advice consisted, Giovanni di Pagolo Morelli's son, Alberto, provided posthumous consolation to his father in a dream. Alberto took ill, according to his father, on 19 May 1406, and endured three weeks of intense pain and agony until his death on 5 June:

> And there is no heart so hard which would not have pitied him, seeing him in such pain. He commended himself repeatedly to God and to His Mother the Virgin Mary, had the *tavola* of Our Lady brought, and embraced it with so many expressions of penitence and with so many prayers and vows, that no heart is so hard not to be moved to great pity to see him. Then he commended himself to his father and to his mother, to his relatives and to those present, with such humility and with such efficacious words that it was a wondrous thing. Finally he died, as has been said. And none of the great help and the many prayers and vows helped. God wanted his life to end.[93]

Morelli then describes his memories of his son in life: how at six he knew the psalter, and at eight and nine was writing letters in the vernacular and exercises in Latin, and had "good memory, good speech, good looks, gentle and mannered." Rather than comforting the grieving parents, these memories were "a grave knife," a knife, it turns out, that could only have been wielded by his son's tormented soul trapped in Purgatory. Morelli then described in some detail the ritual process involved in again contacting his son's soul.[94] Morelli's account combines much that is unfamiliar, without knowledge of Florentine ritual context, with much that is familiar in our own experience of the incomplete resolution of grief. The first anniversary of his son's death, for example, was the cause of special torment.

Certainly Giovanni's son Alberto was able to impart consolation and to calm the anxieties of his father. Once Giovanni had "contacted" the soul of his lost son, which he could do only by undertaking a rigorous self-examination of the connection between his father's mistreatment of him and his own mistreatment of Alberto, he appeared to Giovanni in a dream, saying, "Father, be comforted, for your prayers have passed to the heavens and been accepted in the sight of Our Lord God. As a sign of this you see me here to console you."[95]

Giovanni had four major concerns in this conversational dream involving his son: First, he sought reassurance that his own sins had not brought about Alberto's death. Second, he wished to know if he would have more sons. Third, he asked his son to grant him "good status" in this world, by which he meant wealth and communal honors. Finally, he wanted to know whether to expect "to depart from this life young or old."[96]

Alberto was able to console his father on at least the first, third and fourth counts, with assurances that if he diligently watched over his family "they will remain kind to you." To the fourth question Alberto replied:

> I counsel you to exert yourself to depart old. This would be your salvation and that of your family, and would please God, before whose majesty I will always be favorable to your needs and to those of my faithful and earthly mother.[97]

Alberto undertook this intercession on behalf of his father, one notes, not for his father's soul, but for earthly and material blessings: the preservation of family, freedom from the oppression of guilt, and the acquisition of honors and possessions.[98] To some extent the hopes that Florentines had for the prayers of infants "shining in purity" were directed toward the military, economic, and political prosperity of the Florentine State, which could only occur if citizens courted divine favor by practicing charity toward children. On the individual scale as well, Giovanni sought not only short-term resolution of his grief, but also expressed the broader perspective that his own lack of charity toward Alberto might have been a contributing factor to his constant misfortune and inability to acquire status and power in communal politics.

If the souls of dead children could intervene on behalf of their parental and communal clients to ensure material salvation, so could the behavior and activity of living children contribute to their parents' heavenly salvation. Thus the children of the Innocenti, except for years in which plague intervened, were part of the ritual processions that took place on the feast day of San Giovanni, the patron saint of Florence. A float carried the hospital's children, and the commune underwrote its expense.[99]

The participation of *fanciulli* in the public ritual and religious life of

Florence is now well documented.[100] Such religious enthusiasm, however, was not without its anti-Semitic overtones. When Bernardino da Feltre preached sermons in Santa Maria del Fiore for Lent, advocating that Florentines set up a Monte di Pieta to free the poor from oppressive and usurious loans:

> the children took up hatred against the Jews, and many of those children went to the house of a Jew called Manuellino, who ran a pawnshop. They tried to kill him and to sack the pawnshop.[101]

Similarly, on occasions when the honor of Our Lady was threatened, *fanciulli* came to her rescue:

> On 17 August 1483, it happened that a certain miscreant, not for reasons of disrespect but because he was crazy, went throughout Florence breaking images of Our Lady, including the one on the marble tabernacle of Or San Michele. He defaced the eyes of the Christ child and threw excrement in the face of Our Lady. For which reason the children began to pelt him with rocks, and also...some men threw some large rocks at him, so that they killed him.[102]

These and other excesses, such as monitoring the enforcement of sumptuary laws, were due, Landucci tells us, to "children who loved Friar Girolamo [Savonarola], and who had to correct lax behavior." When these children appeared, "everyone fled...and women went about in complete propriety."[103]

At no time was Savonarola's influence more deeply felt than at Carnival. Landucci writes that a few days before 16 February 1496, "Fra Girolamo had exhorted children to substitute for their usual vandalism the begging for alms and subvention of the shamefaced poor."[104] Thus at the hour of Vespers, instead of pranks, processions occurred in which each quarter carried its own banner. These processions consisted of an image of Our Lady, trumpets and pipers "of the Palagio," and officials from communal government, singing *laude* and crying out "Long live Christ and the Virgin Mary." In addition, these young people carried olive branches "so that truly wise and good men were tenderly moved to tears, saying 'this truly is a work of God!'"[105]

This crowd gathered in the Piazza de' Servi, under the portico of the Innocenti. Landucci estimated that six thousand or more children from the ages of five to sixteen assembled there before embarking on a procession throughout the city that would gather "hundreds" of florins to be distributed for charitable causes. Again such devotion and sanctity moved such spectators to tears. Landucci writes that even some of his own children were among "this chaste crowd."[106]

The choice of the Innocenti's portico was a logical one, as the children of the Innocenti themselves were an important part of this ritual procession. Ghirlandaio's painting *The Adoration of the Magi,* painted in 1488 for the Innocenti, shows not only the traditional gifts of the three kings, but also two injured children clothed radiantly in white garments being presented to the Christ child and the Madonna. In this panel officials of the silk guild and the Innocenti, as well two of the Innocenti's *commessi,* look on. In Savonarola's Palm Sunday processions as well, the five thousand children who attended "were dressed all in white, with olive branches and crosses in their hands as well."[107]

The centrality of children, and the importance of their innocence and example, would not make sense as a sudden development of the last decade of the century. This extraordinary era was, rather, the culmination of a relationship between charity and children of which Brunelleschi's architecture was only the earliest monumental symbol. From their devastating experience of infant and child mortality, Florentines constructed a fortress not of indifference but of charity and compassion. In exploring the limits of grief, Florentines redefined the boundaries of the innocence of children. In Savonarola's view, young children were perfect models for demonstrating the simplicity of the Christian life. A work of art, according to Savonarola, could never be more perfect than the works of nature:

> It follows naturally that works of nature are even more pleasing than works of men. . . . Painters even strive to hide their art so it looks like a work of nature. We also know from experience that the actions and words of children delight everyone, because they have neither artifice nor duplicity, but proceed naturally from their pure form.[108]

After the failure of the Savonarolan regime, and ultimately of the Republic, political authority in Florence shifted its focus from infants, young children, and adolescents as saviours of the State, to the colonization of the energies of its young men. If the organization of care at the Innocenti made more rigid and traditional distinctions between the sexes and among the social orders, religious groups such as Ippolito Gal-antini's Congregation of Christian Doctrine organized schools divided into various classes by age. These schools taught not only Christian behavior, but also the duties of charitable obligation. Yet where these schools segregated by age, they also taught classes for married men and women, who learned from other layfolk the principles of educating their sons and solutions to the inevitable problems of domestic family life. Charity directed toward children by Filippo Neri focused more self-consciously on formal instruction. During the sixteenth century the Buonomini of the Bigallo not only taught a trade to the young men it assisted, but also reading, writing, and choral singing. As Brian Pullan has documented in areas farther north, so in Florence did education and charity acquire a Counter-Reformation sense of moral reform. Confraternities combined disciplined spiritual exercises with the frequent practice of charity. Charitable work targeted specific groups of the morally deficient.

The colonization of the energies of young men had its parallel in the grand dukes' appropriation of charity and of charitable institutions in the service of state building. The adverse fortunes of the Florentine Republic exerted a profound effect on the relationship between the hospital of the Innocenti and the institutions of municipal government. During the fifteenth century, the hospital wielded only the same amount of power on the Florentine political landscape that its benefactors and patrons could muster on the hospital's behalf. Communal government at times took a passive, even antagonistic role, culminating in the 1529 seizure of large tracts of the Innocenti's and Santa Maria Nuova's real estate to finance disastrous military campaigns. Throughout the fifteenth century, it fell to the silk guild to petition the commune for funds or for exemption from taxation, or even for institutional participation in the dowry fund.

In the sixteenth century the Medici grand dukes consciously appropriated the practice of municipal charity in the service of the consolidation of their own political power. After the fall of the republic, Duke Alessandro personally intervened to rescue the Innocenti's devastated holdings in the Tuscan countryside. Cosimo I's efforts at charitable reform succeeded in making social welfare less episodic in its approach, and his municipal intervention had as its goal greater social control and moral reform. In 1533, the Grand Duke Alessandro insisted on the right of the State to nominate the superintendent of the hospital of Santa Maria

Nuova, and Cosimo I deprived the silk guild of its direct control of the hospital, turning the office of the Innocenti's superintendent virtually into another arm of government. In 1541, the Senate of Florence conceded to the Innocenti the creek-bed of the Mugnone from Fiesole to Florence to provide speedier transportation of food from the *contado* to the Innocenti. The Grand Duke also intervened legislatively to punish wet nurses convicted of fraud.

Certainly this sort of intimacy between the hospital's fortunes and the patronage of the grand dukes often reflected close personal ties. Vincenzo Borghini, the hospital's superintendent in the mid-sixteenth century and a collaborator of Vasari, provided the Duke Francesco I with the iconographical plan for his studiolo in the Palazzo Vecchio. Francesco's involvement with the hospital extended even to suggesting that children, during periods when wet nurses were in short supply, should be fed with cow's milk, an experiment that in eighteenth-century France, at any rate, caused a sharp increase in infant mortality. Thus, the effect of direct intervention by the grand dukes was not always salutary. In 1572 the Grand Duke Francesco ordered Vincenzo Borghini to send a large number of boys at the Innocenti to the galleys of Livorno.

Around 1536, at about the same time that the officials of the hospital of Santa Maria Nuova were writing to Henry VIII in England about how that hospital was governed,[109] the officials of the Innocenti drafted a brief explanation of the mission and functioning of the hospital of the Innocenti:

> The hospital of Santa Maria degli Innocenti in Florence is united with the hospital of San Gallo. All three [were built] for the same purpose: to receive children abandoned and exposed at birth, and those sent by their own fathers and mothers or other relatives. Thus they are called *gittatelli*, or "throwaways," or *trovatelli*, "foundlings," and commonly by us, Innocenti. Whether they come here because of poverty or scandal, or because of the death of relatives, or to hide secret acts, or whatever other reason there might be, we treat them as follows: as soon as we receive these creatures they are given to wet nurse and weaned. Then they are welcomed back into the hospital, and we teach the boys, according to their ability, various skills. And there is a school and master for anyone who is skilled at reading and writing. If any soul is discovered who is worth it, he is made to study, and good pupils come of it, even prelates up to the rank of bishop. When

they are hired, at the age of fourteen or fifteen, or however many years is deemed appropriate, they are sent out to those trades they have to learn first.... They always maintain a certain homelike relationship with the hospital, which in any case keeps them under its protection.

As far as the girls are concerned, as the weaker sex, and more vulnerable to dangers, the care is proportionately greater and longer. Once they have been weaned they return to the hospital. They are sent to a special mistress, whom they call mother, and they are taught occupations proper for women: to sew, to cook, to thread silk, to throw, to weave, etc. [They] never leave the hospital except to be married or sent to a convent, in which case they are given dowries with the usual things supplied by the hospital. And if they are widowed, the hospital takes care to recover their dowries, and to remarry them to whomever they wish. In sum, they are never free from total protection, meaning those who behave honestly and well, because those who behave otherwise are no longer received in the hospital... so that, as with infected ewes, they will not spread illness and infect the others. The rest are helped as much as possible. Those who do not wish to marry or become nuns stay the remainder of their lives in the hospital, occupying themselves with the work of the House and the supervision of the family. As long as boys and girls are in the hospital, they are fed and clothed, and their other needs are attended to as children [expect] from their true and natural fathers.[110]

This brief goes on to describe how children are returned to parents, specifically, the ones that come "with a sign or countersign," but the judgment of the prior decides whether a parent may reclaim a child:

But commonly this rule is adhered to, boys are returned without much difficulty, but... the girls are placed more slowly: beyond clarifying their intentions, the kind of person they are returning to is investigated, and if they lead an evil life, or even if such is suspected, they are not given back, not even to their own mothers, to avoid the danger that evil may befall them.[111]

The hospital also required that the parent who wanted a child back should cover the costs of institutionalization "except in cases of extreme poverty." In a sentiment more traditionally associated with Protestant than with Catholic charity, the hospital enforced this policy "not only because it is just and reasonable so to do, but because it avoids the greater harm of making a shop out of a hospital, lest charity become the traffic of layabouts." Not only was the hospital not a shop, it was also, according to the authors of this document, "neither inn, nor hostel, nor refuge for pilgrims, nor a hospital for the sick."[112]

This document underlines both continuity and change. The humanist spirit that had inspired and nourished this institution in the fifteenth century continued into the sixteenth. Yet the authors of this document packaged and categorized daily human experience, affording "the weaker sex" a longer period of care and protection. At the same time, even though the Innocenti had always provided specialized care for children, only in the sixteenth century did a hospital official consciously set forth what the hospital was not. In the fifteenth century, moreover, the hospital relied on adoptive parents to lead the hospital's boys to an important religious or secular post, or to lead a girl to honor and provide her with a dowry. By the sixteenth century the Innocenti had acquired a more recognizably residential character. Hospital administrators expended less effort on sending young boys out for adoption or sending girls out as household help to be dowered and eventually married. Boys learned their skills and their grammar from a master who taught in the Innocenti's school, and were not apprenticed until reaching adolescence, whereas in the fifteenth century boys were apprenticed in middle childhood. Girls often preferred to serve the institution, which in turn assumed a protective stance toward them. If in the fifteenth century the hospital was freer about allowing adoption of girls, and then worked assiduously to keep track of them, in the sixteenth the hospital cloistered its girls from the evil snares lying in wait just over the wall.

Certainly demography must account for shaping the different character of the institution over time. As population growth continued throughout the sixteenth century, the resources of the hospital continued to be strained. By 1552 the annual influx of admissions pressed so insistently that the hospital proposed banning the admission of legitimate children. Surely this same population growth and accompanying decrease in the value and importance of children reduced the demand for apprentices and domestic servants. Yet the hospital's concern for its children did not subside in the face of overcrowding. The hospital noted that often people abandoned children in order to steal their childrens' share of an inheritance. Such people, wrote these anonymous sixteenth-century guildsmen:

are worthy of the severest censure, because they are robbing what rightly belongs to the poor little child, depriving it of knowledge of its true status, and the lack of a countersign makes it impossible to recognize them.[113]

But where in the fifteenth century the prior might send a girl as far away as Viterbo, in the sixteenth:

We find that we have a number of girls between fifteen and twenty-five years of age. They are very pure and have been brought up with great simplicity and religious feeling. They could not be mixed in among persons who have customs different from theirs. . . . Thanks to the help of certain alms, [we have managed] to detach them totally from the wet nurses, who are people of coarse quality . . . so they can no longer mix with our little girls as they used to do.[114]

NOTES

1. Lloyd de Mause, "The History of Childhood" in *The History of Childhood*, ed. Lloyd de Mause (New York, 1974), 1–37. See also Lawrence Stone, *The Family, Sex, and Marriage in England, 1500–1800* (New York, 1977).

2. Lauro Martines, *The Social World of the Florentine Humanists* (Princeton, 1968).

3. Gene Brucker, *The Civic World of Early Renaissance Florence* (Princeton, 1977).

4. Christian Bec, *Les marchands écrivains: Affaires et humanisme à Florence, 1375–1434* (Paris, 1967).

5. Ibid., 98.

6. Archivio dell'Ospedale degli Innocenti di Firenze (AOIF), Ricordanze A (XII,1), fol. 146v, 12 April 1475.

7. AOIF Entrata e Uscita (CXXII,2), fol. 127r, 1 February, 1448 [modern = 1449]; Richard Trexler, *Public Life in Renaissance Florence* (New York, 1980), 369–70.

8. Leon Battista Alberti, *Della Famiglia*, trans. Rene Watkins as *The Family in Renaissance Florence* (Columbia, S.C., 1969).

9. Ibid., 113.

10. Ibid., 47.

11. Matteo Palmieri, *Della vita civile* (Milan, 1825), 222.

12. Alberti, *Della Famiglia*, 30.

13. Ibid., 81.

14. Giovanni Dominici, *La regola del governo di cura familiare,* trans. A. B. Cote as *On the Education of Children* (Washington, 1927), 62.

15. Ibid., 63.

16. Ibid., 64.

17. Christiane Klapisch-Zuber, "Blood Parents and Milk Parents: Wet-nursing in Florence 1300–1530," in *Women, Family, and Ritual in Renaissance Italy* (Chicago, 1985), 132–64, originally published as "Parents de sang, parents de lait: La mise en nourrice à Florence (1300–1500)," *Annales de Demographie Historique* (1983): 33–64.

18. John Demos, *Past, Present and Personal: The Family and the Life Course in American History* (New York, 1986), 42–67.

19. Alberti, *Della Famiglia,* 45.

20. Ibid., 57.

21. Palmieri, *Della vita civile,* 16–17.

22. Alberti, *Della Famiglia,* 36–37.

23. Ibid., 86.

24. Palmieri, *Della vita civile,* 9.

25. Ibid., 15.

26. Ibid., 11.

27. Ibid., 11–12.

28. Ibid., 12.

29. Cited in James Bruce Ross, "The Middle Class Child in Urban Italy," in *The History of Childhood,* ed. Lloyd de Mause (New York, 1974), 190.

30. Palmieri, *Della vita civile,* 9.

31. Alberti, *Della Famiglia,* 61.

32. Ibid., 62.

33. Ibid., 50.

34. Palmieri, *Della vita civile,* 16.

35. Ibid.

36. Ibid., 18.

37. Ibid., 16.

38. Alberti, *Della Famiglia,* 36.

39. Ibid.

40. Ibid., 88–89.

41. Ibid., 59.

42. Dominici, *Regola del governo,* 65.

43. Bec, *Les marchands écrivains,* 286.

44. Ibid., 288.

45. Ibid., 289.

46. Ibid., 290.

47. Ibid., 291.

48. Ibid., 283.

49. Giovanni Rucellai, *Il Zibaldone Quaresimale*, ed. Alessandro Perosa (London, 1960–81), 13.

50. Ibid., 14–15.

51. Alessandra Strozzi, *Lettere di una gentildonna fiorentina*, ed. C. Guasti (Florence, 1877), 57: Alessandra to Filippo degli Strozzi, 26 February 1449.

52. Ibid., 182–83: Alessandra to Filippo degli Strozzi, 6 September 1459.

53. See, for example, Lawrence Stone, "The Massacre of the Innocents," *New York Review of Books* 21 (Nov. 14, 1974): 25–31.

54. Strozzi, *Lettere*, 547–48: Alessandra to Filippo degli Strozzi, 11 January 1465 [modern = 1466].

55. Ibid.

56. Ibid., 4–5: Alessandra to Filippo degli Strozzi, 24 August 1447.

57. Ibid.

58. Ibid.

59. Ibid.

60. Ibid., 591: Alessandra to Filippo degli Strozzi, 8 May 1469.

61. Ibid., 596: Marco Parenti to Filippo degli Strozzi, 21 April 1469.

62. Ibid., 599: Fiammetta to Filippo degli Strozzi, 29 July 1469.

63. Ibid., 12: Marco Parenti to Filippo degli Strozzi, 18 August 1447.

64. Ibid., 9: Alessandra to Filippo degli Strozzi, 18 August 1447.

65. Ibid., 43–44: Isabella to Niccolò di Lionardo degli Strozzi, 17 December 1450.

66. Ibid., 55: Alessandra to Filippo degli Strozzi, 26 December 1449.

67. Ibid., 27: Alessandra to Filippo degli Strozzi, 14 March 1446 [modern = 1447].

68. Ibid., 6: Alessandra to Filippo degli Strozzi, 24 August 1447.

69. Ibid., 45–46: Alessandra to Filippo degli Strozzi, 13 July 1449.

70. Ibid., 51: Marco Parenti to Filippo degli Strozzi, 11 July 1449.

71. Ibid., 45–46: Alessandra to Filippo degli Strozzi, 4 November 1448.

72. Ibid., 86: Alessandra to Filippo degli Strozzi, 22 October 1450.

73. Ibid., 112: Alessandra to Filippo degli Strozzi, 11 December 1450.

74. Ibid., 127: Alessandra to Lorenzo degli Strozzi, 27 February 1452 [modern = 1453].

75. Ibid., 586: Alessandra to Filippo degli Strozzi, 2 May 1469.

76. Ibid., 586: Alessandra to Filippo degli Strozzi, 4 March 1468 [modern = 1469].

77. Alberti, *Della Famiglia*, 49–50.

78. Ibid., 51–52.

79. Ibid., 54–55.

80. For a recent discussion of this tradition, see George McClure, "The Art of Mourning: Autobiographical Writings on the Loss of a Son in Italian Human-

ist Thought (1400–1461)," *Renaissance Quarterly* 49, no. 3 (1986): 440–75.

81. James Banker, "Mourning a Son: Childhood and Paternal Love in the *Consolateria* of Giannozzo Manetti," *History of Childhood Quarterly* 3, no. 3 (1975): 351–62.

82. Ibid., 353.

83. Ibid., 354–56.

84. Ibid., 357–59.

85. Ibid., 359.

86. Strozzi, *Lettere,* 204: Alessandra to Lorenzo degli Strozzi, 2 November 1459.

87. Ibid.

88. Ibid., 196–97: Alessandra to Filippo degli Strozzi, 13 September 1459.

89. Lapo Mazzei, *Lettere di un notaio a un mercante,* ed. C. Guasti (Florence, 1888)1:247: Lapo Mazzei to Francesco Datini, 31 July 1400.

90. Ibid., 1:68: Mazzei to Datini, 21 August 1394.

91. Strozzi, *Lettere,* 196–97: Alessandra to Filippo degli Strozzi, 13 September 1459.

92. Mazzei, *Lettere,* 1:247: Mazzei to Datini, 31 July 1400.

93. Richard C. Trexler, "In Search of Father: The Experience of Abandonment in the Recollections of Giovanni di Pagolo Morelli," *History of Childhood Quarterly* 3, no. 2 (1975): 225–51.

94. See Richard Trexler, *Public Life in Renaissance Florence* (New York, 1980), 172–85.

95. Ibid., 184.

96. Trexler, "In Search of Father," 250–51.

97. Ibid.

98. Ibid.

99. AOIF, Entrata e Uscita (CXXII,2), fol. 127r, 1 February, 1448 [modern = 1449].

100. Rab Hatfield, "The Compagnia de' Magi," *Journal of the Warburg and Courtauld Institutes* 33 (1970): 107–61. See also Ronald Weissman, *Ritual Brotherhood in Renaissance Florence* (New York, 1982); and finally, Richard C. Trexler, "Adolescence and Salvation in the Renaissance," in *The Pursuit of Holiness,* ed. Charles Trinkaus and Heiko Oberman (Leiden, 1974), 200–264.

101. Luca Landucci, *Diario fiorentino dal 1450 al 1516, continuato da un Anonimo fino al 1542* (Florence, 1883), 53.

102. Ibid., 63.

103. Ibid., 123.

104. Ibid., 124.

105. Ibid.

106. Ibid., 125.

107. Ibid., 128.

108. Girolamo Savonarola, *De simplicitate Christianae vitae,* ed. Pier Giorgio Ricci (Rome, 1959), 63.

109. Luigi Passerini, *La storia degli stabilmenti di beneficenza e d'istruzione elementare gratuita della città di Firenze* (Florence, 1853), 851ff.

110. AOIF, Suppliche e sovrani rescritti (VI,1), fol. 138r, n.d. Since San Gallo had been closed in 1529 and Santa Maria della Scala was annexed to the Innocenti in 1536, the document could not be prior to that date. Its chronological position in the volume places it before 1540.

111. Ibid.

112. Ibid.

113. AOIF, Suppliche e sovrani rescritti (VI,1), fol. 462r, *anno* 1552.

114. AOIF, Suppliche e sovrani rescritti (VI,1), fol. 510r, 12 December 1572.

Appendix: Daily Menus of the Ospedale degli Innocenti, 23–26 October 1484

Giovedì a dì 23 d'ottobre la mattina:
-alla tavola de' fanciulli che ssono a ttavola 75 fra maschi e femmine choppie 18 di pane di peso in tutto lib. 32.
-alla tavola della infermeria che ssono bocche 24 choppie 7 lib. 12–3.
-a fanciulli maschi e femine che vanno a bottegha per tutto il di choppie xiiii di pane lib. 24–6.
-alle balie che ssono bocche 13 tra disinare cho' fanciulli svezzi choppie 16 di peso lb. 28.
-alle donne di rifettoio sono bocche 81 coppie 40 di peso lb. 7.
-al rifettoio de' preti che ssono bocche 8 choppie 4 peso lb. 7.
-e per lo sciolvere di fanciulli et altri coppie 18 di pane lb. 31–6.

206–3[lb.]

-e fra ttertti la mattina 16 1/2 quarti di vino.
-e adì detto la sera per la ciena alla tavola choppie 18 di pane peso in tutto lb. 32.
-e alla tavola della infermeria choppia 6 e ne . . . in tutto lb. 16.
-e alle balie coppia 6 di pane.
-e a fanciulli maschi e femine da bottegha che ssono in tutto fanciulli 28 coppie 9 di pane———lb. 14.
-e per la tavola del rifettorio coppie 35 lb. 71.
-e per la tavola de' preti choppie 4 di peso lb. 8–9.

161–9 lb.

in tutto per questo di 23 d'ottobre coppie 195 lb. 368.
-olio . . . tre mezzette cioe a meta della 5 1/2.
-vino per la ciena 1/2 barile.

-legne per tutto lo spedale dallato delle donne pezzi 50.
-fastella 3 di fraschoni pel forno.

Venerdì a dì 24 d'ottobre:
-a fanciulli e fanciulle di chasa per sciolvere choppie 18 di pane in fer-
ingno lb. 42.
-alle balie per sciolvere e desinare et merenda e ciena che ssono 13 balie
e 4 fanciulli svezzi coppie 15 di pane lb. 34.
-all' infermi isciolvere choppie 2 di pane lb. 4.
-a fanciulli piccini per sciolvere choppie 2 di pane lb. 4 1/2.
-a fanciulli e fanciulle che vanno a bottegha choppia xi di pane lb. 24 1/2.
-all' infermi per disinare choppie 14 di pane lb. 28.
-a preti per disinare choppie 4 di pane lb. 12.
-all tavola del rifettoro delle donne coppie 32 lb. 71.
-vino a disinare 12 1/2 quarti.
la sera per la ciena:
-alle che mancho loro di quello per mano choppie 2 di pane.
-all' infermi coppia 6 di pane lb. 11 1/2.
-alla ciena de' fanciulli coppie 20 e parte della rato lb. 22.
-alla tavola de' preti coppie 4 di pane lb. 8 1/2.
-al rifettoro delle donne per la ciena copie 34 di pane lb. 7 1/2.

-2 forme di chacio per tutto questo dì peso di lb. 8.
-olio per condire la cucina et inasalate e lla ciena 1/2 quarto d'olio.
-vino per merenda e ciena 18 1/2 quarti.
-legne per tutto lo spedale per tutto il dì pezzi 50.
-fastella 2 di fraschoni pel forno.

Sabato + a dì 25 d'ottobre:
-adì detto consegneremo a Monna Aghata per questo dì coppia 100 di
pane lb. 191.
-a dì detto coppie 12 di pane in ferigno lb. 31.
-a dì detto coppie 46 di pane lb. 103 1/2.

-olio per il dì quarti due d'olio a misura d'olio.
-vino per tutto il dì barili 1 1/2.
-chacio una forma lb. due.
-fastella 4 di fraschoni pel forno.

Domenicha + *adì 26 d'ottobre:*
-allo sciolvere di tutta la brighata coppie 15 di pane in ferigno lb. 40.
-alla balie per tutto il dì choppie 12 di pane peso lb. 25.
-a disinare pe'fanciulli che furono tutti e fanciulli perche questo di non vanno a botegha choppie 25 di pane lb. 51.
-al disinare i preti coppie quattro di pane.
-al disinare al rifettoro delle donne coppie 37 de pane.
-alla ciena pe' fanciulli choppie 25 di pane lb. 50.
-alla ciena de' preti choppie 4 di pane lb. 8
-alla ciena pelle donne chopie 34 di pane lb. 67

vino per tutto il dì barili 1 1/2.
legene per tutto lo spedale pezzi 50.
olio quarti 2 1/2 a misura d'olio.
charne secche lb. 2

Source: AOIF Ricordanze B (XII,2) fols. 50v–51r,
23 October–26 October 1483

Bibliography

Unpublished Primary Sources

Archivio dell'Ospedale degli Innocenti, Florence (AOIF):

Balie e Bambini (Series XVI)
Contratti (Series X)
Debitori e Creditori (Series CXX)
Entrata e Uscita (Series CXXII)
Filza d'Archivio (Series LXII)
Giornale (Series XIII)
Liber Artis Portae Sanctae Mariae (Series V)
Libro delle Muraglie (Series VII)
Obblighi Perpetui e Commessi (Series LXXVII)
Quaderno del Camarlingo (Series CXXVI)
Ricordanze (Series XII)
Suppliche e Sovrani Rescritti (Series VI)
Testamenta et Donationes (Series IX)

Archivio di Stato, Florence (ASF):

Archivio Mediceo Avanti il Principato
Archivio Notarile Antecosimiano
Arte della Seta
Balie
Catasto
Compagnie Soppressi
Consulte e Pratiche
Diplomatico
Provvisioni Registri
Signori: Carteggi, Missive, Legazioni e Commissarie
Signori: Deliberazioni Fatte in Forza di Autorita Ordinario

Harvard University, Baker Library of Graduate Business Administration:

Medici Collection

Published Primary Sources

Alberti, Leon Battista. *Della Famiglia.* Translated by Rene Watkins as *The Family in Renaissance Florence.* Columbia, S.C.: University of South Carolina Press, 1969.

———. *Ten Books on Architecture.* Translated by James Leoni. London: A. Tiranti, 1955.

Antoninus, Saint. *Summa Theologica.* Verona, 1749.

Bernardino of Siena, Saint. *Opera Omnia.* Florence: Ad Claras Aquas, 1956.

Borghini, Vincenzo. *Considerazioni sopra l'allogare le donne* delli Innocenti fuora del maritare o monacare. Edited by Gaetano Bruscoli. Florence, 1901.

Ciampi, Ignazio, ed. *Cronache e Statuti della città di Viterbo:* Cronache di Nicola della Tuccia. Florence, 1872.

Dati, Goro di Stagio. *Istoria di Firenze dal 1380 al 1450.* Edited by Luigi Pratesi. Norcia, 1902.

Dominici, Giovanni. *Regola del governo di cura familiare,* part 4. Translated by A. B. Cote as *On the Education of Children.* Washington, D.C.: Catholic University of America, 1927.

Dorini, Umberto, ed. *Statuti dell'Arte Por Santa Maria.* Florence, 1934.

Landucci, Luca. *A Florentine Diary from 1450 to 1516.* Translated by Alice de Rosen Jervis. London: J. M. Dent and Sons, 1927.

———. *Diario fiorentino dal 1450 al 1516.* Florence, 1883.

Manetti, Antonio. *Vita di Brunelleschi.* Translated by Howard Saalman. University Park, Pa.: Penn State University Press, 1970.

Masi, G., ed. *Statuti populi et communis Florentiae anno salutis MCCCCXV.* Freiburg, 1778–80.

Mazzei, Lapo. *Lettere di un notaio a uno mercante.* 2 vols. Edited by C. Guasti. Florence, 1888.

Palmieri, Matteo. *Della vita civile.* Milan, 1825.

Rucellai, Giovanni. *Il Zibaldone Quaresimale.* Edited by Alessandro Perosa. London: The Warburg Institute, 1960–81.

Savonarola, Girolamo. *De simplicitate Christianae vitae.* Edited by Pier Giorgio Ricci. Rome: A. Bellardetti, 1959.

Singleton, Charles, ed. *Canti carnascialeschi del Rinascimento.* Bari: Laterza, 1936.

Statuti dell'Ospedale di Santa Maria della Scala di Siena. Rome: Archivio di Stato, 1962.

Strozzi, Alessandra. *Lettere di una gentildonna fiorentina.* Edited by C. Guasti. Florence: Sansoni, 1877.

von Fabriczy, Cornelius, ed. *Il libro di Antonio Billi.* London, 1891. Reprinted from *Archivio Storico Italiano* 7, no. 5 (1891): 299–368.

Secondary Works

Ariès, Philippe. *The Hour of Our Death.* Translated by Helen Weaver. New York: Alfred A. Knopf, 1981.

Banker, James. "Mourning a Son: Childhood and Paternal Love in the *Consolateria* of Gianozzo Manetti." *History of Childhood Quarterly* 3, no. 3, (1976): 351–62.

Bardet, Jean-Pierre. "Enfants abandonées et assistés à Rouen." In Sur la population francaises à XVIIe au XVIIIe siècles: Homages à Marcel Reinhard. Paris: Société de Demographie Historique, 1973, 19–47.

Baron, Hans. "Franciscan Poverty and Civic Wealth as Factors in the Rise of Humanistic Thought." *Speculum* 13 (1978): 1–37.

Baxandall, Michael. *Painting and Experience in Fifteenth-century Italy.* Oxford: Clarendon Press, 1972.

Bec, Christian. *Les marchands écrivains: affaires et humanisme à Florence, 1375–1434.* Paris: La Haye et Mouton, 1967.

Becker, Marvin. *Florence in Transition.* 2 vols. Baltimore: Johns Hopkins University Press, 1967

———. "Aspects of Lay Piety in Renaissance Florence." In *The Pursuit of Holiness,* ed. Charles Trinkaus and Heiko Oberman, 177–99. Leiden: E. J. Brill, 1974.

———. *Medieval Italy: Constraints and Creativity.* Bloomington: Indiana University Press, 1981.

———. Review of *Rich and Poor in Renaissance Venice,* by Brian Pullan. *Journal of Economic History* 32 (1972): 1005–8.

Beckerman, Wilfred. "The Measurement of Poverty." In *Aspects of Poverty in Early Modern Europe,* ed. Thomas Riis, 47–63. Florence: Le Monnier, 1981.

Bergman, Abraham. *The "Discovery" of Sudden Infant Death Syndrome: Lessons in the Practice of Political Medicine.* New York: Praeger, 1986.

Berkner, Lutz. "The Stem Family and the Developmental Cycle of the Peasant Household: An Eighteenth-century Austrian Example." *American Historical Review* 77 (1972): 398–418.

Boswell, John. *The Kindness of Strangers: The Abandonment of Children in Western Europe from Late Antiquity to the Renaissance.* New York: Pantheon Books, 1988.

Braudel, Fernand. *Capitalism and Material Life, 1400–1800.* New York: Harper and Row, 1973.

Brown, Augustus C. "The Eight Surviving Pellegrinaio Frescoes at the Ospedale della Scala and their Social and Visual Sources." Ph.D. diss., University of Pittsburgh, 1976.

Brucker, Gene. *The Civic World of Early Renaissance Florence.* Princeton: Princeton University Press, 1977.

———. "The Ciompi Revolution." In *Florentine Studies,* ed. Nicolai Rubinstein, 314–56. Evanston: Northwestern University Press, 1968.

———. *Renaissance Florence.* New York: Wiley, 1969.

———. *The Society of Renaissance Florence.* New York: Harper and Row, 1971.

Bruscoli, Gaetano. *La storia dello spedale degli Innocenti.* Florence, 1900.

Chamoux, Antoinette. "L'enfance abandonées à Reims à la fin du XVIIIe siècle." *Annales de Demographie Historique,* 1973, 263–301.

Cipolla, Carlo. *Before the Industrial Revolution, 1000–1700.* New York: Norton, 1976.

Conti, Elio. *La formazione della struttura agraria fiorentina.* Rome: Istituto storico italiano per il Medico Evo, 1965.

Cooper, J. P. "Patterns of Inheritance and Settlement by Great Landowners from the Fifteenth to the Eighteenth Centuries." In *Family and Inheritance: Rural Society in Western Europe, 1200–1800,* ed. J. Goody, J. Thirsk, and E. P. Thompson, 192–327. Cambridge: Cambridge University Press, 1976.

Corsini, Carlo. "Materiali per lo studio della famiglia in Toscana nei secoli XVII–XIX." *Quaderni Storici* 33 (1976): 998–1052.

Corti, Gino, and da Silva, J. G. "Note sur la production de la soie à Florence au XVe siècle." *Annales: Economie, Société, Civilisations* 20 (1965): 309–11.

Cunningham, Carole. "Christ's Hospital: Infant and Child Mortality in the Sixteenth Century." *Local Population Studies* 18 (1977): 37–40.

Davis, Natalie. "Poor Relief, Humanism and Heresy: The Case of Lyons." *Studies in Medieval and Renaissance History* 5 (1968): 217–69.

de la Roncière, Charles. "L'église et la pauvreté à Florence au XIVe siècle." *Recherches et debats: Cahier du Centre Catholique Intellectuels Francais. La pauvreté: des sociétés de penurie à la société d'abondance* 49 (1964): 47–66.

———. "Pauvres et pauvreté à Florence au XIVe siècle." In Etudes sur l'histoire de la pauvreté, ed. Michel Mollat, 661–745. Paris: Publications de la Sorbonne, 1974.

Delasselle, Claude. "Les enfants abandonées à Paris au XVIIIe siècle." *Annales: Economie, Société, Civilisations* 30 (1975): 187–218.

de Mause, Lloyd. "The History of Childhood." In *The History of Childhood,* ed. Lloyd de Mause, 1–37. New York: Psychohistory Press, 1974.

Demos, John. *Past, Present and Personal: The Family and the Life Course in American History.* New York: Oxford University Press, 1986.

de Roover, Raymond. "Labor Conditions in Florence ca. 1400." In *Florentine Studies*, ed. Nicolai Rubinstein, 277–313. Evanston: Northwestern University Press, 1968.

———. *Sant'Antonino and San Bernardino: The Two Great Economic Thinkers of the Middle Ages.* Boston: Baker Library, Harvard University, 1967.

Edler de Roover, Florence. "Andrea Banchi, Florentine Silk Manufacturer and Merchant in the Fifteenth Century." *Studies in Medieval and Renaissance History* 3 (1966): 223–85.

Gallavotti, Daniela. "Gli affreschi quattrocenteschi della Sala del Pellegrinaio nello Spedale di Santa Maria della Scala in Siena." *Storia dell'Arte*, 1972, 1–42.

Gavitt, Philip. "Economy, Charity, and Community in Florence, 1350–1450." In *Aspects of Poverty in Early Modern Europe*, ed. Thomas Riis, 79–118. Florence: Le Monnier, 1981.

Geremek, Bronislaw. "La popolazione marginale fra il Medievo e l'era moderna." *Studi Storici* 9 (1968): 623–40.

Gilbert, Creighton. "The Earliest Guide to Florentine Architecture." *Mitteilungen des Kunsthistorisches Institut von Florenz* 14 (1969): 33–46.

Goldthwaite, Richard. *The Building of Renaissance Florence.* Baltimore: Johns Hopkins University Press, 1980.

———. "The Florentine Palace as Domestic Architecture." *American Historical Review* 77 (1972): 977–1012.

———. "I prezzi del grano a Firenze dal XIV al XVI secolo." Quaderni Storici 28 (1975): 5–36.

———. *Private Wealth in Renaissance Florence: A Study of Four Families.* Princeton: Princeton University Press, 1968.

———, and Rearick, W. R. "The Ospedale di San Paolo in Florence." *Mitteilungen des Kunsthistoriches Institut von Florenz* 21 (1977): 221–306.

Hartt, Frederick. *History of Renaissance Art: Painting, Sculpture, and Architecture.* Englewood Cliffs: Prentice Hall, 1969.

Hatfield, Rab. "The Compagnia de' Magi." *Journal of the Warburg and Courtauld Institutes* 33 (1970): 107–61.

Herlihy, David. "Mapping Households in Medieval Italy." *Catholic Historical Review* 58 (1972): 1–24.

———. "Viellir à Florence au Quattrocento." *Annales: Economie, Société, Civilisations* 24 (1969): 1338–52.

———, and Klapisch-Zuber, Christiane. *Les Toscans et leurs familles.* Paris: Fondation nationale des sciences politiques, Ecoles des hautes études en sciences sociales, 1978.

Jochem, Frederick. "The Libri dello Spedale." Ph.D. diss., University of Wisconsin, 1936.

Jones, Alice Hanson. *Wealth of a Nation: The American Colonies on the Eve of the Revolution.* New York: Columbia University Press, 1980.

Jordan, W. K. *Philanthropy in England, 1480–1660.* London: Russell Sage Foundation, 1959.

Kent, Francis William. *Household and Lineage in Renaissance Florence.* Princeton: Princeton University Press, 1977.

———. "The Rucellai Family and its Loggia." *Journal of the Warburg and Courtauld Institutes* 35 (1972): 397–401.

Kirshner, Julius. "Pursuing Honor While Avoiding Sin: The *Monte delle Doti* of Florence." *Studi Senesi* 89 (1977): 177– 258. Also published separately in *Quaderni di Studi Senesi,* no. 41. Milan: A. Giuffre, 1978.

Kirshner, Julius, and Molho, Anthony. "The Dowry Fund and the Marriage Market in Early *Quattrocento* Florence." *Journal of Modern History* 50, no. 3 (September 1978): 403–38.

Klapisch-Zuber, Christiane. "Blood Parents and Milk Parents: Wet-nursing in Florence 1300–1530." In *Women, Family, and Ritual in Renaissance Italy,* 132–64. Chicago: University of Chicago Press, 1985. Originally published as "Parents de sang, parents de lait: La mise en nourrice à Florence, 1300–1500." *Annales de Demographie Historique,* 1983, 33–64.

———. "L'enfance en Toscane au debut XVᵉ siècle." *Annales de demographie historique,* 1973, 99–122.

———. "Fiscalité et demographie en Toscane, 1427–1430." *Annales: Economie, Société, Civilisations* 24 (1969): 1323–28.

———. "Maternité, veuvage, et dot à Florence." *Annales: Economie, Société, Civilisations* 38, no. 5 (1983): 1097–1109.

Knight, Bernard. *Sudden Death in Infancy.* London: Faber and Faber, 1983.

Kristeller, Paul Oskar. "Lay Religious Traditions and Florentine Platonism." In *Studies in Renaissance Thought and Letters,* 99–122. Rome: Edizioni di Storia e Litteratura, 1956.

Lastri, Marco. *Ricerche sull'antica e moderna popolazione della città di Firenze per mezzo dei registri del battistero di San Giovanni dal 1451 al 1774.* Florence, 1775.

Lopez, Robert. "Hard Times and Investment in Culture." *The Renaissance, A Symposium,* 19–32. New York: Metropolitan Museum of Art, 1953.

———, and Miskimin, Harry. "The Economic Depression of the Renaissance." *Economic History Review,* 2d ser., 14 (1962): 408–26.

Manz, Robert. "Almsgiving as Part of Lay Spirituality in the *Speculum Ecclesiae.*" Unpublished.

Marks, L. F. "The Financial Oligarchy under Lorenzo." In *Italian Renaissance Studies,* ed. E. F. Jacob, 123–47. London: Faber and Faber, 1960.

Martines, Lauro. *Lawyers and Statecraft in Renaissance Florence.* Princeton: Princeton University Press, 1968.

———. *The Social World of the Florentine Humanists.* Princeton: Princeton University Press, 1963.

Marzi, Demetrio. *La cancelleria della repubblica fiorentina.* Rocca di San Casciano, 1910.

Mc Clure, George. "The Art of Mourning: Autobiographical Writings on the Loss of a Son in Italian Humanist Thought, 1400–1461." *Renaissance Quarterly* 49 (Autumn, 1986): 440–75.

Mc Clure, Ruth. *Coram's Children: The London Foundling Hospital in the Eighteenth Century.* New Haven: Yale University Press, 1981.

Meiss, Millard. *Painting in Florence and Siena After the Black Death.* New York: Harper and Row, 1964.

Mendes, Manuel, and Dallai, Giovanni. "Nuove indagini sullo spedale degli Innocenti a Firenze." *Commentari* 17, nos. 1–3 (June–September 1966): 85.

Molho, Anthony. *Florentine Public Finances in the Early Renaissance.* Cambridge, Mass.: Harvard University Press, 1971.

———. "A Note on Jewish Moneylenders in Tuscany in the Late Trecento and Early Quattrocento." In *Renaissance Studies in Honor of Hans Baron,* ed. A. Molho and J. Tedeschi, 99–118. De Kalb: Northern Illinois University Press, 1970.

Morris, Colin. *The Discovery of the Individual, 1050–1200.* New York: Harper and Row, 1972.

Morrison, Alan, Kirshner, Julius, and Molho, Anthony. "Epidemics in Renaissance Florence." *American Journal of Public Health* 75, no. 5 (May 1985): 528–35.

———. "Life Cycle Events in Fifteenth-Century Florence: Records of the *Monte delle Doti.*" *American Journal of Epidemiology* 106, no. 6 (1977): 487–92.

Mueller, Reinhold. "Charitable Institutions, The Jewish Community, and Venetian Society: A Discussion of the Recent Volume by Brian Pullan." *Studi Veneziani* 14 (1972): 37–81.

———. "The Procurators of San Marco in the Thirteenth and Fourteenth Centuries: A Study of the Office as a Financial and Trust Institution." *Studi Veneziani* 13 (1971): 105–220.

Mundy, John H. "Charity and Social Work in Toulouse, 1100–1250." *Traditio* 22 (1966): 203–87.

Noonan, John. *The Scholastic Analysis of Usury.* Cambridge, Mass.: Harvard University Press, 1957.

Origo, Iris. *The Merchant of Prato.* rev. ed. New York: Farrar, Strauss, and Giroux, 1979.

Park, Katharine. *Doctors and Medicine in Renaissance Florence.* Princeton: Princeton University Press, 1985.

Passerini, Luigi. *Storia degli stabilmenti di beneficenza e d'istruzione elementare gratuita della città di Firenze*. Florence, 1853.

Peyronnet, Jean-Claude. "Les enfants abandonées et leurs nourrices à Limoges au XVIIIᵉ siècle." *Revue d'histoire moderne et contemporaine* 23 (1976): 418–41.

Phelps-Brown, E. H., and Hopkins, Sheila. "Seven Centuries of Building Wages." *Economica* 22 (1955): 195–206.

———. "Seven Centuries of the Price of Consumables, Compared with Builders' Wage Rates." *Economica* 23 (1956): 296–314.

Piccini, Attilio, "In nome di Dio e del guadagno." *Progress*, 1978, 1–4; an internal publication of the Cassa di Risparmio di Prato.

———. *L'Ospedale degli Innocenti ed il suo museo*. Florence: Becocci, 1977.

Pinto, Giuliano. "Il personale, le balie, e i salariati dell'Ospedale di San Gallo di Firenze negli anni 1395–1406. Note per la storia del salariato nelle città medievali." *Ricerche Storiche* 4, no. 2 (1974): 113–68.

Pinzi, Cesare. *Storia di Viterbo*. Rome, 1887–89.

Ponte, Giovanni. "Etica ed economica nel terzo libro 'Della famiglia' di Leon Battista Alberti." In *Renaissance Studies in Honor of Hans Baron*, ed. A. Molho and J. A. Tedeschi, 283–310. De Kalb: Northern Illinois University Press, 1971.

Postan, M. M. "Some Economic Evidence of Declining Population in the Later Middle Ages." *Economic History Review*, 2d ser., 2 (1950): 221–46.

Provence, Sally, and Lipton, Rose. *Infants in Institutions*. New York: International Universities Press, 1962.

Pullan, Brian. *Rich and Poor in Renaissance Venice*. Cambridge, Mass.: Harvard University Press, 1971.

Ransel, David. "Abandoned Children of Imperial Russia: Village Fosterage." *Bulletin of the History of Medicine* 50 (1976): 501–10.

Ross, James Bruce. "The Middle Class Child in Urban Italy." In *The History of Childhood*, ed. Lloyd deMause, 183–228. New York: Psychohistory Press, 1974.

Rubinstein, Nicolai. *The Government of Florence under the Medici*. Oxford: Clarendon Press, 1966.

Saalman, Howard. *The Bigallo*. New York: New York University Press, 1969.

Savitt, T. L. "Smothering and Overlaying of Virginia Slave-children: A Suggested Explanation." *Bulletin of the History of Medicine* 49 (1975): 400–404.

Schofield, R. S. Correspondence in *Local Population Studies* 9 (1972): 50.

Screech, M. A. *The Rabelaisian Marriage*. London: Arnold, 1958. Southern, R. W. *The Making of the Middle Ages*. London: Hutchinson's University Library, 1953.

Southern, R. W. *The Making of the Middle Ages*. London: Hutchinson's University Library, 1953.

Spicciani, Amleto. "The Poveri Vergognosi." In *Aspects of Poverty in Early Modern Europe,* ed. Thomas Riis, 119–72. Florence: Le Monnier, 1981.

Spitz, René. "Hospitalism: An Inquiry into the Genesis of Psychiatric Conditions in Early Childhood." In *The Psychoanalytic Study of the Child* 1 (1945): 53–74.

Stone, Lawrence. *The Family, Sex, and Marriage in England, 1500–1800.* New York: Harper and Row, 1977.

Tierney, Brian. "The Decretists and the 'Deserving Poor.'" *Comparative Studies in Society and History* 1 (1958–59): 360–73.

———. *Medieval Poor Law.* Berkeley: University of California Press, 1959.

Trexler, Richard. "The Bishop's Portion." *Traditio* 28 (1972): 397–450.

———. "Charity and the Defense of Urban Elites in the Italian Communes." In *The Rich, the Well-born, and the Powerful,* ed. F. Jaher, 64–109. Urbana: University of Illinois Press, 1973.

———. "Death and Testament in the Episcopal Constitutions of Florence, 1327." In *Renaissance Studies in Honor of Hans Baron,* ed. Anthony Molho and John Tedeschi, 29–74. De Kalb: Northern Illinois University Press, 1970.

———. "The Foundlings of Florence." *History of Childhood Quarterly* 1 (1974): 259–84.

———. "Infanticide in Florence: New Sources and First Results." *History of Childhood Quarterly* 1 (1974): 98–116.

———. "In Search of Father: The Experience of Abandonment in the Recollections of Giovanni di Pagolo Morelli." *History of Childhood Quarterly* 3, no. 2 (1975): 225–51.

———. *Public Life in Renaissance Florence.* New York: Academic Press, 1980.

———. "Ritual in Florence: Adolescence and Salvation in the Renaissance." In *The Pursuit of Holiness,* ed. C. Trinkaus and H. Oberman, 200–264. Leiden: E. J. Brill, 1974.

Trinkaus, Charles. *In Our Image and Likeness: Humanity and Divinity in Italian Humanist Thought.* Chicago: University of Chicago Press, 1969.

von Fabriczy, Cornelius. *Filippo Brunellesco: Seine Leben und Seine Werke.* Florence, 1892.

von Hallerstein, H. H. "Grösse und Quellen des Vermögens von hundert Nürnburgen Bürgern um 1500." In *Beiträge zur Wirtschaftsgeschichte Nürnbergs,* vol. 1. Nuremberg: Stadtrat, 1967.

Weissman, Ronald. *Ritual Brotherhood in Renaissance Florence.* New York: Academic Press, 1982.

Zupko, Ronald. *Italian Weights and Measures from the Middle Ages to the Nineteenth Century.* Philadelphia: American Philosophical Society, 1981.

Index